The Collected Plays of
Edward Albee

CW01497618

The Collected Plays o

Edward Albee

volume **3**

1979-2003

OVERLOOK DUCKWORTH

New York • London

First published in paperback in the United States in 2008 by
Overlook Duckworth, Peter Mayer Publishers, Inc.

NEW YORK:
The Overlook Press
141 Wooster Street
New York, NY 10012
www.overlookpress.com
For bulk and special sales, please contact sales@overlookny.com

LONDON:
Gerald Duckworth & Co. Ltd.
30 Calvin Street
London E1 6NW
info@duckworth-publishers.co.uk
www.ducknet.co.uk

Cataloging-in-Publication Data is available from the Library of Congress

Book design and type formatting by Bernard Schleifer
Manufactured in the United States of America

5 7 9 8 6 4
ISBN 978-1-59020-114-5 US
ISBN 978-0-7156-4069-2 UK

Contents

Introduction

THIS IS VOLUME 3 OF A PROPOSED FOUR-VOLUME SET OF MY PLAYS. There are already several plays ready for inclusion in Volume 4—*At Home at the Zoo*, the two-act version of *The Zoo Story*, with *Homelife* an added first act composed 40 years after what follows it; *Me, Myself, and I*, the play about identical twins that I am working on when I am not writing introductions; and *The Lorca Play*, my long-aborning examination of the reasons the fascist government of Spain found it prudent to murder their greatest twentieth-century writer.

So. Volume 4 proceeds and—if I live forever with areas of my brain intact—there may even be a Volume 5. After all, Arthur Miller was writing provocative and experimental plays well into his 80's, and rumor has it that Bernard Shaw was rewriting his earlier plays well into his 90's, simplifying them so he could understand them.

But here we are with Volume 3, which I guess we can call "late-middle period," and which commences with my two most spectacular commercial disasters and includes (along with a one-page additional frippery) several of my most warmly received plays.

I should probably admit here once again that I like all of my plays and find virtues (perhaps hidden to others) in the least appreciated of them. It may be that I am incapable of objective judgment of my work, or it may be that worth and popularity are not always congenial bedmates, and that virtue is seldom its own reward. No matter. Here we are.

Vladimir Nabokov's *Lolita* is a book I have admired greatly for a long time, and when I adapted it to the stage I was determined to render its excellencies—its dark humors, its heartbreaking pathos—intact to the stage. I think I succeeded fairly well, though no one who saw the execrable production the play received on Broadway could penetrate through it to the homage I was paying Nabokov.

The Man Who Had Three Arms is one of my best plays, I believe. It is tough, outrageous, funny, and scalding, and it drove its major subject—critics and how they misuse their power, creating false gods as displays of their power and then, as arbitrarily, destroying them—into fits of apoplexy. I think the play will prove itself one day in a new production.

Finding the Sun and *Marriage Play* are shortish plays of substance—very different in manner—which have been nicely appreciated. *Fragments* is a tricky little play, great fun for actors, the construction of which bewildered many who could not comprehend that dramatic shape need not be linear but could be a vortex, moving from all sides at once toward a culminating center.

Three Tall Women, The Play About the Baby, and *The Goat, Or Who is Sylvia?* brought their author out of critical deep-freeze and into a sunlight that may prove to be as arbitrary as was its preceding dark. I like these three plays a lot (but as I said above, I like them all).

Occupant is an homage to my friend the sculptor Louise Nevelson. People who knew her say I have captured her essence—her ambivalencies, her sense of self—quite well.

So. There we are. On to Volume 4. Thank you for coming this far with me.

—EDWARD ALBEE
Montauk, NY
June 15, 2005

Lolita

ADAPTED FROM THE NOVEL
BY VLADIMIR NABOKOV

Lolita was first presented by Jerry Sherlock at the Brooks Atkinson Theatre, in New York City, on March 19, 1981. It was directed by Frank Dunlop; the scenery was by William Ritman; costumes were by Nancy Potts; the lighting was by David F. Segal; the executive producer was Robert Hartman; and the associate producer was Kee Young. The cast, in order of appearance, was as follows:

IAN RICHARDSON *as* A CERTAIN GENTLEMAN

DONALD SUTHERLAND *as* HUMBERT HUMBERT

BLANCHE BAKER *as* LOLITA

SHIRLEY STOLLER *as* CHARLOTTE

ALAINA WOJEK *as* ANNABEL

MARCELLA LOWERY *as* LOUISE

CLIVE REVILL *as* CLARE QUILTY

BELLA JARRET *as* CONSTANCE

YVETTE HAWKINS *as* HEAD NURSE

COLETTE ALEXANDER *as* NURSE #1

BARBARA WARE *as* NURSE #2

KEVIN CONROY *as* DICK

JOE PAGANO *as* BILL

NORMAN ABRAMS *as* DOCTOR

PROLOGUE

A CERTAIN GENTLEMAN *appears on stage—either before a curtain, or in the darkened set of the scene to follow.*

Good evening.

(Or afternoon, as the case may be)

Ah! I see some of you know me. That *is* comforting. In *my* profession—writer, novelist, playwright, unpopular novelist, playwright, for those of you whose hands have not been beating together just now—in *my* profession any recognition brings tears to the eyes—figurative tears to figurative eyes, to be sure. For we live in an age of drugstore fiction, do we not, and little better drama, art as commodity. No matter. Those of us who toil with precision, dedication and—a little blush here—talent, and are burdened with the kind of mind which is incapable of pandering to the public taste, *yearn,* de temps en temps, to indulge in trash for trash's sake; and we discover, to our dark sorrow, that we do it badly. In any event, it *is* nice to be known, and so, to those of you who were kind enough to applaud, my thanks, and my assumption that you *have* seen one or two of my plays, read one or two of my novels, and have not confused me with someone else.

(To someone particular in the audience)

Hello! Hello there! How nice of you to come. That *was* a splendid dinner party last week! And how witty of you to invite what's-his-name! I had thought he was dead!

(Generally again)

Now. There is a gentleman off there who is dying to talk to you. He is a creation of my mind—one of my lesser creations, perhaps, but mine own—and he has all the vigor and self-possession we authors are so pleased to find our characters sometimes achieve. At the same time, I have found that his interest in himself has transcended mine, has taken directions I am not altogether certain I care to deal with. He is a bit of a trouble, in other words.

(Looks off)

All right! For goodness sake! All right!

(To the audience again)

Such impatience! His name is Humbert. That is, I regret to tell you, both his given name and his family name, as well. Humbert Humbert. It happens in Europe a lot—something familial: third cousins of the same last name marrying. Humbert . . . Humbert.

(Shrugs)

Well, what can you do!? He is very anxious to talk to you because, you see, he has fallen in love.

(ACG [A CERTAIN GENTLEMAN] *very graciously indicates the wings;*
HH [HUMBERT HUMBERT] *enters*)

END PROLOGUE

ACT ONE

SCENE ONE

(HH *comes onstage;* ACG *moves to one side, stays onstage;* HH *has a life-size doll with him*)

HH *(Acknowledges the applause)*
Thank you; thank you; thank you. Good evening.
(Or, afternoon)
Thank you.
(To ACG*)*
You certainly took your time about it.

ACG *(Amused)*
Was I long? I'm sorry.

HH
I don't suppose you plan to leave.

ACG
Leave?

HH
Leave.

ACG
Oh! No; I thought I'd stay about—pull a few strings here and there, manipulate a prop or two, a situation.

HH *(Not too happy about it)*
Naturally.

ACG
Well, I mean—after all.

HH
Naturally.
(To the audience)
Well; as he told you, I am in love. Head over heels? No. Hopelessly? No,

nothing like it. Those expressions cannot begin to do justice to the . . . well, to the overwhelming, gagging sensation of MY being in love. God, what an inadequate term!

(Embraces the doll)

I am in a state of loss, possession, fullness, emptiness, squalor and glory—a state that either can be understood, or cannot. Welcome to the club . . . or: too bad; tough.

ACG

Do you plan to explain the doll?

HH

Pardon?

ACG

The doll. Do you plan to explain it?

HH *(Hugs it to him)*

What doll?

ACG *(Patient)*

All right.

HH

You explain it.

ACG

It's not *my* idea.

HH *(To the audience)*

Ignore him; do your very best to ignore him. He is parenthetical. *I. I* am in love; and love is the subject here. The states of love—we all know about them.

ACG

A lecture?

HH

An exegesis. The briefest of exegeses.

(To the audience)

We all know "rut." Rut, that purely physical passion, where "hello" from the object produces an erection, and "how are you?" an orgasm. We all know about that, and we all know about the pure and hopeless love—that which would perish were life pumped into it. There is, as well . . .

ACG

The briefest of exegeses?

HH

(Ignores ACG, *except for a brief sigh, a closing of the eyes)*

There is, as well, though most often in fiction, the doomed passion of the very great, the . . . powerful, the beloved of the public—the Duchess of Windsor and Joe DiMaggio: Edward the Eighth and everybody's Marilyn, that sort of thing. Then . . . then there are the loves that dare not speak their names. These are usually perfectly rational relationships between people of the same sex, of different colors, and, now and again, with other animals.

ACG

Forgive me; I must interrupt you. A perfectly rational relationship with another animal?

HH

It is theoretically possible.

(To the audience)

I can conceive—I can conceive of conceiving—of such a relationship: a man and his ewe; a lady and her tiger; all things are possible. And, most things are ultimately permissible in this ultimately permissive society of our—most things; but not all.

(He hugs the doll to him, strokes it)

I have—here comes that word again—I have fallen in love, with a girl named Lolita; Lo-lee-ta.

(To the wings)

Will you, uh . . . will you come out, now?

(Lolita enters, with her own doll, regular doll-size)

This . . . is Lolita.

LOLITA

(Casual; to the audience, which fascinates her)

Hi.

HH

Lolita, light of my life, fire of my loins. My sin, my soul. Lo-lee-ta.

LOLITA *(To HH)*

Ohhh . . . bug off.

(She goes into the Haze household set, plops down on a sofa, plays with her doll)

HH

(To the audience)

You . . . you may have noticed that Lolita is . . . well . . . *younger* than most girls. Well, certainly she is no younger than most girls her age; that is not what I meant. It is that she is younger than you might expect one to be who is the object of the . . . breathtaking ardor of one who is thirty-eight years old. Lolita, after all, is . . . eleven.

LOLITA

Eleven and a half!

HH

Eleven and a half. Those of you who are thinking of rising from your seats and muttering up the aisles in indignation, I beg you: stay a moment longer and learn how *really* awful it is. I do not love this girl—this child, this flower, this . . . I do not love this precious as an uncle would, or a dear friend of the family; no, not a bit of it.

(His teeth clenched)

I *want* her! I lust after her!

LOLITA *(Eyes heavenward)*

Jesus!

HH

My groin! Swells! At the mere thought of her!

(Covers his groin with the doll)

Don't look. She is my heart, my mind; she is not in my bed—and that is where I must have her.

LOLITA *(Shakes her head)*

God, you people!

HH *(To the audience)*

And so . . . now you know.

CHARLOTTE *(Offstage)*

Lolita? Dolly?

HH

And that—that voice—is my beloved's mother.

CHARLOTTE *(Comes onstage)*

Lo? Lolita?

(To HH)

Where is that child?

ACG

(To the audience; introduces CHARLOTTE)

Charlotte Haze, the widowed Mrs. Harold Haze, mother of the aforementioned Lolita.

CHARLOTTE

(To the audience; a little flustered)

How do you do, I'm sure.

(To HH)

Have you seen Lolita?

HH

She's over there.

CHARLOTTE

(Moving toward Lolita)

Didn't you hear me calling you? What am I supposed to do, shout my head off?

LOLITA *(Bored)*

I heard you; so'd everybody else.

CHARLOTTE

Come into the kitchen; it's time for your dinner.

LOLITA

I don't want any.

CHARLOTTE

(Grabs LOLITA *by an ear;* LOLITA *shrieks)*

You come into the kitchen with me, young lady, and you eat your dinner.

(They vanish offstage)

HH *(A warding hand up)*

Don't touch that child, you . . .

(Softer; to himself)

Don't touch . . . that child. She's . . . mine.

(To the audience)

You see? She's mine; I said it. I am besotted with love and lust for that treasure of heaven, and I don't know how to go about it. Let me tell you how it happened—how I came to this house, with its double perfumes and cracked mirror images; but let me tell you first a bit about me.

(A change here; light? a mini-curtain? I don't know)

You know I am thirty-eight; you have been told that my name is Humbert Humbert.

ACG *(To* HH*)*

I didn't *know* it was a secret.

HH

I grew up in Switzerland, my family abandoning the Riviera to the Germans and the French collaborators—this was the War, after all—and my childhood was happy, placid . . . Swiss. My father gave me all the information he considered I needed to know about sex when I was twelve and I was thirteen when I met Annabel.

(To ACG*)*

No; her last name was not Lee.

ACG

I didn't say a word.

(*To the audience*)

I didn't say a word.

HH (*To the wings*)

Annabel? Annabel? Are you there?

(ANNABEL *comes onstage; dark-haired, pretty eleven/twelve*)

Ah, there you are, my sweet.

(ANNABEL *curtsies to the audience, giggles*)

Isn't she a pet?

ANNABEL

Can I have your doll?

HH (*Grabs it to him*)

NO!

ANNABEL

Sorry!

HH

I'm sorry; it's just . . .

(*To the audience again*)

Annabel and I came together on a lakeside; our mothers knew one another, I think. She was pretty, you see, and I felt for her things I could not identify.

ANNABEL

Can I go sit down?

HH

No! Stay a moment. You're my *past*.

ANNABEL

All right, Hummy.

HH (*To the audience*)

Hummy! Or—sometimes—Hum-Hum; those were her pet names for me. We met, and all at once we were madly, clumsily, shamelessly, agonizingly in love with each other. Hopelessly, I might add, for we were never alone. Oh, our hands would touch under the sand, and once I brushed my lips against her neck under some pretext.

(ANNABEL *giggles*)

You remember do you? You remember what a time we had?

(ANNABEL *nods*)

We knew what we wanted to do with one another; we knew we would know *how* to do it once we had the *chance* to do it . . . but when was that to be? You see, in Europe, even forty years ago, the world was a more innocent place. Hitler was busy, of course, turning everything to ashes— buildings, dreams, innocence—but still, children—at least of our class— did not go about unescorted, unchaperoned. Had we been slum children of Naples we'd have locked in a minute.

ANNABEL

I love you, Hum-Hum; I want you.

HH

Once, once between two capsized rowboats, we'd gotten our lower clothes undone, and I was on my knees, on the point of possessing her, when two old men rose out of the lake—where, doubtless, they had been swimming —two bearded old men, looking for all the world like that pair on the throat remedy. They saw what I was about to accomplish, and made such a hulabaloo of ribald encouragement that there was nothing left to do but put it all away.

ANNABEL

I did love you, you know.

HH

I know you did, my pet.
   (*To the audience again*)
One night, one night in the garden between our parents' homes, we had been let walk.
   (HH *will use the doll as* ANNABEL, *to demonstrate what he describes, even though* ANNABEL *is standing there*)
Behind a bush we fell to such embracing, her hummingbird tongue in my mouth, I a virgin at thirteen. I grasped the occasion and eased my hand beneath the silk of her little dress,
   (*Demonstrates with the doll*)
through the forest of her underclothes until—at last, finally!—my fingers located what they sought, and, as I touched that fur, the expression on her face in the garden darkness was dreamy and eerie with pleasure and pain.

ANNABEL

I really did love you.

HH

And I took her hand in mine.
   (*Demonstrates with the doll*)
and brought it down, down to the scepter of my passion, to the center of my being, and at the instant of my ejaculation . . .

CHARLOTTE'S VOICE

Annabel?! Annabel?!

ANNABEL *(To* HH*)*

I've got to go. Don't forget me.

(Gets on tip-toes, kisses HH *on the cheek, runs offstage)*

CHARLOTTE'S VOICE

Annabel!? Annabel!?

HH *(To the audience)*

A week later her family took her into Italy on holiday, and four months later she was dead of typhus.

ACG *(After a beat)*

First love.

HH *(Bemused)*

Yes; first love.

ACG

And you have coveted children ever since.

HH

Be fair!

ACG

Well, it's true.

HH

Well, we did have me get married, you will remember.

ACG *(To the audience)*

That's true; he married.

(To HH*)*

What was her name?

HH

Valeria.

(To the audience)

When I married her she *looked* like a little girl, but in two years I had on my hands a large, puffy, short-legged, big-breasted and practically brainless baba au rhum. Not that I really cared. The more into womanhood she grew—or, expanded—the more my thoughts reverted to childhood—mine, Annabel's. I would see glimpses of sweet, dead Annabel in children who would pass—a cheek, an eyebrow a budding breastlet.

ACG

Tsk-tsk-tsk. Dirty old man. At what? Mid-twenties were you?

HH *(To* ACG*)*

I was a dirty old man—to use that term—at thirteen, I suppose.

(To the audience)

Wait, though, I want to introduce an important matter. I want to examine the concept of the nymphet.

ACG

I like the ring of that.

HH *(To* ACG; *uninterested)*

Good.

(To the wings)

Annabel? Annabel, would you comeback out here, please?

ANNABEL *(Peeking in)*

Pardon?

HH

Would you come back out, please?

ANNABEL

I'm dead.

HH *(Patient)*

I know you are, dear, and no one was sorrier than I when it occurred, but, will you be a good girl and come back out here!?

ANNABEL *(Grudgingly)*

Ohhhh; all right.

HH

Good; now stand here; just stand in place.

ANNABEL *(Eyes to heaven)*

All right.

HH

(To the audience. HH *will indicate* ANNABEL *from time to time)*

It is my belief that between the ages of nine and fourteen there occur—little girls—who, to certain bewitched travellers, twice or many times older than they, reveal their true nature——which is not human, but demonic. They are . . . nymphets. Well, you may ask, between those age limits, are not *all* girls nymphets? Of course not! If they were, those of us in the know, we lone voyagers, would have long ago gone insane. And, a normal man, looking at photographs of a group of Girl Scouts, say, would not be able to pick out the nymphet of the group. To do that you have to be an artist or a madman, a creature of infinite melancholy. To sense the deadly little daemon among the wholesome children you have to have a hot bubble of poison in your loins and a super-voluptuous flame permanently aglow in your supple spine. Annabel here was no nymphet to me, when she and I were both children.

ANNABEL

A what? Nymphet?

HH

That's right.

(To the audience again)

After all, I was a faunlet in my own right; we loved each other with a premature love; I was strong, and I survived.

ANNABEL

I didn't. Can I go?

HH

All right.

ANNABEL *(As she skips off)*

Thanks.

HH

You're welcome.

(To the audience again)

But I was marked, you see. Had I been older I would have seen Annabel as the nymphet she was, but I was too young to know. The poison was in the wound, though, and the wound remained open, and soon I found myself maturing in a civilization which allows a man of twenty-five to court a girl of sixteen but not a girl of twelve. In Africa, in India still—in remote areas—grown men are wed to girls of ten, and no one thinks twice, but I am a criminal.

(Shrugs)

So be it. I am ravaged by my first encounter with that poor word, love; I seek it out, again and again. I am a criminal. Tough! I would remind you, though, that when Dante fell madly in love with Beatrice he was a grown man, and she was all of

(Whispers it)

Nine!

(Normal voice again)

And, unless I am mistaken, Dante is still taught . . . at least in our better schools. No matter; here I stand; pedophile; nympholept, unregenerate. And there is a little girl over there

(Indicates the Haze set)

whom I have seen, who has broken my heart and sent my blood coursing . . .

ACG

Those two metaphors will not work together.

HH

In love anything works.

(To the audience)

Come, let me show you how I found my treasure . . . and lost my soul.
Come!

    (He begins to move into the Haze set)

I was looking for a room. I had taken a position at the university.

ACG

This is the address.

CURTAIN

SCENE TWO

    (The Haze household; living room, stairs, terrace)

HH

    (Outside the front door; to ACG*)*
I don't think I even want to ring the bell!

ACG

Oh?

HH

Well, look at the place! That door! The plastic ivy!

ACG

Give it a try

HH *(Sighs; rings)*

All right.
    (Predictable door chimes sound)

LOUISE *(From within)*

Justa minute!

ACG

What is her name again?

HH

    (Takes a card from his pocket)
Haze; Mrs. Harold Haze.
    *(*LOUISE *opens the door)*
Mrs. Haze? Mrs. Harold Haze?

LOUISE *(Rather unfriendly)*

I'm the maid.

HH *(Bonhomie)*

Ah! Then you are not Mrs. Harold Haze.

LOUISE *(A beat)*

You want her? You wanna talk to her?

HH

Well, in theory, yes.

LOUISE *(Unpleasant)*

What?

HH

I said . . .

LOUISE

I'll go get her.

(LOUISE *moves off toward the stairs*)

Miz Haze? Miz Haze?

HH *(To* ACG*)*

Look at the place! Look at the furniture!

(*They are moving within*)

Look at the reproductions! Strong Mexican influence here, don't you think?

ACG

So?

HH

In New England?

CHARLOTTE

(*Appearing at the top of the stairs*)

Yes, Louise?

LOUISE

You're wanted at the front door.

CHARLOTTE *(Starts down)*

I am!? Oh, my goodness.

(*She moves into view at the bottom of the stairs which are, for practical purposes—see later—partially hidden from view*)

HH *(To* ACG*)*

I dread things of this sort.

ACG

Well . . . be brave.

CHARLOTTE *(Sees* HH*)*

Monsieur Hum*bert?*

(*Fr. Pronunciation. No "t"*)

HH
*Humb*ert. Humbert Humbert.

CHARLOTTE *(Glee)*
And I am Charlotte Charlotte Haze Haze!
(She bursts into gales)

HH *(An aside to* ACG*)*
I'm leaving.

ACG
Stick around; it might be fun.

CHARLOTTE
(Coming down from her high)
Oh, my! Oh, my!

HH *(Strained smile)*
Well, I am sure you are *not*: Charlotte Charlotte et cetera et cetera.

CHARLOTTE
No, but what fun!

HH
And I *am* Humbert . . . Humbert.

CHARLOTTE *(Terrible good humor)*
Well, how was I to know!? When the University phoned and said you were looking for a room, they merely said you were a professor of French literary history and language, in residence for a semester . . .

HH *(Mumbles)*
French literary history and language, yes . . .

ACG *(An aside; to* HH*)*
And other courses, if circumstance permits—pedophilia, for example.

HH *(To* ACG*; stage whisper)*
Do be careful; for God's sake!

CHARLOTTE
Is that as long as you will be with us? One semester?

HH
Well, we'll see how it all lies, shall we?

CHARLOTTE
Pardon?

HH
We shall see how I like the University, and how the University likes me.
*(*HH *keeps his strained smile going as much as possible)*

CHARLOTTE *(Fairly gushing)*

Well, a distinguished European like yourself . . . how could they not like you?

HH

You're too kind.

CHARLOTTE

(Looking him up and down)

Not at all; not at all. Come into the living room, why don't you.

HH *(To* ACG, *as they follow)*

This won't do; this won't do at all. Look at it!

ACG

Now, now.

CHARLOTTE *(Showing it off)*

As you can see, my aim is comfort—nothing pretentious; you can see we read; perhaps we don't always put our magazines back where they belong.

(Loud; singsong)

Do we, Louise?

(A confidence; to HH)

Black; well, I'm sure you noticed; uppity; not like the older ones.

(Normal tone again)

But, we plod on; we make do with what we can.

(A crash from the kitchen)

Excuse me, if you will: a little revenge going on out there, I think.

(Goes off)

Louise? What have you done now? Louise?

HH

Get me out of here!

ACG *(Amused)*

Whatever for!?

HH *(Mimicking)*

"Uppity; not like the older ones." Dear Christ! She's probably anti-Semitic, too, probably differentiates between Jews and Kikes—that sort of thing.

ACG

I think it's cozy . . . homey.

HH

You stay here.

ACG

It's the fourth place you've looked at. My feet are getting tired from tramping the pavements of—what is it?—Ramsdale?

CHARLOTTE

(Returning, more gracious than ever)

Do forgive me; no great calamity; she fell off a stool.

HH *(Smiles)*

Well, we know they don't hurt themselves easily, eh?

CHARLOTTE *(Beside herself)*

Especially if they fall on their heads, right?

(She nudges him heavily in the ribs; he winces)

HH

(To himself, pretending paper and pencil)

"Especially if they fall on their heads." I must write that one down.

CHARLOTTE

I keep this room informal because we have our meetings here.

HH

Our . . . meetings?

CHARLOTTE

Our literary club. We girls get together and discuss the newest plays and novels, and "trends," and "historical perspectives," and that sort of thing; we meet twice a month; we have speakers.

(She nudges him again)

I'll just bet you'll be addressing the girls one night—French literary history and language, and all.

ACG *(To HH; an aside)*

Oh, I want to be here for that.

HH *(To ACG; an aside)*

Not a chance in heaven! I would rather marry the woman.

CHARLOTTE

The bedrooms are all upstairs—three of them; mine—which I hope you'll feel free to come and go from as you like—Lo's, and the extra—which would be yours.

HH

I see; yes; well.

CHARLOTTE

It's a nice spot here—not segregated, *actually;* we don't use that word anymore, do we, though there is an understanding with the real estate people.

HH *(False heartiness)*

Very nice; very nice, indeed!

CHARLOTTE

Not too far from the University—a brisk walk, but you have a car, I presume?

HH

No, no; no car. And it does seem to me to be a step far from the campus; I have a bit of a heart problem and . . .

CHARLOTTE *(Will she cry?)*

You don't like it!

HH

It's lovely! It's splendid! Really, it's . . . unique.

CHARLOTTE

I'll bet you say that to all the widows.

HH

W-w-widows?

CHARLOTTE

(Groucho Marx eyebrow movement)
How does that sit with you? Hmmm?

HH

Well, I . . .
(An aside to ACG*)*
Help me!

ACG

Help yourself!

CHARLOTTE

The rental you know already, and, for you, I'd be willing to take even a little less—for all that European charm, and all.

HH

You're really very kind, Mrs. . . . uh, Haze, and it's a lovely spot, it really is, and I'll miss not being at your meetings . . .

CHARLOTTE *(Quite hard all at once)*

What's the matter? Did I say something wrong?

HH

No, no; no; certainly not!

CHARLOTTE

You're not seeing the house at its best, Louise being the way she is; it's really very nice. Let me show you the garden; that might change your mind.

HH

Really, Mrs. Haze . . .

ACG

See the garden, for heaven's sake!

CHARLOTTE

I have such lilies.

HH

Yes; I'm certain you have! Oh, all right, we'll . . . we'll see the garden.
(*The scene begins to shift toward the garden.* QUILTY *enters the living room from the terrace*)

CHARLOTTE

Clare! You sneaky boy! What are you doing here?

QUILTY

Oh, just dropped by; passing by; how are ya, Charlotte? How ya doin'?

CHARLOTTE

Having a talk with Lo, Clare? Is Lo out there?

HH (*To himself*)

Lo?

QUILTY

Yeah, she's doin' her homework. Good to see ya, Charlotte!

CHARLOTTE

Oh! Lest I be rude, let me present you two gentlemen to one another.

HH (*To himself*)

Her homework? *Her? . . . homework?*

CHARLOTTE

Clare, may I present Monsieur Humbert Humbert, new member of the French Department of the University, lecturing here this semester on French language and literary history.

QUILTY

How ya doin', fella?

HH

How do you do!?

CHARLOTTE

And, well, Humbert—may I call you that?—I'm sure you recognize Clare here, better known as Mr. Clare Quilty? Hm? Hm?
(*She is bursting with pleasure and pride*)
Of course you know his plays, and even more his movies?

HH

Ah, yes; well; of course; *The Lady Who Loved Lightning*, right?

QUILTY

Right! Right!

CHARLOTTE

Not to mention. *The Little Nymph, Fatherly Love, Strange Mushrooms* . . .

QUILTY

Aw, come on now, Charlotte!

ACG *(To the audience)*

That's who he is; I thought I recalled that awful face. *Terrible* writer; makes a fortune! Works in films now.

HH

Strange Mushrooms, eh? Well.

CHARLOTTE

Humbert was thinking of taking a room from me, but I don't think he likes our little house.

QUILTY

Too bad; your loss, fella! Gotta go, Charlotte. Nice ta meet ya, Mr . . . ?

HH

Humbert. Humbert Humbert.

(CHARLOTTE *giggles*)

QUILTY *(A beat)*

Sure, sure. Right, right.

(*He exits out the front door*)

CHARLOTTE

Clare comes round all the time; he's spoken to our ladies, oh *lots!* On film, on the novel, on. . . .

HH

Yes; yes, I'm sure. You, ah . . . you have a daughter? Hm?

ACG *(An aside)*

Nicely done; so . . . offhand.

HH *(An aside to* ACG)

Thank you; thank you.

CHARLOTTE

Who? Me? Yes! Of course; Lo; Lolita.

HH *(Very offhand)*

Lolita; charming name. She's in high school!? Ah, but you're too young to have so old a daughter. Perhaps she's in second grade, that's far more like it!

CHARLOTTE *(Laughs)*

Well, come out and see.

(The terrace and garden come into view)

HH

Yes; well; by all means.

(And there is LOLITA, *sunning; bikini, sunglasses;* HH *actually staggers for a moment—unseen by* CHARLOTTE; *he gasps)*

CHARLOTTE

Lo? This is Humbert Humbert.

LOLITA

You're kidding.

CHARLOTTE

I am not kidding. Cover yourself up.

LOLITA

Hi.

CHARLOTTE

That's the skimpiest bathing suit I've ever seen; lucky you don't have much to hide yet.

HH

(A muffled groan escapes him)

Hnnnnnnnn!

CHARLOTTE

Well, that's Lolita, Humbert; and this is my garden. Look at my lilies; just look at them!

HH

(Looking straight at LOLITA, *who returns his glance, unseen by* CHARLOTTE, *who is proud of her lilies)*

Absolutely extraordinary Yes; yes; they're beautiful; beautiful; beautiful;

*(*LOLITA *smiles)*

I think . . . I think if I may have that room after all . . . dear Mrs. Haze . . .

*(*CHARLOTTE *and* LOLITA *go into tableau;* HH *and* ACG *move down stage. The Haze set fades. To the audience)*

And that brings us to the present; that is how I met . . . my love.

ACG

Your would-be love.

HH *(To the audience)*

Yes; my would-be-love. The problem now is: how am I to get at her? How am I to get past that mother of hers? That gorgon at the gate—that gorgonette?

ACG

Just a moment.

HH

Hm?

ACG

What makes you think the child will care? Hanh?

HH *(Transported)*

I've long experience at it. That darling child is a temptress. She is a nymphet!

ACG

No! Really! She looks like an ordinary little girl to me.

HH *(To* ACG*)*

Yes! I'm sure she does!

(To the audience)

And to you, too, as well, I dare say . . . unless. Unless I am not alone? Unless there is one of you out there like me—one of you who knows, one of you who senses the beauty, the thrill, the danger? Is there a pedophile in the house?

(Loud hiss)

How am I to get at her!? HOW AM I TO GET AT HER!? TELL ME!! PLEASE!!

CURTAIN

SCENE THREE

(The set swings to reveal the entire living room. The briefest of blackouts separates this scene from the previous. LOLITA *and* CHARLOTTE *are no longer onstage;* HH *and* ACG *are exactly where they were at the end of the previous scene)*

ACG

And the solution . . .

HH *(To the audience)*

was simplicity itself—marry the appalling Haze woman, kill her, and then—having become my treasure's stepfather, her legal guardian—do with my Lolita whatever I would.

(Leers, shrugs)

As I said . . . simplicity itself, in retrospect.

ACG

I'm glad you added the qualification—"in retrospect." After all, you didn't plan it all out. It fell into your lap, so to speak. You mustn't take credit for it. If anyone is to take credit for it, *I* will.

HH

Very *well*!

ACG *(Purring)*

Very well.

HH *(To the audience)*

I could go on to exquisite length—but I will not!—about how my darling, my Lolita, entwined me in the web of her nymphancy.

(LOLITA *comes onstage, saunters toward* HH)

How my flesh would become electrified at the sound of her voice; how the touch of her hand would bring me to erection, a cut on her grubby, adorable finger to tears.

LOLITA *(To* HH)

Hey; scratch my back.

HH

All right, my pet.

LOLITA

Don't call me your pet; what do you think I am—a dog or something?

HH

No, no; of course not. Where does it itch?

(Begins scratching)

LOLITA

Higher; lower; higher!

HH

Yes yes; yes yes.

LOLITA

Gently!

HH

Yes yes!

LOLITA

For Christ's sake!

HH

Don't swear, darling.

LOLITA *(Awful imitation)*

"Don't swear, darling." What do you think you are, my mother? That's enough; stop it.

(LOLITA *pulls away; lurks nearby, busies herself—there are a number of like encounters coming*)

HH (*To* ACG)

There is, at her shoulder blades, a down—a mist of tiny blond hairlets that drives me mad!

ACG

No doubt.

HH (*To the audience*)

The skin of these—these girl-children! Tender and tanned; not the least blemish. Nymphets do not have acne. Does that surprise you? They gorge themselves on ice cream sundaes; their consumption of junk food would turn the stomach of a goat; they require pizza an hour before dinner. But their skin . . . their skin!

(*To* LOLITA)

You have smooth skin, Lo.

LOLITA

(*Chewing something, offhand*)

Thanks.

HH (*To the audience*)

I have a diary here.

(*Searches his pockets*)

Somewhere, a little diary, bound in black plastic pretending to be crocodile . . . where *is* it?

ACG (*Displays it*)

I have it.

HH (*To the audience*)

Aha. We have a diary here . . .

ACG

An important item, so remember it!

HH

. . . Which lists these encounters with Lolita, these brushes with her nymphancy . . .

ACG (*Reading from it*)

"Her skin! Her skin! How many hours would it take to tongue each precious inch of that delicious hide?" Really, HH; you should be ashamed of yourself!

HH (*To* ACG)

Love makes its own rules.

ACG

No, no! The prose—delicious *hide*?

HH

You write your way; I'll write mine.

ACG

I dare say.
    (Turns a page)
"I may burst; I may burst with passion; Lolita came to me today, complaining of something in her eye . . .

LOLITA *(Approaching)*

Hey, Hum? I got something in my eye. It's right there; I can feel it.

HH

    (Jumping to the opportunity)
Oh, my child! Let me see!

LOLITA

It's so fucking annoying!

HH

Tsk-tsk-tsk-tsk. Such language.

LOLITA

O.K. grandma.

HH

When *I* was a child . . .

LOLITA

I am not a *child!* I'm going to be twelve!

HH *(Rapture)*

I know!

LOLITA

Will you get this thing out of my eye!?

HH *(Peering)*

A Swiss peasant—a Swiss grandma would use the tip of her tongue.

LOLITA

Lick it out? Really?

HH *(Tongue out)*

Yeth; shly try?

LOLITA

Sure; go ahead.
    (Giggles as he does it)
Hey! It works! Goody!

HH

And now . . . the other eye?

LOLITA

Dope!

(Laughs, pushes him, moves away)

HH (To the audience)

That night I dreamt of her face—just that, the image of her face, approaching mine.

ACG (Reading from the diary)

"I long for some terrible disaster. Earthquake! Spectacular explosion. The mother is messily but instantly and permanently eliminated, along with everyone else for miles around. Lolita whimpers in my arms. A free man, I have her. I enjoy her among the ruins." Really; I mean, really!

HH (To ACG)

I am an honest man.

(To the audience)

I am an honest man. Why should I lie? She was driving me crazy. It's that simple. One day . . . one sunny, bee-buzzing afternoon.

(He moves to lawn chair for this)

I had taken my work from the University—the dreadful papers my students kept writing, supposed thoughts on my lectures—I had taken to taking this work outside to grade, as it is put, to be closer to my pet who was—what was her term?—a "sun freak."

(We see LOLITA sneaking up on HH when he is settled)

I was sitting, pretending to be at work, all the while alert to the sound of her, the scent, the nimbus, when all at once . . .

(LOLITA springs from behind, giggling, shrieking, putting her hands over HH's eye's)

LOLITA

Guess who!? Guess who!? Guess who!?

HH

Guess who!? Well, let me see. Whose hands are these?

(LOLITA is squealingly delighted by all this, as HH fondles her variously)

Whose arms are they attached to? Aha! Whose bare little leg is this? Whose knee? Whose little cutoffs have I found now? Eh?

LOLITA (Moving around a little)

Don't open your eyes now. Pucker up; give me a little kiss.

HH (Throaty)

Oh, well, if you insist.

*(*LOLITA *bends over* HH, *kisses him, a little longer than a mere child would, laughs, pulls away)*

LOLITA

O.K. Game's over.

HH *(To the audience)*

I hope my papers covered it, for I had stiffened.
  (To LOLITA; *offhand)*
Come; come sit on my lap for a little.

LOLITA

What for?

HH

Well, it's a nice place to sit.

LOLITA

Looks pretty uncomfortable to me.

HH

You'll like it! You will! Really!

LOLITA *(Grudgingly weakening)*

Well . . .

HH *(To the audience)*

And at that moment—the moment I would have had her in my lap, clothed, no danger, no damage, and I would have spilled into my trousers all my love for my Lolita, a wet run, so to speak, for my true heart's—at that moment . . .

LOUISE *(Appears with a broom)*

Hey! Hey!

HH

Oh, Christ!

LOUISE

Hey, they's a big bug-type-thing down in the cellar, foot and a half long, all kinds a legs, squealing its head off.

LOLITA

Yetccchhh!

HH

Well, Louise, do something about it.

LOUISE

You kidding? I don't do no windows and I don't do bugs. Whyn't you get up off your professorial ass and be the man of the house around here for a little?

*(*LOUISE *exits;* LOLITA *exits;* HH *moves downstage)*

HH

Man of the house, indeed!

ACG

Indeed.

HH

That *was* what I wanted, after all, but there is a distance between bugs in the cellar and buggery in the bedroom.

ACG

Really!

HH *(To the audience)*

And then. And then . . . the ax fell.

(CHARLOTTE *and* LOLITA *enter appropriately here*)

One night, after a lot of screaming and shouting in the kitchen, Lolita and her terrible mother came hurtling into the living room.

LOLITA

I don't wanna go to camp!

CHARLOTTE

You are going to camp!

LOLITA

I am not going to camp!

CHARLOTTE

You are going to camp!

LOLITA

You can't make me! I will not go to that fucking camp!

(CHARLOTTE *slaps* LOLITA; *she shrieks;* HH *starts*)

CHARLOTTE

You will not use that language; I am your mother, and Humbert is a European gentleman.

LOLITA

You trying to kill me or something?

CHARLOTTE

You are going to camp, and that is that!

(LOLITA *bursts into tears*)

HH

Awwww!

CHARLOTTE *(Stern; possessed)*

Leave her alone; we go through this every summer; she doesn't want to go to camp; I make her go to camp; I am the villain; she goes to camp; she loves it; we go through it every summer.

LOLITA

This summer's different.

HH

(*An aside; unheard by* CHARLOTTE, *or* LOLITA)
Oh, my Lolita! My darling!

CHARLOTTE

Why!? Why is this summer different?

LOLITA (*Shrugs through her tears*)

It just is.

HH (*As above*)

Oh, my precious.

CHARLOTTE

Well, you're going, and there's no point arguing. And shame on you, acting like such a child in front of Humbert here.

(*To* HH)

We apologize, Humbert; we have revealed perhaps too much of the workings of our lives.

HH

Oh, no, no; not a bit of it. Really.

CHARLOTTE

After all, you are merely a guest in this house—a welcome, a more than welcome guest, to be sure . . .

LOLITA (*Flings herself on* HH)

Don't let her make me go away! Please! I wanna stay here! I wanna stay with *you*—with both of *you*; I hate camp; I wanna be home! Please! Pllleeeaaassee!

CHARLOTTE

Lolita! You're a disgrace! Untangle yourself from Humbert. He doesn't want you all over him like that. Besides,

(*A strange smile here*)

besides, Humbert is not the man of the house to make such decisions.

(*A hand to her hair*)

There *is* no man of the house, though certainly there is the . . .

(*A questioning look at* HH)

. . . desire for one? Certainly, a man is required in this house.

(*The room fades;* HH *moves downstage;* CHARLOTTE *moves downstage with* HH, LOLITA *exits in the dark*)

HH (*To the audience*)

Well, that was pretty clear, wasn't it? Wasn't that right on the table—or the rug?

ACG *(Shrugs)*

We get what messages we like; we retrieve our own bottles.

HH *(Still to the audience)*

Besides, the awful Charlotte had not been altogether subtle throughout the months of my residence.

CHARLOTTE

(At HH, *moving around him; these short paragraphs are seen as continuous, though separate, incidents)*

How do you like my new dress, Humbert? How does it look at the hips? Does it do things for my bust? Smell my new perfume, Humbert; I got it just for you. Does it do anything for you—anything naughty? Do you think my hips are getting too big, Humbert, or do you European gentlemen like an ample girl, a girl with some heft? We could go to the drive-in tonight, Humbert, since Lolita's got ballet class; we could sit in the car and pretend it was a real date. I might even let you take a liberty or two with me. Why don't you have your breakfast in my bedroom, Humbert? Why don't you just put on your robe and climb up on the bed, and we can watch "Good Morning, America," or whatever?

(She moves upstage, disappearing)

Why don't you do some of these things Humbert? You're not a fairy, or anything, are you? Are you? Hm?

HH *(To the audience)*

And so the idea was put into my head, where it joined the unspoken ideas already lurking there. What better way, after all—what *other* way!?— might I have continued access to the treasure of my life. The capstone, however, was soon put on the arch of my desire, in the form of a letter, delivered by the overly-ubiquitous Louise, shortly after screaming-Lolita was carried off to camp in the car of her beastly mother.

*(*HH *sits on a stool;* LOUISE *and* CHARLOTTE *come onstage together)*

LOUISE

Miz Haze wanted you to have this here letter.

HH

Oh? Is . . . is Lolita gone? Charlotte, too? Mrs. Haze?

LOUISE

They both gone—yellin' and screamin'; just don't *you* start!

HH

Oh; no no.

LOUISE

Here's your letter; I'm gonna leave early today.

HH *(Opening the letter)*

Right; right.

> (LOUISE *exits.* CHARLOTTE *will speak the letter;* HH *will react to it—to its content, to its prose style; grimaces, faces, muggings.* CHARLOTTE *does it straight, of course, never being aware of* HH's *facial reactions)*

CHARLOTTE *(The letter)*

Dearest Humbert; dearest, dearest Humbert: This is a confession: I love you. I have loved you from the minute I saw you. I am a passionate and lonely woman and you are the love of my life. Of course, I know with *absolute certainty* that I am nothing to you, nothing at all. Oh, yes, you enjoy talking to me, you have grown fond of our friendly house, of the books I like, of my lovely garden, even of Lo's noisy ways—but I am nothing to you. Right? Right. Nothing to you whatever. *But* if, after reading my "confession," you decide, in your dark romantic European way, that I am attractive enough for you as a lifelong mate, and that you are ready to link up your life with mine forever and ever and be a father to my little girl, then let me know straight out. If not, then never mind. Destroy this letter and go. Do not forget to leave the key on the desk in your room. And some scrap of address so that I could refund the twelve dollars I owe you till the end of the month. Good-bye, dear one. Pray for me—if you ever pray. Your adoring, Charlotte Haze.

> *(At the end of the letter* CHARLOTTE *withdraws upstage into darkness)*

HH *(To the audience; sighs)*

And so . . . I married her.

ACG *(To* HH*)*

That's rather a touching letter.

> (HH *laughs)*

No; don't laugh; your criminal mind can't fathom it, but she is sincere.

HH

So is a toad!

ACG

You're impossible.

HH

I know.

> *(To the audience)*

And so I married her. She had, after all, begun to make noises about having my darling, my treasure, shipped off some girls' school the coming Autumn—I don't think she *liked* Lolita; I think Lolita made her feel old. So, it was both design and despair which drove me to the altar, if you will—attain the daughter through the mother.

ACG *(To himself; to* HH*)*

The depths to which people will sink.

HH *(To* ACG*)*

Why? You said yourself she was sincere. *I* am sincere; let no man put our sincerities asunder.

ACG

Wily, devious, deeply depraved man; I don't think I like you much.

HH *(Shrugs)*

I am what I am.

(To the audience again)

I must tell you that I got more than I bargained for.

*(*CHARLOTTE *comes on, flimsiest of negligees,)*

Charlotte was—well, I *do* want to be delicate here—Charlotte was a bit of a pig.

CHARLOTTE

Charlotte's sorry she suggested you might be a fairy, Humbert, darling.

HH

That's all right, dear.

(It is clear HH *is embarrassed the audience is witnessing this)*

CHARLOTTE

How far from a fairy can you get, hanh!?

(A heavy nudge in the ribs)

When I told Mr. Haze—dear dead man—when I told Mr. Haze that I wanted it one for one, he was nonplussed, he really was.

HH

One for one?

CHARLOTTE

One for one! *He* has an orgasm, I want one! He comes: *I* come. None of this pile on, puff-puff, squirt, roll off and go to sleep. No, Sir! He comes, I come.

HH

Well . . .

CHARLOTTE

I've always been a liberated woman—and thank you for respecting my honor until after the wedding, by the way, toots—and I don't think Mr. Haze—bless his soul—was quite ready for me.

HH

No; well, perhaps not.

CHARLOTTE

Sex is healthy, I told him, and I expect you to do your nightly duty, yes, I do.

HH

Every night, eh?

CHARLOTTE

Right as rain; regular as clockwork.

HH

A*ha.*

CHARLOTTE

I guess I was into female lib before it ever had a name.

HH *(Empty chuckle)*

Well, yes, I guess you were!

CHARLOTTE *(Hugs* HH*)*

We won't have any problems there that way, you big, sexy teddybear! Oh, you Europeans, you sure know how to satisfy a healthy American girl; yes, you do!

HH

Thank you; thank you. How did . . . how did the poor Mr. Haze . . . pass on?

CHARLOTTE

Oh, he just . . . sort of faded, if you know what I mean . . . faded.

HH

Aha.

CHARLOTTE

You wonderful, dirty man! Let's go up to bed!

(During this next, ACG *snaps his fingers, catches* CHARLOTTE*'s attention; He hands her the black, plastic diary, bows, smiles; she takes it, puzzles, begins to read the entries, begins to redden, quiver, cry)*

HH

(Disentangles himself; rises. To the audience,)

And so, you see, I was not an unsatisfying husband; I fulfilled my obligations, did my nightly duty, as it were, kept my Charlotte misty-eyed and as sated as an unwilling satyr can manage. For every time I rolled on terrible Charlotte, it was my Lolita I had in mind; it was *she* whose furrow I plowed, *she* whose liquids seeped from my mouth, *her* breasts whose aureole I rimmed with my sandpaper tongue. I kept it in the family, you see.

(He becomes aware that CHARLOTTE *is distressed)*

My dearest Charlotte! Whatever is it? What *is* the matter?

*(*CHARLOTTE *approaches, speaking as best she can through her tears, her rage, reading from the diary)*

CHARLOTTE

"That hideous Haze woman! How could I bear to be in the same house with her were it not for Lolita, Lolita whom I desire?"

HH

Where did you get that!? Give that to me!

CHARLOTTE

"Lolita! When will you be mine? When will I caress your soft, sweet naked body?"

HH *(To* ACG*)*

Where did she get that book?

ACG

She finds it among your papers, doesn't she?

CHARLOTTE

"Let me in, Lolita; let me in."

ACG

Isn't that the usual way these women find these things? Most novels *I've* read . . .

HH *(To* CHARLOTTE*)*

Charlotte, my misunderstanding darling . . .

CHARLOTTE

"Every night I sleep with your disgusting mother, my treasure, my love, my nymphet, it is you I am caressing."

(Full fury on HH*)*

You vile, you loathsome man! You monster; you detestable, abominable, criminal fraud!

ACG

My own thoughts exactly.

HH

Charlotte . . . my angel . . .

CHARLOTTE *(Races to the stairs)*

Child molester! Rapist! Filth! You are unspeakable!

HH

Charlotte! Those are notes for a book! It's a work of . . .

(But CHARLOTTE *is gone)*

ACG

Notes for a book!? Indeed!? Who would believe *that!?*

HH

How could you give her that diary!? How could you!?

ACG *(Shrugs; smiles)*
Well . . . plots must turn on something, don't you know.

HH
But, still! That poor woman! What will she do!?

ACG *(Calm)*
I would imagine she will search for and find her poor, dead husband's pistol, and come after you with it.

HH *(Disbelieving)*
No.

   (But CHARLOTTE appears at the top of the stairs, tiny pistol in hand)

CHARLOTTE
You'll never have my daughter, you vile, disgusting man!

HH
Now, now; see here, Charlotte, my darling, put that thing . . .

CHARLOTTE
How could you! Harold Haze shall have his revenge!

HH
Don't shoot me! My God!

   (All at once CHARLOTTE stumbles—in all her lurching—and falls down the entire flight of stairs, the middle part of which is hidden from the audience. Silence.)

ACG *(After a bit)*
Go to her.

HH *(Goes to her)*
Charlotte? Charlotte?

   (He bends over her, lifts her clearly dead, neck-broken form)
She's dead.

ACG *(After a bit)*
Aha.

HH *(Some wonder)*
She's dead.

ACG
Plot, you know.

HH
She's dead! She's dead! It's over!

   (To the audience; leaving CHARLOTTE, moving downstage, with ACG)
She's dead; I am her . . . widower; I am Lolita's stepfather; I am her guardian now; she . . . she's mine. Lolita . . . is . . . mine!

ACG

Not quite yet. Bury the mother first.

HH (*To* ACG)

Bury the . . . oh, my God! A funeral!

ACG

You can play the bereaved.

HH

But I'm so happy!

ACG

Then play at grief; prepare.

HH

Prepare?

ACG

Semper Fidelis and all.

HH

Are you telling me something?

ACG

Are you listening?

HH (*His mind on* LOLITA)

Of course not!

ACG

But your wife!

HH (*Sighs*)

All right. All right, let's get her underground.

(*They move into the next scene*)

SCENE FOUR

(*The Haze living room and environs. All the characters of the play present—except* LOLITA *and* ANNABEL. CHARLOTTE *is in her open coffin. People are slow-moving, quiet, whispering. Improvised dialogue in an undertone except for the speeches indicated.*)

ACG (*To* HH, *to one side*)

My; what a lot of people you know.

HH

Charlotte's.

ACG

Hm? Pardon?

HH

Charlotte's friends. The dear departed was gregarious. The brokeneck was a . . .

ACG

Speak well of the dead.

HH

I am filled with such anticipation!

ACG

Shame!

HH

I know; I know. This is a sad and solemn time.

ACG *(Looking)*

Well, there are folk here who think it *is*.

HH

I *know*—and it *is*. It *is*. And I shall play bereaved husband. I played it while she was alive, God knows, so, why not now?

ACG

Put on a face; someone's coming.

HH

Right; ready.

CONSTANCE

You don't know me . . .

HH

But I know you?

ACG

Steady!

CONSTANCE

Pardon?

HH

I am not myself; I'm sorry.

CONSTANCE

I understand.

HH *(Hysteria underneath)*

Though, if I am not myself, who am I?

ACG

Steady, I said.

CONSTANCE

I understand what you're going through.

HH (*A suppressed laugh*)

You couldn't possibly!

CONSTANCE

I know your grief; I lost a husband once.

HH (*Commiserating*)

Ahhhhhh.

CONSTANCE

You must feel numb—not a sensation in your body.

HH

Well . . .

CONSTANCE

It passes; the vital juices flow again. *Believe* me.

HH

I am more than willing.

CONSTANCE

Dear Charlotte and I, we talked of you; she told me what a splendid man you are—alive, vital . . .

HH

Juices flowing, and all?

CONSTANCE

Hm?

HH

She . . . she thought well of me?

CONSTANCE

She said she'd never known what marriage was . . . until you.

HH (*Modesty*)

Well, dear, dead *Mr.* Haze . . .

CONSTANCE

A cypher! A veritable cypher!

HH

Her very words?

CONSTANCE

No, but I knew.

HH

Aha!

CONSTANCE

She said you brought her to full fruit.

HH *(A tiny pause)*

Well. How grateful I am.

CONSTANCE

Full fruit.

HH

Well.

ACG

Roll with it.

HH *(To* ACG; *an aside)*

I'm trying!

CONSTANCE

Constance, she said to me—I am Constance; I live nearby; I have been away.

HH

How do you do?

CONSTANCE

Constance, she said to me, if anything should happen to me, should my too happy heart give out, should the grim reaper grow impatient, should I seem too happy to be allowed to live . . .

HH

She said all that!

CONSTANCE

I'm paraphrasing.

HH

Aha.

CONSTANCE

Should anything happen to me, she said, come into the breech, dear Constance—after a decent interval, of course.

HH

Do I understand you?
   (To ACG*)*
Do I understand her?

ACG

I think you do.

CONSTANCE

And so, dear man, now is not the time . . .

HH

No, no.

CONSTANCE

. . . but, when your grief is lessened, or when your heart beats again, or when the touch of soft, willing flesh is appealing . . . well, I'm Constance Apple, and I live in the green house down the road . . .

HH

Yes, yes . . .

CONSTANCE

And I am a widow . . . if you get my meaning.

HH

Well, I . . .

CONSTANCE

No more for now. I'll leave you to your grief.

HH

Thank you.

CONSTANCE

I probably shouldn't have spoken at all, nor would I have, had I not seen you staring at me . . . at my poitrine, to be exact.

HH

At your . . . ? Really; was I?

CONSTANCE (*She hugs him*)

Thank you for making our darling Charlotte into a woman again.
(*She moves back into the crowd*)

HH

Well, yes, I . . .
(*To* ACG)
You tax credulity; you really do.

ACG

You doubt her? You doubt these women see the ram in you?

HH

This is a wake!

ACG

I suppose you think badly of these people.

HH

Nonsense; I have been propositioned, have I not? What else would you expect in front of the dead?

ACG

Whose idea was the open coffin? I find that . . . grisly.

HH

The undertaker's. Constance Apple, indeed!

ACG

Be gentle with these people. They're trying to help.

HH

Take my mind off my terrible loss?

ACG

That is what they believe . . . yes.

HH

How do we define a civilization? By its death rites?

ACG

If we like. By whatever conclusion we wish to reach. Here comes your maid.

HH

Louise?
(Turns to her)
Aha; Louise.
(He puts his hand out, in preparation)

LOUISE

I quit.
(She turns on her keel and moves away)

HH *(After her)*

Well.
(To ACG*)*
Well.

ACG

Maybe the widow Apple knows a cleaning lady.

HH

Let it fill with dust—more dust; I don't care.

ACG

Some are leaving; speak to them.

HH

What! A speech?

ACG

Something.

HH *(Under his breath)*

Christ!

(To the gathering)

You've been kind to come—kind to dear Charlotte, for you've barely known me, or not at all. You tell me—you have told me—that I had made her happy; I'm grateful, for Charlotte brought to my life . . . pleasures I had not anticipated.

ACG

Be careful.

HH

And she has left me a treasure image of herself—her darling Lolita.

(Murmurs from the gathering,)

That child . . . my ward, now; my challenge; *my* treasure.

ACG

Be *very* careful, you fool!

HH *(To ACG)*

Hush.

(To the gathering,)

I promise you, I will keep her with me, protect her from sorrow, from all the buffetings.

(More murmur;, a cry or two)

I thank you; I thank you all.

(The gathering begins to disperse, save QUILTY, *who lingers at the open coffin. To* ACG)

Done well? Sincere? Not too. . . European?

ACG

You live dangerously.

HH *(Shrugs)*

How else?

(Claps his hands; comes to life)

Well, now; on to better things!

ACG

Be careful; you still have a guest!

HH

I . . . what!?

(Turns)

Ah . . . the *Strange Mushroom.*

QUILTY

Tough luck, fella!

HH *(Panic)*

What! What's happened!?

QUILTY
(Generally, languid, over-solicitous)
Charlotte, and all.

HH

Oh. That; yes.

QUILTY

Good gal, Charlotte.

HH

Yes; yes.
(Peers into the coffin, waves a little)

QUILTY

Lucky stiff!

HH

Pardon!?

QUILTY
You, fella! Would have tried it with her myself, 'cept . . . well, not exactly my type, ya know what I mean?

HH

I'm sure.

QUILTY
Good woman; good hearty breeding stock. Fell right down those stairs and broke her neck, eh?

HH *(Glances at the stairs)*
Yes; them's the ones.

QUILTY
Sure-footed as a mountain goat, too.

HH

Sir?

QUILTY *(Expansive)*
Weeeeelllll, that's the way it goes. Hey, fella, what're ya gonna do with the little lady, eh?

HH

The . . . ?

QUILTY
Lo. Lolita. How come she's not here?

HH

She's away at camp.

QUILTY

Still!

HH

I phoned them. Lolita is off on a five-day hike into the mountains with her little playmates. I thought it best . . .

QUILTY

Right! Right! Break it to her yourself!

HH

Yes! Right!

QUILTY

Tell her gently . . . open your arms to her, let her cry her little heart out?

HH

Yes; right!

QUILTY

Put your arms around her? Pat her sweet shoulders? Rock her to sleep? Eh, fella?

HH

It seemed . . . it seemed best—gentlest, most humane.

QUILTY (*Expansive*)

Sure! Sure! Good kid, Lolita. You, uh . . . you both coming back here? Hm?

HH

(*Withdrawing, psychologically*)

I . . . I haven't made plans yet. I thought . . . I thought we might take a little trip.

QUILTY

Oh? A little trip?

HH

Yes; see some country. No point bringing her right back here—ghosts, you know—her mother.

QUILTY

Right! Right! A little trip, eh?

HH (*Offhand, a chuckle*)

Oh . . . a little spin.

QUILTY

Nice; nice. Good for you, fella; good for you. Well, see ya around, hunh?

HH

Right!

QUILTY *(Turns to go)*

Oh, give Lo a kiss for me, will ya? Tell her her old homework helper is still thinking about her. Tell her to be in touch.

HH

Sure thing!

QUILTY *(A nudge)*

Well . . . see ya around fella.

    (He exits)

HH *(To ACG)*

Odd man.

ACG

Oh?

HH

I must ask Lolita about him.

ACG

Oh? Whatever for?

HH

Just . . . just curious.

ACG

Are you planning to kidnap her?

HH

I beg your pardon!?

ACG

What is this little trip? This spin?

HH *(A smile)*

Your guess is as good as mine.

ACG

Oh, you sly person.

    (He chuckles, as HH *moves to the coffin)*

A final goodbye?

HH

It seems only . . . proper. Well Charlotte . . .

CHARLOTTE

    (Sits up in her coffin; rage suffusing her face)

I'll see you in hell Humbert Humbert!

HH *(Retreating from the coffin)*

Dear God!

CHARLOTTE

Child molester! Betrayer of trusting woman! Seducer of mother and daughter! Death of your wife!

HH *(Approaching her again)*

For heaven's sake! Be still! There are people!

CHARLOTTE

I'll shout the house down! Cover me with earth and I'll shout it from the grave! Child molester! Seducer!

HH

Be quiet woman! Finally! Be quiet!

CHARLOTTE

I'll see you in hell, Humbert Humbert!

(He lowers the coffin lid on her, pushing her prone)

I'll see you in hell, Humbert . . .

HH *(When that is done)*

Dear Christ!

ACG

And now?

HH

And now? And now Lolita.

CURTAIN

SCENE FIVE

(The motel room swings into place. HH and ACG downstage)

HH *(To the audience)*

Are you appalled that I put the coffin cover down? I'm sorry if you are, but we would have been all night. The scene would never have ended. Besides, Lolita has to be told, does she not?

ACG *(To HH)*

Thoughtful man!

HH *(Still to the audience)*

Yes! I am! My lust is all-engulfing, ravages me, but it does not blind me to my darling's . . . humanity—if you will pardon the word. She is still a twelve-year-old child. And her mother is dead. I have an obligation to that, and I shall accommodate both—my obligation and my lust.

ACG

Your obligation to your lust, did you say.

HH

My obligation *and* my lust.

ACG

Which will come first, I wonder.

HH

I am driven.

(To the audience)

Have you ever been . . . driven? Compelled to a conclusion, an action almost beyond your control—some sudden, impetuous cascade of events startles you by their implications, by their ingenuity? A stock manipulation, perhaps? A tax evasion? An infidelity . . . a fidelity? Of course you have! Then you will not be surprised to learn that the treasure of my loins is, at this very moment behind that door, is showering her filthy, delectable body, rubbing soap over her . . . enough, Humbert! That it was a snap to whisk her away from camp. I told her her mother was . . . ill, was in the hospital, but not to worry, that her adoring Mommykins, my Charlotte would soon get better . . . better and better . . .

ACG

. . . and immediately die.

HH *(To* ACG; *some distaste)*

We did not discuss that.

(To the audience again)

She—my Lolita, my Lolly—seemed . . . mildly concerned; I told her we could not drive it all in one day, that we would stop at . . .

(Indicates the room)

. . . at this, this . . . motel, I believe it is called, this purely American invention? I have never stayed at one. It called itself an Inn. I chose it from the book; it was not far from camp—far enough, to be sure, but not too near the theoretical hospital in which theoretical Charlotte was lying in theoretical ill-health.

(To ACG*)*

I am amazed by this . . . motel thing.

ACG

They are simple; they are cheap; they give a sense of unreality.

HH

Do they differ, one from the other?

ACG

Not usually.

HH

Imagine a life in these.

ACG

Try not to think about it; not yet.

HH *(Smiles; to the audience)*

Is he telling me something? At any rate . . . can you hear the shower?

(Calls)

Soap and water, my darling.

(Back)

It is not that I am fussy. She could come to me, nails ringed in lampblack, her hair a tangle of burrs, and I would lick her clean; she could bury her luscious self in mud and I would tongue a path to my desire. Nymphets always smell of dawn and the dew.

(Shrugs)

I just thought she might like a shower.

ACG

How are you going to go about it?

HH

Hm? Pardon?

ACG

How are you going to *about* it?

HH

Oh.

(Matter-of-fact)

I'm going to knock her out.

ACG

You're going to *what!?*

HH *(Takes out a vial)*

This is a sleeping potion, which I shall give her presently . . .

ACG

A sleeping potion!? Where did you get it, from a gnome somewhere?

HH *(Patient)*

It was my Charlotte's. At times our revels put her in such a state of excitement nothing but this could put her down—nothing; tireless, that tiresome lady. And so I thought it would do for her child—like mother like daughter: knock her out.

ACG

Let me understand this; you plan to render her unconscious, and *then* have your way with her!?

HH *(Great dignity)*

Why . . . certainly. But—before you misunderstand to the point of passing judgement—understand what "way" I plan to have with her tonight.

ACG

Nonetheless!

HH

She will be naked—I'll see to that—and knocked out cold. I . . . do you think I plan to rape her?

ACG

Well, I . . .

HH

This is not a one night stand; I plan a lifetime with this child—however long that lasts, the term of her nymphancy. Six months? A year?

(The bathroom door opens partway)

LOLITA'S VOICE

Hey! Throw me my robe!

HH

Where is it, pet?

LOLITA'S VOICE

In my duffel! Where d'ya think?

(HH goes to the duffel)

HH

In the duffel.

(Puzzled)

What is a duffel?

ACG

The soft one, with straps; I *think*.

LOLITA'S VOICE

Hurry up, will ya?

HH *(Searching; finds it)*

Aha; have it!

LOLITA'S VOICE

Well, bring it here.

HH

Coming, darling; coming Lo.

LOLITA'S VOICE

Don't look! You dirty old man!

(She puts a hand out, grabs robe, slams door. Reopens it)

Thank you.

(Slams it again)

ACG

Dirty old man. Well, she has *your* number. Better watch it.

HH *(Serious)*

No; I think she means that as a figure of speech; I mean, even *as* a figure of speech, she means it as one. Do you follow me?

ACG

I was following an earlier logic. You do not plan to rape the child.

HH *(High horse)*

Most certainly not!

    (Picks up his doll, holds it in front of him as defense)

ACG

You do plan to drug her into insensibility, however, and strip her naked on the bed.

HH

Of course.

    (A pause)

It's very simple.

    (To the audience)

It is really very simple. At a restaurant—a fine one—have you ever had a soup set before you, a fish soup, say, bouride aswim on toasts, as the French put it, a soup so redolent and orange-gold that there is nothing for it but to lower your face to the plate, hover there . . . breathe in . . . and die? Have you never had that?

    (To ACG)

Never?

ACG

I have been . . . tempted.

HH

Then you know! You don't scrabble for your spoon and slurch into the bowl all at once. No; no, you breathe; you absorb; you . . . anticipate.

ACG

Oh; I see.

HH

And so it is with my darling, with my Lo. I shall have her naked flesh . . .

    (Demonstrates with the doll)

I shall run my fingers, my lips, my tongue over each curve and declension of her mind-blinding flesh. I shall kiss each breast, bury my nose in her armpitlets . . .

ACG

Armpitlets?

HH *(Pays him no mind)*

I shall hold her kidskin buttocks in my rough, large hands, and I shall lift her toward me, her downy mound at my nostrils, at my mouth.

ACG *(Tight smile)*

I think I understand.

HH

I shall learn her body—with my eyes, my fingers, my nose, my lips, my . . .

ACG

I think we all understand.
     (To the audience)
Is there any one of you who does not understand? I thought not!

HH *(To the audience)*

After all, we must proceed delicately in these delicate matters. Later, when she is comfortable with me, when her grief and loss have fastened on me in the form of—dare I say it?—love, then there will be time to introduce the matter once again—so to speak.

ACG

You have a way with words.

HH *(To ACG)*

Thank you. Besides, this is to be a night of perfume and passivity. It is not to be a time of tangled sheets, grunts, cries . . . and blood.

ACG

Blood? Blood, you say?

HH

Why certainly. Surely my treasure is a virgin.
     (The theatre fills with many laughters, mocking cries, hoots. HH looks to the flies, the wings for their source. ACG seems oblivious. As quickly as they came they cease)
What was that!?

ACG

What?

HH

Never mind; nothing; a train somewhere; a trick of the wind.

ACG

What did you *hear?*

HH *(Dismissing him)*

Nothing; it was nothing; wind in the willows.

ACG

How appropriate—child and all.

HH *(A sneer)*
What should I have said . . . Laughter in the Dark?

ACG *(Chuckles)*
Very good; very good.

HH *(Ibid)*
Or mentioned that tonight, in a comparative way, my passion burns with a Pale Fire? Though that is but one night's gambit?

ACG *(Chuckles even more)*
Oh, splendid fellow; *do* go on.

HH
. . . That even though it is the American dream—if we only admitted it—it's held in a delicate balance and will soon be all over?

ACG
Very good! Very good!
    (But LOLITA *opens the bathroom door, and emerges, draped in her robe.* HH *drops his doll)*

HH *(Feigns calm)*
Well, there you are. You certainly took long enough.

LOLITA
Well, you wanted me clean, why I can't imagine.

HH
Clean feels good.

LOLITA
Who to?

HH
Pardon?

LOLITA
Hey! Just how sick *is* Mom? Hunh?

HH
Well she'll have to have an operation. It's something abominable—abdominal; abdominal!

LOLITA
Well, when am I gonna get to see her?

HH
We'll get there, dear. Tomorrow, probably.

LOLITA
Well, maybe we oughta call her. Give me the number.

HH
NO!

LOLITA

Hunh?

HH

I mean . . . let her sleep; she's probably sedated for the operation. Let her sleep.

LOLITA

(Looking around the room; matter-of-fact)

What are we supposed to do—sleep in the same bed?

HH

They promised a cot; they said they'd bring a cot.

LOLITA

For who? Who's gonna use the cot?

HH

Why, I will, child. If you're good . . . you can have the bed.

LOLITA

You're crazy, Pop.

HH

Whatever do you mean?

LOLITA

Because, my Dahhhhling, when Dahhhhhling mother finds out, she'll divorce you and strangle *me.*

HH *(Absurd panic)*

Finds out!? Finds out what!?

LOLITA *(A nudge)*

Awwwwww, come on, Dad!

HH *(Attempted stern and fatherly)*

Now, look here, Lo. Let's settle this once and for all. For all practical purposes I am your father. I have a feeling of great tenderness for you . . .

LOLITA

The word is incest, Dad.

HH

(Curiously, genuinely outraged)

Incest! Lolita!

(He reaches out, to embrace her in a fatherly way)

LOLITA *(Wiggles away)*

Let's cut the crap, Dad.

HH *(Nervous)*

Shall we . . . shall we have a little dinner?

LOLITA

You hungry, Dad?

HH

(As LOLITA *moves slowly around him, closer and closer*)
Well I . . . I thought a hamburger, and a choc-choc-choc-chocolate milk-
shake might hit the spot.

LOLITA

What spot you wanna hit, Dad?

HH

Lolita, I . . .

LOLITA

I know what you really want, Dad.

HH

(*Draws the doll in front of him protectively*)
You . . . you do?

LOLITA

Sure thing, Dad.

HH

Then . . . then you tell me.

ACG (*Shakes his head; chuckles*)

Oh, my; oh, my.

LOLITA

Mom's sure gonna kill somebody when she finds out, you sweet, dirty old
man.

HH (*Genuinely panicked*)

Lolita, my child, my darling, my . . . I . . .

LOLITA

(*Standing in front of* HH, *her back to the audience*)
Here you go, Dad.
(*She spreads her arms—See* Tiny Alice—*exposing her naked front
to* HH; *he gasps; slowly, she lets the robe fall from her body, show-
ing us her back, her buttocks.* HH *gasps again*)
Here you go, Dad. What are you waiting for?

HH

(*Hesitates, flings the doll to one side*)
Oh! Lolita!
(*With a cry of ecstasy he throws himself forward, burying his face
in her belly*)

LOLITA *(Looking at her nails)*

That's it, Dad; you got it.

ACG *(To the audience)*

Let me draw a veil over this.

(A half-curtain, already unobtrusively set, flows across the motel set. hiding HH *and* LOLITA. *To the wings)*

Thank you.

(To the audience)

You don't really want to *see* it, do you? You can imagine it. You all *have* imagined it; and you have blanked it from your mind; you may have known it in dreams only, dreams you deny to your waking mind. Don't be angry with *me;* I don't invent these things. We are animals, remember, not far from the baboon, and circumspection is often confused with civilization.

(To HH, *through the veil)*

Are you done? Is your triumph complete?

*(*HH *comes around the veil, shirt half in, tightening his belt)*

HH

My what? My triumph?

ACG

Hmmmmm; your virgin.

HH

Do you know what she told me—*during* it, if you please?—bouncing up and down like a toy, niplets agiggle, riding me like some horse?

ACG

No; what did she tell you?

HH *(Appalled)*

She told me she's been at it for a year.

ACG

No!

HH

At camp! At school! Under the soda foundtain, for all I know!

ACG

I say!

HH

They go at it like guinea pigs—all the little boys and girls, fucking and sucking and God only knows what else!

ACG

That's shocking!

HH

Well, it *is!* It *is* shocking!

ACG

And you so wanted to be first! So much for fish soup, eh? Eh?

HH

I am appalled; I really am. Who raises these children?

ACG

Their parents, usually; your dear, dead Charlotte, in this particular.

HH *(Dead serious)*

She couldn't have known! She couldn't!

ACG

Well, with dear, dead wat's-her-name gone, you're the parent now. I'm sure you'll put a stop to her wanton ways.

HH

How dare they not list you among the Absurdists.

ACG *(Smiles)*

All in good time.

HH

(Offhandedly fingering the doll he has brought with him, under arm from behind the veil)
And how dare you not warn me!?

ACG

Well, all that with the plate of soup, and everything.

HH

You are cruel! Cold and cruel!

ACG

Forgive me the vulgarity, but . . . how was she, hunh?
     (Winks)
Hunh? I suspect there are a number of people who might like to know.
     (Another parody of Rotarian horror)
How was she, hunh?

HH

(To the audience; still holding the doll, utilizing it)
You want to know how she was, hunh!? You want intimate particulars, or will a general rundown do?

ACG

What are you so angry with them for? They haven't done anything to you.

HH

What?

ACG

What have they done to you?

HH (To the audience)

I'm sorry; he's right; I'm sorry. In all my years of nymphet-hunting, nostril-quivering, trouser-bulging lurk in play-yards, buses, school assemblies, never—never, in all my wasted years—has there been such a one as Lolita.

ACG (To himself)

Oh?

HH (To the audience, still)

I have travelled the world; I have nymphetted myself across continents, but this is the ultimate one—the numphet of nymphets, the pure, impure, innocent, practiced, virginal, defiled, knowing, unknowing, final goal of all my searching, the reward of all my longing.

ACG

I see; indeed.

HH (Still to the audience)

Time must stop; she must never grow older.

ACG (To HH)

She will.

HH (To ACG)

Stop time for me? Please?

ACG (Gentle)

How can I?

HH

For just a little? Give me hope?

ACG

Have it while you can.

HH

Promise me! Don't mean it even, but promise me.

ACG

Are you in rut, or are you in love?

HH (Humble)

I am profoundly, blindly, shamelessly, hopelessly . . . in love.

ACG (Sad)

I see.

HH

I am enthralled, wrapped in magic; I shall die of it.

ACG

Poor man; poor satyr.

HH

Help me?

ACG

Have you told her yet? Have you told her her mother is dead?

HH

No, I . . . well, no.

ACG

Profoundly in love, are you?

HH

I don't want to hurt her.

ACG

Lose her, you mean.

HH *(Tight-lipped)*

I'll tell her.

(*He turns on his heel, and goes behind the veil. We hear a wailing; the sound of a child desperately crying. The veil pulls to one side; we see* HH *seated on the bed,* LOLITA *buried in his arms, crying her eyes out. To* ACG)

Pretty sight? Pretty sound?

ACG

Better now than later; better now than never.

HH *(Pitiful)*

Leave us alone?

ACG *(Smiles, a stage whisper)*

I'll give you the illusion of it.

(ACG *ostentatiously tip-toes to one side of the stage*)

I'll be way over here; you'll hardly notice me.

HH

And that will have to do?

ACG *(Gentle)*

And that will have to do.

HH

(*Concentrates on* LOLITA *now; strokes her head, pats her back, tries to soothe her*)

Hush, my darling; hush, Lolita; it's all right; I'm here; I love you; I'll comfort you; I'll hold you close; you'll never have to be alone; it's all right, darling; hush; hush, now.

(LOLITA *weeps more softly now, clutches* HH)

Hush, my pet, let me hold you; there, there now; let me kiss your tears away; let me; there we go; one; and now the other; there; Oh! oh, cry away my precious; yes; yes; there, there, now. Rest; rest your sweet head; yes; yes. Are you comfortable? Here, let me move you; there; sweet angel; cry on my belly; yes. There, there. All better? Getting better? Feeling better? Then rest, my angel. Place your head . . . just a . . . little . . . lower. That's it . . . just a . . . little . . . lower . . . just a . . . little . . . lower.

ACG *(To the audience)*

And time stopped.

(Blackout on all but ACG*)*

CURTAIN

ACT TWO

SCENE ONE

(ACG *alone, in a spotlight; perhaps the veil has reclosed during the previous blackout*)

ACG

And time stopped, and in that holding of a breath a journey began—a journey of five hundred days, five hundred nights, the nights more often better than the days.

(*The veil parts; a new motel room; the bed made differently; new curtains; new picture above the bed*)

LOLITA (*Shrieking*)

You don't love me!

HH (*Helpless*)

I love you!

LOLITA

You say you love me! You don't!

HH

Lolita! Please!

LOLITA

All you want's your goddamn nookie!

HH

Nookie!? Where did you learn that word from—Mummie?

LOLITA

OK. Ass! Your goddamn ass! That better?

HH

Lolita! Darling! Please!

LOLITA

What's the matter? You afraid somebody'll hear? Tough!

HH

Please!

LOLITA (*Cupping her hands*)

Help! Rape! There's a dirty old man in here with a child not thirteen yet! You won't believe the things he makes her do! Help! Help!

HH *(Lunges at her; misses)*

God damn you!

LOLITA

Says he loves her. All he wants is in her pants! He's her father, too!

HH *(Gets her finally; hisses)*

Now you stop that, you little vixen!

LOLITA

Make me!

HH *(Enraged)*

I love you! I love you, God damn it!

LOLITA *(Contempt)*

You don't love me; all you love is my body!

HH

HOW AM I SUPPOSE TO SEPARATE THE TWO!?

LOLITA *(A beat)*

Hunh?

HH *(Calmer)*

How am I suppose to separate the two? I look at you, my heart, my mind are filled with selfless, pure, lovely love. I look at you, my mind undresses you, I smell the perfume of you, and I am on top of you! What can I do about it?

LOLITA

Whyn't you do it yourself once in a while? Hunh? God! I'm getting chafed.

HH

(Ashamed the audience is hearing)

Lolita! Please!

LOLITA *(Ugly)*

WELL!?

HH *(Helpless)*

I adore you.

LOLITA

(To the audience, a mimicking)

Hold it; take it in your hand; oh, isn't that big, precious?; let's go beddy-bye, cudlums, Daddy has a big surprise for you; take it in your hand; put it here, put it there, put it in your . . .

HH

BE SILENT!!

LOLITA *(A beat, a little girl)*

I wanna go home.

HH

You *can't* go home.

LOLITA *(Whining)*

Wwwwhhhhyyyyy!?

HH *(Weary)*

You can't go home.

LOLITA

I miss my friends; I wanna go to school.

HH

Your friends are stupid; you hate school.

LOLITA *(Braying)*

WELL, IT'S BETTER THAN BEING DRAGGED FROM MOTEL TO MOTEL LIKE SOME GODDAMN WHITE SLAVE!

HH

Will you keep that awful voice down!?

LOLITA *(Stage whisper)*

Well, it *is*.

HH

Don't I give you lessons every day?

LOLITA *(Heavy)*

Yeah, you sure do!

HH

School! School!

LOLITA

Yeah; so?

HH

Dolly; precious Dolly; why aren't you happy? I *love* you!

LOLITA *(Reasonable; no nonsense)*

Look, Dad; I'm a little girl.

HH

You are a young *lady*.

LOLITA

I am a little girl, happens not to mind a little fun and games from time to time, but, still, a little girl. I'm supposed to be around kids my own age . . .

HH *(Outraged)*

Like those boys took you into the bushes off at camp!?

LOLITA

At least they didn't make a big thing of it, all that . . . what do you call it?

HH *(Tired)*

Foreplay.

LOLITA

Yeah; that. Wham, bam, thank you, ma'am; simple, pure and simple. Not these *hours* and *hours* of pawing, and licking, and . . .

HH

(Claps a hand over her mouth)

That's enough, young lady!

(She struggles)

That's enough, I said!

(LOLITA *calms down;* HH *releases her)*

HH

Where!? Where are you going?

LOLITA *(Surly)*

I'm going out.

(Laughs)

Oh, listen to you! What are you afraid of? You think I'm going to find me some boys my own age, take off to some bushes, or somewhere . . . ?

(HH *lunges, but* LOLITA *giggles, moves away)*

Don't worry, Dad; I like you old men.

HH

Lolita; I am thirty-nine years old.

LOLITA

Yeah; that's what I said. Give me some money.

HH

You . . . have a call to make, or something? There's a phone right by the bed here . . .

LOLITA *(Mildly disgusted)*

I want to get me a candy bar, Dad. Give Lo her allowance.

HH *(Fishes)*

Here's . . . here's dollar.

LOLITA *(Takes it, looks at it)*

Boy, you sure get it cheap, don't ya?

(Giggles, runs from the room. HH *buries his head in his hands)*

ACG *(gently)*

Why don't you tell her straight out?

HH (*Through his hands*)

Tell her what?

ACG

That you're afraid of losing her; that if you go back, she'll be just another little girl; she'll grow away from you; she'll find her level, and goodbye to all this?

HH

Tell her *that?*

ACG

You dramatize. That is you keep her with you, fleeing fleeting across this country like some criminal . . .

HH

I am a criminal! They would jail me for life, or string me up.

ACG

You dramatize. That if you keep her with you, fleeing across this country, suspending time, she will stay as she is. But will she?

HH

Yes.

ACG

You know better.

HH

Long enough!

ACG

There is never long enough; you know that.

HH

It will become forever!

ACG

And you know better than that, too.

HH

Leave me alone.

ACG

Does she *love* you?

HH

I love her; let me alone.

ACG

But does *she* love *you?*

HH

(*Stares a while before answering; cold*)

I don't want to know. I have found the past, and I will have it while I can.

ACG

When she . . . how can I put this so you'll not panic?—when the time comes for her to . . . go, will you let her? Freely? Gladly? Gratefully?

HH

(Slowly awakening to what is being said)
Go? GO!?
(The glimmerings of paranoia here)
What are you telling me? What is being done? Is she seeing people? Is that it?

ACG

This is not elfinland, dear Humbert, the enchanted glade. This is Boise, if I am not mistaken.

HH

Where would she go!? Is there someone? Where is she right now? What are you not telling me!? Lolita!? Lolita!?

ACG

She is getting candy; she told you so.

HH *(A sneer)*

What would you know!
(He flees out the door after LOLITA*)*

ACG *(To the audience)*

Was that cruel? I was trying to be helpful.
*(*LOUISE *enters, takes a bedspread off, rotates the painting, rotates the bay window)*
Louise? Louise, is that you?

LOUISE

Muh name's Ruta.

ACG *(Suave)*

You look like someone.

LOUISE

Well, I certainly hope so.
(Continues her work)

ACG *(To the audience)*

I could have sworn. There is going to come a time when there will be no Lolita, no Lo, no Dolly. The glade will whither and become sere. Nor will it happen . . . nicely. Lolita is not . . . well, it takes a very special person to be worthy of an unreasonable passion, and Lolita is a . . . well, she is a very average little girl; a trifle careless of her virtue, we might say; not . . . stupid, but not brighter than her poor dead mother; not fit subject for myth, this little miss. I thought I should tell our Humbert so. Am I wrong? You see, Lolita is already . . .

(But the door bursts open and LOLITA *bursts in followed by an angry* HH)

LOLITA

Bullshit! Just plain bullshit!

LOUISE

Mind your tongue, little girl; I'm a religious lady.

LOLITA

Sorry! Hey aren't you Louise?

LOUISE

Muh name's Ruta.

HH

Your name is Louise.

LOUISE

(Slamming the bay window into place)
Muh name is Ruta!

HH

I don't know what you're doing in Boise, Idaho . . .

LOUISE

Muh name is Ruta, and this is Whitefish, Montana. Now, if you will let me pass . . . ?

(She sweeps out)

HH *(To the audience)*

I could swear that was Louise.

LOLITA *(Kicks a chair over)*

Well, as good old Ma used to say, you can't tell one of 'em from another.

HH

Pick that chair up, you ruthless, scheming little . . .

LOLITA

Pick it up yourself, Dad!

HH

Who was that man you were talking to?

LOLITA

What man!?

HH

The man I saw you whispering with, who saw me coming and vanished round the corner.

LOLITA

I don't know what you're talking about.

HH
You're lying through your not very clean teeth!

LOLITA
Prove it! Prove I was talking to a man!

HH
Pr . . . prove it? You're not denying it? Prove it?

LOLITA *(Shrugging: daring)*
I'm not denying and I'm not admitting.

HH *(Enraged)*
WHO WAS THAT MAN!?

LOLITA *(Clearly enjoying it)*
He was. . . he *is* . . . I don't know who you're talking about, Pops.
(HH *hesitates a moment, then slaps* LOLITA *hard. After a moment, standing her ground)*
What is this? Some new trick?

HH *(Slaps her again)*
You like it?

LOLITA *(Considered; deliberate)*
Well, it wouldn't be my first *choice.*
(Tiny smile)
'Course . . . if it makes you *happy,* or anything . . .

HH
(Bursts into tears, envelops LOLITA *in his arms)*
Oh, my darling, my precious, my angel . . .
(They sink on the bed)

ACG
(Shaking his head, chuckling to the audience)
"Oh, my darling, my precious, my angel." I tell you, they behave like grownups.

HH *(Examining* LOLITA's *neck)*
Where did you get that hickey!

LOLITA
What hickey!? What are you talking about!?

HH
I worship your skin! I would *never* bite you! *Who* has been chewing on you!

LOLITA
Well, it's you, stupid.

HH

I would *never* bite you.

LOLITA

You get carried away!

HH (*Even more dogmatic*)

I worship your skin! I would *never* bite you! *Who* has been chewing on you?

LOLITA (*Shrill*)

Nobody Nobody! For Christ's sake!

HH

(*Runs to* ACG *as the motel room darkens*)

She has a hickey! She has a hickey!

ACG (*Very calm*)

My goodness. What next!?

HH

Who did it!?

ACG

Well . . . what does *she* say?

HH (*Quietly hysterical*)

She says *I* did it!

ACG

Did you?

HH

NO!

ACG (*Calming*)

You must have: consider the alternative; you must have.

HH

(*Considers, nods his head; great relief*)

I must have, mustn't I. It has to be me; there's no alternative . . . none I can accept.

ACG

(*Pats his shoulder; nicely, not patronizingly*)

Good boy. Oh, there's a lady there wants to see you.

(ACG *points to* QUILTY, *badly done up as a blowsy, heavyset, middle-aged woman*)

HH (*Shy*)

Me? Whatever for? Who is she?

ACG

Why don't you go talk to her and see?

(HH *moves toward* QUILTY. *To the audience*)

This is a most peculiar scene—doesn't advance the plot, or anything. Interesting, though; watch.

HH

(*Approaching* QUILTY, *who is sitting in a beach chair*)
Good day?

QUILTY

Aha! Mr. Harold Haze?

HH

In a way. At your service.

QUILTY

And how are you enjoying our balmy California weather?

HH

Cali—fornia?

QUILTY

La Jolla here is known for its balm; it is known for its fogs, as well. And its seals. And whales pass; look out to sea; you might catch one.

HH

La . . . Jolla? Whales? Whatever happened to Whitefish, Montana, I wonder?

QUILTY

Went under, I shouldn't be surprised. Look here, Mr. Haze, I don't mean to intrude on your precious time; I see you with your splendid little daughter—arm in arm at Woolworths, hissing intensely at one another at soda fountains; one might confuse you for an odd pair of lovers, if one didn't know better.

HH

Tell me, madam, how does one know better?

QUILTY

We psychologists see all!

HH

Psychologists!

QUILTY (*Fishes in a purse for a card*)
Wanda Blue, child psychologist, at your service, as the saying goes.

HH

Wanda. . . Blue?

QUILTY

Well, not exactly; there's more to the last part, and Wanda is a folie of my own fashioning, but we all create our own identity, do we not!

HH (*An aside to* ACG)

Who *is* this woman?

(ACG *shrugs*)

QUILTY

Wanda, or whatever, Blue et cetera, at your service

HH

How can I help you, Madam? My daughter and I have . . .

QUILTY

Yes, your charming Lolita.

HH

You know her name!

QUILTY

Oh, we talked, and talked, and talked; tete a tete; woman to woman, so to speak.

HH (*Grim*)

I see!

QUILTY

Let me ask you a blunt question, Mr. Haze . . .

HH

Why don't you just call me Harold?

QUILTY

Harold; Harold Haze; that makes your initials HH, does it not. I love alliteration.

(*Swings forward*)

Look here, Harold, what's the matter with that lovely child!?

HH (*Feeling trapped*)

Matter? What matter? Nothing matter.

QUILTY

You're one of those old-fashioned European fathers—probably not even a citizen yet, maybe not even legally in the country, sort of a wetleg—and you might not notice these things, but I see your Lolita as shuttling.

HH

Shuttling?

QUILTY

Indeed! Shuttling between the anal and genital zones of development.

HH

I beg your pardon? What zones?

QUILTY *(Chortles)*

Oh, you old-fashioned, European types; you'd stab your best friend in the back without giving it a second thought, but when the conversation turns to a little girls' matters, you get all blushy and soft.

HH

I assure you, Blue, I have never stabbed anyone in the back; of course I am always willing to make an exception, if it will help.

QUILTY *(Clapping)*

Good! Good old American aggression; you're learning, Harold. By the way, exactly what nationality is Haze? Harold Haze?

HH

Ugandan.

QUILTY

You're pulling my leg!

HH

I wouldn't dream of such a thing.

QUILTY

Oh? You have something against ripe women?

HH

May we get on with this interview, Blue Wanda?

QUILTY

I thought it was Lolita needed help, Haze Harold, but I was mistaken. I was going to suggest the poor darling get out more, see children her own age, go to school, visit her home, be allowed to trip to the little girl's room without you following her, be allowed to make a phone call by herself, talk to elderly priests and other wholesome types in the aisles of department stores without being watched and questioned—hideously questioned, be permitted to develop birthmarks on her neck without dreadful scenes, from her step-father . . .

HH

Step-father?

QUILTY

What!? Are you her true father?

HH

I . . . I . . .

QUILTY

Yes, you don't know who you are, do you, *H.H.*

HH

Blow, Blue!

QUILTY (*Takes out a notebook*)

I'll tell you what report I'll make, Harold; I'm from the state, you know; I was thinking hard on suggesting your daughter be made a ward of San Diego county . . .

HH

You're insane!

(*To* ACG, *beside himself*)

Rid me of this woman!

ACG

You are not enjoying this?

HH

RID ME OF HER!!

ACG (*Sighs*)

Very well. Miss Blue? Will you . . . go off, please?

QUILTY

We tried to help, you clever writer, you.

ACG

I know you did, Miss Blue; bye-bye.

QUILTY

Bye-bye.

(*To* HH)

Watch yourself, Haze, or whatever your name is. There are things lurking behind every tree; moving shadows in every corner; each word is a lie maybe; who can you trust? Bye.

(QUILTY *exits.* HH *runs to* ACG)

HH

It's settled!

ACG

What is settled?

HH

Mexico.

ACG

What is this history lesson. Of course Mexico is settled; the Spaniards came there in fifteen-something, slaughtered the Aztecs and the Mayans . . .

HH

I'm taking her to Mexico! They can't get us there.

ACG *(To the audience)*

This hadn't occurred to me.

HH

I can *marry* her *there!* It's common practice.

ACG

You can't marry the child; that's madness!

HH

And what is *this*!?

ACG

Obsession; delusion; enthrallment.

HH

I'll work; I'll grow marijuana; I'll be rich; we'll have a daughter—Lolita two, and maybe, just maybe, when *she* is twelve and a half . . .

ACG

I can't let you do this.

HH

Then try and stop me!
   (Turns, moves toward the motel set, which has shifted in decor again)

ACG *(To the audience)*

As I told you: they get out of hand from time to time.
   (Waves his hand over the set; calls after HH*)*
A turn in the plot, Humbert! Be careful; you'll bang your head against it!
   *(*LOLITA *is in bed, clearly ill;* LOUISE *is standing by her)*

HH

   (Falls on his knees by the bed)
My treasure! What's wrong? What's wrong; are you sick?

LOUISE

She's sick, all right.

HH

Ruta, what's wrong with Lolita!?

LOLITA *(Weak, but brave)*

Hi, Dad.

LOUISE

Ruta!? Who's Ruta?

HH

You are.

LOUISE

You crazy?

HH

What are you doing in La Jolla, Ruta?

LOUISE

La Jolla!? This is Lovelock, Nevada, and my name's Brigitte.

LOLITA

Brigitte's been awful good to me, Dad. Where you been?

HH *(Falls on his knees by the bed)*

My treasure! What's wrong!?

LOUISE

A hundred and four temperature, that's what's wrong. I sent for the motel doctor.

HH

Get her a specialist!

LOUISE

In Lovelock? She's right; you crazy.

HH

Where does it hurt, my darling!?

LOLITA *(Weak)*

Where doesn't it!?

HH

Is it your precious tummy? Where?

LOLITA *(Heavy whisper)*

I think I have pneumonia, or something.

HH

But yesterday you were . . .

LOLITA

It just came on me, Dad.
  (A knock at the door)

LOUISE

That will be the doctor.
  (She goes, opens the door QUILTY *enters, got up as Groucho Marx imitating Dr. Quackenbush)*

QUILTY

Here I am. Who's sick? You, fella? You look terrible. Where does it hurt?

HH

It's my daughter.

QUILTY *(Goes to* LOUISE*)*

Stick your-tongue out, young lady.

HH

Here! Here! My daughter! Here!
  (Points to LOLITA, *in bed)*

QUILTY *(Approaching the bed)*

Well, why don't you be more specific, fella? Hello there, little miss; what seems to be the matter?

LOLITA

I don't feel good.

QUILTY

Hanh! Who feels good these days, eh? Stick out *your* tongue, then.
  *(*LOLITA *does)*
What's that, a life saver? Maybe that's the problem: sugar in the mouth.

LOUISE

She has a temperature of one hundred and four.

QUILTY

  (Wiggles his eyebrows; to LOLITA*)*
Pretty good, kid; you wanna try for hundred and five?

HH *(Furious; helpless)*

Help her!

QUILTY

Where does it hurt most, dear?

LOLITA

In my chest.

QUILTY *(Wiggles his eyebrows)*

In your chest! Well, let's take a look at the little treasures—the pleasure chest, the chest! That's it; the chest!
  (Looks at HH*)*
Don't peek.

HH

I am her father!

QUILTY

A likely story!
  (Turns back to LOLITA*)*
Now, let's undo these little buttons and . . . oh, my, what a sweet little chest—all those freckles!

HH

What do you think, doctor?

QUILTY

Not bad; not bad at all.

HH

Oh, thank heavens.

QUILTY (*Stethoscope out*)

Now, let's listen a little, shall we? Unh-hunh; unh-hunh; cough for me, dear.
    (LOLITA *does so*)
To one side, sweetheart: we medics aren't made of stone, you know.
    (*She coughs again to one side*)

HH

Oh, my precious.

QUILTY (*Finished*)

This child is sick, pneumonia, probably. Off we go! Up! Up!

HH

Off we go?

QUILTY

To the hospital, of course. What do you want her to do, die?

HH

Die?

QUILTY

These pneumonias, fella . . .
    (*Snaps his fingers*)
. . . just like that!

HH (*Rushes to* LOLITA)

Oh, my darling!

QUILTY

Bring her! there's no time to lose!

HH

Yes, yes; come, my treasure.
    (HH *sweeps* LOLITA *up in his arms, carries her. The set begins to shift,
    taking the motel from us, giving us a huge, empty space filled with
    doctors and nurses, all in white, spaced about the set, in tableau.*)

QUILTY

Hurry! Hurry!
    (*To* LOUISE)
See ya, Louise.

LOUISE

Bye.

LOLITA

Bye, Brigitte.

LOUISE

Bye.

HH

Bye, Ruta.

LOUISE

Bye.

QUILTY

Hurry! Nurse! Doctor! Take this child!
   (DOCTORS *and* NURSES *gently take* LOLITA *from* HH's *arms*)

HH

She'll be all right! You'll be all right, darling!

QUILTY

Of course she'll be all right, fella.

LOLITA

I'll be OK, Dad.

HH

Of course you will, my treasure. Be gentle with her; she's precious to me!

QUILTY

Of course she is. Leave her to us, now; she'll be in good hands.

LOLITA

Dad?

HH

Darling?

LOLITA

When you come to see me, Dad . . .

HH

I'll sleep at the foot of your bed; I'll . . .

QUILTY

Now, now; there are rules, you know.

LOLITA

Dad? When you come to see me, bring me all my things, will you? Pack our bags? Bring all my things?

HH

Of course, my darling.

LOLITA

I don't want to go back to that awful room.

HH

Of course not, precious.

(*A confidence*)

We'll go to Mexico; we'll cross the border; I'll get you a little passport; we'll live in Mexico.

LOLITA

Yeah? Well . . .

(*A fit of terrible coughing engulfs her*)

QUILTY

Quick! Take her!

HH

Lolita!

(*The* DOCTORS *and* NURSES *and* QUILTY *are retreating, walking backward with* LOLITA)

LOLITA

See ya, Dad; see ya; bye . . .

(*Lights down on all that*)

HH

I'll pack! I'll pack!

(HH *races off.* ACG *alone on stage*)

ACG (*To the audience*)

You know how ephemeral all things are, how mutable. That piece of music we made our own with our first or second love, would dance to, pelvis-locked, swaying? Hear it again, years later—loves later—and it is what it always was—trite, manufactured, embarrassing. And that face we love, we live with—our own, or another's? One morning—one night, no matter—we see it and the present is no longer there, only the past and the future—how it looked when we first saw it, how it *will* look when we see it for the last time. You know how ephemeral all things are, do you not. You've learned all that, *haven't* you; you're grown-ups, after all. *Aren't* you. Then pity poor Humbert; pity him; he still believes that we may tread twice the same path. Pity him. Do.

(HH *comes on, laden with baggage The* NURSES *and* DOCTORS *return, without* QUILTY; HH *moves slowly downstage*)

HH (*Happy*)

Lolita? Lolita? I'm packed; we're ready.

A NURSE (*Puzzled*)

Why . . . hello, Mr. Haze. What are you doing here?

HH

How is she? How is she today?

AN INTERN

How is who?

HH

Lolita! My daughter!

ANOTHER

Lolita?

HH *(Laughs)*

Yes; yesterday; pneumonia.

ANOTHER NURSE

Yesterday?

HH

Well, of course; yesterday; certainly it was yesterday?

A DOCTOR *(Remembering)*

Oooooooh, yes; that pretty little girl!

HH

Yes! Yes!

THE SAME DOCTOR

Well, she checked out this morning, didn't she, nurse?

HH *(Head swirling)*

Checked . . . out?

NURSE

Why I think so; let me look it up.

HH *(Panicked)*

Nobody has checked out! She is expecting me! I've come to take her!

NURSE *(Consulting her book)*

Here it is: Dolores Haze, thirteen, admitted with a generalized complaint . . .

HH

Pneumonia!

NURSE

. . . under the instructions of Dr. . . . what is it? Cover? Coverlet? Something.

HH

Pneumonia!

NURSE

Released this morning; yes; I remember now. Her Uncle Gustav came for her.

HH

Her Uncle Gustav . . . ?

NURSE

Yes; I remember; it was so cute; he brought a cocker spaniel puppy for her, and he paid the bill in cash . . .

HH

NO!

NURSE

Oh, and they left you a message; let me see if I can get it right . . .

HH *(A sense of the walls closing in)*

NO! NO!

A DOCTOR

Be calm, sir.

HH

NO!

NURSE

Oh, yes; you were not to worry; they were sorry they missed you; you were to keep warm, and they'd see you at grandpa's ranch as agreed. Yes.

HH *(The staff slowly closes in on him)*

Sorry they'd missed me!? Grandpa's ranch!? Keep warm!? Uncle Gustav!?

A DOCTOR

Take it easy, now.

HH *(Desperate)*

Lolita!?

ANOTHER DOCTOR

Go easy, sir.

HH *(Drops the bags)*

Lolita!? LOLITA!?

AN INTERN

Easy now.

HH

Where is she!? What have you done with her!?

A DOCTOR

You're going to have to leave, mister.

HH

NOT WITHOUT MY LOLITA!

(He rushes the staff, they grab him, force him to the floor, subdue him, during:)

Lolita! Lolita! Lolita!

A DOCTOR *(Finally)*
Do you want a straightjacket, mister, or will you be good?

HH *(After a long pause)*
I'll be good.
(He is released, still on the floor, the hospital staff retreats as before, into dark. HH *alone, with* ACG *to one side)*
I'll be very good.
(He begins to cry a little; sees ACG*)*
What have you done with her?

ACG *(Gentle)*
I?

HH *(Begging)*
Where is she? What have you done with her?

ACG *(So simple)*
She's . . . gone.

HH
(Quiet, despairing determination)
I'll find her.

ACG *(Shakes his head)*
Don't.

HH
I'll find her.
(Begins to crawl toward ACG*)*
No matter what you've done, I'll find her. How *could* you do this to me? I'll find her!

ACG
Believe me; *don't.*

HH *(To the audience)*
I'll find her! You'll see; I'll find her.
(Crying freely now; shaking)
I'll find her; you'll see; I'll find her.

ACG *(Interrupts, to the audience)*
Forgive me? Sorry; he's right; he will. Find her, that is. And he will be very sorry. Let three years pass; our hero has been a busy man.

CURTAIN

SCENE TWO

(The suggestion of an apartment—one room, bed opened from sofa; disarray; books, magazines, bottles, glasses. Noon. RITA *at a card table, with a coffee cup.* HH *by a window, standing, the doll with him; the* YOUNG MAN'S *feet visible;* ACG *to one side)*

HH

Lolita!
    (A call to the heavens)
LOLITA!

ACG (A mocking echo)

Lolita!

HH (Contemptuous)

You've never known love. Help me!

ACG (Detached)

There's no *help* for you. Pedophilia is a disease . . . you just have to . . .

HH

You cannot *call* it that!!

ACG (Gentle)

It is not I; it is . . .
    (Indicates the audience)
. . . they are the ones.
    (Harder)
You can't bed down with a child. Shame on you! Shame!

HH (Simple)

I have none.

ACG

You're lucky she's gone.

HH (Disbelief)

Lucky!

ACG

Change your name; leave the country; go to the moon; maybe they won't catch you.

HH

I'll find her; I'll . . . I'll have her back, I'll . . .

ACG

Flee!

HH

I'll have my revenge on . . . *him,* and then I'll . . .

ACG *(Gentle irony)*

And then you'll forgive her, take her back? Take her to the death house with you? They're executing once again, you know.

HH

We'll travel; we'll . . .

ACG

You've travelled. Flee to the ends of the world?

HH *(Trapped)*

Lolita? Lolita?

ACG *(An echo)*

Lolita; Lolita.

HH *(Revery; a quiet litany)*

Light of my life; love of my love; brown rose, skinned knee, doves to my hand, temptress, innocent child of my waking dreams . . .

ACG *(Unimpressed)*

Etcetera; etcetera.

HH *(Cold; matter-of-fact)*

You *have* never loved.

ACG

I am a happily married man; have been for years; my wife is an adult; we . . .

HH *(A small sneer)*

As I said; you have never *loved.*

ACG *(Smiles)*

Tiresome man.

HH

Leave me be, then.

ACG

Gladly.
(Indicates)
But with all this? Your loneliness, your . . . bereftness?

HH

This lady is my friend.

ACG

And the young man half off the bed?

HH *(Curious)*

I don't quite know who he *is.* I'm sure we'll find out. Perhaps Rita will know.

ACG

Rita?

HH

The lady?

ACG

Isn't she a bit long in the tooth for you? Why, she looks like she may have voted once or twice.

HH

Why don't you just . . .
   (Indicates off)

ACG *(Shrugs)*

As you like.
   (Moves to chair way to one side)
What kind of menage are you managing here, in the depths of your despair?

HH *(After him)*

I manage!
   (To the audience; softer)
I manage. I keep alive—I keep it going, the blood, the bones; I keep afloat, for if I sink . . . what use am I? To myself? To . . . her? To my darling?

ACG *(An echo)*

To my darling.

HH *(To ACG)*

Do hush.
   (To the audience)
This is Rita.

RITA *(Looks up; to the audience)*

Hi.
   (Goes back to her drink)

HH

Rita is. . .
   (Walks toward the audience, for a confidence)
Rita is my life jacket; my buoy; she buoys me; miss pneumatic.

RITA

Watch it, Hubert, I'm not deaf.

HH

Humbert.

RITA

Right.

HH *(To the audience again)*

This is Rita.

RITA *(To HH)*

Hey, who's this guy?
(*Indicates the passed-out* YOUNG MAN)

HH

I thought he might be one of yours.

RITA

I never seen him before.

HH

See if he's dead; if he's alive, wake him.
(To the audience)
Rita and I have been together for three whole years.

RITA

(To the YOUNG MAN, *shaking him)*
Hey.
(She proceeds trying to waken him)

HH

Rita. We met three years ago, nine months after my darling, my treasure,
my Lolita was taken from me. I was drunk; she was drunk; *we* were drunk,
in a bar somewhere.

RITA *(Busy)*

Omaha. I don't know if this one's dead, or not.

HH

Omaha? Perhaps. Why not? Shake him; put a mirror to his lips. If he's
dead we'll have to move.
(To the audience)
You see how I adjust.
(To RITA)
Omaha?

RITA

Near where the trees stop; remember?

HH

Where the trees stop?

RITA *(Moving to find her purse)*

I gotta find a mirror. Sure, don't you remember that guy in the bar? Said he'd take us out in his truck west about fifty miles and show us where the trees stopped?

HH

Just . . . stopped?

RITA

That's what he said. It's a funny country, you know.
(Goes about her business)
Mirror, mirror, mark the fall

HH *(To the audience)*

Omaha, near where the trees stop. I think I remember. Nine months. If you think I wandered aimlessly after my Lolita was . . .

RITA

Snatched?

HH

Don't be unkind.
(To the audience)
*Dis*spirited away. After my reason for living, for dying!, was whisked from me. If you think I was aimless, wringing my hands, whimpering—if you think that of me, you doubt my resolve—my vengeance.

RITA

I think he's breathing. Jesus, he sure isn't pretty.

HH *(To* RITA*)*

Well, be *sure* he's breathing.
(To the audience)
If you think that of me, you doubt my resolve. If you steal my purse, you steal nothing; if you steal my nymphet . . . well, you had better watch out.

RITA

I think this guy's waking up.
(The YOUNG MAN *bolts upright)*

YOUNG MAN

Where am I!?

HH *(To the audience)*
I don't believe it! "Where *am* I!?"

YOUNG MAN

Where am I!?

RITA

You're here; you're here with us.

HH *(To* RITA*)*

What is *that* supposed to tell him, you . . . you silly twit.

YOUNG MAN

Who are you? Where is here? And who am *I*?

ACG

Well; what have you here!?

HH *(To the* YOUNG MAN*)*

Amnesia is more than I can bear. Put on your socks and go away.

YOUNG MAN

Speak, memory! Where am I here? Who are the two of you?

RITA *(A little laugh)*

I guess we all sort of picked each other up last night; I *guess* we did; I can't remember.

YOUNG MAN

You mean we had a . . . a *you* know?

ACG

What is he suggesting?

HH

I believe he was clear—a "you know."

ACG *(To* HH*)*

How *have* the haughty fallen.

YOUNG MAN

Where *are* we?

RITA

Newark, dear.

YOUNG MAN *(Fear and trembling)*

Newark?

ACG

(As if that explained everything)

Ah . . . well.

(To HH*)*

How long have you been in . . . Newark?

HH *(Nonplussed)*

Two months, I think. Is that right, Rita?

RITA

Give or take.

(To the YOUNG MAN*)*

I don't know whether we had a threesome or not, sweetie; none of us seems to be able to remember anything. Does it *feel* like we had one?

HH

Stop pawing the child!

YOUNG MAN

What does one feel like?
(*Suddenly*)
I'm going to throw up now.
(*He heads off to the bathroom*)

ACG (*To* HH)

Pedophilia knows no bounds, I see. (*Sounds of vomiting*)

HH (*To* RITA)

Go help him.

RITA (*Going*)

Why me; why me? Why always me?

HH

Because you're like that; because I love you for it.

RITA (*Exiting to the bathroom*)

We're outa bourbon.

HH (*After her*)

No, we're not you probably hid it.

ACG

You two *do* have a complex little set-up here in—where is it?—Newark?

HH

(*Brushes* ACG *off, with a great sweeping gesture*)
Enough, you! (*To the audience*) Nine months, nine months I searched for my darling.
(*During this next speech,* RITA *and the* YOUNG MAN *will eventually return from the bathroom, will become interested in what* HH *is saying, will finally interrupt him*)
No! Why am I lying to you?

ACG (*To himself*)

Why, indeed!?

HH

I was searching for *him*. Wretched, vile man!, who had stolen my Dolly, who *knew* what . . . who knew she was my only love.
(*Smiles*)
. . . Vile and wretched man. He cannot have wanted . . . he cannot have imagined . . . the breadth of my passion.

ACG *(Offhand)*

Can he not have? *I* imagined it.

HH

It is unimaginable; it can be guessed at, no more.

ACG

Aha.

(RITA *and* YOUNG MAN *have re-entered now, sit on the bed, listen)*

HH

(To the audience again. Of ACG)

Pay him no mind. He had tracked us across country—the fiend?—and so I tracked him—backtracked him, to be precise.

YOUNG MAN

What is he talking about, Ma'am?

RITA

Love and loss, probably. Those are his subjects.

YOUNG MAN *(No comprehension)*

Aha.

HH

Pay *them* no mind. Pay *me.* As I was saying . . . the entire, monstrous plot became clear in my mind—fell into place like a guillotine. All my suspi-cions of my lovely—that she was betraying me, had betrayed me all along —all my suspicions were true. I was *not* mad; we *had* been followed; she *had* arranged it; all of it was true.

YOUNG MAN

What is he talking about? *Who* is he talking about?

RITA

He's a disgusting degenerate, dear; he screws children.

YOUNG MAN

(Hands instinctively to his shoulders)

Of which gender?

RITA

Girls; little girls.

YOUNG MAN

Well, that's a relief.

RITA

Especially if they're his daughter. Right, Hubert?

HH

Humbert, you drunken whore!

RITA

Good enough for *you*! *Too* good for you!

YOUNG MAN *(Awe)*

His very own daughter?

RITA

In a manner of speaking.

HH *(Despair)*

Put a bottle to your lips.
  (RITA *laughs*)

RITA

Go fuck yourself.

HH

Having fucked everything else, you mean?

ACG *(To* RITA*)*

Let him be; he's not the man he was.

HH *(To* ACG*)*

Or will ever be again!
  (To the audience)

I was *not* mad; we *had* been followed, and my treasure had been in league
with it, with that . . . that fiend.

YOUNG MAN *(Generally)*

Is this a ghost story?

ACG *(To the* YOUNG MAN*)*

Well, it's a story of ghosts, or ravings.
  (To HH*)*

You're raving, you know.

HH

I have never been saner; I see it all so clearly, *have* seen it.
  (To the audience again)

In the nine months of my searching I reversed the journey my darling and
I had taken—backtracked, as I said—for I knew now that he, *he* had stayed
in towns with us, or towns nearby, had registered at inns, at motels, a
breath from us, and he must have used a name, and perhaps once . . . only
once, if only once . . . in some slip of the mind, in exhaustion or . . . or
whatever, he had used his own, had signed his name and fate.

YOUNG MAN *(To* RITA*)*

How we gonna find out who *I* am?

RITA *(Offhand)*

Look in your clothes. Have you looked in your clothes?

YOUNG MAN *(Begins)*

No! What a good idea!

HH *(To the audience)*

So, in those nine months, I stopped at precisely three hundred and forty two hotels, motels, inns and tourist homes. I did not stay at them all—naturally, I mean, really!—but I would register, and when I did

(Chuckles a bit at the memory of it)

I would devise some casual pretext to leaf through the place's register.

(Sighs)

And not once did the monster reveal himself. Oh, he left me little messages, horrid jokes, awful, obscene puns in several languages, cunning eruditions.

YOUNG MAN

My clothes don't tell me anything.

RITA

They don't tell you *any*thing?

YOUNG MAN *(Shy)*

They tell me I'm poor, or careless, and don't wash much; maybe I'm religious! Maybe I belong to a sect or something!

RITA *(Interested in* HH*)*

Maybe, hon.

HH

It was all so transparent. In one such register, that of a motel adjacent to the one in which I brought my Lolita to an understanding that there is more than one way to skin a cat, the monster had signed himself as Arsene Lupin. Indeed!

RITA

(Gentle, putting her band on his crotch)

Would it help if I held you here?

YOUNG MAN

I think it might.

RITA *(Looking)*

It *seems* to.

YOUNG MAN

I have a memory of this happening before, but, to whom? And where?

(To ACG*)*

Help me?

ACG

Your memory will never return; don't worry about it; your past was not that interesting; no one is pining for you.

YOUNG MAN (*To* RITA)

Is that comfort?

RITA (*Fondly, fondling*)

Well it will have to do.

HH

I shudder as I think of it . . . of him!

ACG

(*To* HH, *moving into the action; weary*)
I must butt in here.

HH (*Ironic*)

You *must?*

ACG

I could not bring myself *not* to. Does that please you more?
    (HH *shrugs*)
It's about your friend.

HH

Not mine! Well, not mine alone; a fiend for all seasons.

ACG

As you will. Nonetheless . . . how well he knew you!

HH

Yes!

ACG

Well enough to know that you would retrace your steps . . .

HH

Yes!

ACG

Would dog his theoretical tracks . . .

HH

Theoretical!?

ACG

Who knew you well enough to play such an erudite little game!

HH

Yes!

ACG

Who also happened to know you as the compulsive obsessive that you
are . . .

(To himself)

or is that obsessive compulsive?

(Back to HH*)*

Someone, in other words, who knew your deepest guts.

HH

YES!

ACG

And, at the same time, someone completely unknown to you—a shade
glimmering on the edges of your consciousness.

HH *(Offended)*

What are you saying, that I made all this up, that what I've been telling
them didn't happen?

(To the audience: bravura)

Disbelieve me, ladies and gentlemen! I did not retrace my steps! There
were no motels; three hundred and forty two is merely a cabalistic number! My treasure did *not* develop pneumonia, did *not* enter the
Elphinstone General Hospital, was *not* spirited from there by someone
claiming to be her Uncle Gustav!

ACG

Come, come.

HH *(Riding with it)*

I did not awake one wracked and boozy morning to find little miss Rita
here at my side, discover that we had "been at it" as she puts it for an entire
vanished week.

YOUNG MAN

Been at it?

RITA

It's a figure of speech, dear.

HH

I have not looked down from tall buildings with the thought of jumping; I
have not examined my wrists with the idea of . . .

ACG

You do go on.

HH *(To* ACG*)*

Indeed I do!

(To the audience)

I have not known despair and unbearable joy—loss and possession. Rita
does not exist; the young man there has never had a memory to lose; I
never met a Mrs. Charlotte Haze, *or* her nymphet daughter, treasure of
my life.

(Breaks on it)

Lo-Lo-Lo-li-t-t-ta.

(Crushed)

She does not exist; I do not exist; you do not exist.

YOUNG MAN *(To* RITA*)*

Maybe that's *it.* Certainly, that would solve one or two of my dilemmas.

ACG *(To* HH*)*

Shame on you, always looking for the easy way out. It is the *color* you put on things, the readings you give them. No one doubts your Lolita; no one doubts your bliss, *or* your loss.

RITA *(To* HH; *helpfully)*

We all believe in the little girl, Herbert.

HH

Humbert.

RITA

Right!

YOUNG MAN

Humbert?

RITA

That's what he says, dear.

ACG

You see? They even believe your name.

HH *(Glum; to* ACG; *to* RITA*)*

It doesn't matter; I'm indifferent to whether anything exists anymore; nothing matters to me; what can matter?

ACG *(Sighs)*

Well, let me release you from this Purgatory.

(To RITA*)*

Nothing personal.

RITA

To be sure! I don't take offense too easy; I swing with it.

YOUNG MAN *(To* RITA*)*

May I think of you as a mother?

RITA

How about step-mother, honey?

YOUNG MAN *(Cuddles)*

OK.

HH *(To* ACG*)*

You will release me from Purgatory? To what? Tell me, magician; tell me true.

ACG

Release from Purgatory, certainly; release from the unknown. You want to see Lolita again?

HH *(A snort of pain)*

Oh, God!

ACG

Then you shall

    (He snaps his fingers dramatically; LOLITA*'s voice fills the stage)*

LOLITA'S VOICE

Hi, Dad! Hi, Dad! Hi, Dad!

HH

    (Hands to ears; it is unbearable)

Oh, my God!

LOLITA'S VOICE

Hi, Dad! Dad? Dad? It's me, Lolita.

HH

Oh, my sweet, crucified Lord!

YOUNG MAN *(All wonder)*

Where is that voice coming from?

RITA

Hush; I don't think this directly concerns us.

ACG *(To* HH*)*

Take your cowardly hands away! This is what you wanted, isn't it?

HH

    (Removes his hands, reaches for doll)

Oh, God.

LOLITA'S VOICE

(During this speech, HH *makes appropriate sounds—moans, sighs, exclamations of disbelief, etc.)*

Hi, Dad! How's everything? I'm writing you this letter—speech after long silence, right?—I'm writing you this letter to sort of fill you in on things, and because maybe I owe it to you. Well, Dad, I'm married. Right! Right! I'm married, and I'm going to have a baby; how about that! This is a hard letter to write, Dad, but Dick and I have problems. Dick is my husband, Dad, and he's really a swell guy, and he's been promised a big job in Alaska, but until that comes through, we're pretty strapped, so we could sure use some money, Dad. I've gone through much sadness and hardship. This is your Dolly, saying goodbye. Oh! P.S. I haven't told Dick I'm writing this, so address it to me, please: Mrs. Richard Schiller, number ten, Hunter Road . . .

(Her voice fades)

. . . Coaltown, Pennsylvania, Tennessee, Virginia, West Vir . . .

HH

Oh, my God.

RITA *(Dispassionate)*

I guess this is goodbye, eh, Hubert?

HH *(Preoccupied)*

Humbert.

RITA

Right.

HH

Dick? Married? A baby? A . . . QUICK!! QUICK!! BEFORE SHE VANISHES! QUICK!

(He moves toward the wings)

My darling has come back.

RITA *(A small smile)*

Your darling?

HH

Well, she'll come back to me; I'll . . . well. I'll bring her with me I'll . . .

(To ACG*)*

Won't I? Won't I bring her with me? Won't she come with me?

ACG *(A hand out; gentle)*

Come; we'll go see her.

(He and HH *exit)*

RITA

Goodbye, Humbert. You see? I knew it all along.

YOUNG MAN

What a funny name—Humbert. What's his last name?

RITA *(Staring after* HH*)*

The same as his first, dear.

YOUNG MAN

Really? No! Humbert Humbert? Really? No!

RITA *(Rueful)*

Well, at least he has a name, dear.

YOUNG MAN
(Begins to sob in Rita's arms)
Ooooooooohhhhhhh! Oooooooohhhh!

RITA
(Comforting the YOUNG MAN; *after* HH)
Bye, Humbert; take it easy, you hear? Don't expect . . . too much.
*(*RITA's *room fades)*

CURTAIN

SCENE THREE

*(*HH *and* ACG *outside* LOLITA's *house)*

HH
This is unbearable.

ACG
It's your moment of truth, you old bullfighter.

HH
The combination—to see my darling, and to kill the monster.

ACG
Kill? Kill who?

HH *(An awful whisper)*
Dick! Bloated, vile, bald pig! Dick!

ACG *(Amazed)*
Her husband!? You're going to kill her husband!?

HH
He stole her from me, the center of my life.

ACG *(So reasonable)*
Be sure.

HH
I'm sure.

ACG
Be very sure.
(Sees HH *take a small pistol from his pocket)*
Before you fire that ridiculous weapon, be very sure.

(*Quiet advice*)
See your treasure; see Dick.

HH

See Dick? See Dick fall?

ACG (*Gentle*)

See Dick.
(*A light comes on* DICK *and* BILL *in the workshed*)
See Dick there.

HH

Where? Neither of those is . . . what are you telling me?

ACG

The dark one there—the handsome boy—that is Lolita's husband. Is that
your fiend? Your monster?

HH

He's just . . . a boy.

ACG

And Lolita is . . . a girl.

HH

No! She is not . . . a girl. She is . . . she is not "a girl."

ACG

Ring her doorbell, then. Find out for yourself.

HH (*Almost does; withdraws*)

No.

ACG

What! Isn't this the magic wood anymore? Elfinland? What have you lost
. . . besides your nerve?

HH

A sensitive man would understand.
(*He rings the bell. The living room set lights up. A hugely pregnant* LOLITA—*a little older—glasses—and worn looking comes
from the kitchen*)

LOLITA

Just a sec!

HH

I don't know if I can bear this.

ACG (*Macho-imitation*)

Old bullfighter!
(*The door opens*)

LOLITA
(Stares for a moment, open mouthed)
Weeeeeeeellll! For Christ's sake! C'mon in!

HH *(Mumbled supplication)*
I adore you; I loved you the first moment I set eyes on you; I loved you when you left me; I love you now . . .

ACG *(To HH)*
Get ahold of yourself! Behave like a man!

HH
I am!

LOLITA
(Ignoring HH's mumbled outburst)
I said, c'mon in; it isn't much, but it's home, as they say.
(She leads the way into the living rooms)
Dick's down there in the toolshed with Bill—Bill's a buddy from the army; they shot his arm off; he's accident-prone besides. Hey, sit down.

HH
Thank you, thank you. What a . . . what a cozy home.

LOLITA *(Wrinkles her nose)*
Pretty crummy, hunh! You see, I didn't lie to you in my letter.
(Whispers)
I didn't tell Dick I wrote you, so be careful.

HH
You look . . .

LOLITA *(Laughs)*
Older? Well, I am. Hey, listen, Dick doesn't know *anything* about *anything* . . . if you get my drift.

ACG
Her drift?

LOLITA
You're my real father, and I left home to be on my own. OK?

HH *(Begins to grovel)*
Oh, my darling child, I still worship the sight of you, your skin your odor, the tiny, golden hairs on your arm, the . . .

LOLITA
Cut it out! Will you!? Hey, really; here comes Dick. Now, remember, you're my father, my real, true, honest to goodness father.

HH

I can't bear to meet him!

LOLITA

Why not?

HH

He . . . he *sleeps* with you.

LOLITA (*Laughs*)

Well, of course he does; he's my husband. He's not some dirty old man.

HH (*A wounded cry*)

ANNNNNHHHH!

LOLITA (*Shouting*)

Hey, Dick; come on in; guess who's here!?

HH (*A lesser cry*)

Annnnnhhhh.

　(DICK *and* BILL *enter*)

LOLITA (*Shouting*)

Dick! Guess who's here! It's my Dad!

DICK (*Smiles; shakes hands*)

Hey, swell; who'd you say it was?

LOLITA (*Shouting*)

My Dad! My Dad!

　(*To* HH)

Dick's really deaf.

ACG

Aha; the tragic flaw.

HH (*An aside to* ACG)

I hear her shouting at him during love. Oh, God!

DICK

Your Dad. Well; hey! Look, Bill cut his hand on the saw.

LOLITA (*To* BILL)

You've gotta learn to be careful, Billy-boy.

　(*Shouts at* DICK)

I'll fix it; I'll fix Bill's hand. You get Dad a beer.

　(*She heads toward the hall with* BILL)

C'mon, Billy-boy.

BILL *(As they exit)*

All of sudden my hand was where the saw was.

LOLITA

I'll bet!

(They exit. DICK *stands, uncomfortably; hears very little of what is said; goes right on, assuming what people say to him relates to what he is saying)*

DICK

Well, sir; so you're Dolly's Dad.

*(*HH *and* ACG *comment on* DICK's *remarks, assuming he cannot hear)*

HH

In a manner of speaking; yes.

ACG

"Dolly's Dad." I like that.

DICK

Dolly didn't say you were coming . . . or maybe she did. I don't hear too good.

HH

No?

DICK

Pardon?

HH *(Louder)*

NO?

DICK *(Ponders that)*

No, I guess not.

HH *(To* ACG*)*

This will not be easy.

ACG

Nothing good is.

DICK

Pardon?

HH

NOTHING! NOTHING AT ALL!

DICK

Not even coffee? Or a beer?

HH

NOTHING! THANK YOU!

*(*DICK *sits;* HH *sits;* ACG *stays to one side)*

DICK

Well.

HH (*After a moment*)

WELL!

DICK

Pardon?

HH

NOTHING! NOTHING AT ALL!
(*To* ACG)
I can't go on with this.

DICK (*Nods understandingly*)

OK.
(*Pause*)
I guess you'll be staying for a while, talk over old times with Dolly . . .

HH

No, I've just come for a name, just a name.

DICK

. . . so I suppose Dolly and I'll move a mattress into the kitchen while you're here . . .

HH

I'll be gone in minutes.

DICK

. . . we don't have a bedroom, so Dolly and I, we sleep on that couch there.
(*Points to where* HH *is sitting*)

HH

(*An involuntary gasp and start*)
Annnnngh!
(*To* ACG; *stage whisper*)
He has possessed her! Here! Hundreds of times! He has placed those huge hands on her precious buns; he has . . .

ACG

Now, now; they *are* married.

DICK

Oh, yes; it's comfortable; we snuggle up.

HH (*To* DICK: *trying civility*)

Cozy.

DICK

Pardon?

HH *(Shrieks)*

COZY! COZY!

ACG

Cosa; cosa.

DICK

Yes; very; thank you. So, you'll be staying, will you?

HH

NO! NO!

DICK

Well, our house is yours; Dolly's a pretty good cook, too, if you like chili.
   (Laughs)
Naw, that's just a joke.

HH

He has nuzzled her Florentine breasts, his tongue to her dimple-nipples . . .

ACG

I'm ashamed of you.

DICK

She does a fine pork chop, too. She's a swell kid, Mr. Haze.

HH

Who?

ACG

Mr. Haze. Aren't you dead Harold Haze, or something?

HH

Oh. Oh, yes!

DICK

She's really a swell kid; and she's gonna make a swell mother; she really is.

HH *(To* DICK*)*

You have blown her up; you have made her monstrous, you have taken a
tot . . .

DICK *(Smiles)*

Yessireee.

ACG

Stop fingering your gun.

HH *(A whine of loss)*

But she is *mine.*

DICK

Isn't she; makes her look all grown up. Hey, if it's a boy, we're going to
name him after you. OK?

HH

AAAANNNNGHHHH!

DICK

Pardon?

HH

(Gathering himself, slow; deliberate)
THAT . . . WILL . . . BE . . . THE . . . GRANDEST . . . MOMENT . . .
OF . . . MY . . . LIFE.
(To ACG)
There's nothing for it now but to kill myself.

ACG

I thought you were going to kill someone else.

HH *(Snaps his fingers)*
You're right! I forgot!
(To DICK; bellowing)
SO! YOU'RE GOING TO CANADA.

ACG

Alaska.

HH

ALASKA! YOU'RE GOING TO ALASKA!!

DICK

Well, he cut it on the saw; he's, what do you call it, accident-prone.

HH *(Still bellowing)*
WELL! GOOD! GOOD!
(LOLITA re-enters without BILL)

LOLITA *(To DICK)*
Bill's back out at the toolshed. You'd better go see he doesn't do something
terrible to himself.

DICK *(Seems to understand; rises)*
It sure has been good talking to you, sir.
(Laughs)
I guess I oughta call you Dad, or something.
(Kisses LOLITA on the cheek, goes)

HH *(Sort of hysterical)*
Call me Dad, Sure; go ahead; call me Dad.

LOLITA

Dick's nice; he's sweet and gentle and he takes good care of me.

HH *(Through clenched teeth)*
I'm so glad you're happy.

LOLITA
I didn't say I was happy; I'm content; it's all going to be all right.

HH
Who was he? Who was the monster? Who took you from me?

LOLITA
Oh, Christ, what does it matter!?

HH
(Loud enough to shake the heavens)
IT MATTERS!!!! IT MATTERS TO ME!!!!

LOLITA
All right; all right; it was Claire Quilty.

HH *(A sigh; relief)*
Ahhhhhh.

LOLITA
You see? You knew all along.

HH *(A long hissed sound)*
Q-u-i-l-t-y. Aaaaahhhhhaaaaa!

LOLITA
I mean, how come you didn't guess? You saw him enough.

HH
Q-u-i-l-t-y.
(Snapping to)
Of course I knew; I guess I always knew.

LOLITA
Sure; he's as good as anyone else; he'll do, won't he?

HH
Bloated, vile, bald pig. Quilty. Of course.

LOLITA
Or . . . if you didn't like *him,* how about that French professor at school?
You remember the one?

HH
Quilty will do!

LOLITA
You *say.* One's as good as another to me.

ACG

Listen carefully to her.

HH (*Refutation*)

Quilty will do!

LOLITA

Then let it be Quilty.

HH

Since it *was,* you mean. Yes?

LOLITA

Yeah; sure, since it was. Since it was, let it be.

HH (*Great anguish*)

Why Quilty?!

LOLITA (*So simply*)

He was my first love. You always love your first love.

HH (*Horror, though quiet*)

Your first love! Not one of those nice little boys? Not someone your own *age?*

LOLITA

Oh, come on, Dad! *You're* pretty lucky I went for old men.

HH (*Horror*)

Old men!

LOLITA

Quilty used to hang around my mother's; *you* saw him there. He tried to make me when I was ten, but I told him he was disgusting.

HH

Disgusting! Ten! Disgusting!

ACG

Tsk-tsk-tsk. Ten. Imagine!

LOLITA

But later . . .

(*She shrugs, smiles*) . . .

later when he said he loved me, I told him we could go away together. Then you came along, and mother died, or whatever happened to her, and so we hatched up this plot that he'd follow us, and we'd ditch you whenever we could, and . . .

(HH *raises his hand to strike her, stops with arm raised*)

. . . what are you going to do, hit me? 'Cause I was in love?

HH *(Disbelief)*

In love!? You *loved* this . . . this . . .

LOLITA

Man. Yes! He was nice to me; he respected me.

HH

And . . . and you never loved me? At all?

LOLITA

Oh, come on; we had fun, didn't we?

HH

Answer my question. You never loved me?

LOLITA *(After a long pause)*

No; I guess not.

HH *(Long pause)*

I see.

LOLITA

Are you mad at me? I never *said* I loved you, you know.

HH *(Sort of dreamy)*

You never said it?

LOLITA *(Laughs)*

No; *you* said *you* loved *me;* all the *time.*

HH

I'm sure I did.

LOLITA

Anyway . . . that's the way it was; that's the way it is.

HH *(Quietly)*

I see.

LOLITA *(Still a young girl)*

You always told me to be honest.

HH

Oh, yes.

*(Girds himself, manages to get the following out; cold and patiently
—to us—untruthful)*

Well, Dolly, it doesn't really matter, for as you say, I had everything I
really wanted. I never wanted your love—your heart, your *soul,* as you
put it. All I ever cared about was your body. It was pure, simple lust, my
sweet; just that. Us dirty old men don't *love.* We rut; that's all we do. We
never pine, or ache, or any of those things. You were a good lay, little girl;
a good fuck.

LOLITA

(Very long pause; ambiguous)

Right. Well. OK. Right.

ACG *(Gentle; softly)*

Bravo; bravo; indeed.

HH

(Rummages in his pockets; comes up with an envelope; talks briskly, businesslike, but we sense the emotion under it)

I brought you a check here—your mother's life insurance, finally: five thousand dollars which will do you nicely . . .

LOLITA *(Beside herself)*

Five thousand dollars!

HH

And the house is being sold which, after the mortgage, will bring you another tidy sum.

LOLITA

Oh, my God. Wait until I tell Dick! Hey, boy!

(Goes to him, to kiss him,)

You are such a wonderful . . .

HH

(Pulls away from her violently)

KEEP YOUR . . . don't touch me.

LOLITA *(Subdued)*

OK. Right.

HH *(Rises; brisk, old)*

Well . . . this interview is terminated, I think.

(Cold smile)

Loose ends all tied up now.

LOLITA

You'll stay for lunch? I'll put on some chili; I'll . . .

HH

No, I have other . . . no, thank you.

LOLITA

You're so generous; you're really wonderful.

HH

Yes.

LOLITA

Listen, if it'll help you any, Quilty and I never really . . . did anything.

HH

No; of course not.

LOLITA

No; I mean it; really; he was impotent. He took me to this Dude Ranch he had, and he wanted me to go to bed with all these friends of his . . . so he could watch; and he wanted to make movies of it—of me and his friends.

HH *(In a dream world)*

And you refused; of course.

LOLITA

Of course! I mean, God!, what do you think I am!? I was in love with him.

HH *(To himself)*

The world has closed; there is no sense, no reason anymore; the light of my life has gone out.

(To ACG*)*

Have I died?

ACG

Not yet.

HH *(A rueful laugh)*

You never know—a heart like mine; breaks if you look at it.

(Turns to LOLITA*)*

Goodbye; be happy; be a good mother; be faithful to your young man.

LOLITA

You be good; *you* take care; *you* be careful.

HH *(Moves toward the door)*

If you ever change your mind . . . no; never mind.

LOLITA

Hey! Write me?

HH *(Tosses it off)*

Sure! Why not?! Oh, by the way . . . does what's-his-name, Quilty . . . does he still live in Beverly Hills, would you happen to know?

LOLITA

Probably. I don't know. I walked out on him. Why do you want to know?

HH *(Offhand)*

Ooooh, I thought I might drop in on him, talk over old times.

LOLITA *(Smiles)*

Compare notes? Two dirty old men?

HH

You are diminishing.

LOLITA

You can tell him all about what I'm like in bed, and he can tell you. . . .

HH

You are vanishing.

(*Indeed the lights are going down on her*)

LOLITA

Hunh? Pardon?

HH

Goodbye, Lolita.

LOLITA

Hey!

HH (*As darkness engulfs* LOLITA)

You have disappeared.

ACG (*He and* HH *are alone*)

As she appeared; all at once—there and gone.

HH (*Disputing him*)

Flesh and blood. Dirty fingers, scuffed knees, treasure of my life!

ACG

Are you all right?

HH

Of course.

(*It happens at once, an explosion of sobbing, wailing; he falls to his knees; the doll is there; he clutches it to him, wrestles with it; full cries, sobbings, descending, finally into gasps of breath; no words; a full exhalation of agony.* ACG *stands nearby, waiting, until it is done*)

ACG

Done?

HH

With *that*. Forgive me.

ACG

And now?

HH

(*Gets up; the doll held by one of its arms*)

A little trip.

ACG

Beverly Hills?

HH (*A small smile*)

Of course.

(*Scene fades*)

CURTAIN

ENTRE SCENE

(HH *appears alone, in a spot of light, still holding the doll; He speaks quietly, rationally*)

HH

I think I should tell you this, for you may have misunderstood me from before. You may not, I mean, have unencumbered access to the depths of my being. You bring your own vision to a clear view of me; everything is seen as it appears; therefore nothing exists, etcetera, etcetera. But, be that as it may, I want you to know that no matter how it may seem, when I saw my Lolita just now—great with child, worn, old at seventeen, not even a memory of what I . . . as I looked and looked at her, I knew as clearly as I know I am going to die, that I loved her more than anything I had ever seen or imagined on earth, or hoped for anywhere else. You may jeer at me, but until I am gagged and throttled I will shout the poor, sad truth. I insist the world know how much I loved my Lolita—love her—have never known the meaning of love before her, can know only the memory of it hence. I want you to know that. I want you to know that it is love which has moved me, has obsessed me . . . love, no matter what else it may seem. Pure . . . pure love. And now . . . on to murder.

(*He moves into Scene Four*)

SCENE FOUR

(*The scene shifts to the grand hall of* QUILTY'S *manor house.* HH *and* ACG *are there*)

ACG

Do you *really* plan to kill him?

HH

How can you ask?

ACG

Well, it's such a romantic act . . . and noisy.

HH *(Looks about him)*

There's nothing to live for now—except this.

ACG *(Scoffs)*

What nonsense.

HH

Shall I teach again? Shall I search the bars for Rita? Shall I find one of those blow-up dolls with all the proper parts, or shall I . . .

ACG

Oh, goodness! Go on with your messy business.

HH

(Looks about the huge room from where he stands)

Thank you; I shall.

ACG *(To the audience)*

This is love.

HH

Nonsense: this is revenge; this is orgasm—speech after long silence, sound after the mute act. Let me alone.

ACG *(To the audience)*

There's nothing to do with him; he's going to kill; put cotton in your ears.

HH

(To the audience; great intensity)

Does a single one of you blame me for it? Don't answer; please: there may be, and I can't argue. Don't watch it if you're squeamish, but, if you've ever been in love . . .

(QUILTY enters)

QUILTY

(Badly hungover; not seeing clearly)

What *is* all this? Who are all you . . . you; over there?

HH *(To himself; purring)*

There he *is*; Q-u-i-l-t-y. . . Q-u-i-l-t-y.

QUILTY *(Echoes it; softly)*

Quilty; Quilty.

ACG *(To HH; gently)*

There's still time.

HH *(Enraptured,)*

There is no time.

ACG

Look at this place; it's disgusting . . . bottles, spilled glasses, half eaten chickens. This is chaos.

HH *(Still)*

Yes; isn't it.

ACG

Come away.

HH

Go away.

QUILTY

Come away; go away. Who are you people? What do you want?

ACG

Revenge, I think, or is it orgasm?

QUILTY

Are you the phone company?

HH *(Delighted)*

Are we the phone company?

QUILTY

I think that's what I said; odd echo here though.
   (Does it again)
Quilty; Quilty.

HH

Q-u-i-l-t-y . . . Q-u-i-l-t-y.

QUILTY

There it is again. Do you hear it?

ACG *(To Quilty)*

Go back upstairs.

HH

Stay where you are.

QUILTY

Go back upstairs; stay where . . . you *might* be the phone company. Are you Brewster? Is one of you Brewster?

ACG

Go back.

HH

Brewster? Which Brewster you have in mind.

ACG

Do go back.

QUILTY *(To* HH)

Who's your friend? He looks familiar.

HH

You wouldn't believe me.

QUILTY

Oh, I don't know . . . us writers.

HH

I'm not Brewster, friend, you old would-be sodomizer, you.

QUILTY *(Shifty)*

Not Brewster, eh? Not the man from the phone company; not here about those long distance calls. Well, well.

(Sits)

You know, you don't *look* like Jack Brewster, my friend from the friendly phone company: the resemblance is not particularly striking. You look like someone, though—I mean, well, you *must.*

*(Begins rummaging through his pockets—*HH *slaps his hands away)*

HH

Keep your hands in view.

QUILTY

I had some phone bills, I think; lots of long distance calls *I* never made. Patagonia; Philadelphia; Puerto Vallarta; Palestine . . .

HH

There *is* no Palestine.

QUILTY

Of course not; that's what I mean. You mind if I smoke?

HH

On the table there; just keep your hands in view.

QUILTY *(To* ACG)

Your friend has a thing about hands, eh?

ACG

Go back.

HH

Quilty, do you remember a girl called Dolores Haze?

QUILTY *(Thinking hard)*

Dolores . . . Haze.

HH

Dolores Haze: Dolly Haze; Dolly called Dolores?

QUILTY *(Waves his hand a little)*

Hey, that's got a kind of . . . Dolores Haze . . . no, no, I don't think I do. But . . . who cares, hunh?

HH

I do, Quilty; I care; you see . . . I'm her father.

QUILTY

Nonsense, you're not her father. You're some foreign literary agent, some refugee hustling for a buck. Some escapee from the ovens . . .

HH

I am her father, Quilty; she is my child.

ACG

I like your stern parental pose; you wear it well.

HH *(To ACG)*

Thank you.

    (To QUILTY)

I am her father, Quilty.

QUILTY *(To ACG)*

Is he her father? Tell me the truth, buddy.

ACG

In a way of thinking. Sorry to have to tell you that.

QUILTY *(Considers that)*

Well. Well, I'm very fond of children, myself, and fathers are among my best friends.

    (Begins to rise)

However, if you gentlemen will . . .

HH

DOWN. DOWN.

QUILTY *(Sits again)*

You don't have to yell, for God's *sake.* I was just after a drink. You guys want to have a . . .

HH

You've had your last drink, Quilty.

QUILTY

I'm dying for a drink.

    (It sinks in)

My last drink?

HH

Your last drink.

ACG

A communion, it is to be hoped.
   (*To* QUILTY)
I told you: back upstairs.

HH

Your final drink. Think about it, Quilty.

QUILTY

My last drink? My last drink . . . ever?

HH

Ever.

QUILTY (*To* ACG)

Ever?

ACG

It would appear.

QUILTY (*To* HH)

My last drink ever. Hmmmmmm. I think there's a question forming itself here. I don't think I'm happy about it, but there it is. *Why* have I had my last drink ever?

HH

Because I am going to kill you.

QUILTY

Aha.
   (*To* ACG)
You see, I was right. I knew there was a question there; I knew I wasn't going to be happy about it, but when they come there's nothing to be done for it.
   (*Mimics* HH *and himself; falsetto*)
"Why have I had my last drink ever?" "Because I am going to kill you."
   (*Sees* HH *take the gun out*)
. . . Oh, what is that funny little thing you have in your hand there?

HH (*Patient*)

It is a gun. It is what I am going to kill you with.

QUILTY (*Trying to make light of it*)

A gun? More of a gunette, if you ask me. Put it away, you can't kill with that thing—hurt people, possibly, but never . . .

(HH *fires into the rug at* QUILTY's *feet*)
You see what I mean? Give me that silly thing.

HH

Concentrate, Quilty; I want you to concentrate. Try to understand what is happening to you.

QUILTY

I'm willing to try, but it isn't easy without a drink. You know, I think maybe you're Australian—that accent—or *are* you some kind of refugee? This is a gentile's house you know, so maybe you better run along now.

(HH *fires again*)
Ow; look at that; you shot a hole in the chair. You know what upholsterers charge these days? Be careful.

HH

How do you want to go, Quilty?

QUILTY (*To* HH, *sober*)
I beg your pardon?

HH

At once, or in stages? One bullet from the gunette, between your greedy little eyes, or above the ear, a quick snuffing out? . . .

QUILTY (*Pretends to consider that*)
Well, I suppose that might be nice, unless, of course . . .

HH

Or shall I have my pleasure with you? Shoot you in each hand? Each foot? Each arm? A slug in what's left of your liver?

ACG

Oh, come now.

QUILTY

(*Slaps a hand on the arm of the chair; attempts seriousness and sternness*)
My dear sir—stop trifling with life and death. Guns are the tools of the lower classes so give me the thing, we'll throw it away, have a drink and a good laugh . . .

(HH *does not respond*)
You don't take to the idea, eh? Look here, old fellow . . .

HH

(*Takes out a sheet of paper, keeping the gun aimed at* QUILTY's *head*)
Everyone is a writer; I dabble myself. Here; read this.

QUILTY (*Takes it*)

Oh? What have we here? A story line? A precis? Something simple for the studio heads to . . .

HH

It is your death sentence.

QUILTY (*Getting it right*)

My death sentence.

HH

It's in verse.

QUILTY

In verse.

HH

Yes. Verse.

QUILTY (*To* ACG)

My death sentence? In verse? In *verse*?

ACG (*Shrugs*)

I told you to go back.

HH

Read it.

QUILTY

Out loud?

HH

Yes.

QUILTY (*Tries to hand it back*)

I'm not much good at that sort of thing, so why don't we just . . .

(HH *fires again*)

You've punctured my robe.

HH

Read it.

QUILTY

A present from the Shah—in better days.

HH

Read it.

QUILTY

If you'd like to see some other things . . . read it, I see. Right. Well.

(*Clears his throat. Suddenly shifts his tone*)

Look, old friend, I didn't have any fun with your Dolly. Believe me; I'm practically impotent; really; I really am. I gave her a nice vacation; she met some remarkable people.

HH

Read.

QUILTY

Show me your badge. If you're carrying a gun, show me your badge.
Besides, you're a dirty pervert; Dolly said so. She told me the things you
tried to get her to do, and the things you succeeded in. Pretty imaginative,
if I say so myself, especially that idea of yours about . . .

HH

Read.

QUILTY *(Whines)*

I didn't hurt her, did I? Isn't she OK?

HH *(Quietly)*

Read it.

QUILTY *(Sighs)*

Isn't she OK fa Christ's sake? Read it. Well, now.
   (Clears his throat)
      Because you took advantage of a sinner
      Because you took advantage
      Because you took
      Because you took advantage of my disadvantage
That's good, you know; that's damn good. Here.

HH

Read.

QUILTY *(Sighs; reads)*

      Because you took advantage of a sin
      When I was helpless moulting moist and tender
       Dreaming of a marriage in a mountain state
Sort of a cross current of influences there, right? The old T.S.? A little
Edgar A.? Just a hint of . . .

HH

Read.

QUILTY *(Sighs; reads)*

      Because you cheated me of my redemption
      Because you took her
      Because you took her at the age
      When lads are playing with erector sets
A little smutty there, hunh? A little racy?

HH

Read.

QUILTY *(Sighs; reads)*
A little downy girl still wearing poppies
   Still eating popcorn in the colored gloam
As opposed to what? The black and white gloam?

HH

Read.

QUILTY

An active mind is always busy.
   Because you stole her
   From waxy-browed and dignified protector
Who is that? You? I know: read.
   Because you took a doll to pieces
   And threw its head away
   Because of all you did
   You have to die.
Well. Well, sir, that is certainly a fine poem. One of the best *I've* read in a while, let me tell you.
   (To ACG*)*
Not bad for an amateur, what?
   (Hands the poem back to HH*)*
There you are, sir; thank you very much. Now, if we'll just . . .

HH

Do you have anything to say before you die? Anything serious?

QUILTY

Look here, old man, you can't kill me with that thing; it's too little; it's a gun for ladies to shoot one another, not us big sexy men, enh? enh? You might *hurt* me—wound me awfully, spend twenty years in jail for it; then where would you and your little girlfriend be, eh?

HH

Oh, I can kill you with this; I have a pocketful of bullets.
   (Shows a handful to QUILTY*)*

QUILTY

A pocketful of bullets. Well, let me see.

HH

Stay where you are.

QUILTY *(To* ACG*)*
Would you like to . . . you know . . . stop him, or something?

ACG *(Noncommittal)*
He is very willful.

QUILTY *(To* ACG*, very offhand)*
You *do* look familiar.

HH

All right; game's over; last words.

QUILTY

Well now, doesn't time fly by.

HH *(Aiming)*

Nothing?

(From now until QUILTY *is dead—a matter of numerous shots, all described,* HH *and* QUILTY *will move a bit around the huge room,* QUILTY *trying to fend off the bullets, as if they were wasps; he will become weaker, more ineffectual, as the wounds increase in number.* ACG *will move to one side—to be out of range, so to speak)*

QUILTY *(Rises; stays in place)*

Now look here, fella, you're drunk and I'm a sick man—or whatever. Let's postpone this. I need rest and quiet; I have to nurse my impotence; friends are coming in this afternoon.

*(*HH *shoots)*

OW. Jesus Christ, you've shot me; OW. We are men of the world, Humbert, men of the world, in everything—free verse, sex, marksmanship . . .

*(*HH *shoots;* QUILTY *is hurt rather more this time)*

Accccchhhh; that stings, sir. If you bear me a grudge, I'm ready to make amends, even though, my dear Mr. Humbert, in all candor, you were not an ideal stepfather, and I did not force your little protegee to join me.

*(*HH *shoots;* QUILTY *grabs a leg. He snarls the next sentence)*

It was she made me take her from you.

*(*HH *shoots again;* QUILTY *falls to one knee in pain and alarm)*

AAANNNNHHHH. Damn you; damn you, sir. That is very painful, very painful, indeed.

*(*HH *begins reloading, bullets spilling on the floor)*

What are you doing?

HH

Reloading. It only holds seven at a time. Be patient.

QUILTY *(An awful laugh)*

He's reloading; be patient; it only holds seven at a time. You've hurt me enough, sir. Please, no more.

HH *(Aiming again)*

All right; here we go.

*(*HH *shoots)*

QUILTY

AAAANNNNNNNGGGGGGHHHHH. Look, look here: how would you

like this house? It's roomy, cool in the summer, easy to take care of. I'm moving to England, or Florence, forever, in just a day or two, so you can have it.

(HH *shoots, hurts* QUILTY *more; he sucks air through his teeth*)

Gratis.

(HH *shoots again*)

Oh, that hurts atrociously, my dear fellow; I . . . I think you've hit a mainstream of something.

(QUILTY *seems a trifle delirious now*)

I promise you, Brewster, or Humbert, or whoever you are, you'll be happy here. I don't know if you care for the bizarre, but I can also let you have a little house pet, a young lady with three breasts . . .

(HH *shoots;* QUILTY *reacts as if punched a little*)

One of them, the center one, really a dandy.

(HH *shoots again; same reaction from* QUILTY)

Very painful; very painful indeed; most . . . most appalling pain. You won't be bothered. I have a collection of erotica upstairs, photographs of eight hundred and some male organs, examined and measured by the noted French explorer and psychoanalyst, Melanie Weiss . . .

(HH *shoots again;* QUILTY *is clearly near death; hard breathing; blood coming from holes in his body and from the corner of his mouth*)

Ohhhh . . . I have never hurt so much. And to top it off, I can arrange for you to attend executions. Did you know that the electric chair is . . . painted . . . yellow?

(QUILTY *collapses into a heap, dead.* HH *looks at him for a little*)

HH

Yellow.

ACG (From a mental distance)

Pardon?

HH

Yellow.

(*Pause*)

ACG

And now?

HH (Shrugs)

Now? What does now matter? They'll come and find me here; I'll be arrested. I'll say I tried to rob the swine; he was tight-fisted, and so I shot him.

ACG

Twelve times, or whatever?

HH

Small caliber pistol, fat man. *I* don't care what they think; all I care about
is. . .
   (Stops)

ACG

That no one know about Lolita.

HH

Yes.

ACG

Love; loss; revenge.

HH

No; none of it. She doesn't exist. Isn't that right?

ACG *(Shrugs)*

You saw her vanish.

HH

Yes. They'll put me in jail; I'll stand trial for murder;
   (ACG *begins to shake his head, slowly, sadly)*
they'll find me guilty in the first degree, and find me sane to boot! They'll
put me away for life, or kill me. No? Are you saying "NO?"

ACG

Yes. "No."

HH

Well, what do I care about me; then I shall wander the earth. No? I shall
not wander the earth?

ACG

No.

HH

No? What then? Tell me: *you* know everything.

ACG

Yes, but do you want to *know* everything?

HH

Now . . . yes.
   (The doll is nearby; he clutches it instinctively)

ACG

Very well, you will wait here for them, and no one will come, not for the
longest time. And so, to while away the heavy hours, with nothing for com-

pany but the dead Quilty and the twenty flies which have come to feast, with nothing better to do, you will let yourself shift to thoughts of Lolita . . .

HH

Ahhh!

ACG

And, as you have done so often in the past, you will move your hand across your body, down, down to the center of yourself, and you will think of her, and you will harden, and you will take your hand to yourself, and you will spill white on the blood-red floor.

HH *(A kind of orgiastic groan)*

Annnnggggh.

ACG

But your poor heart won't take it anymore, buddy.

HH

Annnnnnnnhhhh!

ACG

It will explode with your orgasm, and down you'll go. Come and go.

HH *(Relieved)*

Ahhhh.

ACG

Has a kind of symmetry to it, no?

HH *(Shivery)*

Yes. And what of Lolita?

ACG

Leave it at that.

HH

WHAT OF LOLITA!?

ACG

(As he tells it, HH *suffers a series of wrenchings, sobs and cries; he twists, descends, the doll clutched to him, to a sitting position, in the rubble of the set. Gentle but factual)*

Lolita? Lolita dies in childbirth.

HH

ANNNNNGGGGGG! [etc.]

ACG

Two weeks beyond term, the baby is born, the mother dies. In great pain and a rush of blood.

HH

ANNNNNGGGGGG! [etc.]

ACG

Well . . . you asked.

HH

And . . . and the baby?

ACG

It lives an hour or so.

HH

ANNNNNGNHH!

ACG

A boy. Before it dies, Dick has it baptized and names it after you.

HH

Ahhh.

ACG

Harold Haze.

HH

   (A cry of irony and anguish combined)
ANNNGGGHH!!

ACG

Isn't that who he thought you were? He's deaf, you remember; a gentle boy, but deaf, and a little slow.

HH

Annngh.
   (HH *subsides into a pile with the doll*)

ACG *(To* HH*)*
And so it all ends, my dear friend.

HH *(Dying)*
Lolita, light of my life, fire of my loins. My sin; my soul. Lo-lee-ta.
   (HH *is still*)

ACG *(To the audience)*
And so it all ends, swept away. Autumn? A sudden breeze? Swept away like leaves.
   (Lights fade)

CURTAIN

The Man Who
Had Three Arms

For
Robert Drivas
1936–86

The Man Who Had Three Arms was first presented by Allen Klein at the Lyceum Theatre in New York City, on April 5, 1983. It was directed by Edward Albee; the scenery was by John Jensen; costumes were by John Falabella; the lighting was by Jeff Davis; the executive producer was Iris W. Keitel; and the associate producer was Kenneth Salinsky. The cast, in order of appearance, was as follows:

WILLIAM PRINCE *as* THE MAN

PATRICIA KILGARRIFF *as* THE WOMAN

ROBERT DRIVAS *as* HIMSELF

(If there is a curtain, the MAN *and the* WOMAN *are discovered sitting onstage,* SHE *stage right,* HE *stage left. If there is no curtain, then let the* TWO *of them saunter on a few minutes before the play is to begin—talk to each other, examine notes, whatever. When it is time for the play to begin—this determined by the* MAN, *when* HE *sees the audience mostly in place—the* MAN *rises, glances off, both left and right, gets his signal, glances at the audience, moves to the podium. House lights still on)*

MAN *(Clears his throat)*

I, uh . . . I believe we can begin now. Are we all assembled? Is . . .

(Glances at those still arriving)

. . . is everyone in his . . . or her . . . ? Perhaps if we waited a few moments more?

(Turns to the WOMAN, *smiles;* SHE *smiles helpfully back)*

Do . . . do take your seats now, if you would be so good. We really should get underway; should we not.

WOMAN

(Whispers at him across the stage)

He's getting very impatient.

MAN

Hm? Oh; yes; well.

(More forceful)

Come now, ladies and gentlemen, let's . . . uh, get our act together, as I think I heard my nephew say the other day.

(Jocular)

All right. Are we ready now? Yes? Fine.

(House lights down)

Then let us begin.

(Takes out index cards, reads from them, and none too well)

It is my pleasure—my *singular* pleasure, sorry—to welcome you here tonight.

(Note: or "this afternoon" as the situation demands)

To welcome you to our presentation, the two hundred and thirty-first lecture in our series "Man on Man." There is nothing sexist in that, you understand—man on man, woman on woman . . . person on *person* we might think of calling it if we were not two hundred and thirty lectures into . . .

(Mumbling)

into a series entitled "Man on Man."

WOMAN

They can't hear you!!

MAN

What?

WOMAN

They can't hear you!!

MAN (Louder)

A series entitled "Man on Man"! Is that better?

WOMAN

Yes.

MAN

Good. Seven times a year for thirty-three years we have gathered here and become participants in the exploration of ourselves in the company, in the *focus* of those illustrious, gifted, intelligent beings whom we have invited here to enlighten us on the subject of . . . well, of ourselves. And what a list!! . . . Albert Einstein, Paul Tillich, Norman Thomas, Herbert Hoover, Robert Frost and Dylan Thomas, and on and on. And I mention only the dead, you notice—the no-longer-with-us-in-person. What an illustrious list! What a grand march of minds across the . . . something of our something.

(Consults his notes carefully)

I sat on my good glasses yesterday, looking for them. I wonder where my good glasses are, I said to myself, sitting to puzzle it out. Sit; crunch. Too late!

(Indicates the glasses HE *has with him)*

These are a power or two less than . . . What a march of minds . . .

(Reads)

across the . . . carbon of our receptive intellects.

(Renewed energy)

We have been taken to areas we dared only dimly imagine, into creativity and creation itself. We are the most fortunate of mortals!

WOMAN *(An embarrassed giggle)*

Really!

MAN

Hm? We are *not?* We are *not* the most fortunate of mortals?

(Considers it)

Well, no: the Christ's disciples, Leonardo's assistants, Jefferson's dinner guests, et cetera, et cetera.

WOMAN *(Sotto voce; corner of mouth)*

Get on with it!

(Broad smile to the audience)

MAN

It is my . . . pleasure, my goodness . . . to introduce you to a lady who, to most of you, needs, as they say, no introduction.

(To himself)

Then why do I introduce her? Why don't I just point in her direction, bow, back off? Why am I here at all? Is all illusion? Do I exist?

WOMAN

Get *on* with it!

MAN

. . . who needs no introduction, our . . . distinguished and be-loved Madame President.

(Applause; HE *bows to the audience, to* MADAME PRESIDENT *and backs to his seat as* SHE *approaches the podium)*

WOMAN

(A gracious bow to the audience, while the applause dies)

Thank you, thank you, thank you, thank you, dear friends.

(Turns to the MAN, *peremptory)*

And thank you, dear friend, for your good words, for your . . .

MAN *(Half rising)*

. . . oh, my dear, think nothing of it; my pleasure, my goodness, my . . .

WOMAN *(Loud, to stop him)*

. . . for your good words!

(Tight smile; to the audience again)

Dear friends. I have one or two announcements to make before we proceed with "the matter at hand"?—if you will forgive my levity?

(No one seems to recognize her levity)

Matter at hand?

MAN (*Chuckles*)

Oh, very good, very good!

WOMAN (*Slightly miffed*)

One or two announcements.

(*Sour acknowledgment of* MAN)

Thank you, my dear.

(*To the audience*)

One or two announcements. You may recall that for tonight's [or today's] meeting, we have had scheduled for the longest time—two years now, I believe—the noted zoologist, Dr. Henry Speedthrift Tomlinson, prize winner—No*bel* Prize winner, to name but one of his big guns!—author, professor, lecturer and whatever else you may care to mention.

Well . . . the other week we wrote Doctor Tomlinson's lecture bureau, since—as is the way of these things—they had been tardy in returning a signed contract, and since we wanted to fête the good doctor as is our wont, and make him as comfortable as a person could want, as is our wont as well. Imagine our surprise—astonishment!—and dismay, then, when we received the following terse, I thought, and not altogether understanding letter from the doctor's lecture bureau.

(SHE *reads*)

"Dear Madame President: We received your letter of [two weeks prior to whatever date it presently is] with . . .

(*Hurries over it*)

astonishment and dismay. Doctor Tomlinson passed away somewhat over a year ago, the precise date being unascertainable since the Doctor's body, he having fallen into an Andean crevasse . . ." . . . which I take to be a crevasse in the Andes . . . "having fallen into an Andean crevasse was not recovered until such time as it was in a state of advanced decomposition." Why do they want to tell me these things!? ". . . decomposition and, indeed, was identifiable only from dental records, and by a locket which contained two photographs, one of the late doctor himself, and the other of . . .

(*Disbelief*)

a large pig."

MAN

A large what?

WOMAN

Pig! Pig!

MAN

A large pig?

WOMAN (*Reads again*)

"You can understand, therefore, why Doctor Tomlinson will not be addressing your group on the evening of [whatever it is]." Yes, well, indeed we can.

(*Reads again*)

"We're certain he would have enjoyed being with you, and we are puzzled only by how the doctor's demise could have escaped your attention, given, as it was, such worldwide coverage.

(*Shrugs*)

I suppose, these days, if one turns one's back for a moment . . .

(*Snaps her fingers*)

. . . the . . . the letter—and *not* an entirely understanding one, as I am sure you will agree by now, went on, concluded by offering us, in Doctor Tomlinson's place, a number of other lecturers in their . . . stable, I suppose it could be called, among whom, it being such an abrupt and confusing state of affairs, we chose yet another doctor, Doctor Abraham Fischman, the internationally famous plastic surgeon, practicing in Mexico, to address us on the topic "Face to Face."

MAN (*A private grief*)

Oh my, oh my, oh my my my!

WOMAN

"Face to Face." Well, and the world is a very strange place. We received a telephone call yesterday morning from the lecture bureau, to say that Doctor Fischman had been arrested in Tijuana and that he would not be with us today either. However, they have, at a moment's notice, and at considerable savings to us, I may add, provided us with tonight's speaker, in anticipation of whom I'm sure your heads are buzzing. One other item first, however: the matter of the poisoned quiche Lorraine and our lawsuit against the Tante Marie Quiche and Cheesecake Company. All of you who are not our newest members will remember that terrible July Fourth, our picnic in the park; our festive tables and our near fatal quiche. Some six hundred of us were felled, were we not! Diarrhea! Vomiting! Wracking headaches! Dehydration! Spasms! It was awful! It was really *awful!* You will recall that we brought suit against Tante Marie even as she—they—had declared bankruptcy and dissolved in spite of the counterclaim that we ourselves were negligent— some nonsense about lack of refrigeration, sitting in the hot sun, et cetera. Well, the case *has* been settled, and we have recovered damages to a sum which al*most*, but not quite covers our legal costs. It has not been one's most reassuring dip into the jurisprudential mire. There is a rainbow of sorts however; the Tante Marie Quiche and Cheescake Company people have resurfaced as a new corporate entity, known as the Frère Jacques Cheesecake and Quiche Company, Limited, and they have offered to cater our next picnic at what they refer to as "wholesale, or near." We have taken this offer under advisement, at least as far as the *cheese*cake end of it is concerned, and we will let you know what we think.

We are taking under similar advisement the suggestion of the Men's Committee that a good old-fashioned Fourth of July calls for hot dogs, potato salad, beer and apple pie, nothing more and nothing less, as the memo came . . . uh, *up* to us. I warn you gentlemen, though, that potato salad can have a life of its own, a crawly one, at that, left out too long.

(*Laughs*)

Well, we will solve it all and let you know in sufficient time.

(*A deep breath*)

Now, what we have all been waiting for, the appearance of our guest speaker. Dear friends, we *have* been fortunate over the years, being witness, as we have, to those who have made our history and shaped our culture, men and women whose accomplishments have wreaked their order on our havoc.

MAN

Oh! What a very nice phrase!

WOMAN (*Genuinely pleased*)

Thank you, *thank* you!

(*To her notes again*)

. . . their order on our havoc and identified our reality by creating it for us.

MAN

Even better!

(*Begins applauding*)

My goodness!

WOMAN (*Trying to cover*)

Our guest today . . .

(*Louder*)

Our guest today, for whom you have been waiting with breath as bated as mine, certainly needs no introduction. His . . . truly miraculous story has been reported in *every* newspaper around the world; he has appeared before august medical bodies, before crowned heads; how famous can you be!? Well, ladies and gentlemen, if you are a man who has—has *had*—three arms, you become pretty famous, indeed!! And a movie of his life entitled *Now You See It, Now You Don't* is scheduled for production in the near future. And so, dear friends, without any further ado, we are proud to welcome into our midst, to hear what he has to tell us, the illustrious, the world-famous . . .

(HIMSELF *appears onstage, bowing, before* SHE *can say his name*)

HIMSELF

Thank you; thank you. Thank you very much. What a pleasure it is to be here. A lovely city. Are you all natives? Any tourists? Yes?

(*Reacts to one*)

Where are you from? Oh? That's nice.

(*To another*)

What about you? Really? How about that!

(*Generally*)

How about a big hand for [whatever]!? So.

I was in Chicago last week, doing my thing—big barn of a place, and they had this legend carved into the proscenium: "You yourselves must set flame to the faggots which you have brought." Who says Chicago isn't a tough town?

Look at your eager little faces. Waiting for revelation, are you? On the subject which has brought you here this [evening? afternoon?] out of what? curiosity? wonder? morbidity?

(*Turns to* WOMAN)

I thank you for the introduction, truly I do. Be careful when you go on a talk show, though: the dumb ones use a club, and the bright ones have a knife. Trust no one, never turn your back, and stay out of alleys. And as for ptomaine if you really want to do it right, lay some boiled shrimp out in the sun; that'll do it. Cut your membership right in half.

WOMAN (*Slightly hysterical*)

Thank you, we'll keep it in mind.

MAN

Oh, now, no, that would be terrible!

WOMAN (*To the* MAN)

Hush!

MAN (*To the* WOMAN, *sotto voce*)

It would! It would be terrible!

HIMSELF

(*Looking across the front row*)

Where is she? Where is she, I wonder; the lady, the girl, usually, who sits there in the front row, almost *always*, wherever, whenever I speak—not the *same* girl, woman, you understand, but of a certain type: plain, more than a little overweight, smock top, jeans, sandals, dirty toenails—sits there in the front row, and, as I lecture, *try* to lecture, try to fill you in, so to speak, make you understand, sits there and runs her tongue around her open mouth, like this,

(*Demonstrates*)

hand in her crotch, likely as not, bitten fingers, lascivious, obscene, does it over and over, all through my lecture, my expiation, my sad, sad tale, unnerves me, bores me, finally wearies me with her longing. Well, I wonder where she is? I don't see her; perhaps you put her type away here. Maybe you have asylums full of them, sitting in their rooms or in the recreation area . . . sitting there in their smock tops, dirty toenails, opening and closing their mouths,

(Demonstrates)

tonguing their perimeters; maybe you've put them all away; maybe you don't "put up with that sort of thing" here. Maybe you have them committed. Good for you! I am committed—hah!—I am committed, usually, on these lecture tours, to a press conference, a "small" dinner beforehand—and, afterwards, to an "informal reception" at which I am pressed to consume undrinkable rosé wine and eat something called cheese food, at which I am slapped on the back and generally touched . . . slap, slap, thump, thump.

(Laughter)

The press conferences I have gotten used to—well, in the way we become used to din, to callousness, or the thought of dying. Your press here is no different from the average, I suppose—some brighter, some not, one sow; the questions—wherever I go—are of such a pattern I'd do as well to hand out prepared answers: "Yes, it *was* quite a surprise growing a third arm; well, yes, children would stare sometimes; did I feel like a martyr? Well, I suppose so; do I miss having a third arm? Yes and no." *Do* I miss it? Well, does one miss oneself? Think about it. Well! These small dinners [lunches, whatever] preceding my lecture—no longer demonstration!

(Laughter)

Thank you, thank you very much; every bit . . . these "small" meals, by which is meant, of course, not that the meals them*selves* are small— tiny carrots, mini-cutlets, string beanettes, et cetera . . .

(Laughter)

Thank you, thank you very much . . . not that the meals are small, nor that the people attending them are small—a congress of dwarfs, a confederacy of midgets.

(Laughter)

Thank you, thank you very much . . . but simply that the *group* is to be limited in number, so as not to exhaust the speaker before the speak—the speech. A manageable group: in other words, anywhere from six to a hundred and fifty.

(Chuckles sadly)

How we live; how we live.

(Imitates a hostess)

"Well, we *did* try to keep it small, but so many people wanted to have a little quiet time with you," my hostess shrieks above the din, the callousness, the forks against the plates, hoots and banter. The average menu at these "small meals" consists of thawed shrimp, overcooked green beans and chicken in musilage; iceberg lettuce!—those who grow it should be horsewhipped!—iceberg lettuce with a choice of dreadful dressings, filled with sugar and sodium something-or-other; and for dessert—far more often than chance would accommodate—a lemonish chiffon of the density of flown hope.

(Some laughter)

Thank you, oh, thank you. That is your average menu. The quenelle, the quail, the walnut oil and the cheese, the perfect berries happen now and again—enough, perhaps, to mourn the death of God.

Once or twice these small gatherings have *been small!* have been civilized and civilizing events, joys of exquisite cuisine, top wines and ravishing exchange. Everything *may* be on its way downhill, may even be giving that destination a new depth, but all is not that way: there are oases. But one of the rules of an oasis would seem to be that the surrounding desert stretches beyond conjecture; otherwise, one would be yawning, saying, "God! yet another oasis! Will they never stop?!" But the way of the world does *not* give us an excess of oases: Beethoven quartets, Mantegna paintings and other waterholes; the phrase "too much of a good thing" is meaningless; it can never happen, therefore cannot be proved. No?

At your average meal the one thing they did not discuss—mention, breathe!—was my arm, back when I had three of them. Maybe it was nothing more than it was not considered fit conversation for the table. War, divorce, money, death, greed, deception, yes—but . . . not an arm.

They would look at me, these people; I would look at *them.* I would unfocus my eyes, finally, stare off into the middle distance—humiliated by my specialness. I hadn't split the atom; I hadn't written fifteen string quartets, or saved the country from itself. I'd grown a fucking third arm! Where's the talent in that?

I used to make little jokes now and again, to try to ease the tension . . . when the food was good, that is . . . "Let not your right hand know what your left hand know what your . . . and so forth." It would get a laugh—peas rolling off forks, butter knives clattering, and so forth. If the meal was *awful,* and it, *I,* was feeling especially awful—hung over, trouble with old number three and its mind of its own, whatever—I would become provocative: stretch and eat at the same time; pass the salt, pepper and bread simultaneously. Produced shrieks, faintings once or twice, a vomiting here and there. Not nice, I suppose, but think about it—what would you have done?

(So reasonable)

And so it was with me—has been. I have seen both, the blinding flash guns, the idiotic, truly idiotic adulation of the vacant . . . *and* the middle distance. Ask me to tell you about the middle distance. Perhaps I will . . . and then again . . .

Signing autographs was interesting. It was! Really, it was! I am, by nature, left handed, which, on occasion, allowed me to sign two autographs at once . . . and, at times, it did not. I never knew, for example, from one day to the next—whether I would be doubled to the right or to the left. "How

can this be?" you ask, scoffing laugh, wise eyes turned to your neighbor;
"How can this be!? The fellow's putting us on." Well, I wish I could
demonstrate it to you. If I could, of course, I'd probably not *be* here—certainly not at *this* price! I have photos, though, which I will be happy to
show you, assuming the equipment is working?

(*This last to the* WOMAN)

WOMAN (*Model calm*)
Well, I certainly assume so.

MAN
I tested it myself yesterday.

HIMSELF
Good!

(*Out*)
Happy? I have photos, as I said, slides, to be precise, which I will show
you, assuming the equipment *is* working, has not taken it into its me-
chanical little head to break down.

(*To the* MAN)

MAN (*Amused.*)
Oh, I say!

(SLIDE: *3 Pornographic slides in succession*)

WOMAN
Gilbert! Gilbert! When the cat's away the mice will play.

HIMSELF
And so much for the informal receptions.

(*Off to* WOMAN, *more or less*)
There is one following this, I believe?

(*Out*)
I'm sure there is. We'll get to mix.
Three arms he had, did he? Well, let's see 'em!

(*Change of tone*)
All in good time. You want the climax at the beginning, a life of de-
tumescence? All right! All right! Jesus!

(*Shows his right arm*)
Here's one.

(*Shows his left arm*)
Here's another. I'm sorry. What can I do? What can I say? You're a little
late. But we've got to lead up to these things. Really, edge up, regular
green beret stuff. Don't worry! I'll show it all to you—all the treasures. I
have a tale will tear your heart out . . . so to speak. After we are done here,
as you move into the lobby, you will find a table, a long one, with photo-

graphs, groups of photographs, booklets, a clinical case study, the coffee table volume, as well as my autobiography—illustrated, naturally! All for sale, all rare, all well worth the small price. And if you see me there, I beg you, please be gentle. I am not a freak. I am an average gentleman—easily injured . . . crushed! I am nothing more—*or* less—than a quiet man who, at one time, for a little, was possessed of . . . an extra arm. I no longer am. Please don't stare at me when we meet as if I were obscene, or deformed. I do not, I no longer bear arms. There is no appendage lurking underneath my jacket: it's gone. I waved it goodbye and it waved back. Gone.

> *(Chuckles to himself)*

I was asked once—recently—if I thought it would return, and, if it would, would that make me happy.

> *(Afterthought)*

Again. This assumes that the first visitation *did* make me happy, that I am less happy now, and *was*, before. I don't know; I really don't know. I have never thought it was man's lot—his right—to be "happy." To be conscious, yes—the pain of consciousness—to be aware of passing through it, that what little repose, less delight and least ecstasy we were granted was a blessing. I was not . . . *un*happy be*fore* it; certainly it changed my life and therefore all my definitions. I *am* unhappy now, though possibly for reasons having less to do with *it* than with *me;* were it to . . . return? Would that make me happy again? Probably not. Well, perhaps I'd best tell you how it all happened—stop skirting, or, more accurately, cuffing the issue. The meal [dinner, whichever] by the way, the one today, on a graph of one to ten was . . .

> *(Very expansive)*

. . . well, what did you think!? Way up there. At least a three! No, I'm only kidding.

> *(To the* WOMAN*)*

Really, kidding.

> *(Out)*

Seven! Eight! It was a smallish group today [or, tonight], nice ladies and gentlemen, and a minister—one of the more . . . relaxed denominations.

> *(Note:The* MAN *and the* WOMAN *will unobtrusively prepare for the roles* THEY *will momentarily assume; may have to do nothing save remove or put on a scarf;* HE *should get a cigarette, a drink and reverse his collar. No rush. Harsh chuckle)*

Hanh! I remember *one* time, *one* meal, back when I still had three arms, where I was seated across from a Catholic priest, ginned up to his elbows, cloth ashed and spotted; he smoked constantly, and his little fingers were all yellow; thin, ridged nails. Are you many Catholic here? Well, he shamed you! There are some who do. His hair was white, and streaked with a yellow identical to his finger stain. He had one eye did not *exactly* pay attention to the other; most of the time it *related*, if not precisely, but, on occasion, it

would develop a will of its own and range about . . . as if it had had a private
sight and was straining to be off after it. "You are an accident of nature," he
hissed at me, the priest, the priest hissed at me over the split pea soup. He
had been eyeing me—so to speak—at the "stand-up," the cocktail hour, but
he had kept his distance. "That's our father so-and-so," my hostess said to me
in her brightest voice when she saw his baleful eye on me. "He is of the old
school."

WOMAN

That's our father so-and-so; he's of the old school.

(Has SHE *risen? I'm not sure*)

HIMSELF

I *sort* of knew what she meant: driven into it—the cloth—driven into it by
tradition, fourth son of an ignorant and impoverished family, promised at
the deathbed of a grandmother, sex terrors, caned, starved, frozen in the
seminary, dreams of glory . . . for a while. "I can make red."

MAN (*Wistful*)

I can make red.

HIMSELF

I can make red. God, do they all dream of it—becoming Cardinals. Pope
even? The sin of pride not necessarily preceding the fall, the fall coming
on by itself, no great height to topple from, merely that there *is* a hierar-
chy, and some are in at the top, and others . . . are not—who your ward
captain is, so to speak. I find it hard to believe—well, there you are!—I
find it hard to believe that there's any of them hasn't shuddered, reddened,
if only once, with the thought of the glory, of the red and the amethyst, the
paradox—most high, most low—has not, only once, squared the shoulders,
stuck out Adam's apple, gulped and offered, "If debasement can be glory,
then the highest can also be my martyrdom: the faith of paradox, the paradox of faith."

MAN

If debasement can be glory, then the highest can also be my . . .

HIMSELF (*Cutting in*)

. . . or some such gibberish! But it fades; the awareness comes, that low is
all, that endless, hopeless drudge and grind and scuff and tatter is the end,
is the service . . . is the "way." We all come to it—in one way or another.
There is not a life, not one—name it if you can!—not a life hasn't seen
futility at the end, up ahead, like a highway turning into sand. No matter
how rich the life, filled, *filled* with joy, and "great doings," the sense comes
that there is nothing except the doing of it, and it fills the mouth with
mold, as good old Melville had it.

(*Out*)

Man A. Man A keeps his eyes closed so as not to see too much, to know too much; man B closes his after he has seen it all, closes with sadness, loathing and relief; and man C—is there a man C?—never blinks, keeps his eyes wide open, staring into the blinding dark.

There were—still are, probably!—holy men in India gaze into the sun from rise to set, never blinking. They have gone blind, of course, years back, the eyes burned out by the glory, but every day they sit, blind eyes staring at the burning, making the slowest of arcs as the earth moves, the sun moves. Man C. Man C is the happiest of men: he has seen the futility; it destroys him; he worships it. His is the only certainty—no hope; merely . . . adoration.

MAN

(Coming up behind HIMSELF, *clergy garb. Hissed)*

You are an accident of nature.

HIMSELF

"You are an accident of nature," he hissed at me: the priest; the priest hissed at me, over the split pea soup.

MAN

I've been watching you.

HIMSELF

"I've been watching you." Over the split pea soup.

(An aside; out, though)

There were saltines for the split pea soup, two to a cellophane package. Is it cellophane any longer? I wonder. Two to a package, cellophane— or whatever—with a red strip for opening. The crackers were not mandatory; God! the soup was like a porridge, or a yellow paste, and the crackers, probably served as a thickener in some dim, gone time, now would . . . sit on the stuff when you crumbled them into *it*—*onto* it. Sit there. Well, one could push them down *into* the glue, lose them *into* it with the round spoon, and there they would stay, little oases of dough in the doughy goo.

MAN *(As before)*

You are an accident of nature.

HIMSELF

And he looked at me, across the shrieking board, cigarette and gin in one hand, cracker crumble in the other, declined his head a trifle, shot one eye off toward our hostess, kept the other focused on my nose. "There is no redemption, then," I said.

(To the MAN)

There is no redemption, then?

(Out)

We freaks, you know. We've got to be careful.

WOMAN (SUGAR LADY)

Ohhhh!

(*Giggles*)

You men.

HIMSELF

"If you would die," he drawled.

MAN (*As* PRIEST *still*)

If you would die—*were* to—then you would have *been* an accident of nature, but no longer, softened, straightened by the great bosom. All is forgiven . . . ultimately.

HIMSELF (*Out*)

If I would only die. One of the comforts, I suppose: in the hospital bed, inventing new definitions of pain, or crumbled over the dinner table, breathless, wrenched with impossible stabbings, one could die; one could die, and in the meanwhile ponder this: it's all a test; God loves you; hi there, Job; love ya, baby; it's all a test. "I love you. Do you love me?" It's a spoiled child, or a lunatic—all the old hat stuff.

Any faith supposes cessation is an answer, well . . .

(*Leaves it unfinished. Grudging*)

Well, for everything there is a reason, for every pro a con and such like; everything transforms: pain into cessation, consciousness into faith. All of this comforts me less than . . .

MAN (*Still as* PRIEST)

How can you eat at the table with other people!?

HIMSELF (*To the* MAN)

I would be happy *not* to eat with you. You fill me with revulsion, a state impenetrable by pity, and I fear for my soul, deed I do, but there it is in my contract; I have no choice. It says it so clearly—not only will you present yourself at the place of assembly, or some other place determined by the sponsor, no later than one hour before the time of your revealing, but you shall, as well, break both bread and your heart either before or after the whatever, at the discretion of the whomever.

(*Out*)

"Revulsion," I said, right at him, "a state impenetrable by pity, and I fear for my soul." And it was amazing!

(*Note: the* MAN *demonstrates what is described*)

He raised his ginned and cigaretted hand in a blessing or a warding off and spread his lips with a bubbling hiss, which chilled the room, the table, at any rate, and would have the soup, were *it* not already on its own way there, did not live a life of its own, a condition I all at once envied—oh, to be soup! "Father X is a man of the old cloth," my hostess reminded me.

WOMAN (SUGAR LADY)

He really is: a man of the old cloth.

(*To* HIMSELF; *tentative*)

Would you like some wine?

HIMSELF (*To her*)

Of course, my dear; whatever you think goes best with the soup.

(*Out*)

I drove my spoon toward the greeny thing and, lo! a crust, or armor, had formed on its surface, and the spoon rebounded, would not penetrate. I suppose if I'd given it a good shove, but I hadn't the heart. White, I think, my dear. The staring eye bulged. "You have no soul, sir."

MAN

You have no soul, sir.

HIMSELF (*Out*)

Well, this *was* something to think about: you have no soul, sir. I was suddenly filled with a childish pride—not to possess a soul! I was, you see, to his way of viewing the world, all at once in a class with kangaroos—unusual to the point of bizarre, therefore beneath, therefore soulless. It was ludicrous, of course, and laughter could have fallen from the mouth . . . like vomit, but it was, at the same time, and in some deeper context, freeing. All the weight was suddenly lifted from me, the guilt, the fear . . . *and* the hope. No more hope; neither salvation nor damnation. I was to one side of . . . everything. I was free to be what I had always been. It was liberating to the point of hallucination.

(*To the* MAN/PRIEST)

If only I had asked you sooner!

WOMAN (*As* SUGAR LADY; *to herself*)

You're not eating your soup.

HIMSELF (*To her*)

I attempted it, Madame. It wanted no part of me.

WOMAN

Would you like another cup?

HIMSELF (*To her*)

I would rather develop a second nose.

MAN (*As* PRIEST)

Wouldn't surprise me a bit. Once it's out of hand . . .

HIMSELF

. . . so to speak . . .

MAN (*Ibid.*)

. . . once it begins, there's no telling: it's like the heresies.

HIMSELF *(Out)*

And this in the midst of all the reforms, this . . . throwback after John twenty-three and J.P.2.

(To the MAN*)*

Eternal vigilance being the price of the cloth?

MAN *(Wintry smile)*

On the button.

*(*MAN *and* WOMAN *exit)*

HIMSELF *(To the* MAN*)*

Right!

(Out)

I tell you these things—I share parts of my past with you—so you will have some sense of how it was back when—back when I was a freak. But I think I'd better tell you HOW IT ALL BEGAN! How *I* all began, to be precise.

(Off)

Are the slides ready? Are the slides ready? Hm? Yes? No? Yes? Good!

WOMAN

Yes!

HIMSELF *(Out)*

The slides are ready. This Is My Life. I was born some [however old the actor playing HIMSELF is] years ago in a town no more than eighteen hundred miles from here, a town like any other town.

(Waits; nothing happens)

Start the fucking slides, will you!?

(Slide show commences.

Note on slides: whenever the text says SLIDE, *the appropriate slide is shown.*

SLIDE: *A town like any other town)*

A town like any other town. Trees.

*(*SLIDE*)*

Houses.

*(*SLIDE*)*

Banks.

*(*SLIDE *of one)*

A bibliothèque.

*(*SLIDE*)*

Four drunks.

*(*SLIDE*)*

One gay.

(SLIDE; *normal face*)

One hideously lonely gay.

(SLIDE: *same, crying*)

Seven voluptuaries.

(SLIDE)

And a drum and fife corps.

(SLIDE: *famous painting of revolutionary corps*)

It was a town like any other town, except . . . except that on [actor's birth-date] in a house on Prune Street,

(SLIDE)

the corner of Prune and Hoover, there was born to my parents . . . me.

(SLIDE: *newborn baby*)

Me . . . a healthy, bouncing baby boy. Not bouncing, actually, literally, not literally bouncing, but healthy and a baby and a boy. I wonder why they say that—"She had a baby." What were they expecting—a sixteen-year-old? An oven mitt?

I grew rapidly and without incident.

(SLIDE: *a three-year-old boy.* HIMSELF *looks at it*)

Photo of me as a three-year-old boy.

(SLIDE: *a three-year-old black boy.* HIMSELF *looks at it*)

Photo of me as *another* three-year-old child?

(*Note: if a black actor plays* HIMSELF, *reverse the previous*)

I hated neither of my parents—that, I think, is more a city habit—and it was only later, much later, that I discovered I had loved them more than I think they had loved me. It's not the sort of thing, though, you can go up and ask them.

(MAN *and* WOMAN *enter*)

WOMAN

Hello, son.

HIMSELF

Hello, Ma.

WOMAN

Dad? Look who's here.

MAN

Hm? Well, my golly, look who's here.

HIMSELF

I have a question I have to ask you both.

MAN (To the WOMAN)

A what?

WOMAN

A question! A question! He wants to ask us a question.

MAN (*Sort of surprised*)

Well, of course! Why not!
  (*To* HIMSELF)
Shoot!

HIMSELF

It's about love.

MAN (*To the* WOMAN)

About what?

WOMAN

Love! Love!

MAN

Well, of course! Why not?

HIMSELF

I know you love me, have loved me, but I think in general I have loved you more.

MAN (*To the* WOMAN)

What does he say?

WOMAN

That we love him; he knows we've loved him.

MAN

Well, of course! Why not?

HIMSELF (*To the* WOMAN)

That's not what I said.

MAN (*To the* WOMAN)

What's that?

WOMAN

He thinks perhaps we have loved one another unequally.

HIMSELF (*To the* WOMAN)

That is not what I said; that is not precisely what I said. I said, I think in general I have loved you more than you have loved me.

WOMAN (*Smiles*)

It will do.

MAN (*To the* WOMAN)

What?

WOMAN (*To the* MAN)

Nothing.

HIMSELF

(*Out; the* OTHER TWO *still standing*).

You see? You can't ask them. The shortest distance between two generations is *not* a straight answer. Well . . . what does it matter—they're dead.

MAN (*To the* WOMAN)

What? What was that?

WOMAN (*To the* MAN)

We died.

MAN (*To* HIMSELF)

Well, of course! Why not?

(MAN *and* WOMAN *re-sit*)

HIMSELF (*To* MAN *and* WOMAN)

Thank you both.

(*Out*)

In any event, I grew; I went to school, I pubed, I developed simultaneous crushes on the Nabokovian girl-child two seats up from me in English class,

(SLIDE: *a nymphet*)

Aha! There is the girl; pretty thing; I have no idea what happened to her.

(SLIDE: *the boy*)

and the captain of the swimming team, a superbly handsome brute of a boy, now senator and, some say, on his way to the Oval Office. He's certainly less handsome now, though no less brutish. I imagine he'll make it.

(SLIDE: *both the boy and the girl*)

This bi of mine, this crush on both sexes, led to nothing, in the sense that while I was possessed by both of them . . . I possessed neither.

(SLIDE *off*)

I settled finally—and naturally, for me—on a heterosexual quest, the usual progression: self-abuse, self-abuse with fantasy, simple dates, complex dates, light petting, heavy petting, "all the way," love and longing, broken hearts and aching nuts, the whole thing. I'm afraid I don't have slides of this.

I graduated high school.

MAN (*Calling*)

Congratulations, son!

HIMSELF

. . . and went off to college.

WOMAN (*Calling*)

Stay warm!

HIMSELF

. . . off, I say, away from the farm,

　(SLIDE: *city*)

so to speak, and up to the city—first city on the way to others, larger, more distant, more . . . complex. It is a progression devoutly to be wished, or some such thing.

　(SLIDE *out*)

I was bright, ambitious, more than a little curious about the world around me, and, soon enough, cosmopolite.

　(To the wings)

Do we have a photo marked "cosmopolite"?

　(Pause)

No? No matter.

　(Out)

Take it on faith, why don't you—soon enough, cosmopolite. You can't go home again, they tell you, by which they mean you cannot become your-self as a child again—until the final senility, and then only in manner. Nor does it matter.

I became a city boy. I graduated from the U.

　(SLIDE: *huge graduating class*)

That's me, seventeen rows from the front, forty-third in from the left.

　(SLIDE *off*)

My parents came to it, *for* it; I was an only child—two would-be sisters died at birth. I have no photos of them. God! who would have photos of dead newborns!? What do you want!?

My parents came to it,

　(SLIDE: *parents*)

came to the city, wondered at it, were polite about its . . . excesses, its dirt, its . . . diversity, by which *they* meant Chinks, Jews, and Spics and all that. Forgive them; they were good people. Agee-ans. "One was my Mother who was good to me; one was my Father who was good to me." James Agee. Remember it? No? Ah, well.

Good folk, but not city; they watched me graduate, smiled, swelled, were truly, *truly* proud—neither had been beyond tenth grade—truly proud, and anxious to be home. They kissed me, hugged me, went to the station, got on the train, went home . . . died. I have compressed time a little—for the sake of narrative.

　(SLIDE: *side-by-side gravestones*)

And there they are.

MAN

Well, of course! Why not!?

　(SLIDE *off*)

HIMSELF *(Out)*

And on I went—bright, *very* bright, and shrewd, and . . . dare I say it? talented, *into* advertising, *up* the ladder. I had my own accounts in *no* time.

(Curiously offhand)

Oh. I married along the way, on one of the rungs.

(SLIDE: *his wife; she must look quite like the* WOMAN; *perhaps the photo is of the* WOMAN *at an earlier age)*

There she is: a pretty, old-fashioned girl.

Will you laugh that we had not been to bed until our wedding? Some of you won't; some of you must have gone the same route—

(Some contempt)

the same old-fashioned "think of it as a gift, a sort of wedding present" manner, the old "who would want a girl who gives it away?" routine. Routine? Unfair! Unfair!

(SLIDE *out)*

Just because your city sluts are pros at twelve doesn't mean the corn and wheat fields don't produce a . . . slower carnality. Everything in its own good time—God's good time; society's good time.

(A confidence)

Look, fucking yourself cross-eyed is a mound of fun, and no mistake about it. Even when *I* was a pup, out in puppyland, there were those girls who took a lineup of the local boys easy as beaten biscuits. We had names for 'em: round heels, easy, everybody's, *any*body's, Saturday night special, et cetera, et cetera. And we *liked* those girls; they were nice, friendly, laughing, with an easy manner and a gentle, willing way in the sack. But it's *true:* we didn't marry them. We married the other ones, and those lovely acquiescent girls fanned out across the land, found husbands—most of them— whom they made happier than chance would have it.

My wife and I had a good and happy life . . .

(SLIDE: *another photo of wife)*

for a while. We were congenial and compatible, and she was a helpmeet in every way. We moved into a lovely house,

(SLIDE *of it)*

and we had our children early,

(SLIDE: *husband, wife, three kids—two boys, one girl)*

so as to get it underway, *out* of the way, and build . . . *build.* My career was a straight line *up,* my prospects were unlimited, and with my wife at my side, the toddlers toddling at my knees, there was nothing but joy and accomplishment and security and predictability—the swift ascent, the long, rich crest, the planned deceleration: easy life and easy cease. And then.

(SLIDE *out*
Pause)

And then it happened, the event which changed my life forever, created me, destroyed me, raised me up . . . and brought me here.

(Tiny pause)

To you. To your stares, your awful receptions, your terrible food, your . . .

(Catches himself)

No; that's not fair: today's meal was nice. Really it was.

WOMAN

Well, we're glad.

HIMSELF

I don't like my salad first, but I am in a minority these days, this land. Appetizer, soup, fish, flesh, salad, cheese, dessert, fruit and nuts. That *used* to be the way of the world. God! I was somewhere in the ["your" if played in the Midwest] Midwest once when they served coffee as soon as we sat down to table—and they drank it! my hosts and hostesses, smiling and sipping while all *I* wanted was another gin, which, come to think of it . . . ?

(To the WOMAN*)*

Is it possible to get a . . . ?

WOMAN *(As herself again)*

I beg your pardon?

HIMSELF

I said: is it possible to have a glass of gin brought up here?

WOMAN *(Appalled, if mildly)*

A glass of gin!? Up here!?

HIMSELF

I feel the need for a nip; I am nip-needy.

WOMAN *(Self-conscious)*

Just . . . go about your business.

MAN *(To the* WOMAN*)*

I could . . . go . . . if you think . . . ?

WOMAN

Certainly not!

HIMSELF

Oh, please!

WOMAN

Sir! You are addressing us!

HIMSELF *(Louder; tense)*

Well, why can't I do it with a glass of gin in my hand?!! If priests do it, why, oh why can't I? It isn't as if I asked for a bottle, for Christ's sake!

MAN *(Rising)*

I'll just steal off . . .

(Begins to do so)

I'll just . . . you know: steal off.

WOMAN *(To them* BOTH*)*

I don't approve!

MAN *(To* HIMSELF *)*

I'll be right back; we'll see what we can do. You stay right where you are.

(Exits)

HIMSELF *(To the exiting* MAN*)*

You are a very helpful old man.

WOMAN

I really don't approve.

HIMSELF *(To her)*

It's not very much to ask!

(Out)

It's not very much to ask. It's not as if I asked for a fucking bottle!

(So reasonable)

Every once in a while a man needs a little nip—and no jokes, please! One can go along quite nicely, sometimes for hours, ginless, joyless, fully in control, and then one needs a nip of gin.

WOMAN

It's unprofessional.

HIMSELF *(To her; and out)*

Balderdash! Show me a contract specifies the speaker can't have a gin if he wants it—needs it—*wants* it. Besides the lecture circuit is strewn with drunks and secret junkies, pill poppers, winos. Take a look at your famous some day: take a look at your big stars—How many do you think've hit fifty-plus intact? Hunh!? Take a look around you.

(Calmer)

Today's meal was nice, the placement of the salad aside.

WOMAN *(Ice)*

We're sorry.

HIMSELF *(To the woman; brutal)*

THEN LEARN FROM IT, LADY!!

(Control regained; out)

Sometimes, one doesn't get to eat at all. Today I did; today was fine.

WOMAN *(Cool)*

Thank you.

HIMSELF

You're welcome.

(Out)

I wasn't too happy about the press, if truth is of any interest.

WOMAN

Oh?

HIMSELF *(To her)*

Only one.

(Out)

The rest was your usual, but there was this one came to the press conference all prepared, not homework-wise, but . . . opinioned. The article was already written; all she wanted was my assent, my agreement to the dismemberment. "You do admit, don't you, that taking money the way you do, for a deformation—a former deformation, at that— blah blah blah." Where's my gin!? I want my gin!! Shit like that; you know them; you know those . . . journal*istes*: they would have been party members in the thirties; they write with spite and polish; they crucify and vilify and get all runny in the name of "good hard journalism." They tend to be prettier now than they used to be: fewer hairy upper lips, less hippiness; manicured for a change, less lesbo, but still killers.

(Smiles)

She's sitting there among you; she's smiling at me, killer smile; she loves the recognition; she hates me for it. She won't be shamed into decency; it'll just move her a little further into shrewd slaughter.

(Waves)

Hello, dear! Look at her! Purring away. Wave back, why don't you? Reveal your sources, so to speak. No? Cunt!

WOMAN *(Outraged)*

Please!

HIMSELF *(To her; curt)*

Sorry.

(Out)

Give me an old-fashioned journalist any time: some drama critic fired from the sports department, say; some borderline psychotic from the foreign desk; some crusty editor doesn't give a shit and does his job, just does his job.

(Points out generally)

Protect us all from *that*.

(Waves)

Hello, dear! Be sure to put something in about the gin; attribute everything to that: "The arm fell off because of the gin," or something like that.

(More general now)

The arm did *not* . . . fall off. Thud! My goodness, look at that! There's an arm lying there amid the sawdust; poor thing, fell off because of the gin, most likely. Speaking of which . . .

(Off)

Any luck? Any gin?

WOMAN

I'm going to phone your agent!

HIMSELF

Good. Maybe she'll talk to you.

(Back)

I should have it put in my contract: let there be gin. I suppose that might . . . diminish my engagements? Make wary the sponsors, warier the already wary? And Christ knows we can't afford diminishment at this . . . blunt point in time, to use the awful phrase. We are diminished already—diminish-ed—our major attraction, you might say, gone as it came. And how long can we plow the furrow of what was? They used to pay me twenty-five thousand dollars an hour. Twenty-five . . . thousand . . . dollars . . . an *hour*—merely to wave it a little, do a few tricks . . . back when I was a freak!

(A confidence)

The fee for a former freak is somewhat less, I dare say you'll believe me when I tell you. I have been had for as little as half a grand. And a tottle of gin, or two.

(Off)

Any luck, old man?

(Shrugs)

The rest of the press was . . . fine: they wondered the usual and I replied the same. *Plus* the lesser usuals—the wife, the kids, do I miss them, the special tailoring, the Pope. You know . . . the usual. "Why are we to believe you met the Pope?" the cunt asked.

(The WOMAN *is uneasy at that word.*
An aside, to the WOMAN*)*

Sorry.

(Back)

—the cunt asked in the midst of all the pleasantries. "Because I have a photo of it, you painted whore," I lisped between my smiling teeth. "And besides," I went on, all oily, "and besides, why would the Pope lie about it?"

Well, that got a laugh from the presslet—score one for *me*—save the killer didn't even blink. She merely decided *not* to write that one down—might show humanity, or wit, or something: wouldn't do; wouldn't fit.

(*Curious pleading*)

I have so much to tell you, so, so much to share. Such wonders . . . such wonder. I will take you with me on such a ride. I do a splendid show for my crust of bread; you'll not be sorry you invited me. It's just . . . I must have a glass of gin.

WOMAN

We're trying.

HIMSELF

Well, it's not good enough; I think you'd better have an intermission.

WOMAN

We hadn't planned on an intermission.

HIMSELF

Well, then, sit there and cross your eyes for fifteen minutes or so. *I'm* going to have an intermission—a gin, and a pee, and a quiet cry—two sobs and a gulp and a freshet of tears in a corner somewhere.

(*Out*)

If you come upon me, my back to you, my shoulders shaking with my sobbing, please leave me be; don't . . . touch me, comfortingly, gently, on the golden spot; don't offer solace. Just . . . leave me be and let me sob it out.

(*Looks at his watch*)

I'll see you, then, at [fifteen minutes from whatever time it is].

(HE *starts off bowing*)

Thank you, thank you, thank you all.

(*Exits*)

WOMAN

(*Making the best of a bad thing*).

I . . . I take it we're about to have an intermission.

(*Walks off*)

CURTAIN

ACT TWO

(Stage bare of actors; set as at end of Act One. Toward the end of the audience return, let HIMSELF *appear in the auditorium, manically urging the audience to its seats)*

HIMSELF

All right, now! Come on! Back to your seats! Don't dawdle! Come on, show on the road! You've paid your money; I've paid my time. Let's get it together! Come on, now! Hurryhurryhurry! Show's about to begin! Up we go!

*(*HE *jumps on the stage, sees no one else there; calls offstage)*

Let's get a move on out there!

(Out)

Back to your seats! No talking; shuffle on, gather round, stir the cauldron, make a wish!

(The WOMAN *comes on, with as much dignity as* SHE *can manage)*

WOMAN

Are we . . . you would like to begin now? Rebegin?

HIMSELF

Where's your friend . . . the geezer?

MAN

(Rushing—for him—on, fixing his fly)

Oh my, oh my, oh my!

HIMSELF

(Loud slapping together of hands)

OK! Here we are!

(To the WOMAN*)*

Any more announcements? Lies? Evasions? Would-be jokes? Denouncements?

WOMAN *(Sitting; great composure)*

Nothing, thank you.

HIMSELF *(Mimicking)*

Nothing, thank you.

(To the MAN*)*

And you?

MAN *(Not quite with it)*

Hm? Pardon?

HIMSELF

Anything from you? Any . . . redundancies?

MAN

I'm not sure I . . .

HIMSELF

Did you have a nice intermission?

MAN

Well . . . *yes,* come to think of it; very nice, indeed. I ran into a couple I
hadn't seen in . . . oh, years: fifteen, perhaps.

HIMSELF

Isn't that nice.
    (Out)
Isn't that nice?

MAN

I had seen them last in Muncie, I think.
    [Unless we are there; if we are . . . Cincinnati]

WOMAN

Do get on with it.

MAN

    (Taking this as encouragement. Out, as well as to them)
Randall and Beatrice Endicott—she a Springfield Endicott, he a Munice-an,
both with the same last name: like marrying one's cousin, I suppose . . . in
a way.
    (Realizing)

WOMAN

May we get on with it?

MAN

Nice people, the Endicotts—philosophers, the both.
    (A nod out)
Nice people.

WOMAN *(To* HIMSELF*)*

Please?

HIMSELF

    (Gracious, having had his fun)
Of course!
    (Out, with considerable energy)

Well; here we are, all refreshed—freshened—ready for revelation, resolution, come what may. *I* enjoyed the interval—intermission. You *did* leave me alone, most of you. I thank you for that. Couple of sneers, two or three blue-hairs shaking their heads; what's-her-name, the actress. One autograph: ten-year-old boy, hideous glasses, likewise suit, teeth like a rabbit. Patted him between the ears. Oh! and our Lady of the Lake came up to me—the lady I was telling you about, the journalist, the journa*liste*? Came right up to me, the baggage! right into the anteroom I'd slid into after the rabbit. "You're good," she said, "you're really good." There was a loathing to it, a condemnation that I dare be articulate, coherent. "You're really good." "So are you," I said. "You've got balls."
The energy of the hatred here, the mutual rage and revulsion was such that, had we fucked, we would have shaken the earth with our cries and thumps and snarls and curses: a crashing around of Gods—chewed nipples, bleeding streaks along the back. Had we fucked . . . Oh, Jesus! what issue! *But* . . . but the only issue was the issue of me, the . . . dismemberment of me. "You've got balls!" I said. And I crashed my hand into her crotch like a goosing twelve-year-old. "Get your hands off me," she said. "Get your filthy hands off me." I withdrew my hand: it had hit rock. "If you'll excuse me," she said, ice, shoving past me. She *is* an impressive lady.

MAN (Chuckling)

You didn't *really* do that.

HIMSELF (To the MAN)

Well my goodness. I certainly hope I didn't. I'd worry about myself if I had.

MAN (To the WOMAN)

He didn't really *do* that.

WOMAN (Generally)

Well, I certainly hope *not*.

HIMSELF (Out)

I didn't really do that? All right.
    (*Calls*)
You can forget it, puddin' pie; it never really happened!
    (*To them all; to himself*)
I am *trying* to be nice; I have *promised* myself I will be nice—and perhaps if I knew what the term *meant*, then perhaps I would be, *could* be. So!
    (*Tiny pause*)
So, all in all, it was an interesting intermission: I was physically abusive to a lady, and contemptuously dismissive of a sincere and well-intentioned boy child. Par for the course.
    (*A confidence*)

I find it hard sometimes to distinguish between my self-disgust and my disgust with others, and I worry about that; I really do, truly do. I mean, I'm a nice person or at least I used to be. It occurs to me: look here, old man, you *really* ought to be able to distinguish between self-disgust and your disgust with others. Give it a good try! Don't mix 'em up like that. I mean, you have no trouble with pity—you can tell self-pity from the Christlike a mile away—well, a hundred yards.

WOMAN

Talk about yourself.

HIMSELF *(to the* WOMAN*)*

I thought I was.

  (Out)

I thought I was!

  (To the WOMAN *again)*

Did you talk to my agent?

WOMAN

They weren't in.

HIMSELF *(Both to her and out)*

Out scouting up new clients, probably. They have me, two sisters used to be on radio, a defrocked Satanist, three defectors from the EPA, an overweight diet expert, the plastic butcher of your next meeting. And, of course, the late, lamented Doctor What's-his-name.

MAN

Plastic butcher.

WOMAN *(Hard)*

Get on with it!

HIMSELF *(To woman; saluting)*

Yes, Sir!

  (Out)

So. I had my cry, too. Remember my cry. Who remembers my cry? My promised cry?
Promise them circuses, eh?

  (To someone in the front)

Do you remember what I said? Before we broke? Remember I said that if you came upon me sobbing in a corner, not to disturb? That it was a way I had and not to worry? Do you remember?

  (Note: If the person says "yes," say: "You do!" If the person says "no," say: "You don't!" If person fails to respond, wing it, choosing what you like)

Splendid; it's those of you pay attention cheers me up in the low times. I had my sob, my cry, my cryette. It was in the anteroom after Miss fourth estate and I had had our set-to, our little chat. I sat on a settee, the edge of it, a spongy thing covered in . . . purple plastic sheen—a kind of iridescence—the sort of sofa gives one second thoughts about the West. I sat there; I put my hands to my dry eyes, to rub them: These lights . . . they strain. I put my dry hands to rub my dry eyes and they came away wet—as if the hands were a signal to the eyes, their coming to them a sign to flood. I discovered I was crying, and therefore I made the *sounds* of crying, the sobs, the gasps, and I let it grow into a full and theoretically satisfying cry. It occurred to me, though, in the middle of it, the cry, that I didn't know *why, why* I was crying. There was so much to choose from! . . . such a wealth of the ludicrous, the painful, the emptying, that I would never know. And I let *that* become the source: thoughts about the source became the source. Isn't that wonderful?—so much to weep over one cannot be sure which one has chosen. Who says we're not a healthy land!

(*Pause; claps hands together once, loud*)

OK!! On we go!

MAN (*Startled*)

What!? What!?

HIMSELF

On with the story! The saga of the man who had three arms! Where was I? Had I brought you up to "the moment"?—the moment that changed my life forever?

(*Fast*)

Ma? Pa? Education? Job? Wifey?

Right! OK! "And then it happened."

This is what you *came* for, isn't it!?

OK? OK?

OK. And then it happened.

One Saturday morning, nearer to noon than not, after a good hot A.M. time post breakfast with my wife—that being second preference only to five P.M.—I had gone to shower. I had shampooed my hair—a thing I did first —and was finishing with my body. I had done my groin—that always first— my armpits, my chest, my legs, my backside and my lower back, and I was ending as I always did—no longer do; I no longer shower; I tub— finishing with my upper back, that awkward area between the shoulder blades. I had my soapy cloth, and I was doing away with a sort of lackadaisical diligence when I felt a . . . a kind of bump—a bump*ette*, to be more exact—between my blades; not a pimple, not a boil, but a . . . small bump; not a mole, nothing on the surface, but a kind of rising under the skin.

I have no photos of this, of course. It was not until later—much later—that the photos started. If you have expected a visual progression of it from the very first, then you will be sadly disappointed—perhaps even to the point of bitterness, in which case . . . tough!

Aha! I said to myself, and what is *this?* What is this bump?

(WOMAN *rises, moves center; appropriate action for the following*)

My wife had come into the bathroom, her eyes dreamy with post-coital mist, her negligee agape.

(*To* WOMAN)

Sweetie?

WOMAN

Mmmmm?

HIMSELF

Will you feel this thing on my back?

WOMAN

What thing?

HIMSELF

Come see; right . . . there, between my shoulder blades.

WOMAN (*Peers*)

It's a bump. It's a little bump. Will you be long?

HIMSELF

What does it look like?

WOMAN (*Peers again*)

It looks like a bump.

HIMSELF

Is it . . . red, or anything?

WOMAN

No, quite a normal little bump. Will you be long?

HIMSELF

No, I'm done.

(*Out*)

And that was that . . . for a little while. I felt it the next day—my bump—following another post-coital shower—it being Sunday—and while it was still there, since there was no pain, apparently no inflamation, I let it go. Well, look: one never lets things "go," entirely. I mean, one is always conscious of something like that, but one becomes *used* to it, if you know what I mean. I had determined that if there were pain, or growth, or redness, or a sudden, instinctive cancer-panic I would hotfoot it down to the doctor—otherwise, not. Let nature take its course—create, cure.

WOMAN

How's your bump?

HIMSELF

. . . my wife said to me another time, maybe a week after I'd first made her conscious of it.

WOMAN

How's your bump? Is it still there?

HIMSELF (*To the* WOMAN)

I haven't paid any attention to it. Why don't you have a look?
   (*Out*)
This was a weekday, eight in the A.M. She looked, looked a bit longer than casual.

WOMAN

Hm!

HIMSELF (*To the* WOMAN)

What! What!?

WOMAN

HM!!

HIMSELF (*To the* WOMAN)

For Christ's sake, woman! What *is* it!?

WOMAN (*Calm; curious*)

I don't exactly know. Why don't you pop down to the doctor?

HIMSELF (*Out*)

I leaned against the sink to support myself. I looked in the mirror and I was gray.
   (*To the* WOMAN; *doomed tone*)
What is it, sweetie!?
   (*Out*)
She chuckled, and her tone was almost amused.

WOMAN (*Chuckle*)

Well, if I didn't know better, I'd say you were growing a little . . . fern, or something.

HIMSELF (*To the* WOMAN)

A fern!

WOMAN

Well, that's certainly what it looks like. Do you want a mirror?

HIMSELF (*Out*)

And she brought over the mirror she uses for the back of her hair, and she positioned it so as I could see the area of my back where whatever was there was . . . well, *there.* I couldn't make anything *out* . . . clearly. I can't see anything, I said.

WOMAN

Well, it's not very large, you know, about the size of my thumbnail.

HIMSELF

(To the WOMAN; *mildly hysterical)*

It's a *plant!?*

WOMAN *(Calm)*

A fern. Or . . . fernlike. Is that better? I'd trot on down to the doctor if I were you, see if you're becoming a vegetable.

HIMSELF *(Out)*

Count on her for calm, for making light, for the even keel, the sense of proportion: good girl! I *called* my doctor, *our* doctor, the family . . . what? physician? I told him I had something funny growing on my back and, in effect, what did he intend to do about it. What he intended to do about it he said, was send me to a specialist, a man who dealt with plants and things growing out of people's backs—according to their wives. Didn't *he* want to see me? No, whatever for? Of course: whatever for?

(Shrugs)

He made the appointment for me, for a week or so later, and I went. I took the day off, which wasn't any problem since I was a full partner now, right *up* there—I was a big boy—or plant, or whatever.

(In this next section—several visits to the specialist—separation is determined by HIMSELF *standing and bending over.*

The MAN *rises, becomes the* SPECIALIST; *the* WOMAN *rises, becomes the* NURSE, *unobtrusively passing the prop table as* THEY *come up. Out)*

The specialist was a dignified gentleman of innumerable years who had trained in Paris and Peking—and I had no reason to doubt him—and had treated among others, he said, Noël Coward, Chou En-lai, one of the Marx Brothers—I forget which, a minor one—the Queen of the Netherlands and, I assumed, Thomas Burpee and the Jolly Green Giant.

MAN *(Jolly)*

So, you have a growth you want me to look at, eh?

HIMSELF *(To the* MAN)

Yes, apparently I have.

MAN

Well, let's have a look, shall we?

(Note: Does HIMSELF *merely bend over a little as the* DOCTOR *examines him each time, or does he bend over the prop table, say? To be decided)*

Mmmmmmmmmmm . . . goodness!

HIMSELF *(Apprehension)*

Yes?

MAN *(To the* WOMAN)

Come here and look.

HIMSELF

What is it!?

WOMAN *(Peering)*

My goodness!

HIMSELF

What *is* it!!?

MAN

Well, I don't rightly know quite yet.

HIMSELF

Take it off!

MAN

What's your hurry? I don't even know what it *is*.

HIMSELF

Is it . . . is it a plant?

WOMAN *(Laughs)*

A what!?

MAN

A what!? A plant!?

HIMSELF

A fern; my wife says it's a fern.

MAN *(Trying to be serious)*

Well, I don't think it's a fern, if that's what you're afraid of. People don't
. . . grow ferns.
  (Second thought)
Well, we *do*, actually, but not from our backs—in *pots*, usually . . .

HIMSELF

I don't understand you people.
  (Out)
Nor did I think I wanted to. The relief of knowing a plant was not protrud-
ing from me was less than I would have hoped.

MAN *(So reassuring)*

All that is growing from you . . . is *you*. Now, I will see you in a week.

HIMSELF *(Out)*

And once a week I returned. On my second visit . . .

MAN

Very interesting. Really very interesting.
  (To the WOMAN*)*
Come see.

WOMAN *(Peering)*

Oh, indeed it is.

HIMSELF *(To the* MAN*)*

What!? What is!?

MAN

It seems to be growing just a bit.

HIMSELF

Take it off!!

MAN *(Reassuring)*

No, no, we'll let it go a little. Come see me in a week.

HIMSELF *(Out)*

He affixed a bandage—a loose one, so as not to disturb the little fellow, as he put it—which made it difficult for my wife to have a look at it, and reduced me to sponge baths and bent-over hair washings. At the end of the fifth week—during which time my attention at the office was less than it might have been—I was determined both to have a look at whatever it was and have it lopped—done away with, excised . . . removed.

(To the MAN*)*

I want it removed!

MAN

What? You want what removed?

HIMSELF *(Gesturing futilely)*

This . . . whatever it is. I want it *off!*

MAN *(Sighs)*

I think we'd better have a little talk.

HIMSELF *(Out)*

This was it! It *was* cancer, one of those swiftly growing ones, lymph nodes already involved, dead in three weeks. Why me!? Why me!? And we sat down, the three of us, all of us on the examination table, sitting on the edge of it. A crossing of legs.

(To the MAN*)*

How long have I got?

MAN

Before what?

HIMSELF *(Little boy lost)*

Before I die?

MAN *(As the* WOMAN *giggles)*

Who knows? Twenty-five years if your heart's good; ten seconds if you get in front of the wrong taxi.

HIMSELF

You mean it's not a cancer!

MAN

Goodness, no! It's not a cancer at all.

HIMSELF *(To the* MAN)

Well . . . if it's not a cancer . . . what *is* it?

MAN

I have been in practice a very long time.

HIMSELF *(To the* MAN)

I know.

MAN

I studied in Paris and Peking.

HIMSELF

I know; I know.

MAN

Noël Coward was a patient of mine.

HIMSELF

I know; you told me.

MAN

And in all my years . . .

HIMSELF *(Out, an aside)*

He was a man took forever.

(To them BOTH)

WHAT IS IT!!??

(Out)

I mean . . . Jesus!

MAN

My dear fellow, what is happening is that . . . well, is that you are growing
a third arm.

HIMSELF *(A beat)*

I beg your pardon.

MAN

A third arm; you are growing a third arm.

HIMSELF *(Rage; hysteria)*

A THIRD ARM!!!???

(Pause. Out; great calm)

This comes as no surprise to *you*, of course; you've been way ahead all
along; you knew about it; I did not. Place yourself in *my* position.

(To a lady in balcony)

For example, Madam, say one afternoon you awoke from a nap, went to your dressing table to . . . to powder your breasts, say, and, lo, there was something between them—a mound, a tiny lump of something. You would panic, would you not? The dread cancer? And what if it grew and grew and your doctor would not remove it—seemed spellbound by the thing? And what if one day it all fell into place, so to speak, developed its own nipple and nimbus—aureole, rather—and it was explained to you—the obvious and inconceivable—that you were growing a third breast, nicely rising between Gertrude and Gloria, or whatever your husband called them; that it seemed a perfectly normal, healthy breast, and that with any luck it would probably stop growing when it attained the size of the others. How would you feel about that . . . eh?

(To a man in the audience)

Or you, sir. What if one day, fumbling into your fly at the urinal, whipping it out to take a pee, you noticed a kind of . . . well, a kind of little lump, or something, right next to it? Oh, shit! A social disease. Some new strain of something brought over from the Orient, resistant to all known medicine! What the fuck am I going to tell the wife!? And it grows, and it grows, *and* the specialist seems fascinated by it, and finally he lets you in on the joyous news you've grown another dick—no bigger than the other one, alas, but there it is.

I ask you . . .

(Out)

I ask you all—wouldn't you be just a . . . tiny bit surprised? Here you have passed your lives in relative content and dignity, with no more falling off of honor or dream or whatever than usual; you have settled into an acceptable pattern—individuality within conformity—and . . . all . . . of . . . a . . . sudden . . . you've become a *freak!* Place yourself in my position: not now . . . *then!*

(To MAN*)*

A THIRD ARM!!!!????

MAN *(Matter-of-fact)*

Yes, a third arm.

HIMSELF *(Faintly hysterical)*

Whose *is* it?

MAN

Why . . . yours, of course.

HIMSELF

This sort of thing doesn't happen!

MAN

Just because it is emerging . . . a little late . . .

HIMSELF

A little *late!!*

WOMAN

Better late than never.

HIMSELF

I . . .
    (*To* WOMAN)
You render me speechless.
    (*Out*)
So, there I was—bearing arms, armed for anything, all those puns I had to put up with later . . . when it all came out, so to speak. But now, here I was, newly armed and up in arms about it.
    (*Gestures for laughter; gets some canned*)
What to do.
Well, indeed, what to do? I had an obligation to it, I was told, and to society. What did they think I was going to do . . . go on tour with it!? God!! My wife had to be told, of course, and right away.
    (WOMAN *rises, becomes* WIFE.
    To WOMAN)
I think we'd better have a little talk.

WOMAN (*Cheerful*)

O.K.

HIMSELF

A . . . a serious talk.

WOMAN

OK.

HIMSELF

You'd better sit down.

WOMAN

What is it . . . you've been cheating on me?

HIMSELF

No.

WOMAN

I've been cheating on *you?*

HIMSELF

No, of course not.

WOMAN (*Relieved*)

What then?

HIMSELF *(Out)*

And so I told her, and she took it rather well—a little disbelief, a little revulsion, a little . . . panic, but . . . all in all, rather well.

(To WOMAN*)*

I think you'd better have a look at it.

WOMAN *(Quiet disbelief)*

Look at it? You want me to *look* at it?

HIMSELF *(Out)*

And so she had her first real look at the little fellow.

(WOMAN *examines* HIMSELF's *bent back*)

WOMAN *(Finally)*

It's kind of cute. Once you get over wanting to throw up it's kind of cute.

HIMSELF

Help me!

WOMAN

I'll try.

HIMSELF

What am I going to do?

WOMAN

Are you waving at me?

HIMSELF

I beg your pardon?

WOMAN

It's waving, I think. Are you waving it at me?

(Giggle)

HIMSELF *(Out)*

And it was here that I had my first sense of the complexity of it all. No, I was *not* waving, but *it was*. It was a baby arm at the moment, and moved spasmodically, as from the impulses of a baby brain. It would come under my control eventually, do my bidding, but never entirely; it retained—right to the very end—a . . . mind of its own.

WOMAN

I'm going to touch it; I'm going to tickle its little palm.

(Does so)

HIMSELF *(To the woman)*

That tickles!

(Out)

And I felt its tiny fingers close on my wife's great tickling finger, and I was aware of sensation.

WOMAN

That *is* cute. Let go; thank you.

HIMSELF *(Out)*

It was a moment of . . . revelation, I suppose is the only word—the wonder of it, of *being*.

WOMAN

What are we going to tell the children?

HIMSELF

Hm? I beg your pardon?

WOMAN

What are we going to tell the children? You can't just grow a third arm without telling the children *some*thing . . . and a lot of other people, too, I should imagine. By the way, which arm is it?

HIMSELF

What do you mean?

WOMAN

Well, is it a right arm or a left arm?

HIMSELF

It's a *middle* arm.

WOMAN

Don't be ridiculous.

HIMSELF

Well . . . which arm does it *look* like?

WOMAN *(Peering)*

That's why I asked. Every time I look at it, it seems to be different. Right now it looks like a *left* arm, but when I was tickling it, before, I could swear it was a *right* arm.

HIMSELF *(Out)*

One of the wonders; truly, one of the wonders. It had, by I knew not what gymnastics, what leverage, the ability to be whichever arm, right or left, it needed or wanted to be. More of that later.

I must describe to you now my state of mind, my view from this particular bridge. I was possessed of a third arm—a growing armlet which, I was told, would reach normal, or arm size, and be content with that. And this was, at the moment, a secret shared only by the doctor, his nurse, my wife . . . and myself, of course. The children had not been told. That it would not—*could* not—remain a secret for long was evident. I had—well, you've seen it—a splendid wife . . . intelligent, level-headed, a no-nonsense, good and good-humored wife; that was a help, but we were not dealing here with your ordinary run-of-the-marriage situation. There was also the vague but

nagging sensation that it was not *me* we were concerned with here . . . but
it. Does that distinction make any sense to you? Oh! and we must add a
sudden complication: my high-paying, permanently secure executive position vanished in a recession retrenchment. And there I was out on the
street. And me with a third arm to feed.

WOMAN (*As* WIFE; *having risen*)
What *are* you going to do—*we?*

HIMSELF
You're going to help me hold it all together until I figure it out.

WOMAN
OK.
(*Afterthought*)
But I still think we ought to tell the kids.

HIMSELF (*Out*)
A cousin of mine—a deadbeat, but inventive—put me in touch with a
man; a man who, he said, could work miracles.
(*The* MAN *moves forward, as* HIMSELF *finishes.*
To WOMAN, *not quite convinced*)
This man can work miracles.

WOMAN (*To* MAN)
And I can keep the kids quiet during nap-time. Howdy.

MAN (*Expansive; oily*)
You must be the little lady. Howdy-do to *you.*

WOMAN
Work miracles, hunh?

MAN
Nah, it just seems like it.

HIMSELF (*To the* WOMAN)
I've told him . . . everything.

MAN
He even let me have a look at the little fella.

WOMAN
Cute, isn't it?

HIMSELF (*To them* BOTH)
It scratched my back this morning.
(*Out*)
It did; I was about to shave, felt an itch, was about to put the razor down,
when all at once I noticed I—it!—was scratching away.

WOMAN

Did you say thank you?

HIMSELF

(To WOMAN; *mildly impatient*)
You don't say thank you to your *arm!*

WOMAN (*Shrugs*)
I don't *know,* way things are *these* days.

MAN

I've drawn up what I think are some pretty good ideas on how we handle this thing. When this comes out it's going to be one big story, one knock-'em-on-their-ass sensation.

HIMSELF (*Uncertain*)
Yes, I suppose *so;* for a little while.

MAN (*Abrupt laugh*)
For a little *while!?* Are you *kidding!?* Man, you're going to be the hottest thing going!

HIMSELF

I am?
    (*To the* WOMAN)
I am?
    (*Out*
    SHE *shrugs*)

MAN

Fucking-A right! There hasn't been a story like this since the crucifixion.

HIMSELF

I'm afraid I don't see the connection between the Lord's agony and my having . . .

MAN

I'm talking news value.

HIMSELF

Oh.
    (*Beat. Out*)
Oh?

MAN

Right! Mister, I can make you the most famous man in America.

HIMSELF (*Pause; some wonder*).

You can?

MAN

Shit! I can make you the most famous man in the *world!*

HIMSELF

You're kidding!

MAN

I kid you *not!* And, on top of it, if we play our cards right . . . I can make us . . . *rich!*

(MAN *and* WOMAN *turn, go to their seats*)

HIMSELF *(Out)*

I want you to understand that the reach of my ambition—*before* all this started—had been grand, perhaps, but not excessive: I wanted a lovely wife, some decent kids, a fine home, a rewarding and well-paying career, the respect of my community and a painless, sleeping death when I was old enough to want it.

(*Shrugs*)

All within reason, the American Dream—the Anglo-Saxon, *Protestant* American Dream, at any rate. *And* I was well on my *way* to it, gathering it all together nicely. And then, of course, the shit hit the fan, with me offering neither one, neither slit nor fan, unless you go with the minority says I *willed* my martyrdom—my monsterdom—drew it out of myself . . . from the pericardial unconscious, I dare say. Believe me! I wanted nothing less than big frog in reasonably big pond, and nothing *more.* I did *not* want what *happened!*

(*Almost choking with sudden rage and tears*)

And you can be *certain* I *never*—in my wildest dreams, *nightmares!*—I *never* wanted to be standing *here*, where I am today!

(*Stops, shoulders shaking*)

WOMAN *(As herself)*

Are you all right?

HIMSELF

A minute!

MAN *(To the* WOMAN*)*

Is he all right? Does he want another gin, do you think?

HIMSELF *(Loud; to them)*

I'LL BE ALL RIGHT!

(*Gathers himself, out*)

But you see, in spite of all I wanted—a splendid life, but with limits—in spite of the really *little* I wanted in return for going through it all . . . it just wasn't to *be* that *way*. I grew a third arm, and my career was destroyed from under me.

What . . . to do!?

My very own Colonel Parker—or so I dubbed him—arranged it all, and I must give him credit . . . he was a *pro.*

> MAN (*Seated; side of mouth*)

Thanks.

> HIMSELF (*To the* MAN)

You're welcome.

(*Out*)

My wife and I agreed that we had to do *something*—the doctor was planning a book *plus* I owed it to medical science *plus* the kids now knew and it's against the law to cut out the tongues of the young *plus* a lot of ugly bills were coming due, and I mean a *lot* and I mean *ugly* mortgage, insurance, school, medical bills, car, food, clothes and on and on and on! Plus I still had three arms.

There was nothing for it, the wisdom went, but to hit and hit hard.

(*Slams fist into hand as, simultaneously, the* MAN *does the same*)

Now, when I say I must give the Colonel credit, I kid you not—as he would say.

(SLIDE: *press conference*)

The press conference he called to unveil my arm was equal to that announcing the second coming or—a less likely event—the democratization of the China.

(SLIDE *out*)

When it occurred, it was a lollapalooza! I vetoed the Colonel's suggestion that it—the arm—be first seen waving a tiny American flag; that—at the *time*—struck me as, well . . . crass. HA!

Well, I needn't remind you how it went. Unless you were in a loony bin somewhere you *know.*

(*Pleasure in recalling*)

Has there *ever* been anything like it? My goodness, I think back to it, the awe—the jaw-dropping, pencil-dropping, *camera*-dropping awe—as I removed my shirt and tie, smiled—shyly, diffidently: truly shy, truly diffident—spread my two visible arms in a kind of combo benediction-greeting, and slowly turned to reveal the eighth wonder of the world. The intake of a thousand breaths; the silence; the *last* silence, and then the tumult! Thank God we had a double line of guards!!

It was unbelievable! The crowds outside my apartment.

(SLIDE: *crowds*)

The riots if I dared go to a restaurant or a movie.

(SLIDE: *riot*)

The ticker-tape parades.

(SLIDE: *ticker-tape parade*)

The medical conventions.

> (SLIDE: *photo of famous turn-of-the-century painting of medical demonstration*)

The presentation of royalty.

> (SLIDE: *someone being received by Queen Elizabeth II*)

The summons from the President.

> (SLIDE: *someone entering the White House*)

The magazine covers.

> (SLIDE: HIMSELF's *face on cover of* Time, Newsweek, People— *1 slide*)

With all of them, I insisted they photograph only my smiling face—the Colonel insisted. There was, as you may have imagined, more than decorum in the Colonel's caution.

MAN (As COLONEL)

I'll make us rich!!

HIMSELF

What *does* a man do?—what is a man to do who had grown a third arm of considerable agility and attractiveness—given the parameters—who, at the same time, has been thrown into unjustified career ruin and financial instability, and who has become—with barely a tap on his shoulder—the most famous man in the world? The answer is so simple—inevitable—as to state itself: make the most of it; get it while you can, and get it big. Does that sound crass to you? A bit . . . grasping? Well, think about it: we do or we do not do, and if there is either excess or regret, which do we mourn the more—that which we *have* done, or that which we have *not?* Eh?

> (SLIDE *out*)

Things were not . . . well . . . *ideal,* however. The kids had been taken out of school and were being tutored privately, at great expense. First it was their schoolmates taunting them—Daddy's a freak; your Daddy's a freak—and then, without much wait, the kidnapping threats began.

WOMAN (As WIFE)

Jesus Christ!

HIMSELF

. . . which led to the guards—the *extra* guards, the ones on top of mine, the four I had at all hours. And if you think the city was paying for my protection, I laugh at you—har, har, har! It was coming out of *my* pocket . . . well, the Colonel's pocket as part of the tab I was running up. Within six weeks of the great unveiling, I was into the Colonel for $78,400!

WOMAN

Jesus!

HIMSELF

The guards, the lawyers, the two-and-a-half-million-dollar insurance policy on "the arm"—in case of loss!

WOMAN

Christ!

HIMSELF

There was a lot of money to be made. And the Colonel told me *our* split would be fifty-fifty.

WOMAN

Jesus!

HIMSELF *(To the* WOMAN*)*

It was fair!

(Out)

It *was* fair: the Colonel was making a fortune for us, and fifty percent of a lot is more than ninety percent of nothing!

WOMAN *(Still as* WIFE*)*

Christ!

HIMSELF *(To* WOMAN*)*

Hussy! Bitch! Abandoner!

(Out)

Ignore her! She left me . . . finally!

WOMAN *(Shrill)*

Tell them how you'd go to sleep and *it* wouldn't. Tell them how it'd wait until I'd gone to sleep—*you'd* gone to sleep—and it would play with me, stroke me, finger me to orgasm.

HIMSELF

Silence, woman!!

WOMAN

And how I would wrestle with it, and it would slap me!

HIMSELF *(Weary)*

No more.

WOMAN

Tell them how you changed; tell them about your ego; tell them about your temper; tell them about the groupies; tell them about giving me the clap!

HIMSELF

Silence!

WOMAN

. . . and the kids, and how you *became.* No one would blame me!

HIMSELF

Please; no more.

WOMAN

No one could take it.

HIMSELF *(Rage)*

All right! You've done it! I've forgotten you! Leave me alone!

WOMAN *(A pleased snarl)*

You haven't forgotten me;

(*Harsh laugh*)

you'd give your right arm to have me back. I'm going to write that book; really, I *am.*

HIMSELF *(Spitting it out)*

Write it! Spill my guts out! You're a little late, sweetheart: who the fuck cares!?

(*Out*)

Would *you* buy her book? Poor wifelet, stands arm in arm in arm with her man some part of the way, then *takes* off, *takes* the kids, *takes* the alimony . . .

WOMAN *(Cold)*

You're behind, by the way.

(*Turns away*)

HIMSELF *(Out)*

Ignore her: She couldn't take the blinding light.

(*Quieter*)

I regret giving her the kids without a fight; I regret everything.

(*More assured—laughter in the dark*)

And I regret nothing. Je ne regrette rien! as the little lady used to say, to sing. Je ne regrette rien! I mean . . . I had a lot of fun! While it lasted . . . I had a ball! Are any of you celebrated? Really . . . famous? Some of you probably are—one or two—and you know what it's like—what happens *within* the awareness of *self* that comes as revelation, the knowledge that one *is* larger than life, at least larger than others; the fact that one can change whole areas of public perception, help alter the course of history. This is not small potatoes. The money, the sex, the adulation, the perks, all those are gravy on the pot roast; the meat is the sense of self. Let us pray.

(*After the pause following "let us pray"*)

Do you find me . . . well, what *is* the word? . . . unsympathetic? Not fit for pity? Yours, or anyone's?

(*Laughs*)

I met someone once said no one ever earned the right—not ever. What about Job, I said. Not even Job, he said: see God. Well, *I* feel bad about *me* now and again; sometimes I just . . . wallow in self-pity, and I think I've earned the right, and anybody doesn't go along, I say fuck 'em!

(*Small smile*)

Or, is that "unsympathetic" too? Probably.

(*Shrugs*)

Fuck it. Anyhow, as I said, things were not . . . ideal.

(*Pause*)

I had a talk with the Colonel.

(MAN *has risen, moves into position.*

To MAN)

What am I going to *do?*

MAN

I don't get you.

HIMSELF

I owe you a fortune; I'm going under fast; I . . .

MAN (*Laughs*)

Oh, that! Well, we're going to sell you, boy!

HIMSELF (*Out*)

And he whipped out a scenario.

MAN

We've worked up some preliminary figures, in case you're interested, and, uh . . .

(HE *fishes out a piece of paper which* HE *shows*)

. . . this looks like what you'll be taking in each week—we'll be taking in.

HIMSELF (*Looks; gasps*)

Jesus Christ!

MAN (*Returning to his seat*).

On we go, boy; gold at the end of the rainbow and silver along the way!

HIMSELF (*Out*)

I won't even tell you the figures he showed me; I am unhappy with envy in myself and I will not be party to it in others. Enough to say it was ransom sufficient to twist the arm of *any* man. And off we went! Well, you watched it. No one has ever ridden higher or loved it more! And the Colonel orchestrated it so beautifully!

MAN (*From his seat*)

Thank you, thank you!

HIMSELF

And I was getting laid a lot. I bring this up—childish or adolescent as it may seem—because it is a matter not everyone comes face to face, or crotch to crotch with. Most people—most of *us*—marry, or carry on long-term relationships of one sort or another, and we cheat now and again, though not as often as either chance or our memory has it; we have reasonably good sex lives: we get by. But with celebrity—with *great* celebrity—the thighs of the world swing open—and I am speaking heterosexually, you understand; our gay brethren have their own images—the thighs of the world swing open, the universal clitoris and the great divide await, *plus* Nabokov's brown rose, *plus* head to turn the head of a martyring saint. And all one has to do is . . . show up. You don't even have to undo your own belt. It all becomes part of a way of life, and has nothing—or little—to do with morality, or fidelity, or . . . anything.

So, I became what he promised, the most famous man in the world. It was a high ride and a good one.

Though, I guess, you can't win them all.

The Colonel was getting rich. Why wasn't I? Answer in thirty words or less. And then the day came, the day I shall remember above all others to the day of my dying, above even the revelation of the identity of the bump growing from my back, above even my first orgasm.

Do you remember that famous story of the identical midgets in the circus,

(SLIDE: *midgets*)

both stars, both in love with the same midget*esse*? How she was wooed by them both, and married one, and the other brooded and bided his time? Do you remember it? These two midgets wore tails and top hats in their act and carried canes—regular little Fred Astaires. Well, all at once the married of the two became morose and developed a far-away expression in his eyes; his wifelet asked him over and over what was wrong.

(*Tiny voice*)

"What's wrong? What's wrong?" And finally he told her.

(*Tiny voice again*)

"I'm growing," he said. Midgets did this sometimes, in middle age—they just started growing: sometimes they grew a foot—not a *third* one, but . . . up. And what it meant was the end of midgethood, the end of employment, the end of marriage, of course, and the end of celebrity. To make it short, the despondent midget killed himself, and his widow married the other one. And at the end of the story it's revealed that the poor little fellow wasn't growing at all, that the other one, the rejected one, was sneaking into the wardrobe every night and sanding just the tiniest bit off the bottom of his rival's cane, just the tiniest bit more each night, enough to persuade the horrified little fellow that he was growing.

(*Cheerful*)

You don't remember that story? My goodness, *I* do!

(SLIDE *out*)

I mention the midgets only to talk about my shirts. Is that unclear? Unclear enough? Let me explain. One day, I noticed in a new batch of custom-made shirts a . . . disparity of sleeve, by which I mean that my two normal, or regular, sleeves had been made too small, too short, for there was a fullness, a largeness in the third one. I mentioned it to the Colonel: I mean, a hundred and thirty-seven fifty per shirt, and they couldn't even make the sleeves of an equal length anymore!

This . . . disparity of sleeve produced in me a normal—enough—attack of celebrity paranoia. Of course, the shirt people were enraged, insisted they made shirts by hand, with great care, that all my sleeves were of equal length, and if I persisted in my calumny I would hear from their solicitor. "You have made my right and left sleeves too short," I insisted. "How else can we account for the third sleeve being too long? If you insist that all three sleeves are of equal length, then one of two things is possible, neither of which is likely: either my right and left arms have suddenly begun to grow—ha, ha, ha!—either that or my central or third arm has suddenly begun to . . .

    (Pause)

And my world . . . fell apart.

Could it be happening? *Was* my arm, my *new* arm, the cause of . . . everything I now valued . . . going away? Was it returning whence, et cetera? Jesus Christ! I measured it carefully—the arm—locked, double bolted in the bathroom—

    (Out)

It was almost a full inch shorter than it had been. Even now I can barely bring myself to think about it, much less talk about it. My arm, my livelihood, my celebrity had diminished—a trifle, to be sure, barely an inch, but, still, diminished. The panic I fell into was . . . well, encompassing. I had to tell the Colonel; there was no choice.

            MAN *(As* COLONEL; *up and in position)*
Jesus Christ!

           HIMSELF *(To the* MAN*)*
It's two weeks now, and it seems to be going at about an inch a week.

                MAN
Jesus Christ!

           HIMSELF *(To the* MAN*)*
I don't know what to do.

                MAN
Jesus Christ!

             HIMSELF
There's that medical convention in Sào Paulo.

                MAN
Jesus Christ!

             HIMSELF
And the three-hand piano recital in Tokyo? I can't even reach the black *keys* anymore with my third arm! I've tried!

MAN

Jesus Christ!

HIMSELF

What am I going to *do!?*

MAN

Jesus Christ!

HIMSELF (*Out*)

Jesus Christ, indeed! What was decided, finally, was *not* to disguise the fact of what was happening, but to make capital of it. The Colonel called an enormous press conference—almost as well attended as the great First— and revealed that the Lord giveth and the Lord taketh away; announced, as well, what was to be, in effect, a farewell tour of the arm. Those who had not seen it: hurryhurryhurry; those who would like to watch it as it lessens, come right on up; last chance! The question was raised as to whether I thought it might re-grow—disappear, and then pop up again, somewhere else: on the top of my head, I suppose. I expressed enthusiasm for the idea, but deep inside I knew better; I knew the jig was up.
The farewell tour,

(SLIDE: *ticker-tape parade*)

at the beginning, fueled by both my world celebrity *and* the new sensation, began splendidly—the crowds, the riots, the usual, but as the attention-getter—the moneymaker, if you will—diminished, so did the audience for it: when it was back to half, so were the crowds; a quarter, a quarter; and when the poor thing was down to a nubbin, waving its little fernlike fingers in a pathetic farewell, I remember once that no more than twenty people showed up, sullen and embarrassed.
And then . . . and then it was gone. My ex-wife sent me a card of condolence.
The Arabs folded their tents and crept off into the night. Shall I describe the falling away of my retinue? There's no need to; you can imagine it. And the Colonel left as well, with not even a farewell, just . . . left. A very wealthy man, he . . . left. Swine.

MAN

Now, now.

HIMSELF

And I! How was *I* left? Well, a meeting with my accountants shed some black light on that: with one thing and another, fees and endorsements out the window, the failed farewell tour, tax disallowances, plus I had been coasting along on anticipated income for quite a while now, when the whole thing was totaled up, I was in debt to the tune of $2,134,625.22, *and,* the accountants wondered, wouldn't I like to pay *them* right away.
Thank God for the insurance policy on my arm—or loss thereof—I mused

out loud. Oh, that, they mused right back, that was taken out in the Colonel's name; that doesn't belong to you; we imagine he's cashed that in already.

(*To the* MAN *as* COLONEL)

Swine!

MAN (*As* COLONEL; *so mild*)

Now, now.

HIMSELF (*Out*)

So, I had been had, had I not. But I was to blame, as well, I suppose: the hog I had been living high off of was of my own devising, was . . . myself. Nor had I carried too many friends along with me to the heights of my celebrity—too rarefied a place for many, and I was startled, when it all came crashing down, by how many people wished me ill, how many had a smug smile at my extremis. I declared bankruptcy, as you doubtless read but may have forgotten; I suffered what is termed a nervous breakdown—Jesus!, who could blame me!?—and for a year and a half I sat, staring off into the middle distance. Remember the middle distance? And I drank a lot, and I cried a lot.

I still drink—oh!? Does he!?—and I still cry. And so, here I am—here we are. And how do you like your blue-eyed boy now, Mr. Death?

(*Pause.*

Harsh tone, claps hands once)

So! Here we are! How did you like the rendition, boys and girls? Did you enjoy your little trip to voyeur's heaven? That oh-so-sad-sad story? Well, good for you.

(*Pause; quiet, growing loathing*)

I think I've finished; I've laid the sorry tale out for you; you've paid your money and you've seen what's left of the freak! Go home! GO HOME!!

(MAN *and* WOMAN *become apprehensive*)

MAN (*To woman*)

Are we done?

HIMSELF

Go home, you mothers!! Haven't I humiliated myself enough for you!?

WOMAN (*Rising, out*)

I think we're done. I would like to thank our . . .

HIMSELF (*Ignoring her*)

You owe me something, you people! You loved me in the good times, and you're fucking well going to love me now!!

WOMAN (*Moving center*)

I really *do* think we're done.

HIMSELF *(Waving her off)*

Get away from me!

(Out, pleading alternating with hatred)

I'm no different from you; I'm just like everyone you know; you love *them:* you love *me.* Stop treating me like a freak! I am *not* a freak! I am *you!* I have always *been* you! I am YOU!!! Stop looking at me!! Like that!!

WOMAN *(Off)*

Will you have them lower [close] the curtain?

HIMSELF

No!! No one leaves!! I am *not* a freak! I'm just like you.

(Gets an idea; begins to remove his shirt)

Look; believe me; I am *you;* I have always been *you;* there's no difference between us.

(Shirt off. . . . has he ripped it off? Perhaps)

One head, two ears, two eyes, one nose, one mouth—though it doesn't always seem that way; one chest, two nipples—vestigal remains of the old self-generating days, most probably. I am just like you! You see!? Stop treating me like a freak! I am not a freak!

(He begins to weep)

WOMAN

(Comes over to him, to comfort)

Yes, yes; of course you are; of course you're not.

HIMSELF *(To the audience)*

Stop looking at me like that!

WOMAN *(As he shudders, weeps)*

Shhhhhhhh! Shhhhhhhh! It'll all be alright.

(She strokes his shoulders, his back)

Shhhhhhh! Shhhhhhhh!

(She notices something on his back)

Oh! Oh, how extraordinary!

HIMSELF

I'm no different from . . .

(becomes aware of her)

What!? What is it!?

WOMAN

(Moving behind him, looking at his back)

Well, I. . . . if I didn't know better—although I *do* know better, or should— if I didn't know better I'd say you . . . had something growing there—on your back.

(To the MAN*)*
Come; come see.

MAN *(Moving in)*

What? What is it?

HIMSELF

(Disbelief and wonder suffusing his face)
Something. . . . Growing. . . . ? There. . . ?

WOMAN *(Pointing)*

See?

MAN *(Peering)*

My goodness! Why, *yes!*

HIMSELF

(Eyes more-or-less heavenward)
It's coming back, you fuckers!
    (Fist upward and clenched)
You'll get yours, you mothers!
    (To the two behind him; joy and pleading)
It's coming back? You can see it?

MAN

Yes! Look there!

WOMAN

Isn't that extraordinary!

HIMSELF *(Eyes closed tight)*

Just wait, world!

WOMAN

Why, its. . . . I think its waving at me, or. . . . yes, look there; its. . . . its wiggling its little toes!

HIMSELF *(A long beat)*

Toes!?
    (A longer beat)
TOES!?
    (A beat. Blackout)

CURTAIN

Finding the Sun

CHARACTERS

ABIGAIL
Twenty-three; mousy brown/blond hair. pinched features;
not tall; thinnish; not pretty, but not plain

BENJAMIN
Thirty; blond, willowy-handsome; medium height

CORDELIA
Twenty-eight; attractive in a cold way; dark or raven hair;
tallish; good figure

DANIEL
Thirty-seven; dark; tall; good-looking

EDMEE
Forty-five, or so; smallish; a together, stylish matron

FERGUS
Sixteen; blond, handsome healthy kid; swimmer's body

GERTRUDE
Sixty; small, gray hair, deeply tanned, thinnish,
elegant outdoors woman

HENDEN
Seventy; big, sprawly man; white hair;
looks like a retired diplomat

SETTING

A beach in bright sun. Eight beach chairs—candy striped or of various colors—spread about, leaving a free area downstage center. A narrow boardwalk upstage with railing.

LIGHT

Bright sun; August, a New England day. Toward the end of the play, a lighting shift; until then, still sun.

COSTUMES

Whatever beach outfits seem most appropriate to each of the characters and the actors playing them. Towels, bags, and the usual beach stuff as well.

AUTHOR'S NOTE

The scenes of the play flow into one another without pause, although a tiny "breath" between them—more a new upbeat than anything else—would be nice.

SCENE ONE

(Rise from black; hold for two seconds. ABIGAIL *and* BENJAMIN *enter; bathing suits, beach stuff)*

ABIGAIL *(Stretching)*
Ah! Find the sun!

BENJAMIN *(Nods; pleased approval)*
Find the sun!
(They begin setting up. CORDELIA *and* DANIEL *enter; bathing suits, beach stuff. They do not see* ABIGAIL *or* BENJAMIN, *nor do they see these two)*

CORDELIA
Find the sun, you said.
(Smiles, stretches)

DANIEL *(Abstracted smile)*
Did I? "Find the sun?" Well? So?
(They begin setting up. EDMEE *and* FERGUS *enter; same action as above)*

EDMEE
Finding the sun should always be your first action, Fergus.

FERGUS *(Feigned puzzlement)*
Not finding a chair with your back to the wall?

EDMEE *(Happy with it)*
Outdoors . . . the sun.
(Looks about)
Goodness, look at all the people!

FERGUS *(Mock concern)*
Gosh, Mother, will we never be alone!?

EDMEE *(Throaty chuckle)*
Oh, hush!
(They begin setting up. GERTRUDE *and* HENDEN *enter; same procedures as others)*

GERTRUDE

Oh, Henden! We've found the sun!

HENDEN

We've found what? Oh! The sun!
    (Sighs)
You're right: we've found the sun.
    (Pause)

ALL (Settling in)

Ahhhhhhhhh!

SCENE TWO

(DANIEL rises, moves down right; BENJAMIN sees him, moves to
him; ABIGAIL has her eyes closed, as does CORDELIA)

BENJAMIN

Is that you!? It is! It's you!

DANIEL

I *thought* it was.

BENJAMIN (Sotto voce)

What are you *doing* here?

DANIEL

. . . though I remember saying to Cordelia—in the car—do you think that's
me?

BENJAMIN

I mean, I was sitting there and there you were!

DANIEL (Quick, mirthless smile)

Seems like old times.

BENJAMIN (Blurting)

Are you here alone? I mean, are you with Cordelia?

DANIEL

No: I'm here with a couple of tricks named Jeremy and Phillip I picked
up in . . .

BENJAMIN (Shy smile)

Oh, come on, Daniel.

DANIEL (Mimicking)

Oh, come on, Benjie-wengie!

BENJAMIN *(After a tiny pause)*
So many people here.

DANIEL
(A hand on Benjamin's shoulder)
I miss you.

BENJAMIN *(Shrugs; smiles)*
I *love you.*

DANIEL *(Nods; removes his hand)*
I love you, *and* I *miss* you.

BENJAMIN *(Giggles)*
I wonder what Abigail will say.

DANIEL
Abigail will say . . .

ABIGAIL *(Seeing* BENJAMIN *gone)*
Benjamin!? Where are you!?

DANIEL
That is what Abigail will say.

SCENE THREE

(BENJAMIN *and* DANIEL *move back to their places as* EDMEE *and* FERGUS *move down left)*

EDMEE *(As they come)*
Having found the sun—the good sun, the clear, healing heat—having *found* the sun, *then* you put your back to the wall.

FERGUS *(Imitation of eager student)*
Aha!

EDMEE
The sun is the source of all life: the aminos and all the rest couldn't have done their work with*out* it, you see.

FERGUS
Aha!!

EDMEE
Look at your civilizations! Africa!—if you call that a civilization—four? five million years ago, in the hottest of the muck, down there, closest to boiling, the *cradle* of it.

FERGUS

We live in New Hampshire.

EDMEE *(Ignoring? Not having heard?)*

And the Mediterranean basin? Greece? Rome? The Parthenon is *not* in Bergin, Norway, my dear.

(Peering)

I wonder who those people are? Nor does the Appian Way run through Tierra del Fuego.

FERGUS

Nor New Hampshire.

EDMEE *(Not angry)*

Be civil.

FERGUS

Oh, Mother!

EDMEE

Everything proceeds comparatively, it is true—there is no light without dark, rest without action, and so forth and so on—and a life in the tropics produces a . . . lassitude which leads to an absence of philosophical inquiry, but nor have the Lapps or the Eskimos given us much beyond some charming little carvings—doo-dads, really; no, time in the sun *and* time away: that's the ticket! Everything comparative; everything in season.

FERGUS

Okay.

EDMEE

Why do you dwell on New Hampshire?

FERGUS

We dwell *in* New Hampshire.

EDMEE

You dwell in your own skin. Do you dwell on that?

FERGUS

A life of acne?

EDMEE

This, too, shall pass.

(Sees GERTRUDE *rising, coming toward them)*

Is that lady coming to talk to us?

FERGUS *(Rising)*

To you.

EDMEE *(Sincerely bothered)*
Oh, Fergus! Maybe you'll like her.

FERGUS *(Moving away)*
Let me know.
    (Nods to the approaching GERTRUDE*)*
Ma'am.

GERTRUDE *(Nods)*
Young man.
    (To EDMEE*)*
Is that yours?

EDMEE
Yes; yes, he is.

GERTRUDE
What is he to you, or am I being nosy?

EDMEE
I beg your pardon? Yes, you probably are.

GERTRUDE
I *always* am. I can't help myself.

EDMEE *(To get it straight)*
What *is* he to me?

GERTRUDE
Henden says to me, you are the nosiest woman in Christendom, and this in spite of that little gouge above the left nostril, that little gouge where they took the cancer off. Would you believe that I've had four skin cancers removed—all from the sun!—and I still won't stay out of it? Don't go in the sun, Gertrude: You know your propensities.

EDMEE
What *is* he to me? Who is Henden?

GERTRUDE
Or, more to the point, who is *Sylvia?* Henden is my husband, my third; the other two I lost—not through carelessness, but time: I marry older men. Henden is the youngest I have married—in distance from *my* age, I mean to say. Henden is only seventy. What is he to *you;* well, what *is* he to you?—the young boy: Is he your son, your nephew, your ward your . . . lover?

EDMEE *(A smile)*
You *should* stay out of the sun.

SCENE FOUR

(EDMEE *and* GERTRUDE *stay where they are,* GERTRUDE *having sat in* FERGUS's *chair.* ABIGAIL *and* CORDELIA *come down right*)

ABIGAIL

He's such a child; he behaves like . . . such a child!

CORDELIA

(Eyes closed; absorbing the sun)

Hmmmmmmmmmmm.

ABIGAIL

He comes back—when I call him—he comes back, plops himself down in in his chair, and starts blathering on about . . . all the *sail*boats, there are *no* clouds, *are* there!, *where* will we go for dinner . . .

CORDELIA

Hmmmmmmmmmmm.

ABIGAIL

Not a word! Not one word about running into Daniel . . .

CORDELIA

Hmmmmmmmmmmm.

ABIGAIL

. . . which meant, naturally, that *you* were here, which information was of interest to *me* . . .

CORDELIA

Hmmmmmmmmmmm.

ABIGAIL

Not a word!

CORDELIA *(Stretching; drawled)*

Well, what would you expect?

ABIGAIL

You would think . . .

CORDELIA

What do you *really expect?*

ABIGAIL *(Too brightly innocent)*

I beg your pardon?

CORDELIA

I know them both as well as you know Benjamin—better, probably. Recall I knew them *before* you, and they were *lovers* then . . .

ABIGAIL *(Too bright)*

Well, they're not lovers now!

CORDELIA

Because they married us, you mean? Remember the leopard.

ABIGAIL

I beg your pardon?

CORDELIA

Do you not *like* me—or are you like that, I mean . . . naturally?

ABIGAIL *(Abrupt laugh)*

Whatever do you mean?

CORDELIA

Your tone, baby.

ABIGAIL *(Haughty)*

I have no idea what you mean.

CORDELIA

Okay. Just remember the leopard.

ABIGAIL

I'm supposed to understand what that means?

CORDELIA

Are you retarded? Leopard! Leopard: spots. A leopard doesn't change its spots.

ABIGAIL *(Snooty)*

I can't speak for you and Daniel, but Benjamin is home with me every night.

CORDELIA *(Dry)*

How *nice* for him.

ABIGAIL *(Pleased; proud)*

I never let him out of my sight.

CORDELIA

They must love you in the men's rooms.

ABIGAIL *(Riding over that)*

You and Daniel may have what is referred to as an "arrangement"—by which is usually implied a moral quagmire—and, to be sure, Daniel may not have . . . adjusted to the world, but Benjamin has seen the follies of his ways, his *former* ways, and . . .

CORDELIA

Oh, bullshit!

(Abigail fumes, moves away)

SCENE FIVE

(HENDEN *puttering,* FERGUS *coming upon him*)

FERGUS

Hello.

HENDEN

Hello.

FERGUS

How old are you?

HENDEN

What an odd question! I'm seventy.

FERGUS

That's what I thought: you're the oldest person here—in the vicinity.

HENDEN

I often am.

FERGUS

And I'm the youngest. I'm sixteen.

HENDEN

Don't be silly.

FERGUS

A lot of people say that.

HENDEN

There is no such age.

FERGUS

Yes, that's what they say. Why are you here?

HENDEN

Why am I *anywhere!?* Luck, I guess; or that's what they call it.

FERGUS

Who do *you* belong with?

HENDEN

Again such an odd question! I am *with* my wife, my Gertrude, the one was talking with the lady you arrived with, I believe; that is who I am *with*. As to whether it is Gertrude I *belong* with . . . well, that would take some mulling.

FERGUS

Mull away.

HENDEN

By which I mean—thank you . . .

FERGUS

You're welcome.

HENDEN

. . . by which I mean that I am very fond of Gertrude, as wives go—though I've had only two—but whether it is she I *belong* with . . . well, that takes some pondering.

FERGUS

What happened to the first one?

HENDEN *(Shrugs)*

She died; after forty-six years of marriage with me she took it into her head to die.

FERGUS

Literally?

HENDEN

Yes; a brain tumor.

FERGUS

Forty-six years is a very long time.
  (Afterthought)
Sorry.

HENDEN

Not in retrospect: only during. And I married Gertrude—though I like her very much—I suppose to *be married,* as much as anything: a continuity.

FERGUS

Hmmmm. I suspect I'm a little young for a sense of continuity. There's a theory afoot, though, that we young and we old have things in common should bind us together against those in the middle.

HENDEN

Heavens! And what *are* those things?

FERGUS

I haven't the faintest. Doesn't anybody swim around here?

HENDEN

The beginning and the end! An alliance! Well, maybe; might work as well as most. Who do *you* belong with?

FERGUS

Well, I'm here with my mother—the lady your Gertrude was talking with—and since I *am* only sixteen and I legally belong *to* her, I daresay I belong *with* her. The day will come, though . . . well, the day will come. Who *are* all these people!?

HENDEN

Well, we've accounted for the two of *us*, for Gertrude and your mother; that leaves the other four.

FERGUS

. . . of those nearby.

HENDEN

Well, surely I'm not to account for the entire coast. The couple over *there*
    (*Indicates* CORDELIA *and* DANIEL)
are Daniel and Cordelia; Daniel is my son—by my first marriage, of course; his wife, Cordelia, is daughter to Gertrude—by one of *her* earliers.

FERGUS

My goodness! You know everything! Who are the others? Do you know?

HENDEN

The other couple? Abigail and Benjamin.

FERGUS

Heaven, you do! Whose daughter and son are *they!?*

HENDEN

No one's—well, someone's, naturally, but none of ours.

FERGUS

Strangers!

HENDEN

Not exactly. Well, perhaps, though they *are* married—to each other! No, the cord binding them to us is, uh . . . a complex twine.

FERGUS

We've heard of that in New Hampshire, I believe.

HENDEN

Abigail did not exist before she married Benjamin, but Benjamin . . . well, he and Daniel, before Daniel married Cordelia, he and Daniel were . . . well, how shall I put it . . . ?

FERGUS

I don't know!

HENDEN

. . . were . . . involved.

FERGUS

I beg your pardon?

HENDEN

Benjamin and Daniel were "involved."

FERGUS (*Trying to sort it out*)

With one another.

HENDEN

Yes.

FERGUS

In a business sense?

HENDEN

How old are you?

FERGUS

Sixteen—but I'm from New Hampshire.

HENDEN (*Understanding*)

Of course. No; in a . . . personal sense.

FERGUS

Yes?

HENDEN

Benjamin and Daniel were lovers.

FERGUS (*Long pause*)

With each other?

HENDEN

Yes.

FERGUS

My goodness.
    (*Considers*)
I believe we've heard of this in New Hampshire. They loved one another?

HENDEN

Certainly.

FERGUS

And gave each other physical pleasure.

HENDEN

As I understand it.

FERGUS

Why are they no longer lovers? Pleasure into pain?

HENDEN (*Slightly standoffish*)

You'll have to ask them that, young man.

FERGUS

Well, I shall!
    (*Afterthought*)
I've not been lovers with *anyone*.

HENDEN

Well, you're sixteen.

FERGUS

Romeo was fifteen, they say, but he was Italian.

HENDEN

When you're older . . .

FERGUS

My hand and I will say good-bye?

HENDEN

Well, will probably develop a more casual relationship.

FERGUS

Oh? Pity.

HENDEN

If you *do* speak to Daniel or Benjamin of their . . . liaison . . .

FERGUS

Yes?

HENDEN

Do be cautious.

FERGUS

Oh?

HENDEN

Well, you *are* very young and very . . .

FERGUS *(Contemptuous)*

Pretty?

HENDEN *(Gently)*

I was going to say "handsome."

FERGUS *(Melting)*

Thank you!

HENDEN

But you are . . . young.

FERGUS

That's very true, sir, but don't forget that I'm . . .

HENDEN *(A hand up)*

I know! You're from New Hampshire.

SCENE SIX

(HENDEN *moves upstage;* FERGUS *crosses to* EDMEE *and* GERTRUDE)

FERGUS *(Moving by fast; to* EDMEE)
Have I got things to tell *you!*

GERTRUDE *(After* FERGUS *goes)*
Who *is* that?

EDMEE *(Pause)*
What?

SCENE SEVEN

(CORDELIA *and* DANIEL *together*)

CORDELIA
I was *so terrible* to Abigail!

DANIEL *(Reading? Sunning?)*
That's nice.

CORDELIA
Do you know what I think it is?

DANIEL *(Ibid.)*
Hmmmm?

CORDELIA
Do you know why I think I'm so terrible to Abigail?

DANIEL *(Becoming involved)*
Well, let's see: Because she's here? because you don't like her? because she's turning Benjamin into a shell—sucking him dry, you should excuse the expression? because she's a self-obsessed, tedious bore of a woman?

CORDELIA *(Considers it)*
Those are interesting.

DANIEL
I thought so.

CORDELIA
But no; I think I'm terrible to her because there she is with Benjamin and I loathe Benjamin and she *doesn't* control him in *spite* of your lies. . . .

DANIEL

You don't loathe Benjamin.

CORDELIA

The two of you are as close now as you ever were . . .

DANIEL

What did you do—you and Miss Abbey—marry us as part of a sisterhood solidarity reform movement? And you're falling out among yourselves? You never told me any of this; you should choose your co-conspirators better.

CORDELIA *(Not to be put off)*

The two of you are as close now as you ever were—which I will probably divorce you for one day . . .

DANIEL *(Harsh laugh)*

You wouldn't dare! Your family'd kill you over the publicity: famous former deb, mainline family heirloom—heiress, sorry!—married to fag, files for annulment, names hubby's former hubby as . . .

CORDELIA

The two of you are as close now as you ever were—which I will probably divorce you for one day—and I'm probably taking *that* out on poor Abigail.

DANIEL

Plus you don't like her.

CORDELIA

Why doesn't she make Benjamin take her to live in Peru, or somewhere?

DANIEL

Because, pussycat, then *we'd* have to move to Peru, too, and you *know* how you are with languages. . . .

CORDELIA

Why doesn't she . . .
    (Stops)

DANIEL

Yes; why doesn't she!

CORDELIA *(Giggles)*

I accused her of following Benjamin into men's rooms!

DANIEL *(Giggles)*

You're not *nice!*

CORDELIA

    (Hand out to him; after a beat)
What *are* we to do?

DANIEL *(Takes her hand)*

Give it some time.

CORDELIA

It's been three years.

DANIEL

Give it some *time.*

CORDELIA

Do you see him secretly?

DANIEL *(Pause)*

No.

CORDELIA

Do you see *anyone?*

DANIEL *(Gently)*

Don't probe.

CORDELIA

I love you, you see.

DANIEL

And I love you.
  (Pause)
I've got a very roomy heart.
  (Pause; then she begins to laugh; he, too)

SCENE EIGHT

(CORDELIA and DANIEL return to their books, or whatever)

EDMEE

(Turning to GERTRUDE both still in their beach chairs. Very casual, informal informational)

Well, now, to answer your question—your pry, to be more accurate, about Fergus. What he *is* to me is too much. He is my son—he *is:* real mother, real son. And since my husband died—his father—he has been the "man" in my life, so to speak. It's four years now since his father dove off the rocks—showing off, as usual—hit some jutting something underwater wasn't supposed to be there, broke his neck, drowned.
  (Shrugs)
These things happen. I haven't thought of remarrying; perhaps I will, later. I've raised Fergus; he's a good boy. There is, I think—there may be—an

attachment transcends the usual, the socially *admitted* usual, that is, by which I mean: given the provocation, Fergus would bed me in a moment. A mother knows these things, even admits knowing them . . . Sometimes. He doesn't know it, or, if he *does* sense it, is polite or shrewd enough to pretend he does *not*. It is more usual for a son to lust after his mother than a mother for her son, so there is little surprise in the information that my interest in bedding Fergus is minimal. I mean, God! I have birthed him, I have held him, rocked him, comforted him, bathed him, scolded him, dressed him, guided him . . . why on earth would I want to fuck him!?

(GERTRUDE *drops whatever she is holding*)

SCENE NINE

(EDMEE *and* GERTRUDE *stay where they are; focus on* ABIGAIL *and* BENJAMIN)

ABIGAIL

Cordelia doesn't like me!

BENJAMIN *(Taking the sun; eyes shut)*

Ohhhhhhh . . .

ABIGAIL

You know perfectly well she doesn't!

BENJAMIN

Well . . .

ABIGAIL

Why don't you tell Daniel to *make* her like me!?

BENJAMIN

Oh, I don't think I . . .

ABIGAIL

Certainly it would make everything easier. I mean, if we're going to live in this proximity, with all the strings and all . . .

BENJAMIN *(Eyes open)*

Oh, God!

ABIGAIL

. . . having her like me, or at least making a good stab at *pretending* to like me, would be a help. *You* don't help.

BENJAMIN

Oh, God!

ABIGAIL

Nor does "Oh, God" help.

BENJAMIN

Oh, God!

ABIGAIL

You and your sidelong glances, your letters you won't let me read, your odd phone calls, your feeble excuses for getting home late, your . . .

BENJAMIN *(Rises)*

Oh, God!

(Leaves her area)

ABIGAIL *(Genuine surprise)*

Where are you going?

SCENE TEN

*(*HENDEN *comes down front)*

HENDEN *(To the audience)*

I get frightened sometimes. Don't you? About dying, I mean? What is the age we become aware of it? That we *know* it's going to happen, even if we don't accept it? It differs with the person, I'm told. The earlier on the better—well, no: I don't mean that young man over there; I don't mean *he* should be burdened with it, not at *his* age, but somewhere in the thirties— forties at the . . . most tardy—it will come on healthy little feet; much later and you're whistling in the . . . light, I suppose. When you reach *my* age you . . . well, you get a little frightened sometimes. Because you're alone. Oh? Really? Wife, if you're lucky? Children? *Grand*children? Yes, certainly, if you're lucky, but you're still . . . alone.

(Taps his head)

Nobody gets in there with you. Greek peasants have a room they keep their coffin in, ready for the day.

(Shrugs)

No difference there from keeping it in the back of your head, the back of your mind. Being seventy gives me a few more years, if we're to believe the actuaries—three, four. That's a help, though it isn't a guarantee, and I feel pretty well. Oh . . . I have the usual: one hip not so hot; arthritis in the neck; something uncomfortable down in my lower gut, fairly steadily; a little . . . loss of sensation in my left arm now and again, and I fainted once, last week, tying my shoes.

(Shrugs)

The usual. I go to my doctor once every year or so. I ask him; he says, "You're getting old!" Well, I *am*. Still. Nothing to be done about it, but I *do* get . . . just a little . . . frightened now and again. Being alive is . . . so splendid.

(*Smiles*)

Ah, well.

(*Moves back to his beach chair*)

SCENE ELEVEN

(BENJAMIN *moves to where* DANIEL *and* CORDELIA *are sunning*)

BENJAMIN

I can't stand it! Can I move in with you two?

DANIEL

May I.

BENJAMIN

May I? *May* I move in with you two?

CORDELIA

No.

DANIEL

No.

BENJAMIN (*A whine*)

Whhhhhyyyy?

CORDELIA

Just because.

BENJAMIN

Aw, come on, guys!

CORDELIA

You made your bed, now sleep in it.

DANIEL

Besides, we *have* someone moving in.

CORDELIA

(*After the briefest catching-on pause*)

Yes; yes, we have.

BENJAMIN (*Mistrustful*)

Who?

CORDELIA

Well . . .

(Looks to DANIEL)

DANIEL

We wrote in to one of those magazines for swingers . . .

CORDELIA

. . . *Swingers Mag*, it's called . . .

DANIEL

. . . that's right: *Swingers Mag*, and we saw an ad in there for a bi stud
wanted to relocate . . .

CORDELIA

. . . six foot seven, two hundred and thirty-five pounds, wrestler's body . . .

DANIEL

. . . goes both ways, into three-scenes or solos, fully reciprocal, light S and
M, no femmes or fatties.

CORDELIA

It seemed like a perfect addition to the house: cheaper than a new play-
room, or . . .

DANIEL

He gets here tomorrow; we paid his way, of course.

BENJAMIN

(After a brief thinking pause)

We could do foursies!

DANIEL

Rub-a-dub-dub, three men and a tub?

CORDELIA

Don't be witty.

BENJAMIN

I don't believe you guys! You wouldn't dare!

DANIEL (Haughty)

And why not, pray?

CORDELIA

Yes, and why not?

BENJAMIN

Because Henden and Gertrude wouldn't put up with it.

(A silence)

CORDELIA

He has a point there.

DANIEL

Mmmmmmmmm; afraid he has.

BENJAMIN

They'd let *me* move in with you, though; they *like me*.

CORDELIA

Tell you what: you go live with *them*.

DANIEL

Right, and we'll send you a subscription to the magazine.

BENJAMIN *(Moving off)*

You guys are no help.

DANIEL *(To Cordelia)*

No help?

CORDELIA *(To Daniel)*

Really?

SCENE TWELVE

(ABIGAIL *and* FERGUS. ABIGAIL *by herself, talking to herself*)

ABIGAIL *(Practicing)*

Benjamin, this can't go on! Benjamin?, you and I have to have a talk.
Benjamin, grow up!

(Faster)

Who do you think I am, Benjamin? Benjamin, just who do you think you
are? I'm leaving you, Benjamin; No, I'll never give you a divorce, you. . . .
you . . .; you're making our lives a shambles, Benjamin; we could have been
so happy together.

(Pause)

Nuts!

(To FERGUS, *who is ambling by, listening, really)*

You're not married, *are* you.

FERGUS

Hello!

ABIGAIL

You're not, are you; of *course* you're not; you're . . . you're an adolescent.

FERGUS

I was going to say, my, aren't you pretty! But that word killed it.

ABIGAIL

What word?

FERGUS

Adolescent. If there's one thing an adolescent doesn't want to be called it's an adolescent—even those of us *know* we're adolescents, accept it, we don't want the word used: we don't like the sound of it. Ad-o-les-cent; it's an ugly word.

ABIGAIL

I'm *sorry!*

FERGUS *(Comforting)*

I *know* you are; I'm *sure* of it.

ABIGAIL

What would you *like* to be called?

FERGUS

Fergus.

ABIGAIL

What a . . . pretty name. I meant generically.

FERGUS

Young man?

ABIGAIL *(Considers it)*

Young man. That has a nice sound. *You* are a . . . young man.

FERGUS

My, aren't you pretty! There; you see? One good turn of phrase deserves another.

ABIGAIL

I don't feel particularly pretty right now.

FERGUS

How come?

ABIGAIL

(Looks about to see if anyone is listening)
I'm . . . married.

FERGUS *(Cheerful)*

I know: to the gentleman over there used to be . . . involved with that other gentleman, who is . . . where? Ah! Over there, with who!—his wife!

ABIGAIL

My God, you know everything, don't you. Do *all* of you know everything?

FERGUS

Who is . . . all?

ABIGAIL

All is too much, most likely.

FERGUS

Have . . . have you and the *other* lady been . . . involved?

ABIGAIL

I beg your pardon!

FERGUS

Have you and the other lady . . .

ABIGAIL

Certainly not!

FERGUS

You make it seem so . . . definite.

ABIGAIL

Well, it *is!*

FERGUS

But why?

ABIGAIL

Cordelia and I are not . . . that *way.*

FERGUS

I see!

ABIGAIL *(Transparent)*

Nor are Benjamin and Daniel.

FERGUS

I see; yes, I see.

ABIGAIL

Far too much!

FERGUS

Ma'am?

ABIGAIL

Who have you been talking to? To Gertrude? To Henden? Gertrude is Cordelia's mother, you know.

FERGUS

Really?

ABIGAIL

Yes, and Henden is Daniel's father.

FERGUS

My goodness!

ABIGAIL

And Gertrude and Henden are married now.

FERGUS

Gracious!

ABIGAIL

And who's the woman you're with?

FERGUS

Edmee? She's my mother.

ABIGAIL

There's too much family on this beach. I'm the outsider.

FERGUS *(Considers it)*

Well, that must give you a perspective.

ABIGAIL

It gives me nothing! It gives me the pip!

FERGUS

Pip is given a lot, isn't it.

ABIGAIL

Stay away from Daniel; he's dangerous.
    (Afterthought)
For that matter, stay away from Benjamin, too.

FERGUS

But . . . why?

ABIGAIL

You're very young

FERGUS

Where is *your* family?

ABIGAIL

They died in a collision.

FERGUS

Oh, I'm so sorry! My mother says the roads are a terrible place.
    (ABIGAIL *inaudible*)
Pardon?

ABIGAIL

Not a car! Not roads!

FERGUS

An airplane!

ABIGAIL

No.

FERGUS *(Puzzles)*

A train, then!

ABIGAIL

No.

FERGUS *(Awe)*

Boats?

(ABIGAIL *inaudible again*)

Pardon?

ABIGAIL

Balloons.

FERGUS *(Pause)*

Pardon?

ABIGAIL *(Too loud)*

Balloons!

(Softer)

Balloons.

FERGUS

My goodness

ABIGAIL

(Still sad and perplexed over it)

They were in central Texas—antiquing—and they came upon a town—I don't know, *some*where—and the shops weren't any good, I guess, and they called me, very excited, and said they were going ballooning, that there was an outfit took people up for an hour ride—hot air balloons, you know?

FERGUS

I *guess.*

ABIGAIL

Be careful, I said. What can happen, they said; what are we going to run into in a hot-air balloon? You never know, I said. Tush, they said, and off they went!

FERGUS

And?

ABIGAIL

Texas is a big state.

FERGUS

Yes.

ABIGAIL

Flat.

FERGUS

Yes.

ABIGAIL

You can see for . . . miles.

FERGUS

I don't doubt it.
    (*Pauses*)
They hit something?
    (ABIGAIL *shakes her head. Awe*)
Something hit *them?*
    (ABIGAIL *nods*)
My gracious!

ABIGAIL

A boy genius! Are you bright? Very bright?

FERGUS

I believe so.

ABIGAIL

Damn your eyes! A boy genius, building his own rocket—out in all that flat-ness—building his very own rocket. You'd think he would *see* something in all that flatness, wouldn't you? Sets the fucking thing off—on its way to Mars, I suppose—and it goes right through the bag of the balloon, and the bag deflates, and down like a shot it goes with my appalled mother and father, back to the flat, flat earth, fast, inexplicably . . . and *Splat!*

FERGUS

Oh, dear; oh, dear.

ABIGAIL(*Controlled*)

I went down—grief and disbelief; the boy genius had such thick glasses—prisms; enormous hands on such a slight boy; enormous hands and these . . . prisms. He said he was sorry.
    (*A sudden explosion of tears*)
And I have to be married to a fairy!
    (*She runs off*)

FERGUS (*To her retreating form*)

Yes . . . well . . .
    (*To himself*)
My goodness.

SCENE THIRTEEN

FERGUS

(Comes forward; speaks to the audience)

If you think it's easy being my age, well . . . you have another think coming, as they say. A New England boyhood isn't *all* peaches and cream, maple syrup and russet autumns. I know it *sounds* pretty good—wealthy mother and all, private school, WASP education. ASP, to be precise. *Are* there any black Anglo-Saxons? It all sounds pretty nice, and it *is*. I'm not complaining; it's nice . . . but it isn't always easy. Being corrupted, for example; now, that's important to a young fellow. Whether he takes advantage of it or not. The corrupting influences really should *be* there; all you should have to do is turn a corner and there you are, all laid out for you, so to speak—fornication, drugs, stealing, whatever; it should *be* there. But if you live in Grovers Corners, or wherever, pop. fifteen hundred and thirty-three, it isn't too easy to come by. You have to . . . search it out. Oh, there's the grocer's youngish widow with her blinds always drawn and the come-hither look, and the mildly retarded girl in the ninth grade has some habits would make a pro blush, *and* the florist with the dyed hair and the funny walk and the mustache for those inclined that way, or at least want to try it. These things are to be *had* in a small town, but not without the peril of observation and revelation. What's missing, I suppose, is . . . anonymity. And there are, after all, some things we'd rather do in private—at least until we're practiced—do them well. The lack of anonymity: Well, in a small New England town, if your family's been there eight hundred years, or whatever, and you're "gentry," *and* you're bright, *and* your mother practically sends out announcements *saying* you're bright and destined for "great things," well, then . . . it's not the same, the nice same, as being able to get it all together behind the barn, so to speak, and then coming out all rehearsed and "ready." "I hear you're getting all A's, Fergus; good for you!" "Your mother says you've decided on Harvard, young fella; well, I hope they've decided on you, ha, ha, ha!" Lordy! Even when I was tiny: "Took his first step, did he!?" "Potty trained is he? Good for him!" Royalty must have it worse, or the children of the very famous. I don't even know what I want to *do* with my life—if I want to do *anything*. If I want to *live* it, even. Do you know what suicide rate has been making the biggest jumps? Kids. Kids my age. I'm not planning to . . . kill myself or anything; don't misunderstand me; I'm happy, relatively happy, as I understand the term. It's just that . . . well, we kids have all sorts of options. You grown-ups aren't the only ones. Think about *that*. Thank you.

(Bows, moves off)

SCENE FOURTEEN

CORDELIA
(Comes forward; alone. To the audience)

I would imagine you've been wondering why I married Daniel, considering everything—Benjamin, I mean. I would imagine you've been wondering; heaven knows, *I* have, now and again. My mother—Gertrude, over there—said to me—how many times?—"Why are you *marrying* that person? I warn you, young woman, you're in for a lot of woe." "Oh, Mother," I'd say, knowing full well what she meant. "I warn you: they don't change; you'll find out!" "Oh, Mother!" Back and forth; Ping-Pong. "I had a cousin married one." "Oh, Mother!" "Scandals; driven from one town to another." "Oh God!" "Mark my words."

GERTRUDE *(From where she sits)*
Mark my words!

CORDELIA *(Out)*

I married him because I love him. Doesn't that seem simple enough? We met; I found him handsome—in his way; sexy—in his way; plus bright plus tender and considerate plus patient plus he cheered me up a lot. I don't mean to suggest that I was greatly in *need* of cheering up; I'm not a manic depressive, or anything. I've had some laughs, some kicks; I've been around—married once before, to a jock, on his way to nowhere as it turned out. I've been around; I know the scene, the score, whatever. But Daniel was special—*is*. I knew he was gay—right off; some women sense these things; others never get the hang of it. I knew he was gay; I knew he and Benjamin were lovers; and I knew I wanted to marry him.

(Shrugs)

Well, I'm a grown-up.

GERTRUDE *(From where she sits)*
Mark my words!

CORDELIA
Oh, Mother!
(Out)

I knew what the problems would be—*are*. I knew the chances. I *know* Daniel sleeps around; well, I'm pretty sure I know it, and I suspect it's with guys. I *hope* it is: I mean, I *like* being his only woman. I mean, if I turn him straight . . . then he'll start in with girls. This way's better. As long as he's careful; as long as he's very careful.

GERTRUDE *(From where she sits)*
You're in for a lot of woe! Mark my words!

CORDELIA *(Laughs)*

Oh, Mother!

(Out)

Every time we're done making love and we have our cigarettes, Daniel'll turn to me and smile and take my hand and say, "Isn't it nice that we're such good friends." Well, I suppose that isn't *exactly* your usual marriage, isn't precisely

(Imitation of jock)

"Hey, babe, that was good for me; was it good for you, too?" Not exactly that, but *I* don't mind. I think I prefer it. I think . . . I think perhaps Daniel is more interested in our friendship than our marriage. I mean, he seems . . . happy enough being married to me, certainly no less happy than when he was—married, I suppose, to Benjamin. And if I lose anything, it won't be the way your usual marriage ends—the friendship goes first, and *then* the marriage falls apart. What I mean is, I think I have a friend, and if one day he thinks that our being married is as silly as it *is* . . . well, then I'll lose the marriage, but I think I'll still have a very good friend.

(Shrugs)

There are worse things in the world to have.

SCENE FIFTEEN

*(*BENJAMIN, DANIEL, FERGUS. BENJAMIN *and* DANIEL *are standing, separate, stretching.* FERGUS *comes up)*

FERGUS

Let's play catch.

DANIEL

I *beg* your pardon!

FERGUS

Let's play *catch.* Here; I have a ball.

(Throws and catches a beach ball)

BENJAMIN

Hey! Why not?

DANIEL

Why *not?* You? Catch something? Herpes is about the only thing you can catch—apparently.

FERGUS

Who's that? May we play?

BENJAMIN

Okay! Okay!

DANIEL *(To* BENJAMIN*)*

Be sure to put your glasses on: you *do* want to catch the ball.

FERGUS *(To* DANIEL*)*

I'll throw it to you and you throw it to him and he'll throw it me.

DANIEL *(Mildly sarcastic)*

Won't this be fun!

BENJAMIN

It *will* be!

FERGUS

Okay; here we go.
    (Throws at DANIEL*)*
Catch!

DANIEL *(Catching)*

Ow! Jesus!

BENJAMIN *(Parody of baseball player)*

C'mon, guy; heave her over here!

DANIEL *(Disbelief)*

Heave her over *here?*

BENJAMIN

Come on; have fun!

DANIEL

Who ever heard of anybody saying anything like that?
    (Underhand toss)
Here!

BENJAMIN *(Sibilant comment)*

Ooooooh! My gracious! Such force!

FERGUS

You guys are *fun!*
    (Catches BENJAMIN*'s fair throw)*
Hey! That's good!

DANIEL *(Jock imitation)*

What's ya name, kid?
    *(*BENJAMIN *giggles;* FERGUS *throws sort of hard to* DANIEL*)*
Ow!

FERGUS

Fergus. Was that too hard?

BENJAMIN *(Jock imitation)*

For a guy like him, kid? You kidding?

(DANIEL *throws very hard*)

Ow!

FERGUS

You guys *are* fun!

(*Natural, casual throwing now; unobtrusive*)

DANIEL

What kind of name is Fergus?

FERGUS

Scots, I believe.

BENJAMIN

I'm Benjamin.

FERGUS

Hi!

DANIEL

And I'm Lucille.

FERGUS *(No change in friendly tone)*

Hi!

DANIEL *(Awe at* FERGUS's *aplomb)*

Wow! No, actually I'm Daniel.

FERGUS

I know. You two are presently married to those ladies over there, although . . . since the two of *you* have been . . . uh . . . intimately involved? . . . there is a question floating around this particular area of the beach as to whether these marriages were made in heaven. I have no opinion on the matter.

BENJAMIN *(To* DANIEL; *false sotto voce)*

The "in-laws" have been talking again.

FERGUS

Are you all good friends, you four? You and your wives?

DANIEL

It varies; it varies.

FERGUS

I . . . wondered.

(*Pause*)

BENJAMIN

Oh?

DANIEL

Oh?

FERGUS

I was having a little chat with . . . well, I guess *your* wife, Benjamin; uh . . . Abigail is *yours?*

DANIEL

Oh, yes; Abigail is his and he is Abigail's.

BENJAMIN

Enough!

DANIEL

Desist? Hold? *Basta?*

FERGUS

You guys are really *fun!*

BENJAMIN

What *about* Abigail?

FERGUS

She's . . .
    (*Tosses ball above his head; catches it*)
well, she's. . . . unhappy?

DANIEL

No kidding!

BENJAMIN (*Gently*)

I *know.*

FERGUS

I'd take care if I were you.

DANIEL (*To no one*)

What*ever* can he mean?

BENJAMIN (*Ignoring* DANIEL's *tone*)

Whatever *can* you mean?

FERGUS

I'd be careful of her; that's all.
    (*Quick subject switch*)
Which one of you guys married first?

BENJAMIN

I did.

FERGUS (*Some surprise*)

Really?

DANIEL

I was planning to when this one decided to do something precipitous. "I'll show *you!*"—*that* sort of thing.

BENJAMIN

Untrue! Untrue!

DANIEL

. . . when he realized that I was serious—that Cordelia and I were going to be married. When *that* sank in, he sort of ran out in the street and hooked on to the first gullible girl he could find.

BENJAMIN

Unclean! Unclean!

DANIEL (*Naggy tone*)

"I'll show you! I'll show you!"

FERGUS (*To* BENJAMIN)

I'd worry about her a little if I were you.

DANIEL

With any luck she might just . . . walk out of our lives, you mean?

FERGUS

Something like that.

BENJAMIN (*More or less to himself*)

That *is* something to think about.

FERGUS

(*Starting to leave, still tossing to himself; a kind of "Okay you guys" tone*)

Okay. Okay.

BENJAMIN

Where are you going?

DANIEL

Where are you taking the ball?

FERGUS

You guys don't need the ball; you've got your own game going.

(*As* FERGUS *leaves, a combination of regret and something private and not too nice*)

BENJAMIN and DANIEL

Aaaaawwwwwwwwwwwww!

SCENE SIXTEEN

(FERGUS *moves behind sleeping* EDMEE, *awakes* GERTRUDE *and* HENDEN)

FERGUS

Have I got things to tell *her!* (*Moves past, out of their view*)

EDMEE (*After a pause; suddenly*)

Who *was* that?

GERTRUDE

Your son . . . or so you say.

HENDEN

What a nice boy!

EDMEE

My son, or so I say?

HENDEN

Bright, too!

GERTRUDE

I mean no offense.

EDMEE (*To Henden*)

Very bright. *Too* bright?—perhaps.

HENDEN

Oh, come sow!

GERTRUDE (*Singsong*)

No offense at all.

EDMEE (*Generally*)

There's danger in consciousness, in too much awareness.

HENDEN

We go through it only once, my dear, or so more tell me than don't—better alert than . . . numb, or not comprehending.

GERTRUDE

(*To* HENDEN; *an old argument*)

You're *certain* of that—that we go *through* it only once.

HENDEN (*To* EDMEE; *chuckling*)

Gertrude is of the opinion that a move away from the big bang theory to the notion that the universe has always existed, in whatever form . . .

EDMEE (*Lazy*)

I don't believe either one.

GERTRUDE *(Mildly startled)*

Oh? Really?

HENDEN

. . . has—what?—permits the concept of . . . cyclism, I suppose it could be called . . .

GERTRUDE *(Fingertips to temples)*

Stop it, Henden.

HENDEN

What? Oh.

EDMEE

(FERGUS *is listening, unbeknownst etc. After a tiny pause)*

It's that Fergus is . . . *so* bright I worry for him. Oh, a mother with a dumb one has her own problems—can he find his way *home*? Won't he be embarrassed to be in the third grade at fourteen? Whatever will he *do* with his *life*? Those *are* problems, and I don't envy a woman who *has* them. But Fergus is ready for college and he's just sixteen. We're going to Europe for a year, to Rome, to Athens, to Dendura, to Istanbul, to let him see it all, begin to relate time to place, fact to theory.

GERTRUDE

Isn't that nice.

EDMEE

You *still* don't think he's my son, *do* you!

HENDEN *(Admonishingly)*

Why, Gertrude!

GERTRUDE *(Too innocent by far)*

I didn't say a word! I haven't said a word for . . . minutes.

EDMEE *(Hard)*

He's not my type, lady! I *told* you that!

GERTRUDE

I didn't say a word!

HENDEN *(To placate)*

What a nice boy he is!

(FERGUS *turns, pauses, exits just before the end of* EDMEE's *next speech)*

EDMEE

You know what bothers me most about him, about Fergus—being so special, being so . . . bright, so beautiful and bright? That he'll turn out . . . less than he promises. I don't want to be around when his hair recedes or his body starts its way to fat; I don't want to see the expression in his eyes when he looks at his life and sees it's not going to be quite what it might have been. Tarnish! That's what I don't want to see . . . tarnish.

GERTRUDE
(Cold; to comfort and destroy)
Well, maybe he'll die young.

EDMEE *(Wistful)*
Maybe.

GERTRUDE
Or maybe you won't be around.

EDMEE *(Ibid.)*
Maybe.

HENDEN
Or, or maybe none of that will happen; maybe he'll . . . *be* . . . everything he might.

EDMEE *(Ibid.)*
Maybe.

GERTRUDE *(Caught up in it)*
My goodness! Wouldn't that be something!

EDMEE
Yes. Wouldn't it.

SCENE SEVENTEEN

(DANIEL *and* HENDEN, *together;* HENDEN *arriving)*

DANIEL
Hi, Dad.

HENDEN
Hello, son.
(Pause)

DANIEL
You should keep your head covered.

HENDEN
Oh?

DANIEL
Burn.

HENDEN
Aha!
(Pause)

DANIEL

Cordelia's over there.

HENDEN

I see; I see she is.
(*Pause*)
Gertrude's over there.

DANIEL

Yes; I saw.

HENDEN

Aha.
(*Pause*)
How is it going?

DANIEL

What?

HENDEN

It! You, Cordelia, Benjamin, what's-her-name, and all that?

DANIEL

"All that?"

HENDEN

All right!!
(*Pause*)

DANIEL (*Shrugs*)

Not bad.

HENDEN

Good?

DANIEL (*Harder*)

Not *bad*.
(*Pause*)

HENDEN

Do you want to talk about it?

DANIEL

You *know* better. (*Pause*)

HENDEN

I am your father . . .

DANIEL (*Explodes*)

Christ! Great, suffering Jesus, do we have to go *on* with this?

HENDEN (*Hurriedly; mollifying*)

No, no, no, no, now . . .

DANIEL (*Continuing*)

Must we go on with it? There is no hope! There is . . . going *on;* there is
. . . getting through it!

HENDEN (*Softly*)

All *right.*

DANIEL (*Continuing*)

There is my *nature* and *Benjamin's* nature, and we are doing what we *can*
about it, though I think we're *idiots.* We have fallen between stools, Father;
we were better perched on our specialness . . . our disgrace, perhaps. Perhaps
not. I don't know—the perch, I mean; not the specialness. I don't know.

HENDEN

I know.

DANIEL (*Ironic*)

But we are *trying.* Jesus, we're trying!! Benjamin is heartbroken and confused; Abigail—what's-her-name to you—Abigail is close to a collapse of
some sort; Cordelia is turning tough and brittle at the same time and is
beginning to drink just a little too much, though maybe that's *in* her; and
I . . . *I* can't keep my hands from shaking, *or* shouting at you, dearest man,
whom I love above all creatures on this earth.

   (*Pause*)

HENDEN

Well.

DANIEL

Yes; well.

   (*Pause. They embrace;* DANIEL *seems to sob;* HENDEN *tentatively hugs
   him, pats him on the back, they separate, go in opposite directions*)

SCENE EIGHTEEN

   (ABIGAIL *and* EDMEE. EDMEE *seated next to a sleeping* GERTRUDE;
   ABIGAIL *approaches*)

ABIGAIL

May we talk?

EDMEE

I suppose we *could.* I don't really *want* to.

ABIGAIL (*About to leave; shy*)

I'm sorry.

EDMEE (*Removing her dark glasses*)

No! *I* am! I'm being rude.

ABIGAIL

Well, a little.

EDMEE (*None too pleasant*)

I like candor in a girl; next to bitten fingernails, I like candor best.

ABIGAIL (*Looks to be sure*)

I don't bite my nails.

EDMEE (*Expansive*)

I don't know what it is about the sea—the beach and the sea: they bring out in me a tristesse I feel no other place. It's not a lugubrious sadness or a grief; no, I described it as I intended.

ABIGAIL

A tristesse?

EDMEE

Yes. I have felt fear in the plains, panic in a church, claustrophobia in the mountains, tearing loss at Christmas with all my lovelies around me, implausible sadness on a summer day, but only here, where the earth and water meet, do I feel this . . . tristesse.

ABIGAIL (*Shy*)

I see.

EDMEE

We have so much to be thankful for, being alive. *Being alive!!* for one! I've never taken much comfort from "what lies beyond," as they put it. I *doubt* it; I doubt the entire proposition, but even if it does . . . occur, the reports are none too encouraging—hellfire for the wicked and a kind of disembodied cloud sit for the rest? What comfort there! What! No dry martinis? No poetry? No . . . no whatever makes it all worth the effort? Perhaps I could accept an eternity of tristesse, sitting here with a magazine, my mind, and some memories.

(*Turns to Gertrude*)

Are you asleep, my dear?

ABIGAIL (*Wistful; lost*)

The water is . . . lovely.

EDMEE

It's the line where it meets; that's the magic! One element into another.

(*Snaps her fingers*)

Just like that! I would love to be able to walk into it—the water—walk down the grade, enter, submerge, walk about, reverse and march right

back to my starting point, all erect, all . . . gliding. I would love to be able
to breathe both water and air.

ABIGAIL

We can . . . in a way.

EDMEE (*Scoffing*)

Oh, masks and tanks and things!

ABIGAIL

No; not really.
   (*Begins to move away*)
Thank you; I enjoyed our talk.

EDMEE (*To* GERTRUDE's *sleeping form*)

Gertrude?
   (*To the retreating* ABIGAIL)
Oh! Oh, so did I! I hope I was some . . .
   (*To herself*)
Well, I hope I was some help.

SCENE NINETEEN

(ABIGAIL *and* BENJAMIN. ABIGAIL *returning*)

BENJAMIN (*Casual*)

Where have you been?

ABIGAIL

Where have *you* been?

BENJAMIN

Nowhere.

ABIGAIL

Me, too.

BENJAMIN

Who were you *talking* to?

ABIGAIL (*Indicates*)

That lady.

BENJAMIN

Her son is called Fergus; he's . . .

ABIGAIL (*She can't help it*)

. . . a little young for you, don't you think?

BENJAMIN

Oh, come *on!* Jesus, can't we even *talk?*

ABIGAIL

I'm sorry!
  (*Softer*)
I *am;* I'm sorry.

BENJAMIN (*Taking her hand*)

How can your *hand* be so *cold?* It's hot out here; how can your hand be so cold?

ABIGAIL (*Withdrawing her hand*)

I'm always cold; I get colder all the time. If you ever held me anymore you'd know.

BENJAMIN

I hold you.

ABIGAIL

Sure!

BENJAMIN (*Anger rising*)

I *hold* you!

ABIGAIL

  (*A burst of self-propelled anger*)
Yes! *You* hold me! But I hardly know it's *you,* and who are you holding *really,* and why do you want to hurt me in bed, and why are you walking away, and . . .
  (BENJAMIN *goes*)
. . . and why am I so cold all the time? . . . And . . .
  (*Raises her hand to the sun; slow, quiet intensity now*)
Why don't you just . . . go out? Burn out? Flare up, sizzle, crackle for a moment, and then . . . just . . . fade . . . bring the ice down on all of us? *I'm* ready; *I'm* cold enough. Go out! I dare you!
  (*Pause; pain*)
Benjamin! Benjamin!
  (*At the end of this scene, and as Scene Twenty begins,* ABIGAIL *takes her towel and exits; none of the others see her exit*)

SCENE TWENTY

(EDMEE, GERTRUDE, *and* HENDEN *in their chairs*)

GERTRUDE

  (*Waking up; an announcement of subject*)
Am I asleep, my dear.

EDMEE *(Pleased)*

Aha!

GERTRUDE

Where is Henden?

HENDEN

(Eyes closed; hat over her face)

Asleep, my dear.

GERTRUDE

Aha.

(*To* EDMEE)

I doze; I slip off into sleepettes. Is it tiny strokes, I wonder—the sleep-ettes? I will be at a dinner party, attentive to my neighbor, and all at once I am aware I have slipped off for a moment. Or I am reading and it will happen. Tiny strokes? Probably not: Simply that I don't sleep much at night; I cat-prowl. Henden and I still have the same room—the same bed!—and he lies there, a wheezing lump, unconscious.

HENDEN

Ah, now . . .

EDMEE *(Literally)*

Tee-hee!

GERTRUDE

. . . and I am awake, almost all the night, dozing fitfully until I am awak-ened by a creak, a chirp, the memory of a dream.

EDMEE

I've done it.

GERTRUDE

I do it as clockwork. I am as familiar with dawn as any farmer, the night as any watchman. I waxed the library table once at three in the A.M. down on my knees in my nightdress doing away at the big claw feet.

HENDEN

Looked grand when you were done.

(EDMEE *laughs*)

GERTRUDE

And I write long letters in the night—wise, instructive, useful—to our leaders, but I seldom mail them: might change the world; wouldn't do—let bad enough alone.

EDMEE

I sleep without moving.

GERTRUDE *(Too bright)*

Who *tells* you?

EDMEE (*Smooth*)

Oh . . . whoever is with me. I have a . . . variety of gentlemen, and one lady, share my night times. I outsleep them; they tell me.

GERTRUDE

Why did you wonder if I was awake?

EDMEE (*Mildly corrective*)

I wondered if you were *asleep.*

GERTRUDE

Oh.
(*Afterthought*)
They are not the same?

HENDEN (*Behind his hat*)

Not exactly.

EDMEE

That . . . that girl was talking to me, the young one. I wanted to help.

GERTRUDE

Abigail?

EDMEE

Is that her name?

GERTRUDE

Abigail. She is married to Benjamin. We know all about that.

EDMEE

Oh?

GERTRUDE (*Hurrying through it*)

It's so tedious. Abigail is married by mischance to Benjamin, who by mischance was lovers with Daniel, who by mischance is now married to Cordelia. Cordelia is my daughter, and Daniel is Henden's son.

EDMEE

Goodness!

GERTRUDE (*Waving it all away*)

They travel in a pack; they are not happy! They worry and bother us.

EDMEE

Gracious!

GERTRUDE

. . . though we have given up trying to solve it all: too much fate; too much irony.

HENDEN

I try . . . now and again.

GERTRUDE

To any end?

HENDEN

You know better.

EDMEE

Perhaps it will all resolve itself. I wonder what she wanted.

GERTRUDE *(Shrugs)*

To whine; to explain; to be comforted; to save her soul. Who knows? Perhaps it will all resolve itself? Yes; well, perhaps; and—then again—perhaps not. And so . . . Henden sleeps and I prowl.

EDMEE

Jack Sprat!

GERTRUDE *(Laughs)*

Yes; in a way.

HENDEN

Jack who?

GERTRUDE

Go back to sleep.

(GERTRUDE *and* EDMEE *laugh, sadly gaily*)

SCENE TWENTY-ONE

(BENJAMIN, CORDELIA, DANIEL, EDMEE *and* GERTRUDE. DANIEL *and* CORDELIA *are right,* EDMEE *and* GERTRUDE *in their chairs left.* HENDEN *is in his chair, back to front.*

BENJAMIN

(Comes down to CORDELIA *and* DANIEL*)*
Hold me, you guys.

DANIEL

Another bout?

BENJAMIN *(Still standing)*

Just hold me.

DANIEL

Come in between.

CORDELIA *(Shrugs; smiles)*

Why not?

(The sun goes behind a cloud; the sky becomes gray)

GERTRUDE (*To* EDMEE)

Are we losing the sun?

EDMEE

Hm?

GERTRUDE

I said . . .

EDMEE

Why, I think we are.

BENJAMIN

There are days when I just don't . . .

DANIEL

Forget it.

BENJAMIN

Why is the sun going away?

DANIEL (*Sad laugh*)

It's one of those *days*.

BENJAMIN (*A child*)

What if it were to . . . go out?

CORDELIA

That'd solve a few things.

DANIEL

It sure would.
(*Sighs*)

GERTRUDE (*About the sun*)

Awwwwwww.

EDMEE

So much for skin cancer.

GERTRUDE (*Cheerful*)

Oh, it'll come back.

EDMEE

You and I should talk about facelift sometime.

BENJAMIN

Let well enough alone, I tell her.

CORDELIA

Well enough?

DANIEL

Indeed.

BENJAMIN
What?

DANIEL
Let bad enough alone, you mean?

BENJAMIN
Something like that.

GERTRUDE *(To* EDMEE*)*
Whatever for? Are you planning one?

EDMEE
One likes to think ahead.

GERTRUDE
I have the skin of a turtle. *I* don't bother.

BENJAMIN
She says I hurt her in bed.

CORDELIA *(Gleeful interest)*
Oh? Really?

DANIEL *(Chuckles)*
Down, girl!

EDMEE
If you are as vain as I am, then you look around the next corner.

GERTRUDE
(A bit chiding, a bit taunting)
What would your Fergie say?

EDMEE *(Laughs)*
Well, then your dreams might come *true*.
(Offhand)
Where *is* he, I wonder?

BENJAMIN
I think one day it'll have to be just . . . the three of us.

CORDELIA
Only if you'll promise to hurt me.

DANIEL
He'll find a way—one way or another.

BENJAMIN
I'm gentle. How about it, guys? The three of us?

CORDELIA
The *two* of you, you mean.

DANIEL

Oh, come on, baby!

CORDELIA

I'll bow *out*; I *will*.

GERTRUDE *(To* EDMEE*)*

Do you think I *should* have it done?

EDMEE

Couldn't hurt.

GERTRUDE

I wonder what Henden would say?

EDMEE

Ask him.

GERTRUDE *(Looks)*

He's asleep. He probably wouldn't notice.

BENJAMIN

The musketeers.

CORDELIA *(Looking)*

There's a crowd down there at the water.

DANIEL

A whale, probably; a shark.

CORDELIA *(Puzzled frown)*

No; no, I don't think so.

DANIEL

Well, why don't you go *see?*

CORDELIA *(Rising, moving off)*

Yes. Yes, I think I will.

(Exits)

DANIEL *(Imitation of a witch)*

Now we're alone, baby!

BENJAMIN *(Sincere)*

Oh, Daniel; hold me.

*(*DANIEL *does, gently)*

EDMEE

There would appear to be two theories about facelift—at least! One is, wait until you're nicely lined and sagged and wattled, and *then* do it. The *other* is, do it often and surreptitiously—never look a day older than when you've begun it.

GERTRUDE
Our skin ages, no matter what you do.

EDMEE
Oh, you have to stay out of the sun.

GERTRUDE
Stay out of the sun!? Are you mad!?

EDMEE *(Chuckles; then)*
There are *people* down there.

GERTRUDE *(Not interested)*
Oh?
    (Intense)
Why doesn't the sun come back?

BENJAMIN
Do we have to go on this way? Can't we go back to how we were?

DANIEL
I don't think so.

BENJAMIN
I *love* you; you love *me*. I don't hurt *you*.

DANIEL
No; we can't.

BENJAMIN
We could *try*.

DANIEL
What do you want to do with the girls? Grow up!

BENJAMIN
I *miss* you.

DANIEL *(Pause)*
I miss *you*.

BENJAMIN
I *love* you.

DANIEL *(Pause)*
I love *you?*

GERTRUDE
Henden?

EDMEE
Let him sleep.

BENJAMIN
It's hope-less, then.

DANIEL

It's hopeless, then. What did Beckett say?: I can't go on; I'll go on?

GERTRUDE

Henden?

(CORDELIA *returns with* ABIGAIL's *towel*)

BENJAMIN (*Puzzled*)

That's Abigail's towel.

CORDELIA

No beached whale; no shark.

BENJAMIN

That's Abigail's!

DANIEL (*Eyes narrowing*)

What's wrong?

CORDELIA

(*Looking back toward the water*)

Abigail tried to drown herself. They stopped her. They have her over a barrel—literally; they're pumping the water out of her. She'll live.

(*Tosses the towel to* BENJAMIN)

Here; this belongs to you.

BENJAMIN (*Awe; not moving*)

She tried to drown herself? Why?

DANIEL

(*He and* CORDELIA *chuckle sadly*)

Oh, God.

GERTRUDE

Henden?

BENJAMIN (*Generally*)

Hold me?

EDMEE

Let him *sleep*.

GERTRUDE (*Senses something*)

Henden!

(*Goes to his chair*)

Henden?

EDMEE

Let him . . .

(*She, too realizes*)

Is he dead?

GERTRUDE *(Long pause)*

Yes; yes, he is.

EDMEE

Poor him; poor *you.*

GERTRUDE

Poor Henden; poor, dear man.

EDMEE *(Quiet panic)*

Fergus!

BENJAMIN *(Not moving)*

I'll have to go to her.

CORDELIA

Let them wring her out. What would you say to her?

BENJAMIN *(Pause)*

Nothing?

GERTRUDE

(To DANIEL, *from where she is)*

Daniel?

DANIEL *(Pause; softly)*

Yes, Gertrude?

GERTRUDE

You'd better come here.

EDMEE

Fergus?

DANIEL

Is it my father?

GERTRUDE

You know. Yes.

EDMEE

Fergus?

DANIEL

I'll come in a moment.

CORDELIA

Oh, Daniel, poor Daniel.

EDMEE

Fergus?

BENJAMIN

Hold me?

DANIEL (*Gently*)

Oh, God.

GERTRUDE

Oh, Henden.

EDMEE

Fergus!!?

BENJAMIN

Hold me!? Someone!?

CORDELIA

Anyone? Here.
  (*Holds him*)

EDMEE

Fergus?

GERTRUDE

Oh, my poor Henden.

DANIEL

Oh, God.

EDMEE (*A frightened child*)

Fergus?

GERTRUDE

He'll come back, my dear; they do. Look! The sun's returning. What glory!
What . . . wonder!
  (*Indeed, the sun is returning*)

BENJAMIN

Daniel?

EDMEE

Fergus?

GERTRUDE

Oh, my Henden.

DANIEL

Oh, God.

EDMEE

Fergus?
  (*Pause*)
Fergus?
  (*Pause; slow fade*)

CURTAIN

Marriage Play

Edward Albee's *Marriage Play* was commissioned by, and received its premiere, at Vienna's English Theatre, Ltd., Vienna, Austria, on May 17, 1987. The cast was as follows:

KATHLEEN BUTLER *as* GILLIAN

TOM KLUNIS *as* JACK

The American premiere of Edward Albee's *Marriage Play* was co-produced by the McCarter Theatre (Emily Mann, Artistic Director; Jeffrey Woodward, Managing Director), of Princeton, New Jersey, and the Alley Theatre (Gregory Boyd, Artistic Director; Stephen J. Albert, Executive Director), of Houston Texas. It was first presented at the Alley Theatre on January 8, 1992 and subsequently at the McCarter Theatre on February 14, 1992. It was directed by Edward Albee; the set and costume designs were by Derek McLane; the lighting design was by Howell Binkley; the movement coordinator was Chuck Hudson and the production stage manager was Susie Cordon. The cast was as follows:

SHIRLEY KNIGHT *as* GILLIAN

TOM KLUNIS *as* JACK

Edward Albee's *Marriage Play* was produced by Signature Theatre Company (James Houghton, Artistic Director; Thomas C. Proehl, Managing Director; Elliot Fox, Associate Director), in New York City, on October 1, 1993. It was directed by James Houghton; the set design was by E. David Cosier; the costume design was by Teresa Snider-Stein; the lighting design was by Jeffrey S. Koger; the fight director was Marty Pistone, and the production stage manager was Kathleen M. Nolan.
The cast was as follows:

KATHLEEN RUDER *as* GILLIAN

TOM KLUNIS *as* JACK

CHARACTERS

GILLIAN
A woman in her early 50s

JACK
A man in his middle 50s

PLACE
A suburban home

TIME
3:30 on a weekday afternoon; late spring

(GILLIAN *sits in a chair, reading, laughing occasionally. After a bit* JACK *enters through the door*)

GILLIAN
(*Looks up from her book; fairly friendly*)
Hello.

JACK (*Pause*)
Hello.

GILLIAN
You're home early.
(GILLIAN *reads, giggles.* JACK *puts his briefcase down, looks at her; looks back to his briefcase*)

JACK
Yes. I'm leaving you.

GILLIAN (*Thinks about it, frowns*)
What do you mean?

JACK
I'm leaving you.
(*Are you an idiot?*)
I'm leaving you!

GILLIAN (*Back to her book; dismissive*)
Of course.

JACK
Laugh if you *want.*

GILLIAN
I wasn't. Not right then. Earlier, *yes.* Before you came in.

JACK
Laugh if you *want.*

GILLIAN (*Cheerful*)
Did you have a bad day?

JACK (*Pause*)
What do you mean?

GILLIAN

Did you have . . . What do you *mean* what do I mean?

JACK

A bad day.

GILLIAN

You *did!* Oh, I'm *sorry!*

JACK

No.

GILLIAN *(To get it right)*

No. No? No what?

JACK

I did not have a bad day.

GILLIAN *(Thinks about that)*

Did you have a *good* day?

JACK *(Pause; suspicious)*

What do you *mean?*

GILLIAN

If you did not have a bad day, then perhaps it follows you had a *good* day.

JACK *(Not friendly)*

Middling.

GILLIAN

What?

JACK

I had a middling day. I'm leaving you.

GILLIAN

Are you having a dalliance?

JACK

A what?

GILLIAN

A dalliance; another dalliance. Are you dallying . . . with someone? Are you having yet another one of your dalliances?

JACK

Dalliance, as in light-hearted romance?

GILLIAN

Well . . . yes.

JACK *(Considers it)*

No.

GILLIAN

Aha. Are you engaged once again in one or several profoundly involved and/or involving relationships—outside of your home, of course—of a deeply romantic and/or sexual nature?

JACK

My dear woman, this is not to be dealt lightly with.

(Thinks about what he said)

With *lightly*; dealt with lightly.

GILLIAN *(An abrupt, hysterical laugh)*

Certainly not! One or several profoundly involved and/or involving relationships of a deeply romantic and/or sexual nature occurring side by side a marriage of some duration and persistence between two heretofore quick and rational people is not a matter to be dealt lightly with, or with lightly.

(Pause)

What do I mean?

JACK

No, I know what you mean, but that is not what I meant, is not what we're about here. What do I mean?

GILLIAN

Yes; what do you mean?

(Afterthought; no rage)

You cringing piece of filth!

JACK *(Smile)*

Now, now.

(Pause)

You *did* hear me say I was leaving? Departing, taking my life and two suitcases . . .

GILLIAN

I recall something of the sort.

(So solicitous)

What *is* it, you poor old thing?

JACK *(Smile)*

Now, now.

(Pause)

You look up one day from your desk; you are sitting there in your usual manner, doing your usual things—and they are neither boring nor exciting: whatever they may have been they no longer are; they are merely your usual things. Well, you look up from them, are amazed by your familiar surroundings, are startled by the stranger who has been your secretary for

fifteen years. You realize your life is about to change . . . profoundly; either
that or you are mad.

GILLIAN *(Too brightly)*
It was an interesting day, then.

JACK
She chirped.

GILLIAN
She chirped.

JACK
And you are not mad; you are, perhaps, if anything, too on target. Yes;
quite interesting; my life is about to change, and profoundly, you say to
yourself—so to speak.

GILLIAN
Profoundly?

JACK
Profoundly! "May I help you? Is there something I can do?" your stranger
of fifteen years says to you. What is her name? Her name is absurdly Irish.

GILLIAN *(Smiles)*
Kathleen O'Houlihan; Kathleen *Begorra* O'Houlihan.

JACK *(Puzzled)*
Is that *it?* Did you make that up?

GILLIAN
Yes.

JACK
Which?

GILLIAN
Whichever.

JACK
"May you *what?*" you reply.

GILLIAN
"May I help you?"

JACK
Don't help. "May I *help* you?" she asked, regarding my preoccupation with
proper concern. "No, no; it's nothing," I replied. Should I have said . . .
well, you can't say—especially to a total stranger, whether you've known
her fifteen years, or not—"No, no, it's everything; I think my life is undergoing the profoundest change."

GILLIAN
Most profound.

JACK

What?

GILLIAN

Most profound; not profoundest. It may be right, but it sounds wrong.

JACK

Pedant! In any event, *can* you?

GILLIAN

What?

JACK

What?

GILLIAN

Can you *what?*

JACK *(Tiny pause)*

Say that: I think my life is undergoing and so on. *Can* you.

GILLIAN

I don't know. *Can* you?

JACK

Do you *try* to vex me?

GILLIAN *(Kittenish)*

Only when you really want me to.

JACK

(Looks at her for a moment, then away)

Perhaps if I'd truly known you I wouldn't have married you. I'm sure if I'd truly known you I wouldn't have.

GILLIAN *(Businesslike)*

Oh, you would have.

JACK *(Considers the rug)*

Probably.

GILLIAN

Arranged marriages are the best—never see the bride until the marriage day, family puts it all together, for social reasons, or business ones; you never see the bride until the altar, and the veil is raised; your heart stops, for there she is—hairy hippopotamus . . .

JACK

So, you send her off for something, something you actually need, though not very much, and you begin to mull it: what the fuck is happening?

GILLIAN

Change of life. You men have it.

JACK *(Irked)*

I *know* we do.

GILLIAN

It's like breasts: you have those, *too,* but you don't think about them; you don't *use* them much.

JACK

I think about my breasts all the time . . .

GILLIAN *(Chuckles)*

You do not!

JACK *(High horse)*

They are an obsession has probably stood in the way of corporate advancement. I'm sure they have; you can't spend all your time in the company men's room, your shirt open, your tie around your back, your fingers to your nipples, deeply tranced, without it affecting your career—high management walking in and all.

GILLIAN *(Far away)*

I wonder when I'll have mine.

JACK *(Snappish)*

You're probably having it; that's probably what's wrong.

(GILLIAN *throws a magazine at him. It hits him, or it does not, preferable does)*

Don't do that.

GILLIAN *(Glum)*

Pick it up.

JACK *(Bored)*

Pick it up yourself.

(Some enthusiasm)

Do you know the feeling? The one I'm talking about?

GILLIAN

Me? Naah! Me!?

(Awful parody)

I look up one day from my stove. I am standing there in my usual manner, doing my usual things—and they are neither boring nor exciting . . .

JACK *(Half-angry)*

All right.

GILLIAN

I look up from my familiar burners and am startled by the object has been my refrigerator for fifteen years. I realize my cooking is about to profoundly change . . .

JACK *(Angry now)*

All right!!
    (Half to himself)
I should have throttled you years ago.

GILLIAN

Poor darling: you have the most predictable crises; you should read more.

JACK *(Gets up)*

I think I'll come in again.
    (Picks up briefcase)

GILLIAN

What! Go out and come back in?

JACK *(Ugly mimicry)*

What!? Go out and come back in?

GILLIAN

He mimicked.

JACK

He mimicked. Yes; go out and come back in.
    (Moves toward the door)
I'll try once again.

GILLIAN *(Mimicking)*

Hello; I'm leaving you.

JACK *(As Jack exits)*

Pay proper attention.

GILLIAN *(After him, saluting)*

Yes, *Sir!*
    (Alone; imitates a child)
You? Weaving witta me!? Oh, no! Say it isn't so!
    (Remembers something; in her usual voice)
Sad husband, sad wife; Sad day; sad life.
    *(*JACK *re-enters)*

JACK *(Looks about)*

Hello.

GILLIAN *(Looks straight at him)*

Hello.

JACK

I'm leaving you.

GILLIAN

Hm? I'm sorry? I was reading; I didn't hear you.

JACK

That was the *last* time; you are *not* reading *now*.

GILLIAN

I thought we were repeating what we . . .

JACK *(Fuming)*

I said I would do it *again!* I said I would come back in and do it again!

GILLIAN

Yes, but . . .

JACK

I did not intend a time warp! The first time you were *reading; this* time you were *not*.

GILLIAN *(Feigned indignation)*

Well! I'm sorry!

JACK

If you will not pay proper attention . . .

GILLIAN

I try! It's hard, but I try!

JACK *(Dogmatic)*

I'm *leaving* you. It came on me today; a bell went off.

GILLIAN

A bell went off?

JACK

Yes.

GILLIAN

Where?

JACK

I beg your pardon?

GILLIAN

Where?! You said a bell went off. Where did it go off?

JACK

In my head. A bell went off in my head. You've heard the expression.

GILLIAN *(Thinks about it)*

Not for years.

JACK *(Not nice)*

Yeah? Where've you been living?
   (Level)
A bell went off in my head; there I was at my desk and all at once it came

to me, crystallized, the . . . made sense of the feelings of doom, the unfocused anxieties, the gnawing discontents, the . . .

GILLIAN

I get the picture.

JACK (*Sincere*)

I hope you *do*.

GILLIAN

Oh, I do!
  (*Tiny pause*)
Feelings of doom? Really . . . *doom?*

JACK

Well, something close.

GILLIAN

Be *precise.* Doom I'll really fear for you, really *worry.* Gnawing discon-
tents? *Well,* what *else* is new? Unfocused anxieties? Hanh!!
  (*Sees him leaving*)
Where are you *going?*

JACK

I'll try it once again; I'll give you one more chance!

GILLIAN(*Mock supplication*)

Weawy? You're gonna give me one more chance?

JACK

To pay *attention!* To be *serious* about it!

GILLIAN

Perhaps we should put in a revolving door.
  (JACK *walks over to her, and raises his arm as if to strike her*)

JACK

Pay.
  (*Pause*)
Attention.
  (*Turns; exits*)

GILLIAN

  (*After* JACK *leaves; curiously uninvolved*)
You have done everything at least once too often.
  (JACK *re-enters*)

JACK

Hello.

(Pause)

I'm leaving you.

GILLIAN *(Shakes her head; clucks)*

Darn! Ya know, I knew it!? I had a feeling!

> *(JACK turns on his heel, exits. GILLIAN turns pages, ignores exit.*
> JACK *re-enters)*

JACK

Hello.

GILLIAN *(Absorbed in her book)*

Oh! Hello!

JACK

I thought I should tell you that . . . . What are you *doing?*

GILLIAN

Hm?

JACK

What are you DOING?!!

GILLIAN *(Cheerful)*

I'm reading.

JACK

What?

GILLIAN

I'm *reading.*

JACK

No! *What! What* are you reading?

GILLIAN

My book.

JACK *(Long pause)*

What . . . book?

GILLIAN

> *(Overly casual; looks at the cover as if she had never seen it*
> *before)*

Oh . . . *The Book of Days; my* book; *The Book of Days.*

JACK

Never heard of it.

GILLIAN

Oh, it's not published.

JACK *(Pause)*

What do you mean?

GILLIAN

What?

JACK

What do you *mean!?*

GILLIAN

What do I mean by it's not published?

JACK *(Calm, but Jack may hit her)*

Yes.

GILLIAN

I mean that it is not published; that is what I mean by it is not published.

JACK

I know.

GILLIAN

Then why do you ask?

(JACK *makes an attempt to grab the book;* GILLIAN *keeps it)*

No you don't!

JACK

I want to *see* it!

GILLIAN

You haven't wanted to see it for years! All the years it's been right here and you haven't wanted to see it.

JACK

What do you mean "all the years"? You've been reading the same book for years and years? What are you, slow?

GILLIAN

Not reading. Writing.

JACK *(Pause)*

Pardon?

GILLIAN

Not reading. Writing.

JACK

What do you mean?

GILLIAN

It is a book I am writing. It is called *The Book of Days.*

(*Shrugs*)

It is a book I am writing.

JACK
(Smiles, almost laughs; mimic)
"It is a book I am writing." You're writing a *book!?*

GILLIAN *(Annoyed)*
Well, don't make it sound like it's something *beyond* me! "You're writing a book!?" *You*, barely brighter than a gazelle, or frying pan, *you* write a book!?

JACK *(Delight)*
A book.

GILLIAN *(Amounting to justification)*
Well, it's not *fiction*.

JACK
What do you mean?

GILLIAN
It's more of a journal—a kind of record.

JACK *(Humoring a child)*
Ohhhhhhhh, a *diary!*

GILLIAN *(Annoyed)*
No, not a diary, not a "dear diary." It's a record, it's a clinical record.

JACK *(Eyeing)*
What a thick book; let me see it.

GILLIAN *(Protecting it)*
NO!

JACK
What do you mean "a clinical record"?

GILLIAN
It's . . . well, it's a set of notations.

JACK
What?

GILLIAN
A set of notations.

JACK
Of what?

GILLIAN
What?

JACK
It's a set of notations.

GILLIAN

Yes! Yes, it is.

JACK (*Losing patience*)

Of what!? Of *what!?*

GILLIAN

Of our making love.

JACK (*Pause*)

I beg your pardon?

GILLIAN

Every time we have made love I have notated it here; I have commented on it—duration, positions, time of day, necessity, degrees of enjoyability, snatches of conversation, the weather.

(*Shrugs again*)

You know . . . a record.

JACK (*Pause*)

I don't believe you. Let me see that!

GILLIAN

No! Why not?

JACK

Why *not!? Nobody* would do a thing like that!

GILLIAN

Why not? Thirty years of marriage, nearly three thousand . . . events.

JACK

Three thousand!!

GILLIAN

Yes; how many did you think?

JACK

It never occurred to me to. . . . A record of three thousand fucks?

GILLIAN

Nearly.

JACK

My God! The book of fucks?

GILLIAN

The Book of Days, actually.

JACK

The what?

GILLIAN

The Book of Days. That's what I call it. I keep it by my chair; I write in it; I read from it; it amuses me sometimes.

JACK *(Cold)*

Read from it.

GILLIAN *(Gay)*

Choose a page.

JACK

What?

GILLIAN

Choose a page; choose a number.

JACK *(Pause)*

At random?

GILLIAN

Sure; be brave; choose a number.

JACK

Eight hundred.

GILLIAN

What?

JACK

Eight hundred!

GILLIAN

Whyever did you choose *that* number?

JACK

You said to choose a number; you said to . . .

GILLIAN

Yes, but . . .

JACK

You said be brave; you said to . . .

GILLIAN

Yes, but . . . eight hundred; so . . . rounded, so . . . predictable.

JACK *(Cold)*

Eight hundred!

GILLIAN

Eight hundred? All right.
  (Opens book, finds page)
Eight hundred, eight hundred, eight . . . aha; eight hundred. "Will he never learn?!"

JACK

Will he never learn *what!?*

GILLIAN

Who?

JACK

I! Will I never learn *what!*

GILLIAN *(Casual)*

I don't know. That was years ago.

JACK

What kind of woman *are* you?!

GILLIAN

You tell me!

JACK

What!?

GILLIAN *(Louder)*

You tell me.

JACK *(Steely)*

Eight hundred and ten.

GILLIAN *(Rifling)*

All rightie . . . . Eight hundred and ten. "Sunday morning, late, warm for the season, coffee on the bedside table, the papers all over; sex hangs in the air—like a moisture, and you know it will happen and you know it will be good and it does and it is."

JACK *(Pleased)*

Oh. I see. That's nice—Hemingway, but nice. Do another one.

GILLIAN

Don't you think you should quit while you're ahead? Hemingway?

JACK

"You know it will be good and it does and it is," or whatever.

GILLIAN

(Looks down at the page, as if inspecting a flyspeck)
That's Hemingway?

JACK *(A little ugly)*

Do another one; do twelve hundred; do twelve hundred and six.

GILLIAN *(Shrugs)*

O.K. Twelve hundred and six.
(Finds it)

Twelve hundred and six; "Nothing much; OK but nothing much."

JACK *(Pause)*

That's it?

GILLIAN *(Business-like)*

Well, some days—some nights—aren't that . . . special; you know?

JACK

(Walks to the other end of the room; regards her)

Then you've been keeping a record of my performance, or my prowess, if you will . . .

GILLIAN

Don't be silly.

JACK

. . . of my performance in bed through all the years of our marriage?

GILLIAN *(So reasonable)*

Yes!

JACK

What kind of woman *are* you!?

GILLIAN

You tell me, remember?

JACK

That's sick.

GILLIAN *(Serious; a little sad)*

No. . . . It's reasonable, and interesting; a record of our touching.

JACK

I'll never be able to go to bed with you again.

GILLIAN *(Pause)*

Well, since you're leaving me . . . what will it matter?

JACK *(Having only half-heard)*

Hm? Pardon?

GILLIAN *(Gentle; triste)*

Since you're leaving me . . . what does it matter?

JACK *(Puzzled)*

Oh. Right.

(Almost regretful)

I'd almost forgotten, for a moment.

GILLIAN

Just because we announce a plan, it doesn't . . .

JACK *(To stop her; but gentle)*

I'm *leaving* you.

GILLIAN

You *are* having a dalliance.

JACK

I don't dally.

GILLIAN

Then this is a siege.

JACK

This is a departure. If I cause you any hurt . . .

GILLIAN

Listen to you!

JACK

. . . any *pain* . . .

GILLIAN

Oh, Jesus!

JACK

You don't take me seriously.

GILLIAN

Oh, I do; I *do*. There was a time I *didn't*. In the beginning—in *our* beginning, I did . . .

JACK

You *do* want me to hit you, don't you?

GILLIAN

. . . and then I realized that perhaps I needn't, and therefore I did *not* . . .

JACK

Right in the chops, as my uncle used to say.

GILLIAN

. . . but it's been growing on me lately—the taking again of you seriously. Oh . . . yes . . . I take you seriously.

JACK

Or was it my grandfather on my mother's side?

GILLIAN

Everyone takes sides. Who is she? Who is the chippie?

JACK

Who's what?

GILLIAN

The chippie; who's the chippie?

JACK

I'm not changing my mind . . . I'm changing my *life.* You must learn the difference.

GILLIAN

Between your mind and your life.

JACK

I *will* strike you.

GILLIAN

I dare say. Poor darling. Poor *me,* while we're at it.

JACK *(Mimicking)*

Who is she? Who's the chippie?

GILLIAN

Yes!

JACK

There's no one! There's everyone, and there's no one. Maybe that's it.

GILLIAN *(Pinning it down)*

No one.

JACK

No one. Not the blonde on the settee, not the brunette rubbing herself against the chair; not this one, not that one, no one . . . except for the lady I am—with no success—having a sad and useless conversation with.
    (Pause)
NO one.

GILLIAN *(Noncommittal)*

I see.

JACK *(Pause)*

So.

GILLIAN

Yes. So.

JACK

Do twenty-six.

GILLIAN *(Preoccupied)*

What?

JACK

Do something. Do twenty-six.

GILLIAN

Why bother?

JACK *(Contained fury)*

Do twenty-*six!*

GILLIAN *(Reluctant)*

You want to go way back there. To our beginnings. Why bother?

JACK

Twenty-six!!

GILLIAN *(Still reluctant)*

Our first two weeks. The liner. Those islands. Why bother.

JACK

Twenty-*six!*

GILLIAN *(Suddenly)*

What I remember most is everyone knew we were honeymooners—what a funny word!—were honeymooners, were screwing each other cross-eyed and maybe even freshly—old fashioned, I mean: virginal until the knot, and all that. Odd about the knot—about knots: tie the knot; undo the knot.

JACK

Twenty-six!

GILLIAN

Hush. Everyone would look at us. What did we do, carry placards?— "Honeymooners; ficky-fack; new at it." It must have been so . . . . obvious. I know we gazed into each other's eyes a lot, heads slightly tilted, moon-cow sounds probably emanating. They all treated us like . . . furry little animals! "Aw! Aren't they cute!!" As if we were retarded in some . . . pleasing way—no drool or wildness, no danger, but . . . childlike. "Awwwww!!! Aren't they cute! Little babies go fuck now?"

JACK

Twenty-six!

GILLIAN

Every time we came up from below—no matter *what* we'd been up to— "Aw, look! The bunnies have been at it! Cute bunnies!!" or if we left our terrible table—remember the Maltese woman? "I have no money," she whined?—if we left our terrible table or the awful games and went below—to fuck, of course—out their elbows went, nudge, nudge.

JACK

Twenty-six!!

GILLIAN *(Ignores him)*

And on the tenders, ship to shore—or shore to ship, for that matter . . . we would hold hands—we held hands a lot then—and they would look at us, at our twined fingers, coo and murmur.

JACK

Stop vamping! Twenty-six, you wanton bitch!!

GILLIAN

Twenty-six? All right; twenty-six.
  (Seeks it)
Twenty-six.
  (Reads to herself a little; giggles)
Oh . . . all right. *(Reads)* "I am selfish by nature, I think, or self-aware, cer-
tainly, to a degree not entertained by many. I have always been so. I am
not ashamed of it; indeed, it sets me apart from—above, I think—many."

JACK

James.

GILLIAN

What?

JACK

Henry James; an attempt at Henry James.

GILLIAN

What?

JACK

What you just read.

GILLIAN

Oh, thank you!

JACK

A poor attempt at Henry James.

GILLIAN

Well . . . some is better than none. Let me see:
  (Reads again)
"But he has taken me to a level of it—"
  (To him, not reading)
of the self-awareness I was talking about before . . .

JACK

I can *follow.*

GILLIAN

You never know—convoluted, James and all.
  (Reads again)
". . . to a level of it I have been unprepared for. Is it simply that no one has
stroked the small of my back just so before? Or is it I know he is harden-
ing as he does it? Is it the terror and longing in his eyes when he is on me?

Or is it that I see I am imagining and knowing the same time the same thing? Is it that I have come into contact with some . . . essence, some animal . . . something?"

JACK

D.H. Lawrence now . . . sort of. What happened to Hemingway? What happened to James?

GILLIAN

I'm eclectic. Do you want me to go on?

JACK

As who?

GILLIAN

Whom?

JACK

Who.

GILLIAN

You say.

JACK

Yourself. Try that; try being you.

GILLIAN

I've *been.*

JACK

Hm?

GILLIAN

I've *been* trying that. No good. It leads to . . . boredom, middle-age panic, dalliance, threats of departure. Perhaps we should put in a turnstile— make some money while we're at it.

(*Gets no reaction*)

No? I've tried myself: thirty years. Don't you . . . recall? Is the image not familiar to you? "Who *is* that lady reading when I come home from wherever."

(*Terrible butch imitation*)

"Stopped off for a coupla beers with the guys; you know—coupla laughs, coupla beers."

(*Parenthetical*)

. . . reeking of bizarre perfume, worn, we take it, by one of more . . . advanced guys.

(*Back to simple imitation of him*)

"Who *is* that lady? I see her everywhere—answering the door when guests arrive, in my bed when I wake up in the morning, legs in the air or butt up

when I'm in the mood. Who *is* she!? She's next to me when I fall asleep—
when I'm home, that is. Who can she be?" I've tried that, sweetie; it doesn't
work. I've tried it for thirty years. Give me another suggestion.

> JACK *(Sad shaking of head)*

You're hopeless.

> GILLIAN *(Pause)*

Well . . . *some*one is, or *some*thing.
> *(Reckless)*

Leaving me, are you!?

> JACK *(Preoccupied)*

Uh-hum.

> GILLIAN *(Quiet; not rapidly)*

You filthy, thoughtless, selfish, aging, wanton, frightened, misunderstanding, vain, foolish memory of the man I prayed would want me.

> JACK *(So weary)*

Oh . . . be still.

> GILLIAN

Leave me; *I* don't care.
> *(New thought)*

Hunh! Thank God the kids are gone.

> JACK *(From a distance)*

What?

> GILLIAN

I said thank God the kids are gone. If they were still here, having to put up
with *this!?* Or is that part of it—the fact that they're gone?—Living their
own lives now?

> JACK *(Reluctantant)*

We'll have to tell them.

> GILLIAN *(Snorts)*

Hanh! *You* tell 'em.
> (GILLIAN *rises, moves to exit*)

> JACK

Where are you going?

> GILLIAN

I'm going to get a drink.

> JACK

You don't *drink*. You don't smoke, and you don't drink.

GILLIAN

Better late than never.

(*Exits*)

JACK

I suppose so.

(*So* GILLIAN *can hear offstage*)

I had a grandmother, teetotaled, everything. Started smoking when she was seventy, took her first drink five years later, became a regular. I suppose she would have taken to the streets when she was eighty if the weather had been better. Nice lady: taught me bridge—Culbertson, that long ago. Nice lady; had a Pekingese—awful old dog, almost as old as she was, though not as nice, couldn't play bridge either; had an adenoid problem . . . the Peke.

(GILLIAN *re-enters; glass and bottle*)

GILLIAN

What Peke?

JACK

My grandmother's.

GILLIAN (*Taking a swig*)

On whose side?

JACK

Mine as often as not. Nice lady.

(*Reading from* GILLIAN'*s book*)

"*Do* I have a special spot? *Is* there such a thing? Has he *hit* upon it—this way and that after all this time!? Will he find it *again*? Should I tell him I have one? At least that he's found it whether I have one or not? Will he believe me?"

GILLIAN

Stay tuned.

JACK

What are you doing . . . drinking it straight out of the bottle? Starting right out big?

GILLIAN

Why do we drink? I mean, why do you drink . . . not for the effect? I thought you drank to get drunk.

JACK

You're a beginner. You drink like that you'll just get sick. You'll throw up and you won't get drunk or anything . . . just messy. Do things right.

GILLIAN

Let *me* handle it. You do the leaving, I'll do the drinking.

JACK *(A warning)*

OK.

GILLIAN

Messy? Do things right? "Hello; I'm leaving you." "Oh, really? *That's* interesting." Don't talk to me about right; don't talk to *me* about messy.

JACK

It isn't that *way*. It isn't "Hello, I'm leaving you."

GILLIAN *(Another drink)*

No?

JACK

No! Don't do that. It isn't that way at all. Things lead up to things, you know; they don't spring . . .

GILLIAN

. . . fully armed from the head of Zeus!

JACK

If you like. Though we may not know it right away. Suddenly we *know*.

GILLIAN *(Sarcastic)*

Tell me about it!

(Tastes her drink)

This stuff is *good*. Why didn't you get me started years ago; I could have done all those Susan Hayward pictures and everything . . .

JACK

It's a realization.

GILLIAN *(About drink)*

It certainly *is*. If I do it right I can get a lot of sympathy. "Poor dear; he drove her to it." "Cheated on her right and left." "He got someone to go to bed with him?" "So it would seem."

JACK

All *right!!*

GILLIAN

Just have to be sure it doesn't look like I like it.

JACK

I have come home to tell you I have had a revelation, and you *dither* at me; you mock, and you—

GILLIAN *(Clenched and tense)*

I am talking so as not to scream!

JACK

I am at my office . . .

GILLIAN

I never realized before how true that was—that cliché.

JACK

I am at my office . . .

GILLIAN *(Mocking; tough tone)*

Tell me about it, big boy.

JACK *(Sighs)*

As I said . . . I am at my office. I look up from my desk; I am sitting there in my usual manner, doing my usual things—and they are neither boring nor exciting: whatever they may have been they no longer are. They are merely my usual things. Well, I look up from them, am amazed by my familiar surroundings, am startled by the stranger who has been my secretary for fifteen years. I realize my life is about to change . . . profoundly. Either that, or I am mad; and I am not mad. I am, perhaps, if anything, too on target. "Yes; quite interesting; my life is about to change, and profoundly," I say to myself, so to speak. "Profoundly!" "May I help you? Is there something I can do?" my stranger of fifteen years says to me. What is her name? Her name is absurdly Irish.

GILLIAN

Kath . . .

JACK

No matter. "May I help you?" she says, her good face puzzled, her eyes, her . . . steady, honest eyes browning on me. "No, no; it's nothing," I say to her. And she stares at me, not believing, wondering what nothing really is. "It's nothing," I repeat. Well, I can't say—especially to a total stranger, whether I've known her for fifteen years or not—"Yes, I think my life is undergoing the profoundest change." *Can* I. Most profound, I know. And so I send her off for something, something I actually need though not very much, and I begin to mull it: what the fuck is happening!? If I am not mad—and I am not—then perhaps it is a collapse of a part of the brain, a stroke even. I am both hot and chill; my palms are sweating—something they have never done, or seldom—my palms are sweating, and the back of my neck is ice; I feel that if I were to turn my head my neck would break off, or crack, certainly, splinter, sending fissures down my spine and radiating. Surely I am all ice—to my wrists, where suddenly I am fire. All ice . . . then fire. And then . . . and then I am . . . levitated, *levitating,* am leaving my body, leaving it where it is and leaving it, all at once, at one and the same time, am hanging there, above myself—as they say we do in dying, or can: hang above ourselves, observe ourselves as we die, unaware that we are observing, unaware that below we have slipped from the intensely conscious state in which we watch. I am aware that I am the object I am studying, that I am my own subject, or object, if you will. I become aware . . . well, yes, that's it! I become aware of awareness I have never known before, of clarity, of . . . revelation, I suppose. Mystics must have it, clairvoyants, the possessed. It all rushes to me, with all its reasons, its causes flying behind it like ribbons, the conclusions I have come to without even being aware I was arriving at them. Turn a corner of your mind, and there you are! There you are, where you want and need to be, without knowing you were journeying there, without knowing, even, that you needed and wanted to be there. Your mind tells you: I have figured it all out, it says, so to speak. Says, indeed! I have figured it all out: these are the conclusions you have come to, have needed to come to. Trust me! These are the proper conclusions. Here it *is;* this is how it is going to be; this is the future.

GILLIAN

Aahhhh!

JACK

Please! And . . . and I sit there, and tears come, for it is so painful, and so sweet, and so . . . emptying. And so I rise from my desk, returning to myself as I rise, and I close the door behind me, gently, and I know I drive home—though that is all mist. I come in here to you, where you are reading. And you look up from your book. And then . . . "I'm leaving you," I say.

GILLIAN *(After a long pause; softly)*

Are you quite done?

JACK

Yes; I think so.

GILLIAN

I *see.*

JACK

Have you listened at all?

GILLIAN

Oh, yes.

JACK

I mean . . . really listened. You can't be drunk yet.

GILLIAN

I wouldn't know.
(Briefly vulnerable)
Would I? I mean . . . not knowing, would I?

JACK

In any event . . .
(Leaves it unfinished)

GILLIAN

Lovely speech.

JACK

Thank you.

GILLIAN

Honest . . .

JACK

Thank you.

GILLIAN

Simple, if flowery . . .

JACK *(Shrugs)*

Well, *you* know . . .

GILLIAN

. . . an attempt at what might be referred to as . . . troof.

JACK

What?

GILLIAN

Troof! An attempt at troof! T-R-O-O-F. Troof.

JACK

You mock everything, don't you?

GILLIAN *(Rising to it now)*

What do you want? What do you expect . . . riveted attention? Hand-folded, eye-wide, mouth-ajar attention!? And then what!? A hand out to pat you sympathetically on the wrists!? "I understand; I understand." Yes? Fuck you!

JACK

You *are* drunk.

GILLIAN

"Don't leave me, precious; I . . . I'll be nothing without you."

JACK

Forget it!

GILLIAN

Fuck yourself! "Don't weave poor widda me! What wid I be wivout great big wu!?"

JACK

I said: forget it!!

GILLIAN

"Tell me 'u wuv me! Tell me I am your own. Hah!

(Heavy mock)

Walk with me; talk with me; tell me I am your own. Hah! Asshole!

JACK

Drunk as a . . . at least you're a cheap date.

GILLIAN

You'll find out!

JACK *(Sighs)*

I dare say.

GILLIAN

Awwww; poor baby! Going through a great big crisis and she isn't there to help?

JACK

Forget it. Just . . . forget it.

GILLIAN

You're not dealing with your run-of-the-mill lady. You leave me you're giving up something pretty special.

JACK

Sure sure.

GILLIAN

Have I gotten too old for you? Too . . . ripe? Are you not up to me anymore? Do I *frighten* you? Are you suddenly taken with men? It happens. Do you lust for your sister? You did when you were ten, you told me. Are you impotent . . . as of the day before yesterday? Have you forgotten who you are? Who *I* am? Who you were I was? Is tomorrow Wednesday? What*ever* is the matter?

(Waits)

No? Nothing?

(Pause. JACK begins slow, deliberate applause. GILLIAN smiles, bows, spreads her arms, curtsies, spreads her arms again; hold it)

JACK

Brava.

GILLIAN

Thank you, thank you.

JACK

Quite a performance.

GILLIAN

Thank you.

JACK *(Sighs; shakes his head)*

All we've been through together—the deaths, the losses . . .

GILLIAN

Don't start.

JACK

Your father's awful dying, that cancer, that . . .

GILLIAN

Stop it!

JACK

After all of that . . . that sharing . . . we come to this? And you don't understand me?

GILLIAN

I understand you!

JACK

No, no, you *don't;* you can't.

GILLIAN

Jesus Christ, you didn't come home here this afternoon to share anything;
you didn't come home here this afternoon to be understood; you came
home here this afternoon to make an announcement and then get out as
fast as you could!

JACK

There are some things that are facts; there are some things we don't
understand but the gut tells us . . .!

GILLIAN

Oh . . . bullshit!

JACK

Yes; well. I think I'll go now.

GILLIAN

NO!!

JACK

Oh, yes.

GILLIAN

You will *not* leave me.

JACK

I have *left* you.

GILLIAN

You will *not!*

JACK

I shall move to a hotel . . . isn't that how one does it?
    (*Momentary self-disgust*)

Jesus!
   (Back)
Isn't that how it's done? I move to a hotel, taking a small bag of irrelevancies with me? I return when I know you're out and pack more sensibly? We agree on a lawyer and let him redefine our life together—

GILLIAN

Yeah, sure!

JACK

. . . We divide our substance; we de-Siamese ourselves into our empty entities . . .

GILLIAN

As the man said: nobody ever talked like that.

JACK

Do be still. We surface, finally, break through the murk—the oozy weeds, poor Billy . . .

GILLIAN

Melville.

JACK

What?. . . Yes . . . we surface finally.

GILLIAN

You're not up to this. Rhetoric is beyond you.

JACK

Yes. Well. You may be right.
   (Rises, if JACK *has been sitting)*
Well.

GILLIAN *(Eyes narrowing)*

Yes?

JACK

Now I go for my little bag, open the drawer where we keep the irrelevancies, scoop up a double armful . . .

GILLIAN

You're not going anywhere.
   (GILLIAN *moves to the bedroom)*

JACK

. . . dump them in, zip it up, look around, sigh . . .

GILLIAN*(Dismissive)*

Why don't you just shut up.

JACK

. . . sigh, wonder, for just an instant, if perhaps the reason is not the final madness . . .

GILLIAN

I said, shut up.

JACK

. . . straighten up, pick up the bag and . . . exit.
(JACK *moves to wherever the bedroom may be*)

GILLIAN

Sit down.

JACK

Excuse me. You're blocking me.
(JACK *moves to one side;* GILLIAN *blocks him*)
I said, you're blocking me.
(JACK *moves to the other side;* GILLIAN *blocks him*)
You're *blocking* me!

GILLIAN

I'll block you!

JACK (*Grabs her by the shoulders*)

Get out of my . . .

GILLIAN

(*Fights to get his hands off of her*)
God . . . damn . . . you!
(*Note: Now begins a serious physical fight, during which* GILLIAN *slaps him hard,* JACK *slaps her hard,* JACK *pushes her out of the way,* GILLIAN *grabs him from behind, they struggle, they fall on the floor, they roll over on top of one another,* JACK *rises,* GILLIAN *grabs him by the leg, dragging him down again,* GILLIAN *gets on top of him, pummels him,* JACK *strikes her,* GILLIAN *falls,* JACK *sits on her arms,* GILLIAN *knees him in the groin, they try to strangle each other, striking at each other, throwing each other around, trying to escape, trying to kill. Naturally, all this will have to be choreographed, to the possibilities of the actors, to the limits of practicality. During it, the following lines will be said, and some others may be said, as required—either repeats or extensions*)

JACK

I'm leaving you!

GILLIAN

You will not leave me!

JACK

It's over! Get it through your head!

GILLIAN

You can't take a life together . . .

JACK

When things are done they are done!

GILLIAN

You stupid, vapid—OW!

JACK

OW!

GILLIAN

I'll kill you rather than let you . . .

JACK

Don't you dare do that . . . OW!

(And so on, and so forth. In any event, they both end up on the floor, winded, wounded. Be sure the fight has grown in intensity and has not been too brief. Finally: Up on one elbow. Can there be blood from his nose, say?)

Well.

GILLIAN

(Slowly to a sitting position. Can there be blood from her mouth)

Yes; well.

JACK

Are you alive?

GILLIAN

I believe so. You?

JACK

Yes; I think so.

(Silence; heavy breathing)

GILLIAN

You're pretty good.

JACK

So are you.

GILLIAN

Sorry about the knee.

JACK

You really get a man where he lives.

GILLIAN

That may be the problem.

JACK

Oh?

GILLIAN

You filth.

JACK

Don't.
    (*Pause*)
Well . . . are you willing to admit this is serious?

GILLIAN

Yes; all right; yes, it's serious.

JACK

I'm leaving you.

GILLIAN

So it would seem.

JACK

You almost killed me.

GILLIAN

I *did* not.

JACK

Yes; you did; you tried.

GILLIAN (*Making little of it*)

I did *not*.

JACK

And you scratched me.

GILLIAN

Awwwww!

JACK

And you bit me.

GILLIAN (*Laughs*)

I *did* not.

JACK

Fanged right in. I'll probably get hydrophobia.

GILLIAN

Thanks! Get a shot; get ten. *Is* that the same as rabies?

JACK

Is what?

GILLIAN

Is hydrophobia?

JACK

Yes.
   (Afterthought)
I *think* so.

GILLIAN

Serves you right—coming home like that, pulling this crap on me.

JACK

It is not crap; it is all true. I'm leaving you.

GILLIAN

I shall pretend otherwise.

JACK

What *good* will it do you?

GILLIAN *(Cold)*

It will allow me to avoid considering that I am being—what is the term?—
"left . . . in the lurch?", left, however, by someone less than the gesture
demands.

JACK *(Sighs)*

All right.

GILLIAN *(Colder)*

If we are to be *left* it should be by someone we shall *miss*, someone whose
leaving will produce a vacancy not only in our bed but in our heart, as they
call it.

JACK

You'll miss me.

GILLIAN

I have missed you for years, and so why not now, you mean?

JACK

Leave off.

GILLIAN *(Colder)*

If I am to be left alone—temporarily, I should imagine, knowing my
. . . charms—it should be by someone I shall *miss*; it should not be
by someone so . . . *small*, whose value is so *little*, about whom I could
not care *less*, whose departure will not bother me in the *least*. You
are . . . *nothing*.

JACK *(Such a rational request)*

Why . . . don't you just . . . *stop* it.

GILLIAN *(Relentless)*

I have lived my life reasonably well. I have been a better wife than you have deserved. I have "hewn" to you far more than you have "hewn" to me. I have seen and denied seeing; I have comforted you when I thought you were despicable and unworthy of comfort. I have smiled at your side when I thought you were a fool and deserving of abandonment.

JACK *(Heavy sigh)*

Oh, God.

GILLIAN

I have held you in the night when you have bolted up in bed in your sleep—HANH!—when you've bolted up still asleep in one of your night-mares. I've held you, comforted you, eased you back down, stroked you back into peaceful sleep, looked at you, known you were . . .

(Shakes her head)

. . . not enough; that perhaps no one is enough.

(Up from comforting to hard)

Certainly not you. So, go on; leave me; *I'll* survive it. You're not big enough for the gesture. You're . . . *nothing.*

JACK

How odd, my *problem* has always been one of too *much.*

GILLIAN

Sure sure.

JACK

Too much, yes. Always, when I was young, at least. Very young. Too beautiful, too lucky, too this, too that.

GILLIAN

Sure sure.

(Suddenly)

Too what!? Too beautiful!?

JACK

(Matter-offact, as if GILLIAN *were mad to question it)*

Yes.

GILLIAN

You? Too beautiful?

JACK

You didn't know me when I was fifteen. When we met I was still very . . . handsome, I suppose . . .

(GILLIAN *starts laughing*)

I was! Stop that!

(GILLIAN *does*)

I pay proper attention to you: you pay proper attention to me.

GILLIAN (*Not at all*)

Sorry.

JACK

You wouldn't call me ugly now—good face, not too much belly, nothing a little more self-respect wouldn't fix. You called me handsome on our second date: "My God, you're handsome!" you said.

GILLIAN (*Wistful*)

I must have wanted something.

JACK

"My God, you're handsome," you said. 'Thank you," I recall replying.

GILLIAN

Taking your due?

JACK

Well . . . something.

GILLIAN (*Triste*)

How have I put up with you for all these years?

JACK

I *was* . . . *handsome*. We were quite a couple: you . . . pert, me . . .

GILLIAN

. . . ravishing?

JACK

Something like that. But at fifteen . . . My God! Didn't I ever show you the photos?

GILLIAN

I guess you just can't have everything. You poor thing.

JACK

I did. Be still.

GILLIAN (*Too much*)

Oh, Jesus!

JACK

I used to glow; they said I glowed.

GILLIAN

Of course.

JACK

I don't doubt it.

GILLIAN

Light up the sky.

JACK

I don't doubt it; I glow now—in private, of course, when I'm by myself.

GILLIAN

(Examining something on her skirt)
Sure sure sure.

JACK

I mean, I'm not going to go around glowing for . . . just anybody. Why waste your glow?

GILLIAN *(Overly enthusiastic)*

Right!

JACK

A glow is special, and you never know how long it's going to last. I mean, you're going along, minding your own business, and you've been glowing now and again—nothing special, not so as to stop traffic, or anything.

GILLIAN *(Bored)*

I understand.
   (Under her breath)
Jesus!

JACK

. . . but you have been glowing, and one day somebody comes up to you— someone you've glowed for, maybe a year or so before—and says: "Glow for me again."

GILLIAN

"You haven't glowed for me in the longest time?"

JACK *(Ignoring her as best he can)*

"Glow for me; glow for me again."

GILLIAN *(Sweet/sour)*

"Little glowworm?"

JACK

What can you do? I mean, you can't say, "Out of my sight! *I'm* not going to glow for *you;* I've *glowed* for you." You can't say that.

GILLIAN

Of course not.

JACK

People deserve better than that. So you say to yourself; OK, why not? And so you try to glow for them. . . . But you can't; there just isn't any glow.

GILLIAN

Glowed out, eh?

JACK

Well, not necessarily, maybe just for now—for *then*, maybe just for then. It'll probably come back, maybe you just don't have any glow in ya right then, as they say.

GILLIAN

Sort of like some other things.

JACK

Hm?

GILLIAN *(Louder)*

Sort of like a lot of other things—ya just don't have it in ya right now.
    (Indicates)
The book is full of it.

JACK *(Too loud)*

What are you *talking* about?

GILLIAN

Success and failure; good times and bad. Some nights you're Mr. Stud himself, and other times ya just don't have it in ya.

JACK

God, you're a vulgar woman I was talking about *glowing!*

GILLIAN *(Rueful smile)*

So was I.

JACK

Anyway . . . I used to glow.

GILLIAN *(Bored and dismissive)*

Sure sure.

JACK

I *did.* I was very special: dogs would fall in love with me, leave home, lie about my family's house and moon, wait for me; bicycles would appear, wheel themselves into the yard. . . . Oh, *God,* I have memories!

GILLIAN *(Very patronizing)*

Yes, you *do!* You have a secret little treasure trove of them, along with your dance cards, your first rubber, three broken hearts . . .

JACK

. . . a wrapped-up ring finger . . .

GILLIAN

. . . the jock strap of the boy you were in love with when you were thirteen but wouldn't . . . a what!?

JACK

A wrapped-up ring finger.

GILLIAN (*After a beat*)

There's no point in talking to you. You'll say anything.
　(*Pause*)
How did you know it was a ring finger?

JACK

You mean . . . was the ring *on* it, or something like that?

GILLIAN

Or something like that.

JACK

Or maybe there was pale where the ring had been?

GILLIAN

*Some*thing like that.

JACK

Yes; well . . . something like that.

GILLIAN

You'll say anything.
　(*Shakes her head*)
Nothing changes.

JACK

Oh, now . . .

GILLIAN (*Shaking her head*)

You would *think* . . . that after a *while* . . . that someone would learn a little *some*thing . . .

JACK

Be careful of a little knowledge.

GILLIAN

Nothing changes.

JACK

Everything changes.

GILLIAN

Which is therefore the same thing, blah blah blah.

JACK

A little knowledge, et cetera.

GILLIAN

What?

JACK

"A little knowledge is a dangerous thing," et cetera. Pope.

GILLIAN

Name the spring!

JACK

What?

GILLIAN

Name the *spring!* If a little knowledge is so fucking dangerous, name the spring from which we are supposed to dip in and drink. Go on; name it.

JACK

A little knowledge is a dangerous thing . . .
    (Remembering)
Drink . . . drink deep or taste not the . . . what?. . . from the something spring.

GILLIAN

Ha!

JACK

Drink deep or taste not the . . . shit!

GILLIAN

HA!

JACK

It will *come* to me. It always does; these things always do.

GILLIAN

You're damned right a little knowledge is a dangerous thing.

JACK *(Ugly)*

It will *come* to me!

GILLIAN *(Casual)*

What was it wrapped in?

JACK

Hm? What?

GILLIAN

What was it wrapped in? The ring finger; a wrapped-up ring finger, you said.

JACK

How would *I* know!? I made it up.

GILLIAN

Of course you made it up. But what was it wrapped in?

JACK *(Annoyed)*

I don't know—silver foil, gauze, newspaper?! I don't know. Hibernian!!

GILLIAN

Newspaper?

JACK

Hibernian!! A little knowledge is a dangerous thing. Drink deep or taste not the Hiber . . . no, that's wrong.

GILLIAN *(Joy)*

Hibernian spring!! Sunshine and breaking buds in Ireland?

JACK

I *said* I was wrong.

GILLIAN *(Glee)*

Hibernian spring!!

JACK *(Really angry)*

Drop it!

GILLIAN *(Little girl voice)*

Yes, Daddy.
     (Normal)
Newspaper? The ring finger wrapped up in newspaper? Like a herring?

JACK

I don't *know!* I made it up; or I dreamed it; maybe I dreamed it.

GILLIAN

One of your nightmares?

JACK

I don't know. I made it up; or I dreamed it.

GILLIAN

I had a dream the other night.

JACK

Oh?

GILLIAN

Yes; I dreamt you loved me.

JACK *(Long pause)*

I *do.*

GILLIAN (*Noncommittal*)

Yes. I know.

JACK

I *do*.

GILLIAN

Well, you may *have*. Oh, what a wangled teb we weave.

JACK

A what?

GILLIAN

A teb; a wangled teb.

JACK

What is *that?*

GILLIAN

You figure it out.

JACK (*Regret*)

There's so much good we've had between us.

GILLIAN

Let it *alone*.

JACK

No!

GILLIAN

Let it *alone!*

JACK

No!! . . . Our first date? That was one of the good times.

GILLIAN (*Far away*)

Was that good? It . . . slips my mind.

JACK

It *was* one of the good times. No, it doesn't.

GILLIAN

May *be*. Was that the awful orchid corsage?

JACK (*Smiles*)

Yes. The awful orchid corsage.

GILLIAN

Why *did* we ever date?—all I knew about you?

JACK

Because *of* it, probably. There were four of us on that date.

GILLIAN

Oh?

JACK

You; me; and the people we pretended to be—were pretending to be. Crowded in that little car, jockeying and all.

GILLIAN

I think we probably should have married *them*—the two we were pretending to be.

JACK

Or, they should have married each other? Perhaps they did.

GILLIAN

I wonder how it went with them. I wonder did it begin fine and stay that way—get better even? Are they your stock happy couple, or was it failure, prison, cancer, and all the rest? Lucky, in any event. At least nobody came home one day and said, "Hi there! I'm leaving you.

JACK

It hasn't been that bad!

(GILLIAN *snorts*)

It hasn't.

(GILLIAN *snorts*)

We've had a good run.

(GILLIAN *snorts*)

Think about the good times; think how lucky we've *been*. We *have* been!

(*Ibid.*)

Concentrate on *them*.

GILLIAN

(*Pretending to try to concentrate*)

On the good times!

JACK

Come on!

GILLIAN (*Grudgingly at first*)

One of the good times?

JACK

Please?

GILLIAN

Ah! Wasn't that something!? Do you remember Venice?

JACK

Of *course* I remember Venice. Nobody *can't* remember Venice; it can't be done.

GILLIAN

No no; I mean the time in Venice *I* remember.

JACK

The first time? The time in the snow—in the gondola with the snow in our hair?

GILLIAN

No no.

JACK

The gondolier muffled like . . . like Charon?

GILLIAN

No no.

JACK

The Grand Canal the River Styx; the silence . . .

GILLIAN

No!

JACK

And the dislocation of it—the amazement—made me wonder why the snow was holding to the buildings—the palaces—but melting on the streets.

GILLIAN *(Giggles)*

. . . on the canals!

JACK

Yes, why the snow was melting on the water!

GILLIAN

Yes.

 (Tiny pause)

No; not that time.

JACK *(A trifle sad)*

Not that time? The tapestried walls of our room beside the opera?

GILLIAN

No.

JACK

The great four-poster bed?

GILLIAN

No! The *other* time.

JACK *(Thinks)*

The time of the floods, fall, the early floods, wading knee-deep in San Marco when the tray floated by, a full espresso and a half-eaten pastry?

GILLIAN

No; the other time.

JACK (*At a loss*)

There *was* no other time.

GILLIAN (*Gay*)

Of course there was!

JACK (*Puzzled*)

No.

GILLIAN

It was an April—before the tourists and the stink—clear; a little windy, but clear.

JACK

I don't remember.

GILLIAN (*Gay*)

Of course you do.

JACK (*Very matter of fact*)

No; no, I don't.

GILLIAN

I arrived *before* you; I don't know where you'd been . . . somewhere; it was one of those times we joined up.

JACK

(*Clear; quiet. Does* GILLIAN *hear him?*)

There was no other time.

GILLIAN

You flew in; I waited for you at the hotel, in our room, bed down, negligee . . .

JACK

Twice. That's all.

GILLIAN (*Cajoling*)

Noooooo . . .

JACK (*Brisk*)

Yes; twice; that's all.

GILLIAN

I waited for you—deshabille—wine and a baby gorgonzola, late afternoon, still warm, bells beginning . . .

JACK (*Sort of sad*)

No.

GILLIAN *(Happy)*

Yes! I heard you in the downstairs hall, the desk; I heard you on the stairs and into the room. I pretended to be asleep; I heard you put your bag down; I heard your shirt rustle: I heard you unzip your trousers . . .

JACK *(Matter of fact)*

It wasn't me.

GILLIAN

I opened my eyes to your advancing form, and . . . no, it *wasn't* you, was it?

JACK

No; it wasn't.

GILLIAN *(Pause)*

I'm sorry. I could have *sworn.*

JACK

I told you: no.
  (Long pause)

GILLIAN

Well . . .
  (Matter of fact)
Oops, as they say.

JACK

Don't say a word.

GILLIAN

Clearly I *remembered* it as you? *Wanted* it to be? Wished it *were?* No?

JACK

You're not helping.
  (Turns; walks away)

GILLIAN *(So simple; so contrite)*

I'm . . . sorry.

JACK *(Pause)*

Sometimes it hurts; sometimes it doesn't matter at all.

GILLIAN

Oh, come on! What are you playing . . . injured party now?!

JACK *(Weary)*

All right.

GILLIAN

Betrayed husband!?

JACK *(Anger rising)*

I said all *right*.

GILLIAN

Faithful provider done in by vagrant . . .

JACK

I said! Enough!

GILLIAN *(Hard)*

I said I was sorry! I was! Take it while you can!
    (Unhappy afterthought)
Take what you can get.

JACK *(Pause)*

I can't stand it when it's you.

GILLIAN *(Weary)*

Oh, God!

JACK

When it's me I understand it and I accept it.

GILLIAN

Sure! Of course!

JACK

I *expect* it of me.

GILLIAN

Macho *man.*

JACK

No! I *expect* it of me. I know what I am, how I am. You know I cheat; I know you know I cheat. It hurts me that you know it; it hurts me that when I'm off you think I'm cheating; it hurts me that you hurt, that you have enough experience of me to suspect, whether I am or not . . . hurt by probability.

GILLIAN

    (Simple, nonrancorous truth)
Once is all it takes.

JACK

And it means nothing! None of it means . . . it means nothing! None of it! What kind of animal *are* we!? We do what instinct tells us—all of us. There *are* monogamous creatures—a few birds, I think, one type of something-or-other, some type of . . . weasel, or something, but that's what instinct tells them. Instinct tells *us*, tells *us*, *too.* Instinct tells us when the mind and the appetite get together it's then time to do it, and with or to whatever is nearby and to be fancied.

GILLIAN *(Dry)*

I love you when you're like this.

JACK

Why does "I love you" mean "I vow not to put this into that?"

GILLIAN

. . . or vice versa.

JACK

. . . or vice versa. "I will not let that be put into this."

GILLIAN *(Looking off)*

No reason *I* can think of.

JACK

I mean . . . what?

GILLIAN

. . . save love, honor and cherish.

JACK

Well, *there* you have something. Love!? I love you, I love you deeply, sadly and deeply, and I am—oh, God! the horrid word—I am "unfaithful" to you. Not that you are not to me. I *honor* you: I will not permit you to be dishonored—it is one of the things I would probably kill for. Cherish? Well, you *know* I cherish you.

GILLIAN

Me, the Mercedes and the free play of your instincts. It won't do. You're not even sophistic: you're dense.

JACK

The joy is all gone from it. The relief, the pleasure of the relief, of the moment, all that's still there, but no joy. Joy is all gone. I do it by habit . . . reflex. Sometimes I look up from it and say, "Why am I here? Am I . . . am I doing this for pleasure? Or by rote. Rutting by rote?"

GILLIAN

Do shut up.

JACK

Hm?

GILLIAN

Do . . . shut . . . up.

JACK

Once . . . once I turned, looked into a face, said: "Why am I here?" Smile; "Comfort," the face said; "To pass the time less . . . emptily?"

GILLIAN *(Very casual)*

Is it always a woman?

JACK *(Not avoiding; preoccupied)*

I wish to be alone in it. I can't stand it when it's *you.* "My wife is married, *I'm* not," a man said to me one time; I was sixteen, a summer job. He was fat, a large man and fat, three chins. "My wife's married, *I'm* not." A wink and a leer. God, who would have fucked him?!

GILLIAN *(Still casual)*

There's someone to fuck everyone. Those don't get it don't want it, or surely don't want it from those they can get. The trick is to want what you can get.

JACK

I don't *want* these people; I have them without wanting them—without wanting *them.* I want relief and comfort and company and coming; and . . . it means nothing.

GILLIAN *(Long pause)*

To whom?

JACK *(Long pause)*

Hm?

GILLIAN *(Long pause)*

Nothing. I'm sorry about Venice.

JACK

Oh?

GILLIAN

I *did* think it was you. I wasn't setting you up. I *did* think it was you when I remembered it. Not at the *time,* you understand: I'm not careless—or near-sighted. A face above me, huffing and all, I can . . . I know who and all, I can . . . I know who it is—the small of a back, a cock, one knows these things in the dark.

JACK *(Truly interested)*

Really?

GILLIAN

Oh, yes. Tactile. The blind have it; women, too.

JACK

Really!

GILLIAN *(Snorts)*

God, you'll believe anything!

JACK *(Defensive; little boy)*

Sometimes we *want* to.

GILLIAN (*Thinks*)

My God, it's my birthday next week. I'll be . . . and what have you gotten for me? What will you have gotten for me . . . my freedom? A ruby ring? Contrition? Two tickets for something I said I didn't want to see? Stay tuned! Do you still care, by the way?

JACK (*Preoccupied*)

What? Pardon?

GILLIAN (*Matter of fact*)

Do you still *care?* Does cause and effect still interest you?

(JACK *shakes his head at her with wonder*)

Do you wonder at the progress any more, or do you assume the pattern works—still works—that whatever damage was begun goes about its business? Proceeds? I ask you this because you must have thought about it some time . . .

JACK (*So weary*)

What are you talking about?

GILLIAN

I mean . . . when you first hurt me—when you first hurt me that I knew you were doing it—you must have known you *had* . . . you must have known you were doing it; and with *what?* pleasure? rue? regret, even?

JACK

You never listen; you humor me; you think you know what everything means—everything I say. I suppose I mean you think you've heard all the resonances. You haven't, you know. You've heard all you're *going* to hear, though, I suppose.

GILLIAN

No! *You* never listen! Your mind is always cocked for something else, something; you don't know what, but something. I see it in your eyes; I see you not listen.

JACK

Animal! Animal Instinct!

GILLIAN (*Weary, quietly*)

Oh, Christ, not that again.

JACK

Instinct tells us everything: that if there are rules run counter to our gut, then *they* are wrong; we are animals, and we smell the kill and the rest is fine unless it gets in the way. We understand it *all* when we become animals, when we give in to it—standing at night in the forest, in the snow when we become the wolf: *then* we understand it. Man *is* different; man *is* the lordly beast. We know these things by gut; when passion dies . . .

GILLIAN (*Once again; weary*)

Passion in a marriage never dies; it changes. When the passion of passion wanes there are all the others waiting to rush in—the passion of loss, of hatred, the passion of indifference; the ultimate, the finally satisfying passion of nothing. You know nothing of passion; you confuse rut with everything.

JACK (*Weary shake of the head*)

No; no, I don't. No, *we* don't: we . . . hunters and killers.

GILLIAN

You know nothing of . . . enough.

JACK (*Energized*)

I have discovered . . . now, don't laugh at me.

GILLIAN

I'm *not*. I *won't*, rather.

JACK

Well, just . . . *don't*. What I have discovered is this: nothing is enough.

GILLIAN (*Under her breath*)

Jesus Christ!

JACK

Please?

(*A hand up*)

Please? All right?

(GILLIAN *nods, or shrugs*)

Nothing is enough . . . for a life, I mean. No matter the challenges, the variety of challenge—contradiction, even—no matter *what* . . . variety or constancy, we come to the moment we understand, if we are *honest* . . .

GILLIAN

. . . with our*selves* . . . or is this not that part?

JACK

This may be one of the last times we'll ever have a chance to try this hard so . . . please be good?

GILLIAN (*Hopeless*)

Sure.

JACK

Life fills us with . . . such a sense of choice—that everything is out there to be done, to be proved: that we live forever, always have forever in front of us . . . to do everything! And we do, and we do not . . . and it all goes.

GILLIAN (*Comforting*)

You do have a gloomy mind. You foolish man with your foolish gloomy mind.

JACK(*A hand up; sad*)

Not now. We come to the moment we understand that no matter what we have done—forget *not* done, forget the . . . avoiders!—no matter what we have done, no matter how satisfying, how brave, how . . . "good," no matter what, *or* where, *or* with whom, we come to the moment we understand that nothing has made any difference. We stare into the dark and know that nothing is enough, *has* been enough, *could* be enough, that there is *no way* not to have . . . wasted the light; that the failure is built into us, that the greatest awareness gives to the greatest dark. That I'm going to lose you, for example—*have* lost you—no more, no less than fingers slipping from each other, that I'm going to lose *me*, *have* lost me—the light . . . losing the light.

GILLIAN (*Pause*)

Oh, poor darling. You know it, too. Then why rush it?

JACK (*Sad; a wry smile*)

Awareness is all?

GILLIAN

Well, it's certainly enough. What would we *do?* What are we supposed to *do,* for God's sake? Are we supposed to get *married* again? *I* can't have children anymore; I can't make a full marriage: I'm shaped to you. You can take up with some chippie, I suppose . . .

JACK

Stop about chippies! This is not about chippies!

GILLIAN (*Not to be deterred*)

You can take up with some chippie, pretend it's love when it's really desperate, and ludicrous and . . .

JACK

Stop.

GILLIAN

You can . . . kid yourself, pretend you don't know how sad you look, how . . . pathetic.

JACK

I said, stop!

GILLIAN

We're not a hundred; we're not "oooooollllllldddd"; we've got some life left in us—some half-life, maybe—but . . . we're thirty years into this . . .

JACK

I know, I know.

GILLIAN

. . . thirty years into knowing what marriage is all *about*—and what it is *not* all about. We *know* things! This is not our *first* marriage, friend; this is *marriage*.

JACK (*Dogmatic*)

Everything has its duration; everything has a time when it goes on for the sake of going on, and . . .

GILLIAN

You're too smart to kid yourself, you know.

JACK (*Rage*)

I *know* I'm smart!

GILLIAN (*Offhand*)

You're so *dumb*.

JACK (*Softer*)

You're impossible.

GILLIAN (*Glum*)

And you're hopeless.
    (*Tiny pause*)
Play games with *your* life; don't play 'em with *mine*.

JACK (*Stentorian; heavy irony*)

Irrevocably intertwined, he cannot make a move without it touches her—nor can she begin a thought without it . . .

GILLIAN (*Toneless*)

Go fuck yourself. Is this really it then? All the years of it? Is this really it? Has everything been leading to this? Is it really mud pies we've been making all this time?

JACK

I suppose.

GILLIAN

Then I hope what's-his-name was right, that marriage does *not* make two people one, it makes two people two—a good marriage, a useful marriage—makes individuals! That when two people choose to be together though they're strong enough to be alone, *then* you have a good marriage. Has ours been a good marriage? Are we two? Clearly we've not become each other; we've become ourselves—I guess we have, and maybe for the first time. With any luck we've not compensated, we've complemented. Well, at least that's how it's supposed to go. Aren't we lucky!? Aren't we wise, rational people!?

JACK (*Preoccupied*)

Yes. Of course.

GILLIAN
Nothing is certain in this world, *is* it? A lot of things are predictable—you, for example, and everything about you—but very little is certain.
(*A silence;* JACK *looks out "window"*)
What?
(*Silence*)
What is it? What? What is it?

JACK
It's time for the garden; it *would* be time for the garden.

GILLIAN
Yes! Go dig the garden; put the garden in.
(JACK *shakes his head*)
Yes! Put it *in!*

JACK (*Hopeless*)
Don't you know what hopeless means?
(*Silence. Rage*)
WHY WOULD I PUT IN A FUCKING GARDEN!!!???

GILLIAN (*Gentle; quiet*)
You put in a garden every year; you always have; it's hopeless every year—everything: the garden, going on, everything. You put in a garden; you do it every year. It is . . . what you do.
(*Leans toward him; loud whisper*)
That is what you do.
(*A silence*)

JACK
Oh, Lord, I long to live by instinct, not just respond to it from time to time. I no longer know whether . . .

GILLIAN
Just . . . scatter some seeds.

JACK (*A sigh*)
Oh, there are times I wish . . . you and I, I mean . . . there are times I wish.

GILLIAN (*Gentle*)
Something will come up.
(*A long silence*)

JACK (*Finally; no emotion*)
I'm leaving you.

GILLIAN

(Long silence; finally; no emotion)

Yes. I know.

JACK *(Long silence; little boy)*

I *am.*

GILLIAN *(Long silence; gentle)*

I know; I know you are.

(They sit, silence; no movement)

CURTAIN

Three Tall Women

Three Tall Women was originally produced by Franz Schafranek and American Producing Director Glyn O'Malley, at Vienna's English Theatre in Vienna, Austria, on June 14, 1991. It was directed by Edward Albee; the assistant director was Eva Weidermann; the set design was by Claire Cahill; the costume design was by Ruth Bell: the lighting design was by Hans Georg Jobst and the production coordinator was Paul Van Der Lubbe. The cast was as follows:

MYRA CARTER *as* THE OLD WOMAN

KATHLEEN BUTLER *as* THE MIDDLE-AGED WOMAN

CYNTHIA BASSHAM *as* THE YOUNG WOMAN

HOWARD NIGHTINGALL *as* THE YOUNG MAN

Three Tall Women received its American premiere on July 30, 1992, at River Arts Repertory, Woodstock, NY. The same case moved to the Vineyard Theatre (Douglas Aibel, Artistic Director; Jon Nakagawa, Managing Director) in New York City, in January, 1994, and later moved to The Promenade Theatre (produced by Elizabeth I. McCann, Jeffrey Ash and Daryl Roth in association with Leavitt/Fox/Manges). It was directed by Lawrence Sacharow; the set design was by James Noone; the costume design was by Muriel Stockdale; the lighting design was by Phil Monat. The General Manager was Brent Peek Productions, the Company Manager was Roy Gabay, and the production stage manager was Elizabeth M. Berther, and later R. Wade Jackson. The cast was as follows:

MYRA CARTER *as* A

MARIAN SELDES *as* B

JORDON BAKER *as* C

MICHAEL RHODES *as* THE BOY

CHARACTERS

A
A very old woman; thin, autocratic, proud, as together as the ravages of time will allow. Nails scarlet, hair nicely done, wears makeup. Lovely nightgown and dressing gown

B
Looks rather as A *would have at 52; plainly dressed*

C
Looks rather as B *would have at 26*

THE BOY
23 or so; preppy dress (jacket, tie, shirt, jeans, loafers, etc)

SETTING

A "wealthy" bedroom, French in feeling. Pastels, with blue predominant. A bed upstage center, with a small bench at its foot. Lacy pillows, a lovely spread. Nineteenth-century French paintings. Two light armchairs, beautifully covered in silk. If there is a window, silk swags. Pastel carpeted floor. Two doors, one left, one right. Archways for both.

ACT ONE

(At rise, A is in the left armchair, B is in the right one, C on the bed-foot bench

It is afternoon.

Some silence)

A

(An announcement from nowhere; to no one in particular)
I'm ninety-one.

B (Pause)

Is that so?

A (Pause)

Yes.

C (Small smile)

You're ninety-*two*.

A (Longer pause; none too pleasant)

Be that as it *may*.

B (To C)

Is that so?

C (Shrugs; indicates papers)

Says so here.

B (Pause; stretching)

Well . . . what does it matter?

C

Vanity is amazing.

B

So's forgetting.

A (General)

I'm ninety-one.

B (Accepting sigh)

OK.

C *(Smaller smile)*

You're ninety-*two*.

B *(Unconcerned)*

Oh . . . let it alone.

C

No! It's important. Getting things . . .

B

It doesn't matter!

C *(Sotto voce)*

It does to *me*.

A *(Pause)*

I know because he says, "You're exactly thirty years older than I am; I know how old I am because I know how old *you* are, and if you ever forget how old you are ask me how old *I* am, and then you'll know."

(Pause)

Oh, he's said that a lot.

C

What if he's wrong?

A

(From a distance; curiously lighter, higher voice)

What?

B

Let it *be*.

C *(Still to A)*

What if he's wrong? What if he's not thirty years younger than you?

A *(Oddly loud, tough)*

You'd think he'd know how old he is!

C

No, I mean . . . what if he's wrong about how old *you* are.

A *(Pause)*

Don't be silly. How couldn't he be thirty years younger than me when I'm thirty years older than he is? He's said it over and over.

(Pause)

Every time he comes to see me. What is today?

B

It's *[whatever day it is in reality]*.

A

You see?!

c (*A bit as if to a child*)
Well, one of you might be wrong, and it might not be him.

B (*Small sneer*)
He.

c (*Quick smile*)
Yes; I know.

A
Don't be stupid. *What* is it? *What day* is it?

B
It's [*Ibid.*].

A (*Shakes her head*)
No.

c (*Interested*)
No what?

A
No it *isn't.*

B
OK.

c (*To* A)
What day do you *think* it is?

A (*Confusion*)
What day is it? What day do I . . . ?
   (*Eyes narrowing*)
Why, it's today, of course. What day do you *think* it is!?
   (*Turns to* B; *cackles*)

B
Right on, girl!

c (*Scoffs*)
What an answer! What a dumb . . .

A
Don't you talk to me that way!

c (*Offended*)
Well! I'm sorry!

A
I pay you, don't I? You can't talk to me that way.

C
In a way.

A *(A daring tone)*

What!?

C

Indirectly. You pay someone who pays me, someone who . . .

A

Well; there; you see? You can't talk to me that way.

B

She isn't *talking* to you that way.

A

What?

B

She isn't *talking* to you that way.

A *(Dismissive laugh)*

I don't know what you're talking about.
  (Pause)
Besides.
  (Silence then A *cries. They let her. It begins in self pity, proceeds to crying for crying's sake, and concludes with rage and self-loathing at having to cry. It takes quite a while)*

B *(When it's over)*

There. Feel better?

C *(Under her breath)*

Honestly.

B *(To A)*

A good cry lets it all out.

A *(Laughs; sly)*

What does a *bad* one do?
  (She laughs again; B *joins her)*

C *(Shakes her head in admiration)*

Sometimes you're so . . .

A *(Ugly; suddenly)*

What!?

C *(Tiny pause)*

Never *mind.* I was going to say something *nice.* Never *mind.*

A *(To B)*

What did she say!? She mumbles all the time.

C

I don't mumble!
   (*Annoyance at herself*)
Never mind!

A

How is anybody expected to hear what she says!?

B (*Placating*)

She didn't finish her sentence. It doesn't matter.

A (*Small, smug triumph*)

I'll *bet* it doesn't.

C (*Dogged, but not unpleasant*)

What I meant was you may have been incorrect about your age for so
long—may have made up the fiction so many years ago, though why anyone would lie about one year . . .

B (*Weary*)

Let her alone; let her have it if she wants to.

C

I will *not*.

A

Have what!?

C

Why you would lie about one *year?* I can imagine taking off ten—or *trying* to. Though more probably seven, or five—good and tricky—but *one!?*
Taking off *one year?* What kind of vanity is *that?*

B (*Clucks*)

How you go *on*.

A (*Imitation*)

How you go *on*.

C (*Purrs*)

How I go on. So, I can understand ten, or five, or seven, but not one.

B

How you *do*.

A (*To* C)

How you *do*.
   (*To* B)
How *what!?*

B

How she goes on.

A *(Cheerful)*

Yes! How you go *on!*

C *(Smile)*

Yes; I do.

A *(Suddenly, but not urgently)*

I want to go.

C

On?

A *(More urgently)*

I want go. I want to go.

B

You want to go?
     (Rises)
You want the pan? Is it number one? Do you want the pan?

A *(Embarrassed to discuss it)*

No. . . . Noooo!

B

Ah.
     (Moves to A)
All right. Can you walk?

A *(Weepy)*

I don't know!

B

Well, we'll try you. OK?
     (Indicates walker)
You want the walker?

A *(Near tears)*

I want to walk! I don't know! Anything! I have to *go!*
     (Starts to fret-weepy)

B

All right!
     (B moves A to a standing position. We discover A's left arm is in a sling, useless)

A

You're hurting me!! You're hurting me!!

B

All right; I'm being careful!

A

No, you're *not!!*

B

Yes, I am!

A

No, you're *not!!!*

B *(Angry)*

Yes, I *am.*

A

No, you're *not!*
       (On her feet, weeping, shuffling off with B's *help)*
You're trying to hurt me; you know I hurt!!

B *(To* C, *as they exit)*

Hold the fort.

C

I will. I will hold the fort.
       (Muffled exchanges offstage. C *looks toward them, shakes her head,*
       looks back down. Continued; both to herself and to be heard)
I suppose one could lie about one year—some kind of one-upmanship, a
private vengeance, perhaps, some tiny victory, maybe.
       (Shrugs)
I don't know, maybe these things get important.
       (She sits in A's *chair)*
Why can't I be nice?

B *(Re-enters)*

Made it that time.
       (Sighs)
And so it goes.

C

Not always, eh?

B

In the morning, when she wakes up she wets—a kind of greeting to the
day, I suppose: the sphincter and the cortex not in sync. Never during the
night, but *as* she wakes.

C

Good morning to the morning, eh?

B

Something to something.

C

Put a diaper on her.

B *(Shakes her head)*

She won't have it. I'm working on it, but she won't have it.

C

Rubber sheet?

B

Won't have it. Get her up, put her in the chair and she does the other. Give her a cup of coffee . . .

C

Black.

B *(Chuckles)*

Half cream and all that sugar! Three spoons! How has she lived this long? Give her her cup of coffee, put her in her chair, give her a cup of coffee and place your bets.

C *(Looks at the chair she is in)*

What chair!? *This* chair!?

B *(Laughs)*

You got it. Don't worry.

C

It must be awful.

B *(Deprecating)*

For whom?

C *(Rising to it)*

For her! You're paid. It's probably awful for you, too, but you're paid.

B.

As she never ceases to inform me . . . *and* you.

C

To begin to lose it, I mean—the control, the loss of dignity, the . . .

B

Oh, stop it! It's downhill from sixteen on! For all of us!

C

Yes, but . . .

B

What *are* you, *twenty*-something? Haven't you figured it out yet?
  (Demonstrates)

You take the breath in . . . you let it out. The first one you take in you're upside down and they slap you into it. The last one . . . well, the last one you let it all out . . . and that's it. You start . . . and then you stop. Don't be so soft. I'd like to see children learn it—have a six-year-old say, "I'm dying" and know what it means.

C

You're horrible!

B

Start in young; make 'em aware they've got only a little time. Make 'em aware that they're dying from the minute they're alive.

C

Awful!

B

Grow up! Do *you* know it? Do *you* know you're dying?

C

Well, of course, but . . .

B *(Ending it)*

Grow up.

A *(Wobbling, shuffling in)*

A person could die in there and nobody'd care.

B *(Bright)*

Done already!

A

A person could die! A person could fall down and break something! A person could die! Nobody would care!

B *(Going to her)*

Let me help you.

A *(Good arm flailing)*

Get your *hands* off me! A person could die for all anybody'd care.

C

(To herself but to be overheard)

Who is this . . . "person"? A person could do this, a person could do . . .

B

It's a figure of speech.

C *(Mildly sarcastic)*

No. Really?

B *(Not rising to it)*

So they tell me.

A (*Flailing about*)
Hold *on* to me! Do you want me to fall!? You want me to *fall!*

B
Yes, I want you to fall; I want you to fall and shatter in . . . ten pieces.

C
Or five, or seven.

A
Where's my chair!
   (*Sees it perfectly well*)
Where's my chair gone to?

B (*Playing the game*)
Goodness, where's her chair *gone* to!? Somebody's taken her *chair!*

C (*Realizing*)
What!?

A (*Does she know? Probably*)
Who's got my chair?

C (*High horse*)
I'm sorry!
   (*Gets up quickly; moves away*)
Your majesty!

B (*Placating*)
There's your chair. Do you want your pillow? Shall I get you your pillow?
   (*To* C)
Fetch her pillow.

A
I want to sit *down*.

B
Yes, yes. Here we go.
   (B *gently lowers* A *into the vacated armchair*)

C (*At bed*)
Which *pillow?*

B (*To* A)
Are you comfortable? Do you want your pillow?

A (*Petulant*)
Of *course* I'm not comfortable; of *course* I want my pillow.

C (*Still at the bed; to* B)
I don't know which one!

B (*Moving to the bed*)

It's two, actually, one for the back
  (*Takes it*)
and this one for the arm.
  (*Takes it; moves toward* A)
Here we are; lean forward.
  (*Positions back pillow*)
That's a girl.

A

My arm! My arm! Where's the pillow!?

B

Here we go.
  (*Arranges arm pillows*)
All comfy?
  (*Silence. Continued*)
All comfy?

A

What?

B

Nothing.
  (*A knowing smile to* C)

C

And so it goes?

B

Un-huh.

C

What a production.

B

You haven't seen anything.

C

I bet!

A (*To* B)

You can't just leave me in there like that. What if I fell? What if I died?

B (*Considers it; calm*)

Well . . . if you fell I'd either hear you or you'd raise a racket, and if you died what would it matter?

A

(*Pause; then she laughs; true enjoyment*)

You can say that again!

    (Amused at seeing C *not amused)*

What's the matter with you?

C

    (Small silence, until she realizes she's being talked to)

Who!? Me!?

A

Yes. You.

C

What's the *matter* with me?

B *(Amused)*

That's what she *said.*

A

That's what I *said.*

C *(Panicking a little)*

What are you all doing—ganging up on me?

B *(To* A*)*

Is that what we're doing?

A *(Enjoying it greatly)*

*May*be!

C *(To defend herself)*

There's *nothing* the matter with me.

B *(Sour smile)*

Well . . . you just *wait.*

A

What did she say?

B

She says there's nothing the matter with her—Miss Perfect over there.

C

I didn't *say* that; that's not what I . . . !!

A *(To* B; *sincerely)*

Why is she *yelling* at me!?

B

She's *not.*

C

I'm *not!*

B

Now you are.

A

You see!?
  (*Confused*)
What day is it?

B

It's [*whatever day it is in reality*].

A

Will he come today? Is today the day he comes?

B

No; not today.

A (*Whining*)

Why not!?

B (*Making nothing of it*)

Oh, he probably has something else to do; he probably has a full schedule.

A (*Teary*)

He never comes to see me, and when he does he never stays.
  (*A sudden shift in tone to hatred*)
I'll fix him; I'll fix *all* of 'em. They all think they can treat me like this. You all think you can get away with anything. I'll fix you all.

C (*To* B; *an aside*)

Is it always like this?

B (*Overly patient*)

No . . . it's often very pleasant.

C

Huh!

A (*Muttering now*)

You all want something; there's nobody doesn't want something. My mother taught me that; be careful, she said; they all want something; she taught me what to expect, me and my sister. She prepared us and somebody had to. I mean, we were girls and that was way back then, and it was different then. We didn't have a lot, and being a girl wasn't easy. We knew we'd have to make our own way, and being a girl back then . . . why am I talking about this!?

B

Because you want to.

A

That's right. She tried to prepare us . . . for going out in the world, for men, for making our own way. Sis couldn't do it; that's too bad. *I* could; *I* did. I met him at a party, and he said he'd seen me before. He'd been married twice—the first one was a whore, the second one was a drunk. He was funny! He said, let's go riding in the park, and I said all right . . . scared to death. I lied; I said I rode. *He* didn't care; he wanted me; I could tell that. It only took six weeks.

B

Good girl!

A

We had horses when we were married; we had a stable; we had saddle horses; we rode.

C *(Mildly)*

Hoity-toity.

A

I learned to ride and I was very good.

B *(Encouraging)*

I'm sure!

C *(Mildly contemptuous)*

How are you sure!?

B

Shhhhhhh.

A *(Childlike enthusiasm)*

I rode sidesaddle and I rode astride, and I drove ponies—hackneys—and I loved it all. He would go with me and we would ride every morning, and the Dalmatian would go with us—what was her name . . . Suzie? No. We had good horses and we showed them and we won all the ribbons, and we kept them in a big case down in the . . . no, that was the other house. We kept them.

(Pause; reinvigorating herself)

And cups. All the silver cups we won, and bowls, and platters. We knew all the judges but that's not why we would win: we won because we were the best.

C *(Under her breath)*

Of course.

B *(Sotto voce)*

Be decent.

A *(Dismissive)*

Oh, she'll learn.

(Back to the memory)

We had horses! I knew all the judges, and I'd go in the ring when we were in the championships, and I'd sit there and I'd watch the horses—I never rode when we were in the championships; Earl did that; he was our rider. I would sit there and watch with the judges. They all knew me; we were famous; we had a famous stable, and when the judging was done they'd tell me if we'd won, and we almost always did, and if they told me, and they almost always did, I'd signal. I'd take my hat off and I'd touch my hair.

(*Does it: touches hair*)

and that way they'd know we'd won.

C (*To* B; *whispers*)

Who!?

(B *shrugs, keeps her eyes on* A)

A (*Very rational; explaining*)

Everyone in our box.

(*Childish again*)

Oh, I used to love it, riding in the morning, going to the stable in the station wagon in my coat and jodhpurs and my derby, and petting . . . what was her name?, the Dalmatian—Suzie, I think . . . no—and mounting and riding off. Sometimes he came with me and sometimes he didn't. Sometimes I went off alone.

C (*To* B)

Who?

B

Her husband, most likely.

(*To* A)

Did you ride when you were little?

A (*A little deprecating laugh*)

No. We were poor.

C (*To* A)

Poor? Really . . . "poor"?

A

Well, no; not really poor; my father was an architect; he designed furniture; he made it.

C

That's not an architect, that's . . .

B

Let it be.

A

He made such beautiful furniture; he was an architect. Strict, but fair. No,

my *mother* was strict. No, they were *both* strict. *And* fair.
   (*This confuses her; she cries*)

B

Now, now.

A

I don't know what I'm saying! What am I *saying*?

B (*Comforting*)

You're taking about horses; you were talking about riding, and we asked:
when you were a little girl . . .   ·

A (*Rational; tough*)

We never rode; the neighbors had a horse but we never rode it. I don't
think my sister ever rode. But I can't swim.
   (*Conspiratorial whisper*)
She drank.

C

When she was a little girl?

B

Oh, please!

A (*Truly innocent*)

What? What are we talking about?

B

Horses. You didn't ride when you were a little girl.

A

You rode if you were a farmer or if you were rich.

C (*Mildly mocking*)

Or if you were a rich *farmer.*

B

Shhhhhhh.

A (*Of* C, *to* B)

She'll learn.
   (*To* C; *ominous*)
Won't you?!

C (*Flustered laugh*)

Well, I dare *say.*

A (*Story again*)

I wasn't rich until I got married, and I wasn't really right then till later. It
all adds up. We had saddle horses; we rode. I learned to ride and I was

very good. I rode sidesaddle and I rode astride, and I drove ponies—hackneys . . .

C

. . . and you loved it all.

B

Shhhhhhh.

A

And I what?

C

You loved it all.

B

You loved it all.

A

I did?

B

So you say.

A (*Laughs*)

Well, then, it must be true. I didn't like sex much, but I had an affair.

C (*Interested*)

Oh?

A (*Suddenly suspicious*)

What! What do you want!?

B

She doesn't want anything.

A (*Off again*)

We used to ride. *He* would go with me—not all the time. Sometimes I would go off alone, or with the dog, part way, never too far from the stable; she had a cat she was in love with. She'd go back, but I'd go on. I had my jodhpurs and my coat and my switch and my derby hat. I always rode in all my costume. Never go out except you're properly dressed, I always say. I'd drive the station wagon from the house—I loved to drive. I was good at it. I was good at everything; I *had* to be; *he* wasn't. I'd drive in the station wagon to the stable, and Earl would be there, or . . . or one of the stable boys: Tom . . . or Bradley.

 (*Long pause*)

Am I doing in my panties!?

 (*Starts to cry*)

B (*Leisurely*)

Well . . . let's see.

(Goes to A*)*

Upseedaisey!

*(*B *raises* A, *who whimpers; cries more.* B *feels under her. Continued)*

Nope, but I bet you're going to. Off you go.

*(*B *helps* A *off)*

C

Hold the fort?

*(*C *goes to window; looks out; looks at bed; goes to it; smoothes the covers.* B *re-enters. Continued)*

Why am I doing this?

B

Because it's unnecessary? Because I've already done it?

C

The princess and the pea, maybe? What's wrong with her arm?

B

She fell and broke it. It didn't heal. Mostly they don't at that age. They put pins in it, metal pins; the bone disintegrates around the pins and the arm just hangs there. They want to take it off.

C

What!?

B *(Matter of fact)*

The arm; they want to take the *arm* off.

C *(Protest)*

No!

B *(Shrugs)*

It hurts.

C

Still!

B

She won't *let* them.

C

I shouldn't *think* so.

B

What do *you* know? She makes us go into the city once a week—to see the surgeon, the one who set it, the one who wants to take it off. God!, he's almost as old as she is. She trusts him, she says. She goes in once a week, and she makes them x-ray it, and *look* at it, and each time the pins are looser, and the bone is gone more, and she tells the old guy—the surgeon—

it's so much better, and she wants him to agree, and he waffles, and he looks at me and I'm no help, and she makes him promise that he'll never take the arm off, and won't let anyone *else* do it either, and he promises—assuming she'll forget? Probably; but she won't. There are some things she never forgets. "He promised me; you were there; you heard him." I think she says that every other day: "He promised me; you were there; you heard him."

(A crack of glass from offstage. Continued)

Oh, God!

(She exits. From offstage now)

Now, why did you do that!? You naughty, naughty girl!. Bad, bad girl!

(Offstage, A *hoots and cackles. Continued, offstage)*

What do I have to do—take everything away from you? Huh!?

*(*A *appears onstage again, hooting and giggling, followed by* B*)*

A

(Drifting, hobbling; very happy; to C*)*

I broke the glass! I took the glass and I threw it down in the sink! I broke the glass and now she has to clean it up! (B *has re-entered)*

B

Bad girl!

A

I broke the glass! I broke the glass!

(Giggles; suddenly her face collapses and she cries; then)

I have to sit down! I can't sit down by my*self!* Why won't somebody help me!?

B *(Helping her)*

Now, now; here we go.

A

Ow! Ow!

B

All right, now.

C *(Under her breath)*

Jesus!

B *(To* C*; settling* A*)*

You're a big help.

C *(Cold)*

I didn't know I was supposed to be.

B *(Sneers)*

Just here from the lawyer, eh?

C

Yes; just here from the lawyer.

A *(Suddenly suspiciously alert)*

What? What did you say?

B *(Matter-of-fact)*

I said—well, what I implied was, since she's here from the lawyer, why should she behave like a human being; why should she be any help; why should she . . .

A *(To c; happy)*

You're from Harry?

C

No; Harry's dead; Harry's been dead for years.

A *(Tears, again)*

Harry's *dead?* When did *Harry* die?

C *(Loud)*

Thirty years ago!

A *(Tiny pause; crying stops)*

Well, *I* knew *that*. What are you talking about *Harry* for?

C

You asked if I'd come from Harry; you asked . . .

A

I wouldn't do anything that *stupid*.

B *(Amused; for c)*

And so it goes.

A *(Clarifying it for the world)*

Harry *used* to be my lawyer, but that was *years* ago. Harry died—what? Thirty years ago?—Harry died. Now his son's the lawyer. I go to *him;* well, he comes to me; *some*times I go to him.

C

Yes; you do. *And* yes he does.

A

Why are *you* here?

C *(Sighs)*

Some things have been . . . misplaced; aren't being done. Some things . . .

A *(Panic)*

Somebody's stealing things!?

C

No no no no. We send you papers to sign and you don't sign them; we call you and you don't call back; we send you checks to sign and you don't sign them; things like that.

A

I don't know what you're talking about.

C

Well . . .

A

None of it's true! You're lying! Get Harry on the phone!

C

Harry is . . .

B (To A)

Excuse me? The "I'll get to it" pile?

A (Suspicious of B now)

What!?

B (Calm)

The "I'll get to it pile?

A

I don't know what you're talking about.

C (To B)

Papers? Checks?

B (Broad)

Oh . . . lots of stuff.

A (Adamant)

There's nothing!

C (To B)

What is there? What is it?

B (To A; patiently)

You have a drawer full; the bills come and you look at them, and some of them you send on and they get paid, and some of them you say you can't remember and so you don't send them, and . . .

A (Defiant)

Why would I send in a bill for something I never ordered?

B (Shuts eyes briefly)

And they send you your checks—to sign? To pay bills? And some of them you sign because you remember what they were for, but some of them— some of the checks—you can't remember?

A

I *what!?*

B *(Smiles tolerantly)*
. . . you don't remember what they're for and so you don't sign them and you put them in the drawer.

A

So?

B *(Shrugs)*
These things pile up.

C

I *see; I see.*

A

Everybody out there's ready to rob me blind. I'm not made of money, you know.

B *(Laughs)*
Yes, you *are.*
    (To C*)*
Isn't she?

C *(Smile)*
More or less.

A *(Conspiratorially)*
They'd steal you blind if you didn't pay attention: the help, the stores, the markets, that little Jew makes my furs—what's her name? She's nice. They all rob you blind if you so much as turn your back on them. All of them!

C
We've asked you: let all your bills come to us; we'll know what to do; let me *bring* you your checks every month; I'll stay here while you sign them. Whatever you like.

A

(A superior smile, but hesitant around the edges)
None of you think I can handle my own affairs? I've done it for . . . when he was so sick I did it all; I did all the bills; I did all the checks; I did everything.

C *(Gentle)*
But now you don't *have* to.

A *(Proud)*
I didn't have to then: I *wanted* to. I wanted everything to be *right,* and I do now; I still do!

C

Well, of *course* you do.

B

Of *course* you do.

A *(Ending it; superior)*

And so I'll handle my own affairs, thank you.

C *(Defeated; shrugs)*

Well; certainly.

B

And *I'll* watch you *pretend* to handle them.

A

And I watch you, every one of you. I used to love horses.

B

It's just people you don't like.

A *(Noncommittal)*

Oh? Is that it? We rode Western saddle, too. It was when he almost died—the first time, the first time I was with him. He had a blood infection. He was hunting, they were all hunting, and a gun went off and it hit him in the arm, the shoulder.

    (Touches hers; realizes the parallel; smiles sadly)

My God!

    (Pause)

They shot him in the shoulder, and they didn't get all the bullet out, and it got infected and his arm swelled up like a balloon and they lanced it and it burst and there was pus all over . . .

C

Stop!

B *(Cold)*

Why? What's it to you?

    (C shudders)

A

. . . and they put drains in it and there weren't any medicines then . . .

B

No antibiotics, you mean.

A

What?

B

No antibiotics.

A

Yes, and it wouldn't go away and it would get worse, and everybody said
he was going to die, but I wouldn't let him! I said No! he is not going to
die! I told that to the doctors, and I told him that, too, and he said all
right, he would try, if I would sleep with him, if I wouldn't leave him alone
at night, be next to him, and I did and it smelled so awful—the pus, the
rot, the . . .

C

Don't! Please!

A

. . . and they said take him to the desert, bake his arm in the hot sun, and
so we went there—we went to Arizona—and he sat in the baking sun all
day—his arm oozing, and stinking, and splitting and . . . in six months it
went away and the arm went down in size and there was no more pus and
he was saved—except for the scars, all the scars, and I learned to ride
Western saddle.

B

My, my.

A

And it was outside of Phoenix—Camelback Mountain; we used to ride out
into the desert. And the movie star was there—the one who married the
young fellow who ran the studio; she had eyes of a different color.

C *(Small pause)*

She had *what?*

A

She had eyes of a different color: one eye was blue, or something, and the
other one was green, I think.

C *(To* B*)*

Who *was* this?
    (B *shrugs*)

A

Oh, she was a big star; she was tiny and she had a very big head. I think
she drank too.

B

You think *everyone* drinks. Merle Oberon?

A

No; of course not! *You* know!

B *(Enjoying this a little)*

How long ago *was* this? Claire Trevor?

A

Oh . . . when I was there; when we were there. She was tiny! She had two eyes!

B

In the thirties?

A

Probably. She had a son; she cooked an egg on the sidewalk; it was so hot. He *told* me.

C *(Lost)*

Her . . . son . . . told you?

A

No! Ours! He was a little boy, too; he played with all the other children: the chewing-gum twins; *that* one.

B

That must have been before the *war.*

C

Which one!?

B

Civil.

A *(Triumphant)*

Thalberg! *That's* who she married. Arnold Thalberg; he was a real smart little Jew.

B (A *To* C; *ironic*)

All smart Jews are *little.* Have you noticed?
  (To A*)*
Irving; *Irving* Thalberg.

C *(Cold)*

I'm a Democrat; I notice a lot of things.

B

Most of us *are;* most of us *do.* But still, it's fascinating, isn't it—grisly, but fascinating. She doesn't *mean* anything by it—or if she did, once, she doesn't now. It just falls out.

A *(Joyous)*

Norma Shearer!

B

Of course!

C

Who?

A *(Laughs)*
What's the matter with all you people!?

C *(Explaining)*
We're Democrats.

A
What?

C
Well, you asked what the matter was.

A
Don't you get fresh!

B
My God! I haven't heard that in a long time.
    (Imitates)
"Don't you get fresh!"

A
My mother would say that to me all the time: don't you get fresh! To Sis
and me. She made us eat everything she put before us, and wash the
dishes; she made us know what being a grownup was. She was strict but
fair. No, that was our father; no, that was both of them.
    (A little girl whine)
They're dead; Sis, they're dead!

C
A small little Jew?

B
At least she didn't say kike.

A *(Back to her memory)*
She would make us write thank-you notes, and take little gifts whenever
we went somewhere, and made us wash everything we wore the night we
wore it, by hand, before we went to bed. Sometimes Sis wouldn't and I had
to do hers, too. She made us be proper young ladies.

C
And go to church twice a day? And pray a lot?

A
What? Oh, yes, we went to church but we didn't talk about it very much.
We took it for granted, I suppose.
    (To B)
How much did you *steal*?

B (*Not rising to it*)

When?

A

Whenever.

B (*Drawling*)

Well, I waited until you were asleep . . .

A

I never sleep.

B

. . . until you were pretending to be asleep, and then I went into the silver closet and took down all the big silver bowls, and I stuck them up under my skirt, and I waddled out into the hall . . .

A

Joke about it if you want to.
  (*A sudden fit of giggles*)
You must have looked *funny!*

B (*Playing along*)

Well, I suppose.

A

Waddling out like that; you probably clanked, too.

B

Yes; I'm sure I did. Clank, clank.

A (*Hoots*)

Clank, clank!
  (*Notices* C *isn't amused; tough*)
You don't think *any*thing's funny, do you?

C

Oh, yes; I'm just trying to decide what I think's really the most hilarious— unpaid bills, anti-Semitism, senility, or . . .

B

Now, now. Play in your own league, huh?

C (*Miffed*)

Well! I'm *sorry!*

A (*Looks right at* C)

I'll have to talk to Harry about you.

B

Harry's dead; Harry's been dead for years.

A *(With increasing self-absorption)*

I know; so's everybody. I don't have any friends anymore; most of them are dead, and the ones aren't dead are dying, and the ones aren't dying have moved away or I don't see anymore.

B *(Comforting)*

Well, what does it matter? You don't like any of them anymore anyway.

A *(Uncomplicated agreement)*

That's true. But you're supposed to like them, to have them with you. Isn't it a contract? You take people as friends and you spend time at it, you put effort in it, and it doesn't matter if you don't like them anymore—who likes anybody anymore?—you've put in all that time, and what right do they have to . . . to . . .

C *(Incredulous)*

To die?!

A

What!?

C

What right do they have to die?

A

No! To not be what they were.

C

To change, you mean?

B *(Gently)*

Let her alone.

A

No! No right! You count on them! And they change. The Bradleys! The Phippses! They die; they go away. And family dies; family goes away. Nobody should *do* this! Look at Sis!

B

What about her?

A

My sister was a drunk.
    (Not friendly)
She was smarter than me . . . no: brighter, two years younger.

C *(Smile)*

Or five, or seven.

A

What!?

C

Nothing.

A

She always got better grades, had more beaux—when we were growing up. Only then; she missed more boats than you can shake a stick at.

C *(Examining her nails)*

I've never shook a stick at a boat.

B *(Dry)*

Well, maybe you should give it a try. Shaken; not shook.

A

We came to the city together, after she finished school, and we had a tiny little apartment, and our mother and our father came to see it, to be sure it was all right, not dangerous, I suppose. It was furnished, but he didn't like it, so he gave us some of theirs, some from the garage. He made the most beautiful furniture: he was an architect. We went out all the time—looking for jobs, jobs that a young lady could accept—being escorted out at night. We were the same size, so we could wear each other's clothes; *that* saved money. We had a little allowance, but a very little one, nothing to spoil us. She was a little shorter, but not much. We kept a list so the boys—the young men, the men—who took us out—we went out with them together a lot— wouldn't know we were wearing each other's. Is that what I mean?

B

Yes; I think so; most probably.

C

Keep awake.

A

"No, no, I wore that at the Plaza; don't you remember? You'd better wear the beads." We had a regular list. We had big feet.

(Silence)

B *(About the non sequitur)*

What!?

C

They had big *feet*.

A

We had big feet. I still do . . . I guess.

(To B)

Do I still have big feet?

B

Yes; yes, you do.

A

Well, I'd never know. I think we liked each other. We used to confide a lot, and laugh, and . . . Mother made us write twice a week—or call, later. We tried sending letters together—one letter together—but she'd make us send two—each of us one. They had to be newsy, and long, and she'd send them back to us with things like "That's not true," or "Don't abbreviate," or "Your sister said the same thing," if she didn't like them. Or spelling. Sis couldn't spell. She drank.

C *(Incredulous)*

Your mother!?

A

What!? No, of course not. My *sister!*

B

Of course.

C

Even then?

A

When?

C

When you . . . when you first came to the city.

A

No, of course not! Later. Well, we'd have champagne when we went out—before the speakeasies. We would drink champagne and nibble on candied orange rind. *He* brings me some, sometimes, when he comes. Or flowers—freesia, when they're in season. It's the least he can do. And he *knows* it!

C *(To B; an aside)*

Who? Who *is* this?

B *(Absorbed with A)*

Shhhhhhh. Her son.

A

We'd go out, but we didn't take each other's boyfriends. She was prim; I liked . . . wilder men, I suppose.

C

Tsk, tsk tsk.

B *(To C; amused)*

Why? Don't you?

A

We never liked the same boys . . . men. I don't think she liked men very much. Well, I *know* she didn't—sex, anyway. We had to make her get married, when she was almost forty—*get* someone for her. I don't think she wanted him; he was a wop.

C *(Shakes her head)*

I don't believe it sometimes.

B

(Sharp, as A *tries to adjust herself in her chair)*
Why not? Wop, nigger, kike? I told you: it doesn't *mean* anything. It's the way she learned things.

C

From these strict but fair parents.
   (B *shrugs)*

A *(She has heard)*
I have Jewish friends and I have Irish friends, and I have South American friends—I *did.* Not Puerto Rican, or like that, but Venezuelan, and Cuban. Oh, we loved to go to Havana.

C *(To* B, *more or less)*
Another world, eh?

B

Uh-huh.

A

I've never known any colored—well, *help,* yes. In Pinehurst they had colored help and we used to visit them there. They knew their place; they were polite, and well-behaved; none of those uppity niggers, the city ones.

C *(Dismay)*

Oh, Jesus Christ!

A

He keeps telling me I can't say these things. I don't know what things he means. He said once he wouldn't come to see me anymore if I said those things. I don't know what things he means. What did he mean?

B

Don't worry yourself. Your sister married an *Italian.*

A *(Confused)*
She did . . . what? Oh, that was later. I always had my eye out for the right man.

C

And she didn't?

A

No; she always thought everything would fall right into her lap. And it *did;* a *lot* . . . I had to work for *everything* nothing came my way. I was tall and handsome; she was tall and pretty, tall but shorter, not as tall as I am . . . was.

> *(Weeps)*

I've shrunk! I'm not tall! I used to be so tall! Why have I shrunk!?

B *(To A; patient)*

It happens with time: we get shorter. It happens every day, too: we're taller in the morning than we are at night.

A *(Still weeping)*

How!?

B

The spine compresses as the day goes on.

A *(Even weepier)*

I don't *have* one. I used to have a spine; I don't have one anymore!

C *(To B; sotto voce)*

What does she mean?

B

She means osteoporosis.

A

> *(To C; ugly; weeping down to sniveling)*

It hasn't happened to you yet? You wait!

B

. . . the spine collapses; you can fracture it by walking, turning around . . . whatever.

A *(Weepy again)*

I used to be *tall!* I've shrunk!

C *(To B)*

I know.

> *(B smiles)*

A *(Off again)*

He was *short.* A lot of my beaux were tall, but he was short.

C *(Sotto voce; to B)*

Who *is* this?

B *(Also sotto voce)*

Her husband, I think.

C

Oh; that's a long time ago.

A

Oh, I knew such tall boys, such dancers. Sis and I would dance all night with all the tall boys. Some of them were show boys—they were fairies—but some of them were regular. We would dance the night away; and sometimes I'd go off.

B *(Smiling)*

Naughty girl!

A

I was the wild one. Sis would say to me, How can you *do* that!? and I'd laugh and I'd say, Oh, come on! I liked to have a good time, but I had my eye out. I always had my eye out.

    (A shift of tone toward bitter)

If I don't have my eye out, who will? I've always had to be on my toes, them sneaking around, stealing and . . . conniving. If I didn't keep my eye out we wouldn't have had *any*thing. His *sister!* That one she married? The first one! The dumpy little . . . dentist was he? What did *he* know about running an office? What did *he* know about handling money? Enough to steal! Enough to line his *own* pockets. And of course the old man kept his head turned the other way because the—what's his name, the dentist—was married to his precious daughter! Oh *that* one! Whining and finagling, wrapping him around her little finger! I had to stay one step ahead of *all* of them. I fixed 'em.

B *(Proud of her)*

Did you?

A *(Confused)*

What!?

B

Did you fix them?

A *(Panicking)*

Who!? Who are you talking about!?

B

The ones you fixed.

A

How do *I* know? I don't know what you're talking about! Fix who!?

B

I don't *know.*

C *(To help)*

The ones who were robbing you blind.

B *(To* A*)*

Yes: those.

A *(Grim)*

*Every*body's robbing me—right and left. Everybody steals. Everybody steals *some*thing.

B *(Without comment)*

Including me? Do *I* steal?

A *(Nervous laugh)*

I don't know. How would I know? He says I should have more money.

B *(To* C*)*

Doesn't your office . . . ?

C

We deal with what comes *in*. There's more than one handles her money. There's plenty of chance, if anyone *wanted* to.

A

Sis used to envy me after I married. She never *did* well. I always had my eye out.

C

You use all your income as far as *I* can see.

A

Well, why not? It's mine.

C

Well, just don't complain. If you wanted an increase in principal, you'd have to . . .

A

I don't complain: I *never* complain. I have you, and I have her,
    (Points to B*)*
and I have the chauffeur, and I have this place here, and I have to look pretty, and sometimes I have the nurses—though they're black. Why *is* that?—and I have all those things . . . I have the cook, I have the . . .

C

I know; I know.

A

They all steal; every one of them.

B *(After a pause; a sigh)*

Ah, well.

A

Sis didn't have her eye out; not like I did. I married him. He was short; he

had one eye; one was glass; a golf ball hit him there; they took it out; he
had a glass one.

C

Which eye?

B (To C; chiding)

Oh, *come* on!

C (Amused)

No, I want to know.
    (To A*)*
Which eye? Which eye was glass?

A

Which eye was . . .? Well, I don't . . .
    (Becomes weepy)
I can't remember! I don't know which eye was the glass one!
    (Full weep)
I . . . can t . . . remember. I . . . can't . . . remember!

B (Moves to A; to comfort)

Now, now; now, now.

A

I can't remember!
    (Sudden venom)
Get your *hands* off me! How *dare* you!

B (Retreating)

Sorry; sorry.

A (To B; tearful again)

Why can't I re*mem*ber anything?

B

I think you remember everything; I think you just can't bring it to mind all
the time.

A (Quieting)

Yes? Is that it?

B

Of course!

A

I remember everything?

B

Somewhere in there.

A *(Laughs)*

My gracious!
   (To C*)*
I remember everything!

C

Gracious. That must be a burden.

B

Be nice.

C

Isn't salvation in forgetting? Lethe, and all?

A

Who?

B

No one.

C

Lethe.

A

I don't *know* her. Well, maybe I do, I just don't have it right now.
   (To B*)*
Is that right?

B

That's *right*.

A

I *loved* my husband.
   (Silly, remembering smile)

B

I bet you *did*.

A

He gave me pretty things; he gave me jewelry.

B

Them's pretty.

A

My God, he said, you're so big, so tall, you'll cost me a fortune! I can't give you little things. And he *couldn't*. I liked pearls and diamonds best.

C

No kidding!

B *(Amused)*

Oh, hush!

A

I had my pearls, and I had some bracelets, and he wanted me to have another—he'd found one without telling me. We wore wide bracelets back then—diamond ones—wide, *this* wide.

    (She demonstrates: two inches, or so)

Flat and wide, the stones in designs, very . . . what? Very what?

B

Ornate.

A

Yes, ornate . . . and wide. We had been out—I'll never forget it, I'll never forget this—we'd been to a party, and we'd had champagne, and we were . . . what? Tipsy? A little I suppose. And we came home and we were on the way to bed. We had our big bedroom, and it had its separate dressing rooms, and—you know—its separate bathrooms—and we were undressing; we were getting ready for bed. I was at my table, and I'd taken off my clothes—my shoes, my dress, and my underthings—and I was sitting there at my dressing table

    (She really enjoys telling this: laughs, giggles, etc.)

and I was . . . well, I was naked; I didn't have a stitch, except I had on all my jewelry. I hadn't taken off my jewelry.

B

How wonderful!

A

Yes! And there I was, all naked with my pearls—my necklace—and my bracelets, my diamond bracelets . . . two, no: three! Three! And in he walked, naked as a jaybird—he was funny when he wanted to be—we were naked a lot, early on, pretty early on. All that stopped.

    (Pause)

Where am I?

B

In your story?

A

What?

B

In your story. Where are you in your story?

A

Yes; of course.

C

You're naked at your dressing table, and *he* walks in, and *he's* naked, too.

A

. . . as a jaybird; yes! Oh, I shouldn't *tell* this!

B

Yes! Yes, you should!

C

Yes!

A

Yes? Oh . . . well, there I was, and I had my big powder puff, and I was powdering myself, and I was paying attention to *that*. I knew he was there, but I wasn't paying attention. I *have* something for you, he said, I *have* something for you. And I was sitting there, and I raised my eyes and looked in the mirror and . . . no! I can't tell this!

B and C (*Silly schoolgirls; ad lib*)

Yes, yes; tell, tell. Tell us! Yes! Tell us!

A

And I looked and there he was, and his . . . his pee-pee was all hard, and . . . and hanging on it was a new bracelet.

C (*Awe*)

Oh, my God!

    (B *smiles*)

A

And it was on his pee-pee, and he came close and it was the most beautiful bracelet I'd ever seen; it was diamonds, and it was wide, so wide and . . . I thought you might like this, he said. Oh, my goodness, it's so beautiful, I said. Do you want it? he said. Yes, yes! I said, Oh, goodness, yes!

    (*Mood shifts a little toward darkness*)

And he came closer, and his pee-pee touched my shoulder—he was short, and I was tall, or something. Do you want it? he said, and he poked me with it, with his pee-pee, and I turned, and he had a little pee-pee. Oh, I shouldn't say that; that's terrible to say, but I *know*. He had a little . . . *you know* . . . and there was the bracelet on it, and he moved closer, to my face, and Do you want it? I thought you might like it. And I said, No! I can't *do* that! You *know* I can't *do* that! And I couldn't; I could *never* do that, and I said, No! I can't do that! And he stood there for . . . well, I don't know . . . and his pee-pee got . . . well, it started to go soft, and the bracelet slid off, and it fell into my lap. I was naked; deep into my lap. Keep it, he said, and he turned and walked out of my dressing room.

    (*Long silence; finally she weeps, slowly, conclusively*)

B (*Eventually*)

It's all right; it's all right.

    (*Goes and comforts* A)

C (*Kindly*)

The wild one.

B (*Still comforting*)

It's all right; it's all right.

A (*Little child*)

Take me to bed; take me to bed.

B

Sure.

 (*To* C)

Help me.

 (*They ease her up from her chair and to the bed during the following*)

A (*Screams*)

My arm! My arm!

C (*Terrified*)

I'm sorry!

A

Bed! I wanna go to bed!

B

All right now; we're almost there.

 (*At bed*)

OK. Here we are.

A (*Full baby*)

I wanna go to bed!

 (*It hurts!*)

Oh! Oh! Oh!

B

All right, now.

 (A *is now on the bed, under covers, sitting up part way. Continued*)

There. Comfy?

C (*To* B)

I'm sorry; I didn't mean to

B (*To* C)

It's all right.

 (*To* A)

Comfy?

A (*Tiny voice*)

Yes. Thank you.

B

(As she moves away from the bed)
You're welcome.

C

I'm not good at . . . all that.

B

You'll get there.

C

I can't project.

B *(Comforting)*
Well, think of it this way: if you live long enough you won't have to; you'll
be there.

C

Thanks.

B

And since it's the far past we're supposed to recall best—if we *get* to the
future—you'll remember not being able to project.

C

As I said: thanks.

B *(Pause; sighs)*
A-ha.

C *(Pause)*
What happens now?

B *(Eyes closed)*
You tell *me.*

C

You're the one works here.

B *(Smiles; eyes still closed)*
As I said: *you* tell *me.*
(Silence)

A

*(Propped up; eyes opening and closing from time to time, eyes
wandering; very stream of consciousness)*
The things we're able to do and the things we're *not.* What we remember
doing and what we're not sure. What do I remember? I remember being
tall. I remember first it making me unhappy, being taller in my class, taller
than the boys. I remember, and it comes and goes. I think they're all robbing me. I *know* they are, but I can't prove it. I think I know, and then I
can't remember what I know.

(*Cries a little*)

He never comes to see me.

B (*Mildly*)

Yes, he does.

A

When he has to; now and then.

B

More than most; he's a good son.

A (*Tough*)

Well, I don't know about that.

(*Softer*)

He brings me things; he brings me flowers—orchids, freesia, those big violets . . .?

B

African.

A

Yes. He brings me those, and he brings me chocolates—orange rind in chocolate, that dark chocolate I like; he does *that*. But he doesn't love me.

B

Oh, now.

A

He doesn't! He loves his . . . he loves his boys, those boys he has. You don't know! He doesn't love me and I don't know if I love him. I can't *remember!*

B

He loves you.

A (*Near tears*)

I can't remember; I can't remember what I can't remember.

(*Suddenly alert and self-mocking*)

Isn't *that* something!

B (*Nicely*)

It certainly *is*.

A (*Rambling again*)

There's so much: holding on; fighting for everything; *he* wouldn't do it; *I* had to do *every*thing; tell him how handsome he was, clean up his blood. Everything came on *me*: Sis being that way, hiding her bottles in her nightthings where she thought I wouldn't find them when she came to stay with me for a little; falling . . . falling down the way she did. Mother coming to stay, to live with us; he *said* she could; where else could she go? Did we like each other even? At the end? Not at the end, not when she hated me. I'm helpless she . . . she screamed; I hate you! She stank; her room stank; she stank; I hate you, she screamed at me. I think they all hated me, because I was strong, because I *had* to be. Sis hated me; Ma hated me; all those others, *they* hated me; *he* left home; he ran away. Because I was strong. I was tall and I was strong. *Somebody* had to be. If I wasn't, then . . .

(*Silence;* A *is still, eyes open. Has she shuddered a little before her silence? After a bit* B *and* C *look at one another.* B *rises, goes to the bed, leans over, gazes at* A, *feels her pulse?*)

C (*Looks over after a little*)
Is she . . . oh, my God, is she dead?

B (*After a little*)
No. She's alive. I think she's had a stroke.

C
Oh, my God!

B
You better call her son. I'll call her doctor.

(C *rises, exits right, looking at* A *as she exits;* B *strokes* A's *head, exits left.* A *alone; still; silence*)

CURTAIN

ACT TWO

("A" is propped up in bed. [Actually, a dummy with an exact life mask of the actress playing A; same costume as A's in Act One. We must believe it to be A; a breathing mask over nose and mouth helps this]

Some silence. B and C enter, opposite from their exits at the end of Act One and dressed differently from the way they were. C seats herself. B goes to the bed, looks at "A")

B *(General)*

No change.

C *(Wistful)*

No?

B

That's the way it goes.

C *(Shudders)*

Yes?

B *(Grim)*

Something to look forward to.
    (No response from C. Continued)
No?

C *(Hard)*

I don't want to *talk* about it; I don't want to *think* about it. Let me alone.

B *(Sharp)*

It's worth thinking about—even at *your* age.

C

Let me *alone!*

B

    (Wandering about; touching things)
It's got to be *some* way . . . stroke, cancer or, as the lady said, "heading in to the mountain with a jet." No?
    (No response. Continued)
Or . . . walking off a curb into a sixty-mile-an-hour wall . . .

C

Stop it!

B

Or . . . even worse; *think* about this . . . home alone in the evening, servants off, him out, at the Club, sitting home alone, the window jimmied, *they* get in, little cat feet and all, *find* you, sitting there in the upstairs sitting room . . .

C

I said: *stop* it!

B *(Smiles)*

. . . find me sitting there in the upstairs sitting room, going over invitations, or whatever . . . bills; come up behind me, slit my throat, me thinking, Oh, my God, my throat's being slit, *if* that, if there's *time* for that.

C *(Animal growl of protest)*

Arghhhhhhhh!

B *(Tranquil)*

I'm almost done. Or I hear them . . . you hear them, turn around, see them—how many? Two? Three?—fall apart, start screaming, so they have to slit your throat, my throat, though they may not have planned it that way. All that blood on the Chinese rug. My, my.

C *(Pause; curious)*

Chinese rug?

B *(Very natural)*

Yes, beige, with rose embroidery all around the edges. We get it at auction.

C

I wouldn't know.

B *(Momentary surprise)*

No; of course not; you *wouldn't*. You will, though—the rug, I mean. Clearly nobody slits your throat, or mine, for that matter.
     (Considers it)
Might be better.

C *(Rue and helplessness)*

You have things to tell me, I suppose.

B

Oh, I certainly do. But, then again, I don't know everything either, *do* I?!
     *(Gestures towards "*A*")*

C *(She looks, too)*

I'll do a will; I'll do some paper won't let me go on if I get like that.

B

There *aren't* any . . . *weren't* any then, I tried. You can't get your way in this world.

*(A enters during this next, from left. A is dressed in a lovely, laven-
der dress; sling gone)*

C

There *must* be one. You have your way in everything and then you can't at
the last? There *must* be!

A

There *must* be what?
*(She is thoroughly rational during this Act. B and C are not sur-
prised to see her)*

C

A living will.

A *(Observing "A")*

I was going to, but then I forgot, or it slipped my mind, or something. He
kept saying, Make one! He has one for himself, he says. I meant to; nothing much to do about it now. Any change?

B

No, we're . . . just as we were; no change.

A

I wonder how long *this'll* go on. I hope it's quick. What's-her-name took six
years; not a move, not a blink, hooked up, breathed for, pissed for.

B

Do I know her?

A

No; after your time, so to speak.

B

A-*ha*.

A

A lot of money—a *lot*. The kids—hah! Fifty the youngest—the "kids" dis-
agreed. They wanted to see the will first, the lawyer wouldn't *show* it to 'em,
they came down on both sides—*kill* her off! *keep* her going! Not pretty.

C *(Really beside herself)*

Stop it! Stop it!

A *(To a naughty child)*

Grow . . . up.

B *(Smiles)*

She will; she does.

A

Well; yes; of course. And so do *you*.

C *(Rage)*

I will not become . . . *that!* (Points to "A")

A *("Come off it")*

Oh, *really.*

B *("Oh, really!")*

Come *off* it.

C

I *won't.*

B *(Smiles)*

What do you plan to *do* about it?

A *(Amused)*

Yes; *that's* interesting.

C *(To A; pointing to B)*

Nor will I become *this.*

B *(A hoot)*

Hah!

(C *comes down front and speaks to the audience.* A *and* B *relax, comment from time to time, react with each other, etc.)*

C

I *won't.* I *know* I won't—*that's* what I mean. That . . .

(Points to "A")

. . . *thing* there? I'll never be like that.

(B *hoots;* A *shakes her head, chuckles. Continued)*

Nobody could. I'm twenty-six; I'm a *good* girl; my mother was strict but fair—she still *is; she loves* me; she loves me and Sis, and she wants the very best for us. We have a *nice* little apartment, Sis and I, and at night we go out with our beaux, and I *do* have my eye out for . . . for what— "the man of my dreams"? And so does Sis, I *guess.* I don't think I've been in love, but I've been loved—by a couple of them, but they weren't the right ones.

B *(Rue; to herself)*

They never *are.*

A *(Purring)*

Hmmmm.

C

Mother taught us what the right one would be. We have fun with the others—dancing, staying out late, seeing the sun up sometimes. Things get a little . . . involved now and again, and that's fun too, though Sis doesn't think so as much as I do. They get involved, but they never get very . . .

serious. I have my eye out, and we do have our *jobs.* We're mannequins: the fanciest shop in town!

B

I don't want that *known!*

A (To B; pleasantly chiding)

Oh, stop; it was fun.

C

We go into work and we put on these lovely frocks, and we walk elegantly around the store,

  (Imitates)

among the ladies shopping, sometimes with their men, sometimes not, and we stop, and they touch our dresses—the silk, the fabric—and they ask us questions, and then we pass on to another group, to another section. We twirl, we . . . sashay.

  (She does so; B imitates; A, too, but sitting. Continued; to A and B)
We *do!*

B

Oh, I *know.*

A

Yes, we *know;* do *we* know.

C (To the audience again)

Don't look at them; don't . . . listen to them.

  (A and B laugh a little. Continued)
We wear our beautiful evening gowns, and we parade about, and we know there are people looking at us, studying us, and we smile, and we . . . well, I suppose we flirt a little with the men who are doing it—the husbands, or whatever.

B (To A; mock astonishment)

Flirt?! You!?

A

Me!? Flirt!?

B (Sashays; twirls)

Wheeeeee!

A

  (Claps with one hand; her knee, probably)
Brava! Brava!

B (Still sashaying)

Wheeeeee!

C

Stop it! *Stay* out of my life!

B

Oh! My dear!

A *(To C)*

I remember it differently, little one. I remember more . . . design. I remember a little calculation.

B

Oh, yes; a little calculation; a little design.

C *(To audience)*

Don't listen to them. Design? What are they talking about?

B *(Cheerful)*

Never mind.

C *(To audience)*

They don't *know* me!

B *(Looking at A; mocking)*

Nooooooooooo!

C

Remember me!

A *(Also mocking)*

Noooooooooo!
  (C *claps her hands over her ears, shuts her eyes. Continued)*
Oh, all right, dear; go on.
  (C *can't hear. Continued; louder)*
I said, go *on!*

B *(Loud)*

She says go *on!*, honestly.

C

I am a . . . good . . . girl.

B *(To A)*

Well, yes; I suppose so.

A

And not dumb.

C

I'm a good girl. I know how to attract *men*. I'm *tall;* I'm striking; *I* know how to do it. Sis slouches and caves her front in; I stand tall, breasts out, chin up, hands . . . just so. I walk between the aisles and they know there's somebody coming, that there's somebody *there.* But, I'm a *good girl.* I'm not a virgin, but I'm a good girl. The boy who took me was a good boy.

(C *does not necessarily hear—or, at least, notice—the asides to come*)

B

Oh, yes he *was.*

A

Yes? Was he?

B

You remember.

A *(Laughs)*

Well, it *was* a *while* ago.

B

But you *do* remember.

A

Oh yes, I remember him. He was . . .

C

. . . sweet and handsome; no, not handsome: beautiful. He was beautiful!

A *(To B)*

He was; yes.

B *(To A and herself)*

Yes.

C

He has coal-black hair and violet eyes and such a smile!

A

Ah!

B

Yes!

C

His body was . . . well, it was thin, but *hard;* all sinew and muscle; he fenced, he told me, and he was the one with the megaphone on the crew. When I held him when we danced, there was only sinew and muscle. We dated a lot; I liked him; I didn't tell Mother, but I liked him a lot. I like him, Sis, I said; I really like him. Have you told Mother? No, and don't *you;* I like him a lot, but I don't *know.* Has he? . . . *you* know. No, I said; no, he hasn't. But then he did. We were dancing—slowly—late, the end of the evening, and we danced so close, all . . . pressed, and . . . we were pressed, and I could feel that he was hard, *that* muscle and sinew, pressed against me while we danced. We were

the same height and he looked into my eyes as we danced, slowly, and I felt
the pressure up against me, and he tensed it and I felt it move against me.

B *(Dreamy)*

Whatever is *that?* I said.

A

Hmmmmmmmmm.

C

Whatever is *that?* I said. I *knew*, but Whatever is that, I said, and he
smiled, and his eyes shone, and It's me in love with you, he said. You have
an interesting way of showing it, I said. Appropriate, he said, and I felt the
muscle move again, and . . . well, I knew it was time; I knew I was ready,
and I knew I wanted him—whatever that *meant*—that I wanted *him,* that
I wanted *it.*

B *(Looking back; agreeing)*

Yes; oh, yes.

A

Hmmmmmmmmm.

C

Remember, don't give it away, Mother said; don't give it away like it was
nothing.

B *(Remembering)*

They won't respect you for it and you'll get known as a loose girl. *Then* who
will you marry?

A *(To B)*

Is that what she said? I can't remember.

B *(Laughs)*

Yes you can.

C

They won't respect you for it and you'll get known as a loose girl. *Then* who
will you marry? But he was pressed against me, exactly against where he
wanted to be—we were the same height—and he was *so* beautiful, and his
eyes shone, and he smiled at me and he moved his hips as we danced, so
slowly, as we danced, and he breathed on my neck and he said, You don't
want me to embarrass myself right here on the dance floor, do you?

B *(Remembering)*

No, no; of course not.

C

I said, No, no; of course not. Let's go to my place, he said, and I heard
myself saying

(Incredulous)

I'm not that kind of girl? I mean, as soon as I said it I blushed: it was so . . . stupid, so . . . expected. Yes, you are, he said; *you're* that kind of girl.

B

And I was, and my God it was wonderful.

A

It hurt!
   (Afterthought; to B)
Didn't it?

B *(Admonishing)*

Oh . . . well, a little.

C

You're that kind of girl, and I guess I was. We did it a lot.
   (Shy)
I know it's trite to say your first time is your best, but he was wonderful, and I know I'm only twenty-six now and there've been a few others, and I imagine I'll marry, and I'll be very happy.

B *(Grudging)*

Well . . .

A

We'll talk about happy sometime.

C

I *know* I'll be very happy, but will I ever *not* think about him? He was long and thick and knew what I wanted, what I needed, and while I couldn't do . . . you know: the thing he wanted . . . I just *couldn't:* I *can't.*

B *(Stretches)*

Nope; never could.

A *(Sort of dreamy)*

I wonder why.

C *(Very agitated; upset)*

I tried! I wanted to do what . . . but I choked, and I . . .
   (Whispered)
I threw up. I just . . . couldn't.

A *(To* C)

Don't worry about it; don't worry about what can't be helped.

B

And . . . there's more than one way to skin a cat.

A (Puzzles that)

Why?

B

Hm?

A

Why is there more than one way to skin a *cat?*

B (Puzzles that)

Why not?

A

Who needs it!? Isn't one way *enough?*

C (To the audience; still; simply)

I just want you to know that I'm a good girl, that I was a good girl.

B (To C)

You meet him in two years.

C (Self-absorbed)

What? Who?

B (Pleasant)

Your husband. We're what—twenty-six? We'll meet him in two years.

C (Making light of it)

The man of my dreams?

B

Well, a man you'll *dream* about.

A

For a long, long time.

C

Like the boy I was . . .?

A

Well, yes, he was wonderful, but then there's life.

B (To A)

How long?

A

Hm?

B

How *long?*

A

Long enough.
    (To B*)*
You're . . . what?

B

Fifty-two.

A *(Calculating)*

I marry when I'm twenty-eight; you're sixty-six when he dies.
   (To C; smiles)
We have him a good long time.

B *(Musing)*

Another fourteen years.

A

Yes, but the last *six* aren't much fun.

C

That's almost forty years with one man.

B *(To C; chuckles)*

Well, more or less: more or less one man.
   (To A)
No? Not much fun?

A

Not much.

C

How *is* he? Have I *met* him?

B

The one-eyed man? The little one; the little one-eyed man?

A *(Chuckles)*

Oh, now.

C *(Confused)*

What?

B

The one we meet at the party—Sis and me. Sis is with him, but I see him
looking over at me.

A *(A pleased recalling)*

Yes!

B

Sis doesn't much care, I don't think.

C

More or less? What is this more or less?

A

Hm?

B *(Mildly annoyed)*

I beg your pardon?

C

I said almost forty years with one man; you said, more or less; more or less
one man.

B

Oh? Ah! Well, what are you expecting? Monogamy or something?

C

Yes! If I care: yes!

B *(To A)*

Remember monogamy?

A *(Pretends to puzzle it)*

No.

   (New tone; to B)

You can talk about monogamy, if you like—pro and con, if you like. Leave
me out of *that* one.

B *(General)*

Infidelity is a matter of spirit—isn't that what they say? Aside from bad
taste, disease, confusion as to where you live, having to lie all the time—
and remember the lies!

   (To A)

God, remember the lies?

A

Hmmmm. Well, there wasn't much, not *too* much.

B

Except for the groom, eh?

A

Oh, my! The groom.

C

Why do I marry him?

B

Who—the groom?

   (A and B laugh)

C

The one-eyed man! I marry the one-eyed man!

B

Yes, you do.

C

Why!?

B *(To* A*)*

Why do I *marry* him?
  (To A*)*
Why did I *marry* him?

A *(To* B*)*

Why did I?

B

Hmmmmmmmm.

C

Tell me.

B

Because he makes me *laugh*. Because he's little and he's funny looking—
and a little like a penguin.

A *(Has she thought this before?)*
Yes! Quite a bit like one.

B *(Generous)*
Well . . . especially in his bib and tucker.

C *(Some panic)*
Why would I marry him if I'm going to cheat on *him?*

A *(Smiles)*
Why would you marry him if he's going to cheat on *you?*

C

I don't *know!*

B

Calm down; adjust; settle in. Men cheat; men cheat a *lot*. We cheat *less*,
and we cheat because we're lonely; men cheat because they're men.

A

No. We cheat because we're bored, sometimes. We cheat to get back; we
cheat because we don't know any better; we cheat because we're whores.
We cheat for *lots* of reasons. Men cheat for only one—as you say, because
they're men.

C

Tell me about him!

A

Don't you want to be surprised?

C

No!

B

You've seen him, or . . . he's seen *you*. I don't think you've met him. He's something of what they call a playboy—at least in *my* time, not yours. He's rich—or his father is—and he's divorcing his second wife; she's just plain bad; the first one drank; still does.

A

That one dies eventually—eighty, or something; pickled; preserved.

C *(Timid again)*

What's he like?

B *(Expansive)*

Well . . . he's short, and he has one eye, and he's a great dancer—'cept he keeps running into things, the eye, you know—and he sings like a dream! A lovely tenor—and he's funny! God, he's funny!

A *(Wistful)*

Yes; yes, he was.

B *(Please)*

And he likes tall women!

A *(Still wistful)*

Yes; yes, he did.

C *(Uncertain)*

I *have seen* him?

B

He tells me—I think I remember—he tells me he saw me with Sis before he dated her, that I was taller, that he had—you'll forgive the joke—his eye on me.

(To A)

Didn't he tell you that—that he had his eye on us?

A *(True)*

I can't remember. He was going with that comedienne did the splits, the eight-foot one.

B

Well, you put a stop to that soon enough.

A

Once you got your claws into him you mean?

C *(Puzzling)*

Why did I *like* him? Is funny enough? Is having a voice, is dancing enough?

B

Don't forget one eye.

A

Oh, he was *nice;* we liked him a lot.

C

Liked? Liked him a lot.

B *(Looking right at* C*)*

Oh, stop it! You're twenty-six years old, which is not a tot; there *is* the future to look out for . . .

A

. . . and he *is* rich, or is going to be: rich family.

C

I don't *believe* this.

A *(Sharp)*

Our father *dies.*

B *(About her father)*

I *loved* him.

C

No! He doesn't!

B

*Every*body does.

A *(To herself)*

Except me, maybe.

B *(To* C*)*

Except *us.*

C

I *love* him!

B

Well, that should be enough to keep the old heart going: Jesus, she loves me; how can I go and die on her?

C

Is it . . . quick?

A *(Pensive)*

I don't remember.

B

Not bad: heart *failure,* fluid in the lungs, some bad breathing; oh, God, the terror in the eyes!

(C *begins to weep;* B *notices. Continued)*

We did that, yes. We cried when Dad died. I cried; Sis cried; Mom went out on the porch and did it there.

A *(Loss)*

I don't remember.

C

What happens to Ma?

B

She holds out; she stays on alone for almost twenty years, and then she moves in with us.
    (To A)
How does it go?

A *(Toneless)*

What? She becomes an enemy. She dies when she's eighty-four—seventeen years of it, staying up in her room in the big house with us. The colitis, the cigarettes, the six or seven Pekingese she goes through. I stopped liking her.

C

I *couldn't!*

A *(Shrugs)*

She becomes an enemy.

B *(Interested, but not too much)*

How?

A *(Sighs)*

She comes to resent me; she starts to resent getting old, getting . . . helpless—the eyes, the spine, the mind. She starts to resent that I have—*we* have—so much, and that I'm being generous—*we're* being generous. She snaps at everything; she sides with Sis; she criticizes me.

B *(Some awe)*

She wasn't *like* that.

C

No! She *couldn't* be.

A

I don't care. Forget I told you. She never moved in; she's still alive up there in the country, in the same house, she's a hundred and thirty-seven now, does her own baking, jogs three times a week . . .

B

All right; *all* right.

A *(To B)*

There's more. You want to hear it?

(B *shakes her head. Continued; to* C)

Of course *you* don't.

(C *shakes her head. Continued*)

No, of course not. Anyhow, you marry him.

C (*Getting it straight*)

I do.

A

Yes; he's fun, and he's nice.

B

He sings . . .

A

He dances . . .

B

. . . and he's rich, or going to be . . .

A

. . . and he loves tall women.

B

And you suddenly realize you love short men.

A

Penguins.

(A *and* B *both giggle*)

B (*Still to* C)

And it goes all right. His mother doesn't *like* me—doesn't *like* you—at all, but the old *man* does.

A

He certainly does! "You're tall; I bet you're hot stuff."

B (*To* C)

You win him over.

(*To* A)

You know, I think the old buzzard had letch for us?

A

Yes; *I* think so.

B

And, boy did he want a *grand*son.

A

Oh, that made him happy.

C *(Wonder)*

I have children?

B *(None too pleasant)*

We have one; we have a boy.

A *(Same)*

Yes, we do. I have a son.

(He appears in the right archway, stands stock still, stares at "A" on the bed)

B *(Seeing him; sneering)*

Well, fancy seeing you again.

(Sudden, and enraged, into his face)

Get out of my house!

(He doesn't react)

C *(Rising)*

Stop it!

(Moves toward him)

Is . . . is that him?

B

I said, get out of my house!

A *(To B)*

Do be quiet.

(To C)

Let him alone; he's come to see me.

(He goes to "A," sits on a chair left of her, takes her left arm; his shoulders shake; he puts his forehead to her arm, or it to his forehead, becomes still. Does not react to anything about him until indicated. Continued)

That's it; do your duty,

C

He's . . . my goodness. How nice; how handsome, how very . . .

B

You wouldn't say that if you knew!

A

Shhhhhhh.

B *(To A)*

She wouldn't!

(To him)

Filthy little . . .

A

Shhhhhh. Shhhhhh. I don't want to think about *that*. He came back; he never loved me, he never loved us, but he came back. Let him alone.

C

He's so young.

A

Yes . . . well. This is how he looked when he went away, took his life and one bag and went off.

> *(To B)*

No?

B

> *(To his back; less venom, but mixed with hurt)*

You wore that coat the day you left. I thought I told you to get your hair cut!

A

Yes; yes, he did; he wore that coat. I'm leaving, he said, and he took one bag.

> *(Pause)*

And his life.

C *(Bewildered)*

He went away from me? Why?

B *(Bitter)*

Maybe you changed; they say you changed; I haven't noticed.

> *(To A)*

He comes back? He comes back to me—to me? I let him?

A

Sure. We have a heart attack; they tell him; he comes back. Twenty-plus years? That's a long enough sulk—on both sides. He didn't come back when his father died.

B *(Scathing)*

Of course not!

A

But he came to me. They call me up and they tell me he's coming to see me; they say he's going to call. He calls. I hear his voice and it all floods back, but I'm formal. Well, hello there, I say. Hello there to you, he says. Nothing about this shouldn't have happened. Nothing about I've missed you, not even that little lie. Sis is visiting; she's lying drunk and passed out upstairs and not even that little lie. I thought I'd come over. Yes, you do that. He comes; we look at each other and we both hold in whatever we've been holding in since that day he went away.

You're looking well, he says; and You, too, I say. And there are no apologies, no recriminations, no tears, no hugs; dry lips on my dry cheeks; yes that. And we never discuss it? Never go into why? Never go beyond where we are? We're strangers; we're curious about each other; we leave it at that.

B

I'll *never* forgive him.

A (Wistful, sad)

No; I never do. But we play the game. We dine; he takes me places—mother, son going to formal places. We never . . . reminisce. Eventually he lets me talk about when he was a little boy, but he never has an opinion on that; he doesn't seem to have an opinion on much of anything that has to do with us, with me.

B (Clenched teeth)

Never!

A (To B)

Or with *you.*

(*To* C; *and sad smile*)
Or *you.*

C

Did we . . . did we drive him away? Did I change so?

B (Rage)

He left!! He packed up his attitudes and he *left*!! And I never want to see him again.

(*To him*)
Go away!!

(*Angry, humiliated, tears*)

A (Very calm; sad smile)

Well, yes you *do*, you see. You *do* want to see him again. *Wait* twenty years. Be alone except for her upstairs passed out on the floor, and the piano top with the photos in the silver frames, and the butler, and . . . be all alone; you *do* want to see him again, but the terms are too hard. We never forgive him. We let him come, but we never forgive him.

(*To him*)
I bet you don't know *that* . . . *do* you!

C (To A)

How did we change?

(*To him*)
How did I change?

(*He strokes "A's" face, shudders a little*)

B

Don't bother yourself. He *never* belonged.

C *(Enraged)*

I don't believe it!

B *(Furious)*

Let it *alone!*

C

No! How did I *change!?* What *happened* to me!?

A *(Sighs)*

Oh, God.

C *(Determined)*

How did I *change!?*

B *(Sarcasm; to the audience)*

She wants to know how she *changed.* She wants to know how she turned into *me.* Next she'll want to know how I turned into *her.*

(*Indicates A*)

No; I'll want to know *that; maybe* I'll want to know that.

A

Hahh!

B

Maybe.

(*To* C)

You want to know how I changed?

C *(Very alone)*

I don't know. *Do* I?

B

Twenty-six to fifty-two? Double it? Double your pleasure, double your fun? Try *this.* Try *this* on for size. They *lie* to you. You're growing up and they go out of their way to hedge, to qualify, to . . . to evade; to avoid—to *lie.* Never tell it how it is—how it's *going* to be—when a half-truth can be got in there. Never give the alternatives to the "pleasing prospects," the "what you have to look forward to." God, if they did the streets'd be littered with adolescent corpses! Maybe it's better they don't.

A *(Mild ridicule)*

They? *They?*

B

Parents, teachers, all the others. You *lie* to us. You don't tell us things change—that Prince Charming has the morals of a sewer rat, that you're supposed to *live* with that . . . *and* like it, or give the appearance of liking it.

Chasing the chambermaid into closets, the kitchen maid into the root cellar, and God knows *what* goes on at the stag at the Club! They probably nail the whores to the billiard tables for easy access. Nobody *tells* you any of this.

A *(Laying it on)*

Poor, poor you.

C

The root cellar?

B *(To* A *and* C*)*

Hush. No wonder one day we come back from riding, the horse all slathered, snorting, and he takes the reins, the groom does, and he helps us dismount, the groom does, his hand touching the back of our thigh, and we notice, and he notices we notice, and we remember that we've noticed him before, most especially bare chested that day heaving the straw, those arms, that butt. And no wonder we smile in that way he understands so quickly, and no wonder he leads us into a further stall—into the fucking *hay,* for God's sake!—and down we go, and it's revenge and self-pity we're doing it for until we notice it turning into pleasure for its own sake, for *our* own sake, and we're dripping wet and he rides us like we've seen in the pornos and we actually scream, and then we lie there in the straw—which probably has shit on it—cooling down, and tells us he's wanted us a lot, that he likes big women, but he didn't dare, and will he get fired now? And I say, No, no of course you won't and for a month more of it I don't, but then I do; I do have him fired, because it's dangerous not to, because it's a good deal I've got with the penguin, a long-term deal in spite of the crap he pulls, and you'd better keep your nose clean—or polished, anyway—for the *real* battles—for the penguin's *other* lady folk, the *real* ones—the mother who "just doesn't like you" for no good reason except her daughter hates you, fears you and hates you—*envies* and therefore hates you—dumpy, stupid, whining little bitch! Just *doesn't* like you—maybe in part because she senses the old man's got the letch for you and besides, no girl's good enough for the penguin, not *her* penguin; the first two sure weren't and this one's not going to be either. Try to keep on the good side of the whole wretched family, stand up for your husband when he won't do it for himself, watch out for all the intrigue; start *really* worrying about your sister who's really stopped worrying about herself— about *anything,* watch your own mother begin to change even more than you're aware *you* are, and then try to raise that!?

(Points to him)

That!?—gets himself thrown out of every school he can find, even one or two we haven't sent him to, sense he hates you, catch him doing it with your niece-in-law *and* your nephew-in-law the same week!? Start reading the letters he's getting from—how do they call it?—older friends?, telling him how to outwit *you,* how to survive living with his awful family; tell him you'll brain him with the fucking crystal ashtray if he doesn't stop getting letters, doesn't stop saying anything, doesn't stop . . . just . . . doesn't . . . stop? And he sneers, and he says very quietly that he can have me put in jail for opening his mail. Not while you're a minor, I tell him; you just wait, I tell him, you just wait; I'll have you thrown out of this house so quick it'll make your head spin. *You're* going to fire me, he says, quietly, smiling; You going to *fire* me too!? Just like you fired *him?* He's good in bed, *isn't* he! Of course, *you* wouldn't know about *bed*, he says. He gets up, stops by me, touches my hair. I thought I saw some straw, he says; sorry. And he walks out of the solarium, out of the house, out of our lives. He doesn't say good-bye to either of us. He says goodbye to Mother, upstairs; he says goodbye to the Pekingese, too, I imagine. He packs one bag, and he leaves.

 (To him; rage)

Get out of my house!!

 (Pause; to C*)*

Does that tell you a little something about change? Does that tell you what you want to know? . . .

C (Pause; softly)

Yes. Thank you.

 (Silence)

A (Curious)

You want some more?

C

No, thank you.

B

I shouldn't *think* so.

A

Yes, you *do; you want* more.

C (Trying to stay polite)

I said, no, thank you.

A

That doesn't cut any ice around here.

 (Points to B*)*

How you got to *her* is one thing; how you got to me is another. How do you put it . . . that *thing* there?

 *(Points to "*A*")*

C

I'm sorry.

A

Well . . . maybe.

B

Yeah, I've got a few doubts about *that* route myself.

A

You!

B

Yeah; well. I'm not so bad. There's been shit, but there've been *good* times, too. Some of the best.

A *(Oddly bright)*

Of course; there are always good times: like when we broke our back.
   (To C*)*
You break your back.

B *(Laughs a little)*

Yeah; you sure *do.*

C *(Scared of this)*

I do?

B

Snap!

A *(Smiles)*

Well, not exactly. Snap! Really!

B

I should *know;* it was *only* ten years ago, and . . .

A

Riding, yes; jumping. We never liked jumping—hunters; saddle horse, yes, hunters, no. Brutes, every one of them, brutes or hysterics; but hunters it was *that* day, entertaining some damn fools. Brisk, burned leaves in the air, smell of burning, just dawn; mist on the ground, dawn all green and yellow.
   (To B*)*
We didn't like our *mount,* did we?

B

No.

A

No, I didn't *like* her; she was hysteric *and* a brute.

C

When do I learn to ride? I mean really *ride.*

B

It goes with the marriage.

A

Yes, I didn't trust her; I'd ridden her earlier that fall; she was stupid and cantankerous, shied at a moving shadow.

(To C)
I said to him, you go on, I'll stay; you go on.

B

Yes.

A

But he looked so hurt I said, Oh, all right, and off we went, into the wood, the green, the gold, the mist knee high to a . . . to your knees! Stupid *cow* of a horse! Couldn't she see the fence in the mist? Did she come on it too fast and shy like that? Over we *went!*

B

Over we *went.*

C

Oh, no!

A *(To B)*
Could have broken my *neck,* I suppose. Lucky.

B

Well, yes, there *is* that.

A *(To B)*
We never mounted a hunter again, did we?

B

Nope.

A

Damned cast weighed a ton! And you know what I thought about most?

B *(Remembering)*
Who's he doing it with? who's he got cornered in what corner? what hall-way? who he's poking his little dick into?

A

That he might leave us, that he might decide to get one isn't broken.

C *(Awe)*
What kind of man *is* this!?

A *(To C)*
Man-man.

B *(To C)*
Man-man.

C

How was this happy time? Good times, you said?

B *(To C)*
Oh, well, we proved we were human.

(To A*)*

No?

A *(To* B*)*

Of course.

(To C*)*

We were fallible. Once you fall—whether you get up or not—once you
fall, and they see it, they know you can be pushed. Whether you're made
of crockery and smash into pieces, or you're bronze and you clang when
you topple, it makes no never-mind; it's the plinth is important.

B *(To* C*)*

To translate . . .

C

Thank you.

A *(Sweet smile)*

Thank you.

B

To translate . . . you can go around fixing the *world,* patching everything
up—*everyone*—and they're *grate*ful to you—grudgingly, but grateful—but
once you fall yourself, prove you're not quite as *much* better than they are,
than they thought, then they'll *let* you go right on doing everything for
them, fixing the world, etcetera, but they won't hate you quite so much . . .
because you're not perfect.

A *(Very bright)*

And so everything's *better.* Nice and better. Doesn't that make it a good
time? He *doesn't* leave you for something else; he's sweet and gives you a
big diamond ring, and you don't have to get back up on a hunter anymore.
Doesn't that make it a happy time?

C

Do I get to shoot the horse?

B *(Laughs)*

I *beg* your pardon!?

A *(Whoops)*

Whooooooo! Never occurred to me!

*(*A *and* B *laugh together)*

C *(Grit)*

I'll never become you—either of you.

B *(Looks at* C*)*

Oh, stop!

(*To* A)

And the great ring—the big diamond? You don't wear it anymore?

A (*Suddenly sober*)

Gone.

B (*Sobered too*)

Oh?

A

I *sold* it.

B

Oh?

A (*A little bitter*)

I've sold *everything*. Well, not everything . . . but most. Money doesn't go as far these days? Money doesn't go *anywhere!* I have no money. I have *money*, but I eat into it every year; every year it's less.

B

We should cut back; we should . . .

A

Don't talk to me about cutting back! It's all paste! It's fake! All the jewelry sitting in the vault, in the bank? It's all fake!

C

Why is it there? Why do you . . . why do we *bother?*

A (*Contempt*)

Huh!

B (*To* C, *then to* A)

Because we take it out and we wear it? Because the fake look as good as the real, even feels the same and why should anybody know our business?

   (*Specifically to* A)

No?

C

Appearances?

B

Appearances? That which appears to be?

C

I mean, who are we trying to impress?

A

Ourselves. You'll learn. I took the big diamond in. When we bought it—when he brought it in for me, he said . . .

B

. . . this is a perfect stone; I've never seen a better one. You ever want to sell this you bring it back to me I'll give you better than you paid for it. He patted my hand. Pat-pat.

A

Pat-pat. And so I took it back—after he died, after the cancer and all, after all that. They looked at it; they said it was deeply flawed, or it was cloudy . . . or something.

B

Sons of bitches!

A

They offered me a third of what he paid for it, and the dollar wasn't worth half of what it had been?

C *(To A)*

Didn't you sue?
  (To B)
I mean, what can we do? We just can't . . .

A *(Accepting)*

What can you *do?* There's nothing you can *do.* You go *on;* you . . . eat *into* yourself. Starving people absorb their own bodies. The money's there—the investments are there, except less each year; it absorbs itself. It's all you've planned to *count* on *isn't;* the extras?

B *(To A)*

The big diamond, eh?

A

The big diamond . . . *and* most of the rest. Well, what does it matter? It's all glitter.

C *(Protest)*

No! It's more than that! It's tangible proof . . . that we're valuable . . .
  (Embarrassed)
that we're valued.

A *(Shrugs)*

Well, it's gone; all the glitter's gone.

B *(Rue)*

Yup.
  (Waves)
Bye.

C

Are there any *other* surprises?

B (*Grating laugh*)

Oh, yeah; lots!

A

Oh, my dear; you just wait.
   (*Over toward the bed*)
She hides the money. Whatever she gets for the jewelry she keeps in cash, and spends a little whenever there isn't enough of the regular. There's a lot; she can't spend it all—without people knowing what she's doing, I mean. She hides it, and then eventually she can't remember where she hid it, and she can't find it . . . ever. And she can't tell anybody.
   (*Silence*)

B (*A little shy*)

Is the cancer bad?

A

When is it good?

C

How bad?

A (*Mocking*)

Fill me *in;* fill me in!
   (*To* C)
Pretty terrible!
   (*To* B; *softer tone*)
Six years; I told you that; it takes him six years from when he knows it—when they tell him he has it—to when he goes. Prostate—spreads to the bladder, spreads to the bone, spreads to the brain, and to the liver, of course; everything does—the *ancients* knew something. It's all right at first—except for the depression, *and* the fear—it's all right at first, but then the pain comes, slowly, growing, and then the day he screams in the bathroom, and I rush in; I expect to see him lying there, but no, he's standing at the toilet, and his face is filled with horror and he points to the bowl, and I look, and it's all pink in there, that the blood is coming with the urine now. And it's all downhill from there: the pink becomes red, and then there's blood in the bed, at night, as I'm lying with him, holding him; and then there's . . . no! Why go on with it!?
   (*To* C; *ugly*)
It's terrible! And there's nothing you can do to prepare yourself! I don't like you; you deserve it!

C (*So softly*)

Thank you.

A (*Quietly dismissive*)

You're welcome.

C

I don't like you either.

B *(Pause)*

And so it goes.

> *(Silence.* A *moves to the bed, sits on it, opposite from him.* A *speaks directly to him; now he can hear her, can respond)*

A

I had a premonition. I know you say there's no such thing, but I *had* one. It was I died.

> *(His hand up. Continued)*

Oh, stop it! You don't think I'm going to? You can hardly—wait! Just you wait! I died, you see, and when I did it—when I died—I was all alone . . . no one there in the room with me—the hospital room: I was back in that awful hospital!

> *(Suddenly weepy)*

Why didn't you take me *out* of there!? Why did you leave me in that . . .

> *(He tries to touch her, to comfort her. Continued)*

Don't you touch me!! There I was, and I was in a coma, in and out, in and out. Sometimes I'd wake up and wonder who I was, and *where* I was, and who were all those people looking at me? Sometimes I wouldn't wake up . . . not all the way, and I'd half try, and then I wouldn't. You brought me flowers, you brought freesia. You know I love freesia; that's why you bring them to me, because I *love* them! Why do you do that!? You hate me; why do you do that!? What do you want!? You *want* something. Well, you just wait. You'll get what's coming to you. In my premonition I knew I was dead, and it didn't seem to matter any, and I was all alone. There was no one there with me and I was *dead!* No one! Just the chauffeur and the maid. I was there an hour, and I was *dead,* and then *you* came in, and you had your flowers, your freesia. You came into the room, and they were there, and I was dead, and you stopped at the door of the room, and you knew right away, and you stopped and you . . . *thought!*

> *(Loathing)*

I *watched* you *think!* And your face didn't change.

> *(Wistful)*

Why didn't your face ever change? And there you were, and you thought, and you decided, and you walked over to the bed, and you touched my hand, and you bent down, and you kissed me on the forehead . . . for them! They were there and they were watching and you kissed me for *them!*

> *(Softer)*

And then you stood up, still holding on to my hand, as if . . . what? You didn't know what to do with it? You held on to my hand, and my hand wasn't warm anymore, was it? My hand was cold, *wasn't* it?

(*Pause*)

Wasn't it?

(*He looks at her once more, shudders, weeps, looks back at* "A." A
moves away from the bed)

B (*Softly*)

And so it goes.

C

(*To* A; *slowly, with great emphasis, but no anger*)

I . . . will . . . not . . . become . . . you. I will *not*. I . . . I deny *you*.

A (*Mildly amused*)

Oh? Yes? You *deny* me?

(*To them all*)

Yes? You all deny me?

(*To* C)

You deny me?

(*To* B)

I suppose you do too.

(B *lowers her gaze. Continued*)

Yes; of course.

(*To him*)

And of course, *you* deny me.

(*He looks at her. Continued; general*)

Well, that's all right: I deny you too; I deny you all.

(*To* C)

I deny *you*,

(*To* B)

and I deny *you*,

(*To him*)

and, of course, I deny *you*.

(*General*)

I'm *here*, and I deny you *all*; I deny every *one* of you.

C

Is it like this? What about the happy times . . . the *happiest* moments? *I
haven't* had them yet, have I? All done at twenty-six? I can't imagine that.
I had *some*, of course, some of what probably will *be* the happiest even when
I get to the point I can begin to think about looking back without feeling silly,
though God knows when *that* will be!—not feeling silly—if *ever*.
Confirmation, for example, that wonderful time: the white dress Mother
made, Sis all jealous and excited, jumping up and down and sulking at the
same time. But even now, you see, I'm remembering, and what I'm remem-

bering doesn't have to do with what I *felt*, but what I remember. They say you can't remember pain. Well, maybe you can't remember pleasure, either—in the same way, I mean, in the way you can't remember pain. Maybe all you can remember is the memory of it . . . remembering, remembering it. I *know* my best times—what is it? happiest?—haven't happened yet. They're to *come*. Aren't they? Please? And . . . and whatever evil comes, whatever loss and taking away comes, won't it all be balanced out? Please? I'm not a fool, but there *is* a lot of happiness along the way. *Isn't* there!? And isn't it always ahead? Aren't I *right?* Aren't I? I mean . . . all along the way? No? Please?

(B *comes to the right or left of* C, *leaving center free for* A *later.*
B *shakes her head to* C, *not unkindly*)

B

Silly, silly girl; silly baby. The happiest time? Now; now . . . always. This must be the happiest time: half of being adult done, the rest ahead of me. Old enough to be a *little* wise, past being *really* dumb . . .

(*An aside to* C)
No offense.

C (*Looking forward: tight smiles*)
None taken.

B

Enough shit gone through to have a sense of the shit that's ahead, but way past sitting and *playing* in it. This *has* to be the happiest time—in theory, anyway. Things nibble away, of course; your job is to know *that,* too. The wood *may* be rotten under your feet—your nicely spread legs—and you'll be up to your ass in sawdust and dry rot before you know it, before you know it, before you can say this is the happiest time. Well, I can *live* with that, *die* with that. I mean, these things happen, but what I like most about being where I am—and fifty *is* a peak, in the sense of a mountain.

C (*An aside*)
Fifty-two.

B

Yes, I know, thank you. What I like most about being where I am is that there's a lot I don't have to go through anymore, and that doesn't mean closing down—for *me*, at any rate. It opens up whole vistas—of decline, of obsolescence, peculiarity, but really *interesting!* Standing up here right on top of the middle of it *has* to be the happiest time. I mean, it's the only time you get a three-hundred-and-sixty-degree view—see in all directions. Wow! What a view!

(A *moves to center*, B *and* C *stay where they are*)

A

(*Shakes her head; chuckles; to* B *and* C)
You're both such children. The happiest moment of all? Really? The happiest moment?

(To the audience now)

Coming to the end of it, I think, when all the waves cause the greatest woes to subside, leaving breathing space, time to concentrate on the greatest woe of all—that blessed one—the end of it. Going through the whole thing and coming out . . . not out *beyond* it, of course, but sort of to . . . one side. None of that "further shore" nonsense, but to the point where you *can* think about yourself in the third person without being crazy. I've waked up in the morning, and I've thought, well, now, she's waking up, and now she's going to see what works—the eyes, for example. Can she *see?* She *can?* Well, good, I suppose; so much for that. Now she's going to test all the other stuff—the joints, the inside of the mouth, and now she's going to have to pee. What's she going to do—go for the walker. Lurch from chair to chair—pillar to post? Is she going to call for somebody—anybody . . . the tiniest thought there might be nobody there, that she's not making a sound, that maybe she's not alive—so's anybody'd notice, that is? *I* can do that. I can think about myself that way, which means, I suppose, that that's the way I'm *living*—beside myself, to one side. Is that what they mean by that? I'm beside myself? I don't think so. I think they're talking about *another* kind of joy. There's a difference between knowing you're going to *die* and *knowing* you're going to die. The second is better; it moves away from the theoretical. I'm rambling, aren't I?

B *(Gently; face forward)*

A little.

A *(To B)*

Well, we *do* that at ninety, or whatever I'm posed to be; I mean, give a girl a break!

(To the audience again)

Sometimes when I wake up and start thinking about myself like that—like I was watching—I really get the feeling that I *am dead,* but going on at the same time, and I wonder if she can talk and feel and . . . and then I wonder which has died—me, or the one I think about. It's a fairly confusing business. I'm rambling.

(She gestures to stop B)

Yes; I know!

(Out)

I was talking about . . . what: coming to the end of it; yes. So. There it is. You asked, after all. That's the happiest moment.

(A looks to C and B, puts her hands out, takes theirs. Continued)

When it's all done. When we stop. When we can stop.

CURTAIN

Fragments
(A Sit-Around)

AUTHOR'S NOTE

While *Fragments* is a play—looks like a play, sounds like a play, acts like a play—an unnerving number of critics (not audiences, I hasten to add) have declared that it isn't a play as they understand the term, and, therefore, it can't *be* one.

While the problem *is*, I think, theirs—the critics'—I have decided to call the piece a sit-around, and let the critics figure out what *that* means. Certainly, anyone who decides to mount *Fragments* will not be accused of not doing a "play." (While they may be criticized for mounting a "sit-around," there are only so many of the world's problems I can solve)

A NOTE FOR DIRECTORS

Common sense should determine the stage movement. Let groups form
and un-form, but let it be so casual we're not aware of it.

I have found (in directing this piece three times) that the actors' instinct
as to spatial relationships usually works fine.

Do *not* be specific about "where we are" or who the characters "are"; they
are who they portray, and they are where they are. Be casual, be informal;
let the piece build its own tensions and overall shape.

Fragments was originally commissioned by, and received its world pre-
miere at, Ensemble Theatre of Cincinnati (David White III, Artistic
Director), in Cincinnati, Ohio, on October 10, 1993. It was directed by
Edward Albee; the set design was by Kevin Murphy and Ruth D. Sawyer;
the costume design was by Rebecca Senske; the lighting design was by
James H. Gage and the stage manager was Suann Pollock. The cast includ-
ed Michael Blankenship, Gordon Greene, Dale Hodges, Paul Kennedy,
Mack C. Miles, Regina Pugh, Lee Walsh, Julia White.

Fragments was produced by Signature Theatre Company (James
Houghton, Artistic Director; Thomas C. Proehl, Managing Director; Elliot
Fox, Associate Director), at the Kampo Cultural Center, in New York City,
on April 8, 1994. It was directed by James Houghton; the set design was
by E. David Cosier; the costume design was by Teresa Snider-Stein; the
lighting design was by Colin D. Young and the production stage manager
was Elliot Fox. The cast included Angela Marie Bettis, John Carter, Paddy
Croft, Lou Ferguson, Cheryl Gaysunas, Edward Norton, Joyce O'Connor
and Scott Sowers.

CASTING

WOMEN
WOMAN 1 must be younger than
WOMAN 2 who must be younger than
WOMAN 3 who must be younger than
WOMAN 4

Ideal ages:
  WOMAN 1 — 25
  WOMAN 2 — 30
  WOMAN 3 — 40
  WOMAN 4 — 65

MEN
MAN 1 must be younger than
MAN 2 who must be younger than
MAN 3 who must be younger than
MAN 4

Ideal ages:
  MAN 1 — 20
  MAN 2 — 30
  MAN 3 — 45
  MAN 4 — 55-65

NOTE: Man 2 must be cast with an African-American actor; beyond that, let common sense determine casting.

ACT ONE

(Chairs in a semicircle. As lights fade up, eight actors enter greeting each other, each carrying a small hardcover book.

Note: In this scene each of the actors is assigned set speeches—specific proverbs. Between the reading of each proverb, each of the others is requested to make some comment about that proverb if anything comes to mind—ironic, flippant, supportive, whatever. These may vary from performance to performance, but I imagine some of them will become set. Be free with it)

MAN 4 *(To the others)*

OK. Let's begin, shall we?

(To the audience)

Fragments; Act One.

(To the others)

Let's do some proverbs; I'll begin. He that has been bitten by a snake is afraid of a rope.

WOMAN 4

Never put your doctor in your will.

WOMAN 2

Forgive everyone but yourself.

WOMAN 3

It's a good idea to have friends both in heaven and in hell.

MAN 2

Three may keep a secret if two of them are dead.

WOMAN 1

If it were not for hope the heart would break.

MAN 3

Never marry for money; you can borrow it cheaper.

WOMAN 2

When you can step on nine daisies at once, Spring has come.

MAN 1

Everything helps, said the wren, as she pissed into the sea.

WOMAN 4

It's a sad burden to carry a dead man's child.

MAN 3

You cannot prevent the bird of sadness from flying over your head, but you can prevent it from nesting in your hair. Chinese.

WOMAN 4

Only a fool isn't sad at least once a day.

WOMAN 1

If you can't bite, don't show your teeth.

WOMAN 4

Save something for the man who rides on the white horse.

MAN 2

What does that mean?

WOMAN 4

I have no idea.

WOMAN 1

The absent get farther away every day. Oh, isn't that true!

MAN 2

If you can't ride two horses at once you shouldn't be in the circus.

MAN 3

A good scare is worth more than good advice.

WOMAN 3

Don't teach your grandmother to suck eggs.

MAN 3

I beg your pardon?

WOMAN 2

He who sups with the devil should have a long spoon.

WOMAN 4

A wicked man is his own Hell.

MAN 2

People have the greatest faith in things they don't understand.

WOMAN 2

The apple never falls far from the tree.

MAN 1

Cut off a dog's tail and it will still be a dog.

WOMAN 4

Aren't you strange.

MAN 1 *(Shrugs)*

That's what it says, lady.

WOMAN 4

When the cuckoo comes to the bare thorn, sell your cow and buy you corn;
but when she comes to the full bit, sell your corn and buy you sheep.

MAN 1

What the hell does that mean!?

WOMAN 4

Well, I . . .

MAN 1

I mean, it doesn't even rhyme!

WOMAN 4 *(Indignant)*

I'm sorry!

MAN 3

The mother of a coward doesn't worry about him.

MAN 2

Right on.

WOMAN 2

That's pretty cynical.

WOMAN 1

An arrow shot straight up falls on the shooter's head.

MAN 2

Not if he moves.

MAN 4

There are more old drunkards than old doctors.

WOMAN 4

No one knows what will happen to him before sunset.

MAN 3

A rich man's joke is always funny.

WOMAN 4

Cynical! Cynical!

MAN 3 *(Shrugs)*

I didn't write it.

MAN 2

A woman's advice is nothing much, but he who doesn't take it is a fool.

MAN 4

If you would like to know the value of a million dollars, try to borrow it.

WOMAN 2

Dunder do gally the beans.
  (*A silence*)

MAN 2

What?

WOMAN 2 (*Rather proud*)

Dunder do gally the beans!
  (*A pause*)

MAN 1

Dunder do gally the beans.

WOMAN 4

Yes, that's the best one.

MAN 2

We have the greatest faith in things we don't understand?

WOMAN 3

Naturally!

MAN 4

Anybody want to make one up?
  (MAN 4 *begins to gather all the books and places them Up Right*)

MAN 1 (*Hand up*)

It's an ill wind that blows nobody?

WOMAN 1 (*Offended*)

Really!

MAN 2

  (*Answering* MAN 1 *in a way*)
He who lives by the proverb shall die by the proverb?

MAN 3

I have a Cuban one.

WOMAN 4

In Spanish?

MAN 3

No; in English. It doesn't matter whether elephants fight or make love—
the grass still gets trampled.

WOMAN 2

I'm trying to relate that.

MAN 1

To something?

WOMAN 2

Of course!

MAN 4

Here's another one: He who swims with sharks should expect the water to turn red.

WOMAN 4

I have a Zen one . . .

MAN 2

Will it help?

WOMAN 4

Probably not. If you understand . . . things are just as they are; if you do not understand . . . things are just as they are.

(*Bit of a pause*)

MAN 4

No, that *doesn't* really help much, does it.

MAN 1

It's Zen, for God's sake!

WOMAN 1

Still . . .

MAN 2 (*Raises his hand*)

I have a poem, if you think it will help.

WOMAN 1

Poems don't very often do that—help, I mean.

WOMAN 2

I read a book of something called "Helpful Poems" once, I think; or "Healthful Poems"; maybe that's what it was.

MAN 2 (*Sighs*)

Never mind.

MAN 4

No! No; do it. Do your poem.

MAN 3

Really? It's a poem you wrote!?

MAN 1

Yeah; people do that, you know.

MAN 2 (*Not exactly pleasant*)

Yes; it's a poem I wrote. All by myself, without help from parents or teacher.

WOMAN 4

I want to hear it; we all want to hear it.
        (*Generally: Yeah; right; etc.*)

MAN 2

All right. "Exercises" It's called . . . "Exercises."

WOMAN 4

What? It's called what?

MAN 4 (*To* WOMAN 4)

EXERCISES!

WOMAN 4

Ah!

MAN 2

    Take your head off.
    Hold it in front of you with both hands,
    Eye level so to speak,
    Then throw it as high as you can
    —as high as you dare the first time—
    Straight up!

    Don't panic!
    Keep your eyes closed!
    Think about watching it
    Tumbling and spinning.
    —Keep your eyes closed!—
    Coming to rest for that dancer's instant
    Plummeting . . .
    Catch it, you fool!
    There;
    Now put it back on
    Right side up eyes front.

    Sit down and rest for a minute.
    (*A tiny pause*)

WOMAN 1

Well! That was just wonderful!

MAN 2

Second stanza . . .

WOMAN 1 (*Tiny*)

Oh.

MAN 2

    Take your head off again.
    Hold it in front of you with both hands,

Eye level so to speak,
Then throw it as high as you can
—even higher than before—
Straight up.

Don't panic!
Keep your eyes *open* this time!
Watch yourself down there
In all the tumbling and spinning
—keep your *eyes* open, for God's sake!—
come to rest for that dancer's instant . . .
Plummet!
Make your hands catch you!
There;
Now make them put your head back on
Right side up eyes front.

  Sit down and rest again.
  (*Longer pause*)

WOMAN 2 (*Generally; loud whisper*)
Is that it?
  (*Generally: Shhhhhhh! etc.*)
Well, I just wondered.

MAN 4 (*Sincere*)
Well, that's . . . that's very good.

MAN 1
That isn't the kind of poem *I'd* write.

WOMAN 1
It's so . . . so sophisticated, so . . . subtle!

MAN 2 (*Wryly amused*)
What were you expecting . . . Vachel Lindsey's *The Congo*, for Christ's sake? I suppose I could have done some tap with it.

WOMAN 1 (*High horse*)
That's not what I meant!

MAN 2 (*Forgiving*)
I know; I know. Do you think it helped?

WOMAN 4 (*Comforting*)
Poetry helps in subtle ways; you don't think it has, and then . . . bang!

MAN 4
I think it helped; I think it helped a lot.

(Sees WOMAN 2, *with her eyes closed, tossing something imaginary into the air).*

What are you doing?

WOMAN 2 *(Coming to)*

Hm? What? Oh, I was practicing the poem . . . "throw your head in the air . . ." or whatever.

MAN 4 *(Chuckles)*

Well, all right; you do that later. Edward Albee, who wrote this play, wanted you to know about this charity auction—a sort of celebrity auction he was asked to participate in.

WOMAN 3

Oh?

MAN 4

It was called Eggstravaganza, or some such thing.

MAN 1

How cute!

MAN 4 *(To* MAN 1*)*

Now, now; never tell other people how to run their lives—their charities, at any rate. It was for a perfectly *good* charity, he says, and he gets asked to do that sort of thing a lot, he says.

MAN 2

Unh-hunh; unh-hunh.

WOMAN 2

I've never done that.

MAN 1 *(Looks at her oddly)*

Of course not!

WOMAN 1

It must be fun!

MAN 4

He remembered that they sent him—and all the others they asked, he imagined—a largish plastic egg shell, sort of broken open, with some colored felt pens, so he could decorate it as he wanted, and sign his name, too.

WOMAN 4

That must have been a pretty big egg shell, plastic or not—an ostrich egg?

MAN 4

I'm not sure. In any event . . .

MAN 1

Why didn't he just send a book of one of his plays, or something? I'm sure he's got stacks of them—remaindered, and all.

MAN 3

Now, now.

WOMAN 3

Yes: now, now.

MAN 4

I have no idea. Anyway apparently what they asked for was this . . . *egg* shell, all decorated and signed. And so, he did it . . . appropriately, and so did a lot of other celebrities.

WOMAN 2

What exactly is a celebrity these days?

WOMAN 3

Someone who gets asked to sign egg shells and such. Shhhhh!

WOMAN 2

Oh!

MAN 4

Perhaps a hundred . . . celebrities, and he did it, and . . . put it out of his mind.

MAN 1

. . . As a proper celebrity *would.*

MAN 4

Yes.

WOMAN 4 *(To* MAN 1*)*

There are *limits* to you.

MAN 1 *(To* WOMAN 4*)*

Oh? There *are? I* haven't found them.

MAN 4

May I finish this, please?

MAN 1

Oh, yeah.

WOMAN 4

Certainly.
   ("Have I stopped you?")

MAN 4

And he said that one day he got this mimeographed page of paper with— oh—lots of names on it.

WOMAN 3

Mimeographed?

MAN 4

Well, Xeroxed is what he meant, probably.

MAN 3

Faxed, most likely.

MAN 4

Thank you. And there were all these names on it—not alphabetized, though—with dollar amounts next to them, and a little thank you note, and he figured out that the dollar amounts were what everybody's eggs had gotten at the charity auction—what they had gone for.

(*Smiles*)

WOMAN 1 (*Urgent*)

. . . and!?

MAN 4

(*Thinking about something else*)

Hm?

WOMAN 1

And!?

MAN 4

Oh. Well, and naturally he looked to see where he was—who got bid more for than him, who got less—you know: natural curiosity.

WOMAN 1

AND!?

MAN 4 (*Smiles at her*)

And . . . he made a note of the interesting ones, and was surprised that he'd done better than Glenn Close.

WOMAN 3

No!

MAN 4 (*Nods*)

Unh-hunh; and better than Victor Borge . . .

MAN 3

Well, that's no surprise; isn't Victor Borge dead?

WOMAN 4

Very!

WOMAN 1

Shhhhh!

MAN 4

. . . and that he'd done better than Erma Bombeck . . .

WOMAN 2

Now, I can't believe that! Better than Erma!?

MAN 2

Well, funny things happen.

WOMAN 2

Still!

MAN 4

. . . and a lot better than Mortimer Adler.

MAN 1

Than who?

WOMAN 4 (*To* MAN 4)

Really!
  (*To* MAN 1)
Where have you been?
  (*To* MAN 4)
Better than Mortimer Adler?

WOMAN 1 (*To* WOMAN 3)

Who *is* he?

WOMAN 3

He was a . . . is a . . . never mind.

MAN 4

Better than Jay Leno, better than Ralph Nader . . .

MAN 2

Oh, come on!

MAN 4

Yep; better than Donald Trump, better than Willard Scott . . .

MAN 3

. . . Even as we speak.

MAN 4

. . . and better than Ted Danson . . .

MAN 1

Where was this thing held—on Mars?

WOMAN 3 (*Giggles*)

Oh, hush!

MAN 4

. . . and a lot of others, better than a lot of others, but those were the
interesting ones.

MAN 2

Who did he do worse than?

WOMAN 1

Yes!

MAN 2

Whose egg did better?

MAN 4

Well, he thought that was *very* interesting. Aside from some people he'd never heard of—some locals, I guess—he was most impressed by three who'd done better—whose eggs had done better.

WOMAN 3

An important distinction.

WOMAN 4 (*To herself grumpy*)

Better than Mortimer Adler. Really!

MAN 3

Who did better? Whose egg did better?

MAN 4

Jean-Claude Van Damme, for one; Jean-Claude Van Damme did better.

MAN 3

Well, I suppose that figures.

MAN 2

Who else?

MAN 4

The Grateful Dead; they did a lot better.

MAN 2

Well . . . naturally.

MAN 1

Of course.

WOMAN 1

And who else?

MAN 4

The one that got him the most, the one that impressed him *most* did better than he did—whose egg did better than he did . . . than his did—was . . . Don Knotts.

(*Pause*)

MAN 3 (*Disbelief*)

No!

WOMAN 3

You're joking.

MAN 2

Don Knotts!?

WOMAN 2

Where was this thing held?

MAN 1

Mars.

WOMAN 2

Oh; right.

MAN 4 *(Pinning it down)*

Don . . . Knotts.

WOMAN 2

I declare.

MAN 4

He said that's the sort of thing puts it all in perspective for him—shrinks the head a little bit, as he put it.

WOMAN 4 *(Shaking her head)*

I swan.

MAN 3

Don Knotts.

WOMAN 2

I . . . I like Don Knotts.
    (They all look at her)
I do!

MAN 1

Anybody do just the same as he did?—get bid for the same?

MAN 4

Yes; there were three; three got the same bid he did.

MAN 1

And . . .?

MAN 4 *(Without comment)*

Tim Conway, Ann Landers, and Oliver North.
    (Silence)

MAN 3

I don't think there's anything more to say.

WOMAN 4

No. No.

WOMAN 3

No; certainly not. Poor Mr. Albee.

WOMAN 4

Yes; poor Mr. Albee.

MAN 1

Oh, these theatre people, the trouble they've seen.

WOMAN 3

I tell you.

MAN 3

I had a dream the other night: I went to the *theatre*—that I went to a *play*.

WOMAN 4

    (Pause; not very interested)

Oh?

MAN 3 *(Mimicking)*

Oh? Yes, that I went to the theatre.

WOMAN 4 *(Attempting interest)*

I see!

MAN 3

The curtain rose . . .

WOMAN 1

Was it a musical?

MAN 3

Hush. The curtain rose on a stage littered with chairs—severe black ones, a long table-like thing, and a harridan on a kind of trolley.

WOMAN 1

I *like* musicals. I really *do*.

MAN 3

That's nice. She didn't *do* much for the longest time, just . . . sort of trollied around, her face and hair powdered grey, powder puffing from her. Then, at the crack of a slapstick . . . twelve other actors filed on stage and got in a line against a wall and stood there while the harridan trollied around.

WOMAN 1 *(Cheerful)*

Musicals are so. . . . I don't know—comic strip and vulgar and simple-minded. . . .

MAN 3

Please? Then at every crack of the slapstick, one of the actors would . . . *do* something—not very much, take three steps, say, in a kind of slow, slow motion.

WOMAN 1

. . . except the ones aim above their station—lots of clever orchestration, older women and no hummable tunes; those ones win prizes, but they aren't much fun.

MAN 3

Nobody touched, and several people would do things in unison—but very slowly, you understand. And all the while no one was saying anything: not a word; not a sound.

WOMAN 1 *(Slightly patronizing)*

Well, it certainly wasn't a musical!

MAN 3 *(Looks at her strangely)*

No, no, of course it wasn't!

WOMAN 1

With no one saying a word! Musicals are *full* of sound—not much fury, of course—but full of sound, talking and singing and dancing and running about and . . .

MAN 3

It wasn't a musical! Are you going to listen?

WOMAN 1 *(Patting his hand)*

Of course, of course; go on with your little story. All these people were *milling* . . .

MAN 3

Very . . . *slowly*. With gestures like . . . this.
  (Does a slow, slow arm raise)

MAN 2

They did that a lot? That sort of . . . thing?

MAN 3

Yes; usually one and the another. Not like the Rockettes, or anything. . . .

WOMAN 4

I *love* the Rockettes!

MAN 3

But . . . random. One . . . and then another . . . somewhere. Sometimes they walked a little, and then lay down, or something.

MAN 1

But very slowly.

MAN 3

Yes. Very slowly.

MAN 1

And no one said a word.

MAN 3

Yes. Not a word.

WOMAN 3

How . . . how long did this . . . go on?

MAN 3

Oh . . . twenty minutes?

WOMAN 3 *(After a thinking pause)*

Really?

MAN 3

Yes. Really.

MAN 1

Then what happened?

MAN 3

Well, the slapstick cracked and all the lights went out.

WOMAN 4

Well, I should think *so!*

MAN 3

Then they all came on again . . . the lights.
   (Wonder in his voice)
Then all the actors very slowly moved all the chairs and the table-like thing a sort of quarter turn, and the harridan turned in her trolly, and all the other actors, very slowly, lined up against *another* wall, and all the lights went out, again.

MAN 2

Very slowly?

MAN 3 *(Bemused)*

No; the lights would generally come on and go off rather briskly.

WOMAN 1

It happens that way in musicals, too—very brisk! Lights on! Lights off! Music! Singing! Dancing!

MAN 3

This was *not* a musical.

WOMAN 1

Certainly not, not without music, though that may come next, the price of everything and all.

MAN 2

Then what happened.

MAN 3

Well, after they'd very slowly moved all the chairs and the table-like thing and all. . . .

WOMAN 2

. . . *and* the harridan.

MAN 3

. . . *and* the harridan. Oh you *are* following; good. They all lined up and the lights went off, and then the slapstick went again and all the lights came on again, and . . .
   (Some wonder)
and the whole thing started all over again.

MAN 2 *(Beat)*

What do you mean?

MAN 3

Well, it was almost as if they'd planned it.
   (Gestures with this)
They did the whole thing again, the entire twenty minutes, exactly as they'd done it before, very slowly, and it was as though the entire audience—all eight of us—had moved a quarter turn around, except it was the actors had . . . and the set.

WOMAN 4 *(Thinks about this)*

My gracious.

MAN 3

They did it all again—the same twenty minutes.

MAN 1 *(Pinning it down)*

Precisely the same way. No differences at *all*.

MAN 3

Yes. None. Except a quarter turn.

WOMAN 4

And all in silence.

MAN 3

Yes. All in silence.

WOMAN 4

I almost don't dare ask this: What Happened Then?

MAN 3

I woke up!

WOMAN 3

Well, I should hope *so!*

MAN 3

I assume that sooner or later someone would have *said* something. Not that I stayed asleep to see—or *hear,* rather.

WOMAN 4

Well, certainly in a musical they would have.

MAN 3 *(Shrugs)*

Some nights your sleeping self just . . . moves into the *avant garde,* I suppose.

WOMAN 1

In a musical that never happens: in a musical the unexpected is always predictable. The musical is *premised* on the *derriere garde.*

MAN 4

You *will* go on about musicals.

WOMAN 1

I *love* them!—especially when they're old-fashioned, and derivative, and cartoonish, and cynically fashioned, and a thorough waste of time.

MAN 4

I see.
    (Pause)
Do you *dream* about them?

WOMAN 1

Good heavens, no! I go to see them! I'm a regular . . . audience.

WOMAN 3

We need . . . fewer of you, I think.

MAN 4

What's the matter?

WOMAN 4

Oh, nothing. I was just thinking . . . about . . . *stuff.*

WOMAN 3

What? What . . . "stuff?"

WOMAN 4

Things vanish sometimes like in dreams and we're not even aware they're gone, or that they ever were—that we used to be around them and take them for granted.

MAN 4

Oh?

WOMAN 4

Yes: Knife grinders, for example.

MAN 4 (*Some wonder*)

Knife grinders! The men who ground knives!

MAN 1

Who?

WOMAN 4 (*Dismissing him*)

You're all too young to remember knife grinders. They went the way of the Good Humor truck—before it.

WOMAN 3

I remember *them!*

MAN 3

So do I.

MAN 2

I think *I* do.

WOMAN 4

. . . The three-times-a-day mail delivery—oh, all *sorts* of things.

MAN 2

What *about* knife grinders?

MAN 4

And organ grinders: they're gone, too.

MAN 1

Who'd want to grind an organ?

MAN 4

Little old Italian men—Sicilian, probably—with a hurdy-gurdy type thing on a pole, which they'd turn with a crank and it played a tune.

WOMAN 4

And they had a little monkey with a cap and a little tin cup . . .

WOMAN 1

I've seen pictures!

WOMAN 2

Yes! So have I!

MAN 4

And you'd give a penny or something to the monkey—in his cup—and the little old Italian man would say thank you, or grazie.

(*Remembers*)

My goodness.

MAN 1

Or you'd give a penny or something to the little old Italian man—in his cup—and the monkey would say thank you, or grazie, my goodness. Maybe they'll come back.

MAN 3

Sure; all the homeless, and all; they need work.

MAN 2

How in the hell are the homeless supposed to afford a . . . what is it?

MAN 4

A hurdy-gurdy.

MAN 2

. . . Much less a monkey. Be sensible.

MAN 3

Yeah, I suppose.

WOMAN 2

Maybe there's a warehouse filled with hurdygurdys!

MAN 2

And monkeys? Give up.

WOMAN 2

I'm trying to be helpful.

MAN 2

Well . . . you're not getting there.

WOMAN 2 (*Offended*)

I'm sorry!

MAN 2 (*Dismissive*)

Skip it.

WOMAN 4

Does anyone remember knife grinders?
     (*To* MAN 4)
Besides you?

MAN 4

I doubt it.

WOMAN 4 (*To the others*)

For your information—for your education, to be more precise . . .

MAN 2

Thank you.

WOMAN 4

You're welcome. You would be in your kitchen—certainly in your apartment, for this would happen in the city—and you would hear the bell, the handbell, the one with the clapper, and sometimes the call "knives to grind; knives to grind," and you would know the knife grinder was out-side—even without his call; the bell was enough—wheeling his knife-grinding cart down the street. And you'd go into your knife drawer to see which of your knives needed to be sharpened.

MAN 3

What about those gadgets you roll your knives over?

WOMAN 2

. . . or the electric ones?

MAN 4

Oh, this was before all that.

WOMAN 4

Yes, and while you probably had your own knife grinder—the sword-like one you dueled your knives against?—the man who would do it for you was so much better: the knife grinder.

MAN 4

Yes; he had a big pumice wheel suspended on his cart—I guess it was pumice—and he set it moving with a foot treadle . . .

WOMAN 4

. . . Yes, and you brought your knives out and he would sharpen them—so sharp you had to be careful. He was so good sometimes you brought out knives that didn't really need to be sharpened: he was so good.

MAN 2 *(Pause)*

What brought all this up?

WOMAN 4

Oh, I don't know . . . thinking about hand crafts, maybe; thinking about all the little things people set themselves out to do then. How much more . . . community there was.

MAN 4

Yes; organ grinders, knife grinders, people in gas stations who knew how to fix cars . . .

MAN 3

. . . Doctors who made house calls . . .

MAN 2

. . . Plumbers who made house calls . . .

MAN 4.

Yes; things like that.

WOMAN 4

Things like that. You get to a point you miss things—once you get past the point you realize you're missing things but you don't know what they are—if you ever *do* get past that point.

MAN 3

Hunh.

MAN 2

Hunh.

MAN 4 *(To WOMAN 3)*

You seem preoccupied, too.

WOMAN 3

Well, yes; I am.

WOMAN 4

Oh?

WOMAN 3

I had the . . . oddest time at my doctor yesterday.

WOMAN 2

What was it?

WOMAN 3

Well . . . I was in for my annual—good girl that I am: you know, we don't want any surprises if we can help it—I was in for my annual, and I've known Sam a long time—he's our doctor—and he's a *good* doctor. We went to Mexico with Sam and his—what?—

(Does visual quotes)

his "niece?" once; he's a good guy. He tried to get funny with me once— oh, a long time ago—at a party; maybe it was just flattery; anyway, nothing serious. He's a good guy: bright; serious.

(Laughs)

He said to me once, "My shallows run deep."

MAN 1

I don't think that's original with him.

WOMAN 3 *(Only mildly interested)*

Oh? Anyway, I was there for my checkup—breast exam, x-rays, pelvic stuff—you know, the usual.

WOMAN 4

Yes; yes.

WOMAN 3

And . . . and he came back in at the end—I was still on the metal table, sit- ting there, buttoning my blouse—and he seemed sort of . . . preoccupied, or puzzled maybe. "Would you mind taking off your shirt and bra and stuff again for me?" "Hey, for you? anything!" I joked. And I did, and he asked me to stand, and I did, and he looked at me—at my breasts—ten feet off, I guess, and he looked very puzzled, and he sighed and said I could put it all back on, and he shook his head. "Oh, my God!" I said—*aloud.* I'd meant to say it to myself, but it came out . . . *aloud.* "Oh, no, no, he said, "It's not . . . *that;* I'm sorry if I . . . it's not *that.*" "What *is* it, then!?" I said. "Well," he said, and I could see he was . . . confused, or something. "What *is* it?" I said. "Well," he said, shaking his head a little, "you seem to have a kind of . . . reversal. I noticed it, well, I noticed *something* when I was looking at your x-rays—your scans. Your fallopian tubes looked sort of funny— nothing *wrong,* but funny. Then I took a look at your kidneys and I noticed the same thing—they look *reversed.*" "I beg your pardon!?" "Your kidneys are reversed; so are your tubes; the left one's where the right one should be, and vice versa." "*What!?*" "And so it occurred to me maybe your breasts were, too." "Where *what* too!?" "Reversed." "You're kidding." "No; no, I don't think so. Your kidneys sort of . . . turn out. Kidneys look like ears, you know, and they're supposed to face in; and . . ." and here he pointed at my breasts, ". . . and your nipples turn *in* a little bit, where normally they should head *out* some; you're sort of . . . pigeon-nippled." "You're crazy," I said, quite . . . level, I thought, considering.

WOMAN 2 *(Whispered)*

Run! Run!

WOMAN 3

"No, no," he said, sort of unconcerned. "They're just *reversed;* no problem. Of course, if you ever *do* get anything wrong—with your breasts *or* your kidneys—and they want to take one off, or out . . . I'd tell them." "Tell them what!?" "Hm? oh . . . I'd tell them, or, rather, I'd *ask* them. I mean, if they said they wanted to take out your left kidney, or whatever, I'd be sure to ask them *which* left kidney, or whatever, they meant."

WOMAN 1

Crazy as a loon!

WOMAN 4

Yes!

WOMAN 3

"I mean, *left* to them is *right* to you, and so on. I mean, if one day you went in and said, 'I'd like my left kidney removed, please'—just as an example—and you didn't make it clear you meant your *right* one, well, then, they might just . . . take out the wrong kidney. *Then* where would you be? Hm?" I was buttoning up fast, and I'd picked up my purse, and I'd turned to go when he said, real casual, "Do you have a good eye and ear man?"

WOMAN 4

No!

MAN 1

Pigeon-nippled?

MAN 3

Crazy, hunh?

WOMAN 3 (*Almost apologetic*)

Well, that's what *I* thought, but . . . well, then, I started thinking about it, and . . .

MAN 1

You mean it could be?

MAN 2

No!

WOMAN 3 (*Uncertain*)

Well . . .

MAN 4

At the very least I'd get a second opinion.

WOMAN 3 (*Still uncertain*)

Well, I *plan* to, but Sam and I have been together for *so long* . . .

WOMAN 2 (*Whispered*)

Run!

WOMAN 1 (*Nodding*)

Get a second opinion; and get a *woman* doctor.

WOMAN 3

Yes; yes; well, perhaps I will. But you can understand why I'm . . . pre-occupied.

WOMAN 1

I certainly can.

MAN 1

I was thinking about something too. I wonder why we do some things together and some things we don't.

WOMAN 1

What do you mean, she said?

MAN 1

Oh, I was thinking about eating and shitting.

WOMAN 4

You weren't!

MAN 3

My goodness!

MAN 1

Yes; I was. Eating is refueling, right? We eat because we need fuel; it's bio-logical. All the social stuff we've added to it is extra.

WOMAN 3

They call it civilization.

MAN 1 (*Dogmatic*)

We eat because we need fuel. If we didn't eat we'd either become fashion models or we'd die.

WOMAN 4

Yes, but . . .

MAN 1

If we didn't eat we'd die; so every day—if we're lucky, if we're some of the lucky ones unlike the homeless—we eat; we do it three-four times a day, and we get re-fueled. It keeps us going—proteins, carbs, all the rest. We need it, therefore we do it. Biological.

MAN 4

Granted.

MAN 1

And two things happen when we take on fuel . . .

MAN 2

Yes.
    (*An aside*)
I don't know that I want to know this.

MAN 1

We use some of it—we absorb it—and some we don't. Some we pass on as waste—liquid waste, solid waste.

WOMAN 4

Everybody knows this.

MAN 1

Yes, I know everybody knows it.
    (*To* WOMAN 1)
You do know it, don't you.
    (*She is about to reply, but he goes on*)
We all know it, but that's not the question. The question is: we've made one of these into a social event—eating—and the other—shitting—into something shameful. Why do we do that?

MAN 2

Oh, lord!

MAN 1

No, why do we? Why don't we go all by ourselves into little locked rooms and eat our food, and then all get together in a big party . . . and shit? I'm serious.

WOMAN 2

Well, eating is nice . . .

MAN 1

Unh-hunh; and shitting isn't.

WOMAN 2

No; no, it isn't. Food tastes good; it smells good . . .

MAN 1

. . . And the other doesn't. Have you tasted it? How would you know?

WOMAN 2

Don't be disgusting!

MAN 1

When did we decide that food smelled good and shit didn't? Is that part of civilization, too? Communal eating isn't done among all the animals, you know.

MAN 4

This is a ridiculous conversation!

MAN 1

Well, I'll be happy to drop it when someone comes up with an answer. We screw in private—most of us, anyway—we go off to be alone, or private for a lot of lovely things.

WOMAN 3

Cats cover their shit.

MAN 1

Yes, and dogs don't; of course, dogs are domesticated. I think cats do it to hide their traces.

WOMAN 1 (Proud)

And we don't.

MAN 1

Oh, sure; we invented flush toilets to keep the predators away. Can't someone be sensible here?

MAN 3

Why do you . . . care?

MAN 1 (Sing-song)

Why do I care, why do I care? Like the mountain: because it's there.

WOMAN 4

Well, young man, if you keep on like this, you'll probably develop a reputation so that people won't want to eat with you—much less do anything else!

WOMAN 3

I've never eaten with him.

WOMAN 1

Neither have I! And I don't plan to.

MAN 3 *(To* MAN 1*)*

There's a reason, friend; there's a reason for everything; don't . . . trouble yourself: There's enough other stuff out there to keep you busy.

MAN 1 *(Cheerful)*

I worry about that stuff. You want to know some other things I've been worrying about?

OTHERS *(More or less together)*

No. Certainly not! etc.

MAN 1 *(Hand up to stop them)*

OK; OK. Jeez! You guys!

MAN 4 *(After a bit; remembering)*

At camp we used to do it in the woods.

MAN 1

What: screw?

MAN 4

No; the other.

MAN 1

No shit!

MAN 4 *(Sort of sad)*

We used to use leaves; I was a very little boy.

WOMAN 3 *(Gentle)*

And it was a very long time ago.

MAN 4

Yes; oh, yes. Yes, it was. I still go off in the woods sometimes, when I'm in the country—just to pee. Off in the woods, all by myself. It's a very good feeling. I feel very . . . natural.

MAN 1 *(Nice)*

Well, there. You see?

WOMAN 2

We had an Irish wolfhound once . . .

MAN 1

What brought this up? All the talk about shit?

WOMAN 4

I love Irish wolfhounds!

WOMAN 3

Yes! So do I! There's nobody sweeter!

WOMAN 1

Wolfhounds frighten me.

WOMAN 3

Why?

WOMAN 4

Yes: why?

WOMAN 1 *(Shrugs)*

They . . . just do—Hound of the Baskervilles and all.

WOMAN 4 *(Scornful)*

That was a *Mastiff*; that wasn't an Irish wolfhound.

WOMAN 1

Really? Oh.

WOMAN 2

Harry was a great dog, a really great dog.

WOMAN 3

They'd be lap dogs if you'd let 'em.

WOMAN 2

Harry *was!* Well: wanted to be—all hundred seventy-five pounds of him.

WOMAN 1 *(Slow awe)*

One hundred and seventy-five pounds!?

WOMAN 2

A really great dog: friendly, obedient . . .

MAN 1

A regular boy scout.

WOMAN 3

Hush!

WOMAN 2

Better! Better than a boy scout; better than just about anyone. They don't live very long—Irish wolfhounds. Eight is usual; eight years and then they go.

WOMAN 1

You just get them and they die!

MAN 1

Not like butterflies, for Christ's sake: two weeks, or something.

WOMAN 1

I know, but . . .

WOMAN 2

Eight years isn't long if you love someone.

MAN 3 *(Commiserating)*

No; of course not.

WOMAN 2

Harry lived to be *twelve*.

WOMAN 1

That's wonderful!

WOMAN 3

Amazing!

MAN 4

Old age, hunh?

WOMAN 2

I'm not so sure. Well, yes, he was old, but I think it was more the Bush Senior years did him in. The more that went on, the greyer he got, the stiffer, and finally he just . . .sighed one of his big deep heavy sighs and . . . expired.

MAN 2

He should have waited until Bush Junior: that would have done him in real quick.

WOMAN 4

And just when you thought all that was over . . .

MAN 1

Those Republicans . . . you've got to drive stakes through their hearts.

WOMAN 2

And we had this property in the country—we still do—and Harry lived there—with *us*—

WOMAN 4

We assumed that.

WOMAN 2

Yes, and we decided to bury him on the property.

MAN 3

It was a big property.

WOMAN 2

Yes, very big, and so that's what we did.

MAN 2

What?

WOMAN 2

We buried him on the property.
    (Pause)

MAN 2

Well, that's a very interesting story.

WOMAN 2

Wait! I'm not done!

MAN 2

Oh.

WOMAN 2

We'd had cats and when they died we . . . well, we disposed of them—threw them away, I suppose.

WOMAN 1

Oh, no; really.

WOMAN 2

I'm sorry; but we did. Oh dear; maybe there's some terrible . . . *lack* there somewhere, some kind of *inhumanity*. I can't remember what we used to *do* with them.

MAN 4

No, now; no.

WOMAN 3

No; you . . . well, they were . . . over; done.

WOMAN 2

Yes. But with Harry it was different. Not because he was a dog and the others were cats—I love cats, too; I really do—but it was just different.

MAN 4

You related more.

WOMAN 3

Yes.

WOMAN 2 (*Vulnerable*)

Is that it? I hope so. He was more like . . . us.

MAN 1

. . . Ate out of a bowl on the floor, had fleas, shat in the garden.

WOMAN 3 (*Giggling*)

Oh, stop!

WOMAN 2 (*Going off*)

Maybe it was the size, that he would stand up on his hind legs, put his paws on my husband's shoulder, look him right in the eye . . .

MAN 2

"Woof-woof . . . look here, you, about that food you're feeding me . . . Woof-woof."

WOMAN 2 (*Laughs*)

Stop! No, that he was so *BIG*. So we decided to bury him on the property. And when he died—we were with him: I stroked his nose and my husband held on to one of his paws: I don't remember which one; it doesn't matter . . . which paw, not which husband—when he died they asked us what we wanted done with his body—he passed on at the vet—and we weren't certain, and so we said we'd let them know—to hold on to him for us.

WOMAN 4

Yes; of course.

WOMAN 2

And so we agreed to bury him on the property—his property, *was*—out in a stand of pines beyond an outdoor sculpture he used to pee on.

MAN 3

Everybody's an art critic.

WOMAN 2

It seemed like a perfect spot.

WOMAN 4

Yes.

WOMAN 2

And I suppose it was four or five days, and so we called them—the vets— and asked them to bring Harry over, that we were digging a grave for him. And we were, just the two of us, and it was hard work, let me tell you! Irish wolfhounds are *big dogs*. And so we dug a big hole—oh, five feet deep, and three feet wide, and maybe five feet long . . . six. It was a lot of work, but when we'd got it done we were very proud, let me tell you.

WOMAN 1

Of course you were; and rightly so.

WOMAN 2 (*A little grim*)

Yes. And so the van from the vet's came into the driveway, and we told them where we'd dug the grave.

WOMAN 4

Didn't you check to see if it was OK? I mean, burying a dog on the property?

WOMAN 2

It never occurred to us—our property, our dog.

MAN 4

Well, I mean, what if it had been Aunt Sarah?

WOMAN 2 (*Very confused*)

Well . . . I mean . . .

(Suddenly rational)
We didn't *like* Aunt Sarah.

MAN 4 *(Shrugs)*
Oh. Well. OK.

WOMAN 2
And so they brought Harry over from the driveway to the . . . the gravesite, and he was all wrapped in plastic. It was awful!

WOMAN 4
Well, they had to put him in something.

WOMAN 1
Yes, but plastic.

MAN 2
A plastic shroud?

WOMAN 2
Yes! It was awful! And they set him down beside the grave, and asked if they could help, and we said no, he was our dog, we'd take care of it. And they left. And we could see Harry through the plastic, sort of like you could see a face under ice—under maybe an inch of ice.

WOMAN 1
Nooooo!

WOMAN 4 *(To WOMAN 1)*
Calm down, dear.

WOMAN 2
But that wasn't the worst of it.

MAN 3
It wasn't?

MAN 2
No?

WOMAN 2
No. The worst was this: When we tried to put Harry in the hole—the grave—we discovered he was frozen . . . solid!!
   (Pause)

MAN 3
Frozen solid?

WOMAN 3
Solid?

MAN 4 *(Wonder)*
Frozen solid!

WOMAN 2

Yes! Frozen solid. They'd frozen him . . . so he'd keep.

MAN 2 (*Cautious*)

Well, of course . . . if you think about it

MAN 3

Sure!

MAN 1

What else were they going to do?

WOMAN 2

I know! But frozen!

WOMAN 4

You poor thing!

MAN 1

He was *dead!!*

WOMAN 2

Hard as a rock! Frozen solid. There were only two choices—put him in the ground frozen or . . . thaw him out.

MAN 1

You didn't!

WOMAN 2

Thaw him out? No; we had no idea how long that would take, and where we would do it . . . out in the sun? And would he stink, and was there danger, and would it be legal?

MAN 2

If anything was.

WOMAN 2

Yes! It was just too . . . gruesome; so we decided to bury him as he was— ice cold; frozen solid.

MAN 3

Probably the best idea.

WOMAN 2

That's what *we* thought, and that's what we set about to do.
   (*Pause*)

MAN 4

But?

WOMAN 2

But there was a bit of a problem.

WOMAN 4

Oh?

WOMAN 3

What was it?

WOMAN 2

They'd frozen him lying down, of course, like he was asleep, his paws, his lovely paws not straight out, but curled a little, like when he was asleep.

WOMAN 4

Awwwww.

WOMAN 1

That's sweet.

WOMAN 2

Yes, but they'd left his tail straight out; they hadn't curled it around him.

MAN 1

Yes?

MAN 2

And?

MAN 3

And so?

MAN 4

Yes; go on.

WOMAN 2

It was straight out; frozen solid and straight out.

MAN 1

Yes.

WOMAN 2

We dragged him over to the hole—the grave—and saw we couldn't get him in.

MAN 4

You mean . . .

WOMAN 2

Yes; there wasn't room for his tail in what we'd dug. His tail stuck out two feet beyond the hole.

WOMAN 1 *(Pause)*

My goodness.

WOMAN 3 *(Pause)*

Well.

WOMAN 4 *(Pause)*

What did you do?

WOMAN 2

We saw there were only two choices—extend the grave another two feet, or . . . I can't say it.

MAN 3

What!? What can't you say!?

WOMAN 2 *(Blushing—if possible)*

Either extend the grave another two feet or . . . or snap his tail off.

MAN 1 *(Pause)*

Like a fucking icicle.

WOMAN 2

Yes.

(Pause)

WOMAN 4

My goodness.

(Pause)

MAN 4

I suppose we'd better ask what you did.

WOMAN 3 *(Accusing)*

Oh, really!

WOMAN 2 *(Proud)*

We dug an extra two feet, of course. We added a section to the hole we'd dug—a section five feet deep, and two feet long, and six inches wide—an extension I guess you'd call it, just big enough for his tail.

(Pause)

MAN 2

Well, no point in digging any more than that; I mean, no point in digging a hole an extra three feet wide for a six inch wide tail.

MAN 3

No; none at all.

WOMAN 2

And we lowered him gently, and put his collar in with him, and his bowl . . . and some dog biscuits. And we covered him with earth, buried him deep and put the sod back on top.

MAN 1 *(Pause)*

That's fucking touching; it really is.

MAN 3

Yes; yes, it is.

WOMAN 3

Very.

MAN 4

Yes; yes, very.

WOMAN 1

Did . . . did you put up a marker, a gravestone?

WOMAN 2

No; we knew where he was.

WOMAN 1

Yes, but . . .

MAN 2

For what? In case other dogs wanted to come and visit?

WOMAN 1

I just . . . asked.

MAN 1 (*To* MAN 3)

What's the matter with you?

MAN 3

Nothing.

MAN 1 (*Urging him to talk*)

Come on.

MAN 3

Nothing you can help with.

MAN 1

Oh?

MAN 3

Just . . . me, myself and I.

MAN 1

Yeah?

MAN 3

I've got this problem with me and the mirror—my mirror.

MAN 1

No kidding. Who doesn't?

MAN 3

I look at myself in the mirror and I see that I'm not looking back at myself. I'm seeing . . . *him.* I'm seeing *him* looking at me, looking through me to himself, to see the reflection in his eyes of himself looking at himself through me. I . . . I begin to vanish.

MAN 1 (*Quietly comforting*)
Hey.

MAN 3
I look at him in the mirror and I see that he's not looking back at me. He's looking at himself. He's seeing through me to himself. I think I begin to vanish even more. It isn't true, you know, that we all see what we want to.

MAN 1
Awww; come on.

MAN 3
I turn my back to the mirror, and I sense that he's done it, too—turned his back? I can't be certain, but I think he has. I wonder if he's waiting for me to turn. I wonder . . . if I turn and look, whose eyes will be looking at whose eyes, who will be looking *through* whose eyes . . . and to whom. I don't dare turn . . . because I know I won't be there . . . that I'll have vanished.
(*Silence*)

MAN 1 (*Factual*)
You're right; you better work this out yourself.
(MAN 3 *sits; looks at the others with a combination of fear and hatred; rises*)

MAN 3
What are you all looking at!? Hunh?

WOMAN 1
Talking about Harry reminds me of something *we* did.

WOMAN 3
What was it?

WOMAN 2
Yes! Tell us!

WOMAN 1
Well . . .
(*Blushes*)
No, I can't! It's too . . . oh, it's too awful! I mean, it has me humiliated to the point I get . . . numb when I think about it.

MAN 2
De-numb yourself.

MAN 4
Let it out.

WOMAN 3

It might help.

MAN 1

. . . even if it doesn't.

WOMAN 1

Well, all right.
(Sighs)
We had this wonderful old Siamese cat. He was seventeen, I think. He'd survived thyroid cancer, and, oh, so many things. He was a great cat! We'd gotten him when he was under a year from some people were moving and were going to have him put down. Well, finally, he just lay there on the floor in the kitchen, near the exhaust from the . . . refrigerator. Just lay there.

MAN 3

Was he dead?

WOMAN 1

No; not quite. He'd hardly move though. You'd pick him up and he was all limp, and he'd try to jump up on the bed, and he'd miss and fall back down, and his eyes were jaundiced . . .

WOMAN 3

That was one sick cat!

WOMAN 1

Well, yes! I mean, he'd been one sick cat for two years—what with one thing and another, but this was clearly . . . it.

WOMAN 4

Poor thing.

WOMAN 1

Yes. We lugged him to the vet one final time, and they put an IV in his neck and wrapped him all up—he looked like a little baby—and tried to save him, but they couldn't. And he died.

WOMAN 4

Poor thing!

MAN 1

You referring to the cat or her?

WOMAN 4

It's an all-purpose phrase.

MAN 1

Gotcha.

WOMAN 1

And we thought about it and decided to have him cremated.

WOMAN 3

Oh, that's nice.

MAN 2

Why? Why is that nice?

WOMAN 3

If you think it's nice, it's nice. I mean, what are you going to do—what *she* did?
 (*Points at* WOMAN 2)
Just . . . throw the cat *away?*

WOMAN 2

I'm sorry! I'm so sorry!

MAN 4

It's all right; it doesn't matter.

WOMAN 1

And so we had him cremated, and when we picked him up at the vet—his
ashes—there was this nice box, all done up with pretty ribbon, and with a
little card attached. It said "Jake"—that was his name . . .

WOMAN 4

Jake: nice.

WOMAN 1

"Beloved pet of . . ."; and with our name. I . . . I ripped the ribbon and that
card *right* off the pretty box. Pet, *indeed!* Pet! I *hate* that word. He was my
. . . Jake was my . . . darling boy. Pet, indeed. I ripped it *right* off.

MAN 3

Well, so? Your privilege.

MAN 2

No harm.

WOMAN 1 (*Tentative*)

Weelll . . .

WOMAN 4

You mean . . . ?

MAN 4

Something . . . happened?

WOMAN 3

Is this the "numb" part?
 (WOMAN 1 *nods*)
Oh, dear.

WOMAN 2

You might as well tell us.

WOMAN 1 *(Tiny voice)*

Do I have to?

MAN 1 *(Casual)*

No, no; we can go on to something else.

WOMAN 1 *(Intense)*

I have to!!

MAN 1 *(Hands up in defense)*

OK! OK!

WOMAN 1 *(Quieter)*

I have to. We had a friend who died; he was killed, actually, in a car crash—not his fault, late at night, someone drunk, head on.

WOMAN 4

Oh, my.

WOMAN 1

All mangled, head severed; terrible thing!

WOMAN 2

God!

WOMAN 1

Both killed, but our responsibility was our friend. There was no family: wife dead, no children, parents gone, only child. He was our best friend, closest, and so it fell to us—the tidying up of it all.

MAN 4

Of course.

MAN 2

What are friends for?

WOMAN 1

Yes; well; we had him *cremated*—which he'd told us he wanted, if anything ever happened, told us a long time ago. He was from Boston, and he rowed the Charles—the Charles River—a lot, all by himself, a single scull. And he wanted his ashes . . . sprinkled . . . onto the Charles, from one of the bridges.

WOMAN 4 *(To MAN 4; an aside)*

I have a sense of what's coming.

MAN 4 *(Puzzled)*

Oh?

WOMAN 1 *(Sighs heavily)*

And . . . we were on our way to the lake—to our summer place—and we stopped off in Boston, and at two one morning we went out to one of the bridges—we had the box of his ashes . . .

WOMAN 3 *(Quiet disbelief)*

Oh, no.

WOMAN 1

. . . and we took the sack of his ashes from the box, and we looked around to see no one was looking, and we . . . sprinkled his ashes from the bridge into the Charles River—goodbye, and such.

MAN 4 *(Getting it)*

Oh.

WOMAN 1

And so, we went on to the lake for our summer. We unpacked, and I found Jake's ashes after a while—a week, maybe—the box of Jake's ashes, and I buried the sack with his ashes in it in a big, wonderful blackberry patch he used to sit in.

MAN 3

That's nice.

WOMAN 1

Well, yes, I suppose; you do something, you like to do it right.

MAN 1 *(After a silence)*

And?

WOMAN 1 *(Another heavy sigh)*

And . . . and a few weeks later it suddenly struck me.

MAN 4

No!

WOMAN 1

Well, I wasn't sure: *had* I mixed the boxes up? *Had* I buried our friend deep in the blackberries, and *had* I sprinkled Jake into the Charles River at two in the morning? *Had* I? I'd thrown the boxes *away*.

WOMAN 4 *(Mouth sound)*

Tsk-tsk-tsk-etc.

WOMAN 1

I said to myself, I *couldn't* have done a thing like that; of *course* not!

MAN 3

No, of course not.

WOMAN 2

Of course not.

WOMAN 1

Of course not, and I probably hadn't. I'll never know, though; I mean, I'll never know; I'll never be sure. Every time we're at the lake and I look at the blackberry patch . . . I wonder. And I get all numb. Am I crazy?

WOMAN 4

No; no, of course not.

MAN 1 *(Thorough disbelief)*

You really think you may have mixed them up?

WOMAN 3

Let her be.

WOMAN 1 *(Helpless; hopeless)*

I don't *know;* I'll never *know.*
     (Pause)
The blackberries are wonderful.

MAN 4

And the Charles River flows right on. It doesn't matter. What can it possibly matter?

WOMAN 1

You're right, I know; I *know.*
     (Pauses)
Still.

WOMAN 3

Yes.

WOMAN 2

Yes.

WOMAN 4

Yes.

MAN 4

I think it's time for an intermission.
     (Actors file off as lights fade)

CURTAIN

ACT TWO

(Actors return in the reverse order in which they left. The projected title Act Two *appears. As* Act Two *fades, lights rise)*

MAN 4 *(Out)*

Fragments; Act Two.
   (To WOMAN 1)
You feeling better?

WOMAN 1

Yes; thank you.

MAN 4

That was quite a scene you made there.

WOMAN 1 *(Shrugs)*

Yeah, well . . . you know.

MAN 1

My turn! I want to do one. I want to do a scene.

WOMAN 3

He wants what?

WOMAN 4

To make a scene; he wants to make a scene.

MAN 1

Do one; I want to do a scene.

MAN 4

Oh, right.

MAN 1

People want me; people have *always* wanted me. When I was a baby people couldn't keep their hands off me, off my crib, my blankets, my . . . perambulator. Isn't that a good word? People tried to kidnap me, to steal me out of my carriage, come in windows in the dead of night, stand by my crib and breathe there in the dark, just staring at me. A woman came to my crib when I was very tiny—barely born—and she leaned over me—she was old and when she leaned her face fell toward me—and she made those sounds people do over babies . . . and she cooed and ticked, and she had a necklace, giant opal, a pendant hung from leather, a pendant opal the size of a testicle, and it swung above my face, its fire blazing in my mind and in my eye as she ticked and cooed, her face falling toward me. I remember—I remember everything, from always—I remember I smiled and I reached my tiny fingers toward the stone and I reached it and I held on and I wouldn't let go—perhaps couldn't is what I mean. I had the strength of a magnet and my little teeny fingers were iron and I grasped the stone and she hung there for she couldn't move, she couldn't rise up. There was nothing for it, and so she undid the thong from around her neck and let me have the opal. There was nothing for it. I have it still—somewhere . . . I think.

(Shrugs)

It's always been like that. I've never wanted for anything, and I've never wanted anything . . . enough to need it, I mean. Things . . . people . . . present themselves and I take them for the taking, not that I need them, not that I want them. "Take me! Take me!"

(Shrugs)

OK. So I take.

(Laugh)

Once there was this man loved his daughter—I mean, not in a healthy way. She was thirteen—sweet thirteen, remember it?—and exactly that: long honey hair, emerald eyes, glorious, the slightest down, lips you couldn't believe, lithe, slim, the woman's body beginning, but boy, too; girl as boy becoming girl. Jesus, was she good. And he lusted after her, the father did. That guy went round with a hard-on; really! And she didn't know it? A real young thirteen. I could see what was up, so to speak: I was across the street with a nice man paid my way and everything. I was pretty young myself— what, fifteen? But I knew my way around—I'd been on the street a couple of years. Well, yeah; sad. My parents died, you see, going too fast, after a lead, or something; right into a buttress. Sad. Nice people.
Anyway, this guy was taking care of me; he didn't want anything I couldn't give him with my eyes closed, so it was OK. The father—the girl's father— came to me one day and said, "I noticed you've noticed. I notice you've noticed my daughter." I allowed as to how I had. "I notice you've noticed how my loins ache for her, how I am . . . riddled with passion and self-disgust." I allowed as to how I had. "I notice you've noticed she doesn't notice," he said. I allowed as to how I had. "That she is filled with an innocence, a purity commensurate with my lust, transcending it." I allowed as to how I'd noticed; I mean, this guy's lech was life-long and a front yard wide! Forget the bulge in his pants; his death wish rose around him like a balloon, like an aura. And he told me what he wanted me to do. "I want you to take her from me," he said. "I wish to be bereft. I need loss! I will be happy only filled with despair. I want you to lock her away somewhere,"—and his voice started getting sort of . . . throaty here—"spirit her off, put her from me; I want you to have her! I want you to tie her to bed-

posts and . . . have her! I . . . want you to run your tongue along her thighs, I want you to cup her buttocks and . . . bury your face in her. I want you to force open her mouth, and . . ." Well, you get the picture. "And I want you to come and tell me what you've done. I won't hurt you; I promise. I want you to take her prisoner, and *have* her! and *HAVE* her! and come and tell me what you've done; tell me the sounds she makes, how she moans on the bed, the feel of her saliva as she . . ." I mean, this guy really went on—stroking himself and breathing hard. "Look," I said to him, "I mean, look mister . . . I'm fifteen years old. How am I going to do all this, and why should I, why do I want to?" Besides the guy who was . . . taking care of me, as they say, wouldn't react too well to any sort of arrangement like that. I mean, he had certain . . . rights and prerogatives that would run counter to . . . well, you know what I mean. I didn't tell the father any of *this*, of course, 'cause it might have fucked up his fantasy, if you know what I mean. I mean, he wanted a molester for his daughter—baby one—but he didn't want any kind of pervert. Not that I *am*, you understand, or *was*: it's just I've always known how to put butter and bread together—a useful thing to know if you're on your own . . . or on somebody else's if you come right down on it. "You want to because I want you to," he said, an awful smile starting on his face. "I notice everything," he said. "I know that man you live with, he's abducted you, hasn't he!? Nothing escapes me." I played all wide-eyed and innocent, but he wasn't to be had. He said he'd bring the cops down on us, have the poor guy locked up for kidnapping and me stuck in a reform school or an orphanage, whichever worse he could work out. I lied, and begged a lot, but he wouldn't be put off. "Of course," he said, "of course, there's a way out of all this." There was? What was it, I wondered. So we worked out the deal. The kid—the daughter—moved in with her aunt who was stone deaf and didn't see too good and was up to a quart of gin a day—usually by two in the PM, and was then either goofy or prone. The kid was moved in with this treasure, and I was free to come and go as I wanted. Naturally, Daddy left it to me to work out the details of the deflowering—though defoliation was what he was really into—befriending the kid, sousing up the aunt, whatever I wanted, so long as I reported back to *him* twice a week with all the juicy details—the tieings-up, the whispered protests, the foreplay, and the biting and all, the penetrations, the humiliations. Boy, let me tell you, I had to read up a lot! I mean, *I* wasn't going to plow the little girl; I liked her, she was sweet, and I mean, we were little kids; besides, my "old man" . . . well, you understand. I kept reading up on all the stuff my . . . protector had in his porno library, and I'd sort of translate it into hetero terms, and I'd spin such yarns?—every degradation I could dig up: whippings, blood, weird positions, whatever. It wasn't fun to watch him—the father—what he'd do while I told him what I was doing to his sweet baby. And then one day . . . and then one day, after about a month of this shit, I came into his house and sat down on the sofa next to the easy chair he always waited for me in—Kleenex, hand ready. And I sat down on the edge of the sofa, good little kid that I was, and I told him a story. I told him:

(Gentle now)

Last night your daughter and I went walking in the flower garden in the park—early evening, really—and she let me hold her hand as we walked. The birds had gone to sleep, or were beginning to, and it was very still, the crunch of the gravel underfoot as we walked. And we held hands and our arms twined and she put her head against my shoulder as we walked. "Yeah, yeah!" he said, eyes bulging, mouth open, hands . . . you know. "Go on; go on!" And we stopped by the swan lake, I told him, with the moon rising on it, and, way across, the band in the bandstand playing a slow tune—you could barely hear it, even in the still. And we stopped, and we both turned, and she let me kiss her. It was . . . it was wonderful; our lips just brushed, and it was wonderful. "Yeah!? Yeah!?" And then we walked back home, I told him, to your sister's—really, mister, your sister isn't fit to take care of your daughter—we walked home, and we stood on the porch for a moment, and I looked into her lovely eyes, and she touched my cheek with her fingers and smiled and went inside. His face pulled up from slack, turned hard, and white, and his eyes narrowed and he said to me, his voice in his throat, "Don't you ever tell me a story like that again! Do you hear me?!" And he grabbed my wrist and twisted. "Don't you ever tell me a sick story like that again! How dare you make mock of me!? That's sick! That's . . . disgusting!!" I had to tell him: I had to tell him I'd never touched her, that I loved her, that she was the sweetest, purest most beautiful creature I'd ever seen, that I'd made up all the stories I'd told him and couldn't I go now please?

(Pause)

And he started to hit me, he started to beat up on me, and he howled like . . . like some prehistoric beast, and he clubbed me around, and he kicked me, and . . . he banged me up against the wall and started choking me. I did the only thing I could: I kicked him where he lived, and he gasped, and looked at me startled and slowly fell to the carpet, grasping at his groin. "I'll get you," he said—I could hardly hear him—"I'll kill you." Well, there was nothing for it: I left town at midnight—lots of tearful stuff from my protector, but I lied and told him I'd be back—and I turned tail and just kept right on going.

(Triste)

I never saw the lovely girl again. I mean, I never saw the *town* again, or her father—thank God—or my . . . the guy; but, especially, I never saw that lovely girl again. My cheek has a warmth to it, though, a glow. I still feel her fingers brushing me. Perhaps it's a wound; perhaps there's a wound there.

WOMAN 3

Well.

MAN 4

Yes: well. That's very . . .

WOMAN 4

Yes; yes, it is.

MAN 1

Oh?

MAN 4

Yes; very.

WOMAN 4

Indeed; yes.

WOMAN 3

Yes.

MAN 1

Well. Thank you.

MAN 2 *(Parody)*

People want me; people have always wanted me.

WOMAN 1 *(Parody)*

When I was a baby, people couldn't keep their hands off me.

MAN 2

There was this woman; she had a necklace—a pendant opal the size of a testicle.

WOMAN 1

A what?

MAN 2

A . . . you heard me.

MAN 1

OK, guys!

MAN 2

I've never *wanted* anything . . . enough to need it, I mean.

WOMAN 1

Take me! Take me!

MAN 2

Once there was this man loved his daughter.

WOMAN 1

Ohhhhh!

MAN 1

Aw, come *on!*

MAN 2

I notice you've noticed how my loins ache for her.

WOMAN 1

Ohhhhh!

MAN 2

I wish to be bereft. I need loss! I will be happy only filled with despair.

MAN 4 (*Gently admonishing*)

That's not very nice, now.

MAN 2

I want you to have her, and *have* her!

WOMAN 1 (*Enlightenment*)

Ohhhhh!

WOMAN 3

No; no, it isn't.

MAN 2

Look, mister, I'm only fifteen years old.

WOMAN 1

Ohhhhh!

MAN 3

OK! OK, now!

MAN 2

Yeah?! Yeah?!

MAN 3

Yeah!

MAN 2 (*Hands up*)

OK! OK!

WOMAN 1 (*Disappointed*)

Ohhhh!

MAN 1

You can't say *anything* around here.

WOMAN 3

Yes, you *can;* you *can.*

MAN 1 (*Uncertain*)

I don't know.

MAN 4

Let's all calm down.

WOMAN 1 (*Mildly apologetic*)

Right.

MAN 2

Right.

MAN 1

Right.

(*A silence*)

MAN 2 (*Generally*)

I'm sorry; I *am;* I'm truly sorry.

(*Chuckles*)

It's just I couldn't help myself. "People want me; people have always wanted me!"

(*Chortles*)

Indeed! *I* never get stuff like that: "People have *always* wanted me!?" I have had *persons* want me, now and again—my *lady* wants me; but people? No. Not even in Trinidad. Now and again, *some*one would want me, but never . . . people. If you're black—I'm black? You noticed?

OTHERS

Yes, yes; we've noticed, etc.

MAN 2

Oh, good. If you're black most people don't *want* to see you—much less Mr. Ellison's not being *able* to see you. And if they *do* see you, it's not often *you* they see—you personally. I was acting in Cincinnati not long ago—a good play, racially mixed cast, a theatre up in the park, and another guy in the play—he was black, too—took a walk one early evening, in the park, on our day off, and I guess the sun must have set too fast—too fast too quickly—for the cops arrested him—for being black, for being in the park. He wasn't wandering around with a big knife; he wasn't exposing himself to little baby girls; he was walking in the park—on a Sunday, by George! Well, it *was* Cincinnati. I guess he could have said, "People want me; *cops* want me, anyway; cops have *always* wanted me." But that's special, *isn't* it.

(*To* MAN 1)

So, forgive me.

MAN 1 (*Gentle*)

Hey; don't bother.

MAN 2

No, no. I'm sorry; really.

WOMAN 2 (*With a page of something*)

I cut out an article I thought might be some help, might be helpful . . . if one ever needed help, that is: might as well be prepared for whatever, no?

MAN 3 (*Glum*)

Sure. Right on, girl.

WOMAN 2

It's an article suggests the more we call each other funny names, the more chance our relationships will have of . . .

WOMAN 4

Can't you be sensible about anything?

WOMAN 2 (*Dogmatic*)

The article is very serious—imbecile, perhaps, but serious. It's by a psychologist who has been collecting nicknames for over ten years now, nicknames of married couples and . . .

MAN 3 (*Rising to leave*)

I haven't got time for this.

WOMAN 2

No! Listen! "We call our mates according to our desires," he says, or, writes, actually. "They're shorthand signals; they signal our special bond. They express warm, cuddly feelings," he says. He says we shouldn't be afraid of them; he gives examples.

MAN 3

Really?

WOMAN 4

Don't encourage her.

WOMAN 2

He says that nonsense words are a nice throwback to our childhood.

WOMAN 3

Like what?

WOMAN 4

Don't encourage her! Doesn't anybody listen around here?

WOMAN 3 (*To* WOMAN 4)

No.
   (*To* WOMAN 2)
Like what?

WOMAN 2

I appreciate the vote of confidence.
   (*Looking, reading*)
Well . . . wabbit; chickywicky . . .

MAN 3

What!?

WOMAN 2 (*Over-enunciating*)

Chicky wicky. (*Goes on*) Babycakes, snuggums, honey bunny . . .

WOMAN 3

Well, those are catchy.

WOMAN 2 *(Goes on)*

"Our private language is rich with sexual imagery," he goes on, "especially when couples begin to explore each other's bodies."

MAN 2

Who would do a thing like that?

WOMAN 2

Oh, hush.
    (Reads)
Sugar lips, sizzle hips, belly button blower, armpit nuzzler . . .

MAN 3

Belly? Button? Blower?

WOMAN 2

Well, that's what it says.

MAN 4

How extraordinary. I'm trying to conceive of a relationship in which that would occur, much less help.

WOMAN 2 *(Reading)*

Pinkydinks, wuzzy, kissikins, cuddlebumps, love rhino, camelspit . . .

WOMAN 3

Camelspit! Oh, my God! That's it!
    (Generally)
Hello there, camelspit!

WOMAN 1

I suppose if one didn't do it too much in public it might . . .

MAN 1

Right!

WOMAN 3

I love camelspit! It's so much . . . warmer than . . . fuckface, or you filthy wanton bitch, or . . .

MAN 3 *(As if with a checklist)*

You prefer camelspit to that!? All that!?

WOMAN 3

Well . . . sort of.

WOMAN 2

I had another list here somewhere.
    (Begins to look for it)

A list of anecdotes.

(*Keeps looking*)

Unless I lost it—or whatever.

MAN 1

Somebody probably stole it.

(*Shrugs*)

People steal things. They'll steal anything.

WOMAN 3

I had a teacher did it—was one: a kleptomaniac.

WOMAN 4

Funny word.

MAN 3

It's from the Greek.

WOMAN 1

How do you know such things?

WOMAN 2

Not how: *why*.

WOMAN 3

She stole chalk and erasers, from school. I think it was simply she didn't want to teach any more.

MAN 3

Shoplifting is what they call it—when they want to get a laugh. My *father* did it.

WOMAN 4

No!

WOMAN 2

Really? *Really!?* He *did!?*

MAN 3

I suppose he was classic—persistent and all; and certainly there wasn't any economic motive, or anything—I mean, he was president of the savings bank of the town we lived in, and . . .

MAN 1

He didn't shoplift *there*, did he?

WOMAN 4

Oh, really!

MAN 3

No, no, he didn't, and what's really interesting is what made him *do* it. Most shoplifters are women, you know.

WOMAN 1

No; I didn't know that.

MAN 2

Is that so!

MAN 3

—Distinguishing shoplifting from straight stealing, I mean.

MAN 4 (*Pinning it down*)

From economically motivated stealing.

MAN 3

Yes. Most shoplifters *are* women.

MAN 1

Maybe that's because they *shop* more—more than men do.

WOMAN 1

Yes; of course!

MAN 3

Sorry, ladies. Shoplifting in men's stores is way down there—as a percentage, and in women's shops it's really, really high.

WOMAN 2

Well, of course! Women's things are . . . prettier.

MAN 2

Your father *really* was a shoplifter?

MAN 3

He had a room at home he called his study. I guess it was a library—I mean, it had books in it, and all; and it had two big closets. "Stay out of my closets!" he used to say—if any of us kids was nosing around in his study there, bothering him, while he was at his desk—work he brought home with him—"Stay out of my closets!" One of them we couldn't have gotten into if we'd really *needed* to—he kept it locked. "Why do you want a locked closet?" Mother asked him once. "What do you keep in there—a harem?" "Just a lot of stuff," he said. "Just a lot of stuff. Now . . . just let it be."

MAN 4

Boy, *I* would have tried to get in there.

MAN 3

We were *good* kids.

MAN 2 (*Joshing*)

Ohhhhh!

WOMAN 2

A harem? Really!?

WOMAN 4 (*To* WOMAN 2)

I think that was a metaphor.

WOMAN 2

Really??

MAN 3

Yes; yes, it was. They were one of those couples never . . . *did* anything. I knew it in my bones—

(*Smiles*)

as they used to say.

WOMAN 4 (*Smiles, too: a memory*)

Knew it in my bones.

MAN 3

And one day, out of the blue . . .

(*Smiles at* WOMAN 4)

as they used to say . . .

WOMAN 4 (*As above*)

Out of the blue.

MAN 3

One day, out of the blue, early evening, Ma and us kids were at home, waiting dinner for Dad, when the phone rang, and Ma went and answered it, and then she came in, with her coat on. "Your father's been arrested," she said . . . real flat, no expression.

WOMAN 2

No!

MAN 3

She went off, and we stayed there, in the dining room, wondering who he'd killed or . . .

(*Shrugs*)

whatever.

WOMAN 3

You poor babies!

MAN 3

Well, I was sixteen, but I know what you meant, and thank you. And it turned out, of course, that he hadn't killed *any*body, just that he'd been arrested in the 5 & 10 with a dozen coat hangers up under his coat.

MAN 1 (*Disbelief*)

Hangers?!

MAN 3 (*Oddly bland*)

Yes; wire hangers; a dozen of them.

WOMAN 2

What a way to go!

WOMAN 4 *(To get it straight)*

Wire . . . hangers.

MAN 3

Everybody was pretty good about it—the cops, the judge, the five and dime, the . . . bank people, the neighbors. Oh, there were a lot of bad jokes, but . . . everybody was pretty good about it—except Ma, maybe.

WOMAN 1

Oh?

MAN 4

Oh?

MAN 3

I mean, she was fine—supportive, protective, but . . . I couldn't see as far into her eyes as I used to—nowhere near as deep. It was as if she'd closed a venetian blind behind her eyes; you couldn't see into her head anymore.

MAN 1 *(After a bit)*

What about the closet? What was in the closet?

WOMAN 1

Yes!

MAN 2

Yes! what?!

WOMAN 2

What!?

MAN 3 *(A little shy)*

Everything—more stuff than you'd ever expected to see, millions of . . . things, nothing big; nothing valuable; nothing that would matter. He unlocked it for us—just us, the family; the cops came later and hauled it all off—and it was pretty amazing, I guess: Floor to ceiling—cans of shoe polish, spools of thread, tire irons, placemats, wisk brooms, Easter cards, condoms —boxes of them, and they weren't as easy to come by back then . . .

WOMAN 2 *(Whispers; to herself)*

For the harem.

WOMAN 4 *(Smiles)*

Shhhhh!

MAN 3

. . . wind-up clocks, outfielder's mitts, and . . . everybody thought this meant something—something significant . . . bibles, maybe a hundred bibles—Gideons, all snitched from hotels he'd stayed at over the years . . .

MAN 4

They're *free:* you can *take* them.

MAN 3

Yes; I know. And more stuff . . . none of it meaning much—meaning *any-thing*, I guess.

WOMAN 2 (*Quiet awe*)

Did he say why?

MAN 1

Did he?

MAN 3 (*Shrugs*)

Oh . . . not really. We looked at it all, all piled up, floor to ceiling, and he walked away sort of and said, kind of distant . . . "Well, there it is; I thought it might come in handy."

(*Small pause*)

He didn't go to jail or anything. Life went on . . . more or less.

WOMAN 4

My goodness.

MAN 4

Yes.

WOMAN 1

Yes. I know you think I'm strange already . . .

WOMAN 3

Oh, now . . .

MAN 2 (*Mild sarcasm*)

Us? Nooooo.

WOMAN 1

. . . but there's probably something else you ought to know.

MAN 4

Let her do it.

WOMAN 1

Thank you. As I said, I know you think I'm very strange . . .

MAN 1

It's just that you shouldn't give a crowd like this a lead-in like that.

WOMAN 1

I see; well.

WOMAN 3

Dear . . . go on.

WOMAN 1

. . . That I'm very strange, but . . . I talk to plants.

MAN 3

Oh! How sixties.

WOMAN 1 *(Silence)*

I said . . . I talk to plants.

MAN 3 *(To fill the silence)*

Do they . . . do *they* talk to *you?*

MAN 1

. . . too?

MAN 3

Yes.
   (To MAN 1*)*
Thanks.

MAN 1

Welcome.

WOMAN 1

Well, I don't know. I mean, that *would* be polite, but . . .

WOMAN 2

When do you talk to them?

MAN 2

And what do you say? And which ones do you say *what* to?

WOMAN 1 *(Nervous laugh)*

Whoa! You're getting ahead of me.

MAN 1

It's just our. . . . Oh, I don't know: our boundless enthusiasm, I guess.

MAN 4

Let her do it.

MAN 1 *(Salutes)*

Right.

WOMAN 1

Can I talk now? Yes? Good!

MAN 3

When did we stop her? When have we ever . . .

WOMAN 4

Be good!

WOMAN 3

. . . Or at least be quiet.

MAN 3

Sorry.

WOMAN 1

Well, it all began when I was sitting at home one afternoon, and I had the tube on . . .

MAN 2

(Shakes his head; false sympathy)
I don't know; more calamities happen that way . . .

WOMAN 3

Isn't that wonderful the way we call things? I had a grandmother called it an icebox!

MAN 3

What!? Called the TV an icebox?

MAN 1

What was she . . . senile?

WOMAN 3

No! The Frigidaire! She called it an icebox!

MAN 1

The Frigidaire? Do you mean the refrigerator?

WOMAN 3 *(Rather defiant)*

I suppose.

WOMAN 4

I *do* call it an icebox.

WOMAN 3

Well, there. You see?

WOMAN 1

. . . and I had the tube on, and I switched over and there was this woman talking about . . . talking to *plants!* Talking about talking to *plants!* And it was fascinating! She said they *liked* it, that it makes them . . .

MAN 1

Secure, and loved, and . . .

WOMAN 1

Grow! It makes them grow!

MAN 4

It's our breathing out on them . . . the carbon dioxide.

WOMAN 1

Well, I know that. Of course it's the carbon dioxide . . . gives 'em a real . . . jolt.

MAN 3 *(Getting it straight)*

It doesn't have anything to do with what you say to them. "Hello, you big, handsome plant!" or whatever. That doesn't have anything to do with it.

WOMAN 1

No; of course not. I'm not that silly. Anthropomorphic to a fault, I'll admit, but there are *limits*.

WOMAN 4 *(To* MAN 1*)*

Why don't you say, "We're grateful."

MAN 1

We're grateful.

WOMAN 1

. . . Which doesn't stop me from doing it, anyway. I give names to them— most of them—and little histories . . . and we talk about—oh, I don't know —about what the day's like, and are they happy that close to the window— on the sill—and would they rather be watered AM or PM, and—oh, I don't know—just . . . talk.

MAN 3 *(To* MAN 2*, more or less)*

Well . . . I don't suppose that can be . . . harmful, exactly.

MAN 2

No, no, probably not.

WOMAN 1

. . . And it tickles me—doing it.

WOMAN 4 *(Pause)*

I used to talk to my carpet.

MAN 3 *(Pause)*

No.

WOMAN 4

Yes; yes, I did.

MAN 4 *(Pause)*

Is there more to that?

WOMAN 4

Nothing I think you really want to know.

WOMAN 1

It doesn't hurt, you know . . . talking to plants.

MAN 1

What about carpets—talking to carpets?

WOMAN 1 *(Pause)*

I'm not sure I have an opinion on that.

WOMAN 3

I can't see what harm it would do.

MAN 2 *(Shrugs)*

I talk to my *car.*

MAN 3

Well . . . sure! Naturally!

WOMAN 4

I suspect my carpet may have been deaf, come to think of it.

WOMAN 3

Yes, well . . . very possible.

WOMAN 4

In any event, nothing I said to it made any difference.

MAN 3

Just kept getting dirty, hunh?

WOMAN 4 *(Haughty)*

That wasn't the subject of our conversation.

MAN 3 *(Pause)*

Oh?

(Silence)

Oh.

WOMAN 1

One plant started getting all droopy, and dropping things, leaves, and buds and all, and I kept talking to it—to cheer it up, to give it encouragement: "Oh, what do you want to do that for?" and so on.

MAN 1

Maybe it was deciduous.

MAN 4

Those are trees: trees are deciduous.

MAN 1

Not plants?

WOMAN 2

And certainly not carpets!

MAN 3

And certainly not carpets what!?

WOMAN 2

Deciduous: carpets aren't deciduous.

WOMAN 4

Yes they are—can be. Mine was . . . very.

WOMAN 1

It perked up for a while and then said—flat out—"To hell with it," and
. . . shriveled.

MAN 4 (*Mildly embarrassed*)

That's . . . that's a shame.

WOMAN 1

So—anyway: I talk to plants.
 (*To* WOMAN 4)
And you talk to carpets.

WOMAN 4

Did.

WOMAN 1

Did.

WOMAN 4

Now I wouldn't give one the time of day.

WOMAN 1 (*Cheerful*)

Well . . . it takes all kinds. You see?

WOMAN 3

It certainly does. I was at a party once, and a famous old movie star was
there—
 (*The others gather around her excitedly*)
What am I, Mother Goose? I was at a party once, and a famous old movie
star was there—not just an "old star," but a very, *very* old star, a silent
movie star, maybe the first silent movie star. She—it was a female star—
she had a sister, and they were stars together way back then; the sister
died. Well, they're both dead now, but the sister was dead by the time I
met the one that wasn't . . . dead, that is.

WOMAN 4

Don't tell me it was the . . .

WOMAN 3

Shhhhh! Don't say the name!

WOMAN 4

But . . . was it?

WOMAN 3

Yes, but don't say it. It was a dinner party, at someone's house, outside of
the city. Rich people—nouveau, I think, but it doesn't matter. They
thought they were running some kind of half-assed salon—has-beens,

never-weres, almost-made-its, whatever-became-ofs—you know: you take what you can get. And somehow they'd gotten this . . . famous old star lady to come to the dinner. Well to be truthful, I think they paid her; I'm sure they did.

MAN 2

How do you know?

WOMAN 3

Instinct. I'm never wrong.

MAN 2

Oh, I see.

WOMAN 3

She was so fragile. At cocktails, she just sat there—she was deaf, too—and when people tried to talk to her she'd nod and smile and laugh a little, or shake her head. She hadn't heard a damn thing, but she faked it—the way people on the podium fake being awake during speeches. She was good. But at the table, between salad and dessert, the host went into his act; he'd already toasted the "very distinguished"—everything being relative—long, elaborate toasts, which demanded a reply, of course, these replies being praise of the host and hostess, the house, the distinguished blah-blah-blah-blah. They've since divorced, by the way, the loser getting stuck with the kids—spoiled rotten little monsters. Anyway . . .

MAN 3

Why did you *go* to this party? I mean, if you don't like the *people* . . .

WOMAN 4

If you only went to parties where you liked the people you'd stay at home most of the time.

(*To* WOMAN 3)

Right?

WOMAN 3

Right.

MAN 3 (*Considers it*)

Oh.

WOMAN 3

Anyway . . . I also go because I learn, by the way: I'm a student "of our times." Anyway, he'd left our lady to last—a mark of honor, of course: the final act. The host, he toasted her—long, elaborate—and she knew he was doing it; she was aware of that much anyway. And when he finished— something like "and we're so proud to have you grace our table"—and all eyes turned to her, friendly if fixed smiles, and we all waited . . . for her reply. I saw something in her eyes—at least I think I did—something puzzled and rummaging; she knew she was expected to talk, to say some-thing. And . . . and it was as if she'd been turned on, as if a button had been pushed, for she suddenly started, in her tiny voice, "Well, no, he wasn't exactly a *tall* man, though he gave one that impression: I remem-ber once when he was directing me in . . ." and on and on she went, a whole paragraph, a whole long paragraph. It had nothing do to with any-thing, and it was clearly a set piece. She was finished, finally, and did her shy little smile again. There was a small, awful silence, and then the man to my right—to try to save the situation, I think—bellowed at her, "Tell us how silent films were different from talkies!" She focused on him, gathered herself up and said, "I *would* have married him, I think, except my sister wanted him; but he didn't want her; she didn't know he was gay. *He* knew *I* knew, and I didn't care, but nobody ever told my sister, and so her heart was broken . . ." and on and on—another long, long set paragraph. And she would stop . . . just stop when she got to the end of it. It was as if someone wound her up, and she went. The *party* wound down after that, as you might imagine—some early departures—looks at watches, feignings of great surprise. She sat there at the table a while—oblivious, waiting for dessert, possibly. God! I hope they paid her a lot to come there.

WOMAN 2

That's so sad!

WOMAN 4 (*Mild sarcasm*)

Oh? Really?

WOMAN 2

Yes!

WOMAN 3

I hope they paid her a great deal.

MAN 4

Now, I have something I need to say about myself. I don't think of myself as . . . young . . . anymore. I mean, I'm not a fool, and though our famous three score and ten has been upped to seventy-five, I think—as an aver-age, that is, lifespan for us men, we men—still, I've seen far more than I'm likely to, anomaly aside. I mean, I'm nicely over fifty . . .

MAN 1

HANH!!

WOMAN 3

Now, now.

MAN 4

I said "nicely." I'm nicely over fifty, *VERY* nicely, but . . . well, I've never thought of myself as . . . old.

WOMAN 4

No! Of course not!

MAN 1

Such a help.

WOMAN 3

(As WOMAN 1 and WOMAN 2 giggle)
No, now!

MAN 4

I used to think that middle age was something I'd get to one day, while young—or youngish—stretched on and on . . .

WOMAN 4

I know; I know.

MAN 4

. . . and middle age was just around the corner; but last night, not far from here, right out on the street, I was walking along, mulling, or just absorbed, and there was a young couple, a boy and a girl, really, a black boy and girl, at a bus stop, and they were arguing, I think . . .

MAN 2 (Not too pleasant)

Black, were they?

MAN 4 (Puzzled)

Yes. Why?

MAN 2 (Mild sneer)

Oh, nothing.

MAN 4 (Pause, then)

. . . arguing . . . about something, I don't know what, when the girl said "Ask him!" And I realized she meant me—ask ME. And the boy said, sort of sneering, "Ask him!? Ask that old man!? What would he know!?"

MAN 2

My, my.

WOMAN 4

Oh, dear.

MAN 4

. . . And while I didn't walk into a lamppost, or anything, it did throw me some. I mean . . .

WOMAN 4

You poor thing.

MAN 2 (Quietly mocking)

Poor thing.

MAN 4

I mean . . . what have I done?. . . Gone from being young—youngish—feeling young—youngish—gone straight into old age? I mean . . . what!

WOMAN 4

Young old age. Is that a help?
 (WOMAN 1 *and* WOMAN 2 *giggle*)

MAN 4 (*Considers*)

Not much. How can I have missed middle age like that?

MAN 2

Black, were they?

MAN 4 (*Fading off*)

. . . Or at least the awareness of it.
 (*Remembering to reply; no comment in it*)
Yes; black. "Ask *him!?* Ask that old *man!?* What would *he* know!?
 (*Shakes his head*)

MAN 3

I've *always* been middle-aged.

WOMAN 3

Is that a fact?

WOMAN 1

I'm going to be youngish forever.

MAN 1 (*More or less to himself*)

I must try to remember not to die young.

WOMAN 2

It's all one . . .
 (*Unsure*)
isn't it?

MAN 4

I have gotten to that age when my contemporaries—my friends, my loved ones, my acquaintances—are dying around me.

MAN 1

Hanh! Me, too!

MAN 4

No, I mean what they refer to as a normal death.

MAN 1

There's no such thing!

MAN 4 *(Placating)*
I know; I know. I mean people my age.

MAN 1
So do I!

MAN 4
I know! People the age people are *supposed* to die, the age when it's not
. . . unusual. Of course, people die all around one, the . . . startlements, and
the accidents; but no; I'm talking about the time when all the "protective
others" start falling away and you're left all naked. There are two theories
about doctors, you know; if you have a young one you're likely to have a
man—or a woman, I suppose—right up to date with all the theoretical
answers . . . fresh, and not weighed down or discouraged. The other
theory is to have a doctor *older* than you—someone between you and
death chronologically.

MAN 2
That's silly!

MAN 3
Either *way.*

MAN 4
I know; yes, I know. And, of course, when you get to a certain age it's hard
to find a doctor older than you are.

WOMAN 4 *(Generally)*
When I was twenty-two I had a doctor who was eighty-eight. He had a
lovely office, beautiful tools—instruments I mean—though they did look
a little . . . antique.

MAN 3
. . . but, then again: so did he, no?

WOMAN 4 *(Admitting)*
Yes.

MAN 2
Why did you have him? I mean, why did you have *him.*

WOMAN 4 *(Shrugs)*
He was the family doctor; he'd been that . . . forever. I don't think he was
much good . . . much help, but of course when *he* was trained there wasn't
much doctors could do: they came just before the priests. He lived to be a
hundred and six.

MAN 1
Was he still *practicing!?*

WOMAN 4 *(Pensive)*

I don't know; I moved to another city.

MAN 4

You can know all about death; you can have accepted all that—the inevitability, the logic of it—but when they start to go away all around you, there's a . . . bleakness you can't imagine—can't have imagined. And I have reached that age. It's really quite lonely.

WOMAN 3 *(Matter of fact)*

Lear-like.

MAN 4

Oh, not that grand . . . but lonely.

WOMAN 2

I know I'm supposed to be thinking about all . . . *that*—becoming . . . adjusted, but I *can't*. I just can't *bring* myself.

WOMAN 4

You're young; wait

WOMAN 2

I know; I know.

MAN 1

How lonely are you?

MAN 4 *(Pause)*

Very.

(Somewhat shorter pause)

Sometimes I wonder why we all go through our lives without touching one another very much. Everyone I know who's died I know I haven't touched enough, no matter how much I have—or been touched enough by them.

MAN 1 *(Pause; gently)*

Do you want to be touched?

MAN 4 *(Shy)*

Yes please.

(The others move to touch him; some embrace, some stroke, others just . . . touch. After they do so they move back to where they were. Take your time with this)

MAN 2 *(After)*

Yes?

MAN 4 *(Pause)*

Yes.

(Pause)
Thank you.

THE OTHERS *(Quiet)*
You're welcome.

MAN 4

(Pause: suddenly breaks it with a laugh—a little rueful, but a laugh)
Once upon a time there was a man who believed that nothing was impossible.

WOMAN 4
There was probably a woman who believed that, too.

MAN 4
Oh? Yes?

WOMAN 4 *(Hedging a little)*
Well . . . maybe.

MAN 4
I'm pretty sure—
(Pause)
that there is a way to get through it—so long as you know there's doom right from the beginning; that there is a time, which is limited, and woe if you waste it; that there are no guarantees of anything—and that while we may not be responsible for everything that *does* happen to us, we certainly are for everything that *doesn't;* that since we're conscious, we have to be aware of both the awful futility of it and the amazing wonder. Participate, I suppose.

MAN 3 *(Some sarcasm)*
Let me write this down.

WOMAN 3
Shhhhh!

MAN 4
Do that. Or keep it levitated, anyway. "Once upon a time there was a man who believed that nothing was impossible."
(To the others)
Now you do one.

WOMAN 2
Forgive everyone but yourself.

WOMAN 3
It's a good idea to have friends both in heaven and in hell.

MAN 2

People have the greatest faith in things they don't understand.

MAN 3

No one knows what will happen to him before sunset.

WOMAN 1

If it were not for hope the heart would break.

WOMAN 4

Only a fool isn't sad at least once a day.

MAN 1

Dunder do gally the beans.

MAN 4

Yes; exactly. Thank you. *Fragments*: The End.
(*Lights, fade to black*)

CURTAIN

The Play About
the Baby

The Play About the Baby was given its world-premiere production, directed by Howard Davies, at London's Almeida Theatre in 1998. It was subsequently presented in the United States—in a production directed by Edward Albee—in April 2000 by the Alley Theatre, Gregory Boyd, artistic director, Paul R. Tetreault, managing director.

The Play About the Baby premiered in New York City at the Century Center for he Performing Arts (J.C. Compton, founder and director; William Ralph Odom, managing director) on February 1, 2001, produced by Elizabeth Ireland McCann, Daryl Roth, Terry Allen Kramer, Fifty-Second Street Productions, Robert Bartner, and Stanley Kaufelt, in association with the Alley Theatre. It was directed by David Esbjornson; The set design was by John Arnone; the lighting design was by Kenneth Posner; the sound design was by Donald DiNicola; the costume design was by Michael Krass; the general manager was Roy Gabay; the production manager was Kai Brothers; and the production stage manager was Mark Wright. The cast was as follows:

KATHLEEN EARLY *as* GIRL

DAVID BURTKA *as* BOY

BRIAN MURRAY *as* MAN

MARIAN SELDES *as* WOMAN

ACT ONE

*(Two chairs, identically placed not far from center, slightly diago-
nally toward one another, walking space between them. Nice light;
neutral background.)*

*(BOY and GIRL both seated, GIRL hugely pregnant, she stage right,
he stage left; hands folded, facing out)*

GIRL *(Not moving; calm)*

I'm going to have the baby now.

*(BOY and GIRL exit left. Sound: Growing labor; medical preps
and encouragement. Growing pain and moaning; screams with
accompanying sounds; slap; baby crying. Silence. BOY and GIRL,
no longer pregnant, enter. Quietly)*

There.

BOY *(No comment)*

It's the miracle of life.

GIRL

Yes; yes; it is.

BOY *(Turns to her)*

Did it hurt a lot?

GIRL *(Touches her dress at the knee)*

They say you can't remember pain.

BOY

A-ha.

GIRL *(Pause)*

Yes; yes, it did.

BOY

You *can*, then.

GIRL

As I remember.

BOY

I broke my arm before I knew you. Did you know that?

GIRL

Not that I remember.

BOY

Yes. Well, I did.
   (*Sound: cry of baby offstage left*)

GIRL (*Rises*)

Feeding time.

BOY

In here.

GIRL

All right.
   (*Exits left, behind* BOY)

BOY
   (*Sort of to her, but as if she were still there*)
It wasn't exactly I broke it; it was more they broke it for me. Not that they
said we'll break it *for* you if you *want* us to—if you can't do it for your*self*.
   (*Considers*)
More they just broke it—not *for* me, but rather as if I'd asked, though I
hadn't. They did break it, though I hadn't asked.
   (*Afterthought*)
I'm sure if I'd asked they would have been . . . well, eager, I guess. That's
only a supposition, though.
   (*The* GIRL *re-enters from left, already feeding the baby; she sits
   again, chair right. We do not see the baby, merely its blanket.*)

GIRL

Very hungry.

BOY

I'll want some; remember.

GIRL (*Slightly ironic*)

Line up!

BOY (*Matter-of-fact*)
I'd come from the gym and I was pumped.

GIRL (*Looking down*)
V . . . e . . . r . . . y hungry.

BOY

The bloodrush, the endorphins . . .

GIRL (*To the* BOY)

I love your body; I really do.

BOY (*Little wiggle of eyebrows*)

I know; I know you do.

(*Back to previous tone*)

. . . and I was walking back to the dorm, and I had my gym bag and my stuff and I was . . .

GIRL

When you let me lick your armpits I almost faint, I really do.

BOY

It tickles.

GIRL (*Smiles*)

You start getting hard.

BOY

Yes: it tickles.

(*Previous tone*)

And I was in the alley between the gym and the science building and there were these guys I'd seen at the Hopeless Mothers gig at the arena when I was taking tickets there? And I'd spotted them trying to sneak in and I'd called the guards on them . . .

GIRL

I like your left armpit better than the other.

BOY

Well, the other arm got broken; I was *telling* you.

GIRL

You think that's . . . OW!

(*Reaction to baby at breast*)

BOY

Let *me* at it for a while. *I* won't bite!

GIRL (*Oddly*)

Not now.

BOY

I think I like both your breasts equally.

GIRL

What happened?

BOY

Hm?

GIRL

You called the guards on them—on the guys.

BOY

Oh, and the guards roughed them up a little, and they said "We'll get you, motherfucker!" The guys—not the guards. To me; they said it to me.

GIRL (*Looks at him*)

Yes: of course the guys, and of course to you.

BOY

And that's what they did.

GIRL

What?

BOY

They got me, motherfucker. They said, in the alley there, hey, you're the one put the guard dogs on us, aren't you. I said yes, I was; guards, not guard dogs.

GIRL

Not a wise answer.

BOY

Which?

GIRL

Either; both.

BOY

Never lie. Besides, they knew. Yes, I am, I said. You guys could have paid—benefit and all. You guys could have paid.

GIRL

What was the benefit?

BOY

Mother's Milk.

GIRL

Ah.

BOY

Yeah, I know, I know, they said—kind of apologetic; we shoulda paid. No hard feelings I said. Hey, no way, no way, they said. And I put my hand out: no hard feelings I said.

GIRL

Less wise.

BOY

I know; and I think I knew what was going to happen, but too quick to stop it.

GIRL *(Looks at baby)*

Baby's full.

(Rises, goes off left, behind BOY*)*

BOY

(As she exits; as previously)

I put my hand out, and I'd just come from the gym and my forearms looked great.

(Begins to demonstrate)

And the big guy put his hand out and shook hands with me and swung around and cracked my arm against his knee and . . . Crack! And oh shit it hurt! Have fun taking tickets, the big one said, and the others laughed, and I was on my knees, and it hurt so much I was crying, and one of the others came up on me, and he unzipped his fly and what was he going to do . . . piss on me? I don't know; and the big one said leave him alone and they walked off.

(Pause)

Maybe he *wasn't* going to piss on me; maybe he was going to . . .

*(*GIRL *re-enters from left)*

GIRL

All asleep.

(Observes him on his knees, his disturbance)

BOY *(Still preoccupied)*

I don't know what he was going to do! It hurt so! They hurt me so!

GIRL

(She kneels in front of him, baring a breast.)
Shhhhhhh.

BOY *(Softly; almost pleading)*

He hurt me so.

GIRL

Come toward *me*.

BOY

(His left hand on her breast, his right arm hanging limp; still on his knees)

. . . and the other one came toward me . . .

GIRL

Here. Do this.

BOY

(His words becoming mumble as he fastens his mouth on her breast)

. . . and he undid his fly, and I don't know what he was going to do. I don't know if he was going to . . .

GIRL

Shhhhhh. Shhhhh. Shhhhh. Come. In here, in here.

(*GIRL leads* BOY *off left.* MAN *enters, comes center and stands behind and between the chairs.*)

MAN (*Out; smile*)

Hello there!

(*Gestures off left*)

Boy, girl? Yes?

(MAN *observes chairs; passes hand over stage right chair with finger of right hand; smells right hand fingers; considers; looks off left. Addresses audience; sighs*)

Ah . . . youngsmell! Have you ever noticed when you're driving somewhere you've not been before—directions, of course—it always takes longer than you think it should, that you've passed it, or not turned left when you were supposed to? And yet, when you're coming home, or whatever, *after* you've been there—the place you didn't know how to get to, but had directions—you're amazed at how much shorter the trip is?

(*Fingers of left hand over stage left chair; smells fingers; eyebrows waggling; whispers*)

Youngsmell. Have you noticed that? Not youngsmell; how much shorter the trip is? I'm not sure whether it's it *does* take longer to get there, or it's it just seems so.

(*To someone in particular*)

Have you noticed that? Hm?

(*If no answer, go on; if there's an answer, improvise briefly*)

I don't think it's merely that it *seems* so, though it may seem that way—which may be the same thing but I don't think so: that which we *feel* we've experienced is the same as we have?

(*Dismissive*)

Naaaaah! Reality determined by our experience of it? Or our *sense* of experiencing it? Naaaaaaah!

(*Smells both hands together, then right, then left, then both again.*)

Eeny-meeny-miney-moe! Have you ever noticed when you're talking to someone you should know, but don't, at a cocktail party, say, and you try to lead the conversation to remind you who they are—who you're talking to—they won't do it? They won't let you go there? Do they know what you're trying to do and are doing a kind of "Fuck you. You don't remember me? Well, fuck you; just hang there!" Or are they so absorbed seeing you again, remembering *you*—perfectly, of course: your name, the stuff you did to your wife—that it would never occur to them you're twisting in the wind? Once, I was at a party; well, no, I was *giving* it, and I was being a good host—introducing people to people, putting types together I thought would be good for one another or, sometimes, just a hoot, or plain wrong—and I'd been at it for a while— it was a big party—and I was groggy, I guess, and there was this tall, older woman next to me—she'd sort of come over from another group—and two dykes came up—middle-aged, neither one diesel, neither one lipstick, real centered ladies—and I'd known them for years, and they were Jo and Lu, good simple, non-specific names: none of this Josephine and Lucille shit—and I did my host act, and I turned to introduce them to the older woman standing next to me, and I looked at her, and I knew she was familiar, but I couldn't, for the life of me, remember who she was, and I said, "Jo, Lu, this is . . . this is . . . " and Jo laughed and said, "We *know* your *mother*, dear."

(To someone specific)

Fall through the floor!! Ever done that!?

(General again)

I suppose that was the worst—so far!, though I'm looking forward with a kind of dread—fascinated dread, you know? After Jo and Lu had chuckled off, Mother looked at me sort of funny and said, "You didn't know who I was, did you?" "Oh, come on, Ma!" I said, hearty guffaw. "No, you didn't," she said, just the fringiest little bit sad, and she walked away. It didn't *change* anything between us; we were OK, but I think it was the first time I realized we were both adults. She died three years later.

(To someone in particular; laughing)

No! Not from that!

(General again)

Nobody dies from not being remembered.

(Change of tone; more interior)

From being forgotten, yes, very probably, but not from not being remembered.

(Pause)

Or are they the same *thing*?

(Thinks)

No; not quite.

(Energy rising)

So! Anyway! I bring all this up because . . . well, clearly because I wanted to bring it up, and I dare say there was a . . . Yes! Of course! Driving somewhere you'd never been before, that was it; that started it all.

(Smells fingers of both hands again)

Ahhh! How things fade—memories, photo-memories sometimes, last, though, usually. *Scent.*

(Spells it)

S . . . c . . . e . . . n . . . t.

(Sad now)

All fades, all dissolves, and we are left with . . . invention; *reinvention.* I
wonder how I'll remember

(Gestures about him)

all of *this*? But, since I'm not *there* yet—so to speak—have not, haven't
remembered it . . .

(Brisk)

well, first we *invent*, and then we *reinvent.* As with the past so the future—
reality, as they laughingly call it? Who was it said "our reality"—or something—"is determined by our need?" "The greater need rules the game?"
The reality? I guess that was *me.* All those "naaaahs" before? Remember
the "naaaahs"? Just a trick. Pay attention to this, what's true and what isn't
is a tricky business, no? What's real and what isn't? Tricky. Do you follow?
Yes? No? Good.

(Shrugs)

Whichever.

(Begins to exit)

Woman.

(As MAN *exits, stage left,* WOMAN *enters stage right, rather briskly;
sees* MAN *exiting.)*

WOMAN (After exiting MAN)

Wait; wait!

(He exits)

Am I late?

(To audience now)

Am I late!? Am I on time!?

*(*BOY *enters, wearing a towel only;* WOMAN *sees him. To the* BOY;
concerned)

Am I late?

BOY (Mildly puzzled)

Hello?

WOMAN

Hello. Am I late?

BOY (Matter-of-fact)

I wouldn't know.

(Afterthought)

Would I?

WOMAN (Fretful)

I don't *know!*

BOY

(Wipes his mouth; licks his lips; smiles)
I've been mountain climbing.

WOMAN *(Overly bright)*

Have you!

BOY

Yes.

WOMAN

You hardly seem dressed for it.

BOY *(Looks at his towel)*

Oh, I put this *on* . . . put it around me.

WOMAN

(Tiny pause as BOY *doesn't continue)*
Oh? A*ha!*
(Pause)
Where? Where did you put it on? I don't mean around your waist; I mean
. . . where?

BOY *(Points left, over his shoulder)*

In *there.*

WOMAN

No, I mean . . .
(Pause)
A*ha.*
(Pause)
Do you know who I am?

BOY

No.

WOMAN

A*ha.*
(Pause)
Are you certain?

BOY

I'm not?

WOMAN

A*ha.*
(Silence)
Mountain climbing?

BOY (*Recalling; eyes closed, perhaps?*)

It's all jungle as you approach—well, as you imagine it: warm, warmer, moist; but you move through it, past all that, eventually, reluctantly, of course; you're coming up from the south—from below—and you see them up ahead, looming, but there is a lot to get through first, as I said, in the jungle there—the ridges, and the great declivity. God!, and it's so hot and moist and . . . and . . . thrilling, and . . .

WOMAN

I've never done it.

BOY (*Looks at her oddly*)

Oh?

(*Considers it*)

Well, quite probably not; not too many women do . . . what? ten percent? I mean: I don't know you.

(*Afterthought*)

Do I?

(*Answers his own question*)

No; no, I don't think I do. So, no, you may not have—certainly not these; certainly not.

(*Holds invisible melons toward her; on with his story*)

And . . . do you mind if I get hyperbolic here? Even *more* hyperbolic?

WOMAN (*Cautious*)

I don't . . . *think* so.

BOY

Even more than I have been? I didn't think you would. And there are the deep ravines, and the ridges, and there are a lot of temptations! Well, one in particular—two! Two!! And you *do* stop there on your climb, on your ascent.

WOMAN

To rest.

BOY

Oh?

(*Chuckles*)

No, not exactly; more to delve, I guess; to explore; to absorb; to die a little. But you look up—over the great sloping hill with all its jungle, and there they are!

(*Sighs*)

My goodness, there they are.

WOMAN (*Helping*)

Snow-capped, jagged . . .

BOY (*Slightly more disapproving*)

Who *are* you, lady!?

WOMAN

Not snow capped? *Not* jagged?

BOY *(Quiet)*

No; of course not: lovely, curving slopes, almost twins. You go between them; there's moisture there; you breathe; you press your ears gently between them and it's the sound of giant seashells.

WOMAN *(Gets it)*

Ohhhhhhh! Ohhhhhh, I see! *Those* mountains; *that* climbing.

BOY *(Puzzled)*

Yes, of course. What else?

WOMAN

(*Half to the* BOY, *half to herself*)

Hyperbole: of course.

(*Out*)

I should have known.

(GIRL *appears from left, naked, or as naked as the actress will allow*)

GIRL *(To* BOY)

What are you doing? Are you coming back in? What are you doing?

BOY *(Over his shoulder)*

Yes; right away.

GIRL *(Pointing to* WOMAN)

Who is that?

BOY *(Simply)*

I don't know.

GIRL *(Considers it)*

Oh.

(*Considers it further*)

Well, leave her there where you found her and come back in. You're not finished; you're not there yet.

BOY *(Backing left)*

Yes, I know.

(*To* WOMAN *now*)

Yes; goodbye; I'm not there yet.

(*They exit—*BOY *and* GIRL*—leaving* WOMAN *standing.*)

WOMAN *(Waves)*

Farewell, intrepid traveler.

(*Waves off*)

Farewell!

(*Out*)

Where there's a boy, there's a girl, no?

(Shrugs)

Usually.

(Looks at the audience)

Well. I . . . uh . . . well, I suppose you'd like to know who I am, or why I'm here.

(Some uncertainty)

Well, I'm with *him*;

(Gestures off left)

that's why I'm here; I'm with him. The man; not the boy. The man indicated me as he exited, said "Woman" and exited. Remember? That's why I'm here—to be with him. To help . . . *him*; to . . . assist *him*.

(Hand up, palm out, to abort protest)

I'm not an actress; I want you to know that right off, though why you'd think I *was*, I mean automatically think I *was*, I don't know, though I *am* a trifle . . . theatrical, I suppose, and no apologies *there*. I *was* Prince Charming in our all-girl school production of *Snow White*, and while the bug may have bitten, it never took.

(Chuckles)

Nor—and forgive the seeming discontinuity here—nor am I from the press. That's the first thing I want you to know—well, the second, actually, the first being . . . having been . . .

(Trails off; starts again)

Oh, I am a very good cook, among other things. I became that to please my husband, my *then* husband, who was in the habit of eating out, by which he meant . . . alone . . . without *me*. It occurred to *me* that if I . . . well, it was no good: Alone, to him, meant *specifically* not with *me*, though with others, with lots of others. And the great feasts I'd prepare . . . would be for *me*. Alone. I became quite heavy, which I no longer am, and unmarried, which I am to this day. I trust he is still eating alone . . . all by himself . . . facing a wall.

(Pause)

No matter. Really: From the very first week, come dinnertime, he would put the paper under his arm, say "Bye, bye," or whatever, and . . . no matter. I *have* had journalistic dreams, though I am not a journalist—dreams of *being* a journalist, that is, and quite awake; not asleep. I went so far one time as to take a course; and my assignment was to interview a *writer*, to try to comprehend the "creative mind" as they call it.

(Firm gesture)

Don't try! Don't even give it a thought! There seems to be some sort of cabal going on on the part of these so-called creative people to keep the process a secret—a deep dark secret—from the rest of the world. What's the matter with these people? Do they think we're trying to steal their tricks? . . . would even *want* to!? And all I wanted to do was . . . under-

stand! And, let me tell you!, getting through to them—the creative types?—isn't easy. I mean even getting *at* them. I wrote politely to seven or eight of them, two poets, one biographer, a couple of short story writers, one female creator of "theatre pieces," etcetera, and not one of them answered. Silence; too busy "creating," I guess.

(On a roll now)

I remember finally I bribed someone into giving me this one guy's agent's name—this novelist?—and persuaded the agent to call him and see if *I* could *call* him?, and maybe *talk* to him?, and finding out I could *do* that—with no guarantees, naturally—and calling, and hitting the brick wall of the novelist's male secretary. I don't *mean* anything by that, of course.

(Heavy wink)

In any event, hitting *that* brick wall, having to repeat everything I'd said to the agent, and being told by the M.S.—the male secretary

(Heavy wink)

—they'd get back to me, and waiting until finally they *did*—I mean, *really*, who did they think they were . . . *both* of them!? Finally, the M.S. *did* call me—I was in the touchy stages of a soufflée, naturally—telling me that *he* was there . . .

(Does fingers as quotes)

"Himself" that is: the famous novelist . . . and he *was* going to talk to me—"himself" was—and I held the receiver to my ear, expecting what?—something other than a voice? I don't know—a choir of some sort? I held, and then his voice came . . . "Here I am," it said—*he* said—"Here I am." Odd, no? And the voice wasn't friendly, or unfriendly, gruffer than I'd thought it would be, perhaps, just . . . noncommittal. "Here I am; I'm here." I almost hung up, but I didn't. I mean, I'd gotten this close, and if I hung up who *knows* when I'd get another . . . *you* know. "I'm here," he said. And I rushed through what I wanted. "I'm studying the creative process, and I want to do it with *you*, through *you*—watching *you*, understanding *you*." "You want to watch me while I *write?!*" he said, sort of incredulous, and I could sense the phone being passed back to the M.S., or just hung up, or tossed over his shoulder, or whatever. "No! Wait!" I yelled. Silence. "I'm waiting," he finally said, no emotion at all. And I tried to explain what I really wanted.

(GIRL, chased by BOY—naked, or close—goes from stage left to stage right, a sweet chase, giggling, etc. The WOMAN senses, sees them.)

What?! What was that?! Did two people just run nakedly across the stage, giggling? Yes? Well . . . why not? Where was I? Oh: "What I really want is to watch you . . . uh . . . move your words from your mind to the page." "You're not serious," he said, sort of . . . fading away. "Oh, wait! Please; please!" I said—shouted, really. "I *do* want to study you! I so want to watch you move your words from your mind to the page." The sentence was beginning to sound strange to me. I heard a kind of chuckle from him . . . bitter, was it? Contemptuous? "Well, that wouldn't be much fun for anybody but *you*, *would* it . . . you underfoot, banging into people, asking a lot of ridiculous questions, studying everything, being an absolute . . ." "I'd be a mouse! I'd be a mouse!" I said—

(Shrugs)

mouse-like, I suppose. "Yeah, sure!" he guffawed at me, right over the phone. "Oh please; oh, please!" I whimpered.

(An aside)

Have you ever noticed the way we say everything twice when we're upset? "I'll be a mouse, I'll be a mouse;" "Oh, please, oh, please!" Have you noticed that? *I* have. "Will you? Will you? It'll only take a couple of weeks, and . . . " "I'd rather die," he said quietly . . . and he hung up.

(Indignation)

What kind of people *are* they?! I mean . . . what kind of people *are* they, these . . . these . . .

(GIRL and BOY repeat their previous stage cross, but from stage right to stage left. Noticing)

Two people just ran nakedly across the stage again, did they not? Giggling? No?

(Businesslike)

Well, then; now you know who I am *not*, what I do *not* do. As for who I am and what I *do* do, stay tuned.

(MAN enters)

You've had me standing out here, vamping away . . .

MAN *(Amused)*

Shhhhhhh; shhhhhhh. It's fine; it's fine. Come along now.

WOMAN

What were you doing?

MAN

Research? Peeing? Reparking? Whatever.

(Indicates off left)

Boy and girl.

WOMAN

Yes; I noticed.

MAN

That's them. "That's they" doesn't sound right, though it is.

WOMAN

No, it doesn't. That is them, eh?

MAN

Yes. How innocent they are.

WOMAN

Yes.

MAN

Pure.

WOMAN

Yes.

MAN

You'd think it was Eden, wouldn't you.

WOMAN

Yes. You would.

MAN

Yes.
     (*Takes her hand; indicates out*)
Say bye-bye.

WOMAN (*Out*)

Bye-bye.
     (*They exit.* GIRL, *followed by* BOY, *comes out, peers after the* WOMAN)

GIRL

Who *is* she? Who *is* that woman?

BOY (*Looking after her*)

Very strange.

GIRL

Yes.

BOY

I tried to talk to her.
     (*Correcting himself*)
She tried to talk to *me*.

GIRL

And?

BOY

Very strange. She asked me if I knew who she was.

GIRL

What did you tell her?

BOY

That I didn't.

GIRL

Maybe she'll go away.

BOY

Maybe.

(*Smiles*)

Can I chase you some more?

GIRL (*Giggles*)

No! No, you can't! It was fun!

BOY

Yes; yes it was.

(*Decision*)

I'm going to chase you some more.

GIRL (*Delighted*)

You'll catch me. I'll let you catch me.

BOY

Will you let me roll you over, lay you down, and do it again?

GIRL (*Giggles*)

Maybe.

(*Shyly sings:*)

> Roll me over,
> In the clover
> Roll me over
> Lay me down

(BOY *joins in; they both sing.*)

GIRL and BOY

> And do it again.

BOY

I like being on you.

GIRL (*Nice*)

I've noticed.

BOY

I like being *in* you.

(*Quickly*)

You've noticed; yes, I know.

GIRL

Yes.

BOY

I like sleeping with you.

GIRL

Yes.

BOY (*A smile*)

I like sleeping *in* you.

GIRL

Yes.

BOY

Saves time.

GIRL

Yes. Who *is* she? Who *is* that woman?

BOY

Is she familiar?

GIRL

No, not exactly. I mean, she looks like a *woman*, but no; not at all; not famil-
iar at all.
   (An afterthought)
A photograph, maybe?

BOY *(Shrugs)*

She looks like a lot of people.

GIRL

Yes.
   (Abruptly)
Does she?

BOY

You don't. *You* look like *you*.

GIRL *(Preoccupied)*

Oh? Does that make me happy?

BOY

It should.

GIRL

Oh, well, then, it probably does.

BOY *(Takes her wrist)*

Come with me.

GIRL *(Mild concern)*

Where?

BOY

In there.
   (Indicates stage left)
I want to *do* something.

GIRL *(Greater concern)*

What?!

BOY

Something new; something we've never done.

GIRL *(Slightly worried)*

There *isn't* anything.

BOY *(Pulling her)*

I *read* about something. Don't fight me.

GIRL *(Some alarm)*

What *is* it?! What is it you want to do?

BOY

Relax into it.

   (Lets her wrist go; hands to his chest, mock eloquence)

You're my goal; you're my destination. You are my moon and sun and earth and sky and . . .

   (Breaks tone)

on and on, and so on and so forth.

   (Grabs her wrist again)

C'mon!

GIRL

No! What! What *is* it?!

BOY *(An enthusiastic confidence)*

It hasn't been done for centuries; three religions outlawed it in the Middle Ages. C'mon!

GIRL *(Reluctantly giving in)*

W . . . e . . . l . . . l.

BOY

You'll *love* it.

   (Mock tone again)

You are my goal; you are my destination.

   (Normal tone again)

C'mon, girl, let's go!

GIRL

   (Allowing herself to be dragged off)

Not in front of the baby; whatever it is, not in front of the baby.

BOY

(Slightly annoyed, as they exit) OK; OK.

   (After BOY and GIRL exit, MAN enters from right, playing blind.)

MAN

   (To the audience, but not looking at it, of course, and not facing it.)

The chairs should be right ahead of me . . . right . . . *here!*

   (Wrong)

No. Further?

(Bumps against stage right chair)

Ow! Yes; there it is.

(Opens eyes, turns to face audience)

Did she give you a good time? Spin a splendid yarn? Yes? Good. She's good at that; she's very good at that. Have you ever done this?—pretended to be blind? I don't mean to offend those of you in the audience who *are* blind—physically blind, that is—though there are seldom many of you at plays—*blind*; deaf, yes; blind, seldom; which surprises me, since most good plays come at you "by the ear," so to speak; but, then again, so do a lot of bad ones—by the ear. The tactile is underdeveloped in the sighted—in the seeing—for the most part. I was at a museum in London a few years ago—at the Royal Academy, I *think*—and I came upon a sculpture exhibit set up especially for the blind. There were maybe twenty pieces in the exhibit—faces, abstract forms, a few animals—and there were guides about to help the blind get *to* the pieces; there were roped walkways, as well. The blind were asked to touch the sculptures, investigate them, while the guides would assist—the name of the artist, the materials, the subject if need be. I watched for a little, saw the wonder, the enthusiasm of the blind, their smiles, little cries, and then I decided to do it myself—be blind and go through the exhibit by touch only. I closed my eyes, and a guide came up to me, to help me. "I'm not blind," I said, "except I'm pretending to be, to see it, so to speak, as a blind person would. Will you help me?" This being Britain—*or* me being lucky—she chirped at me: "Of course! But be sure you keep your eyes tight shut!" And so I did, and it was fascinating—to see with my fingers, with my hands, to touch, as we sighted do in the dark, the way the blind do in their endless dark—in *their* light. There was a copy of that famous bronze sculpture of the wild boar in Florence, the one sitting on its haunches, front legs up?

(Demonstrates with his arms)

The one with the bronze penis rubbed golden by the hundreds of years of Florentine men touching it—for good luck, for potency.

(Wonders)

What about the women? Do *they* touch it? Have they touched it for centuries, at night, perhaps, in the dark? "You're coming upon the Florentine boar," she chirped—really, she *chirped*. "Be sure you touch its bits and pieces, for good luck." "Its *what*?" I said. "Its . . . you know, its *thing*," she said. "Oh, right," I said. I'd done it in Florence when I was there; but this was different; this felt very different.

(Sudden shift; very offhand)

Have you seen the baby? Cute, no? They love it, *don't* they—the baby.

(Some puzzlement)

They really *love* it. I wonder how much they love it? How much they need it? Perhaps we should find out. As the lady said, stay tuned.

(Puzzles more)

Hunh!

>   (*A beat*)

Ah, well; off we go.

>   (MAN *exits.* GIRL *enters, speaks off to boy.*)

GIRL

That wasn't funny! Well, certainly not as funny as you thought it was—was going to be.

BOY (*Entering*)

Sorry.

>   (*Not really*)

GIRL

It wasn't!

BOY

Sorry!

GIRL

Mean it!

BOY (*Genuine*)

Sorry.

GIRL (*Grudging*)

Well . . . maybe. I don't think I *like* being thought of as a destination, by the way.

BOY (*Nice*)

What would you *like* me to think of you as—if not as a destination? I always *aim* for you: you *are* a destination—*my* destination. I remember when I saw you for the first time—when I was biking along—I saw you lying there on the stretcher, all unconscious—I said—well, to myself, more than to anyone—"*That's* the one; *that's* my destination."

GIRL (*She's heard this before.*)

That's sweet.

BOY

. . . and I said to myself, "When she wakes up—if she wakes up—I'm going to be there, and I'll be the first person she sees, and she'll love me; she'll want me and she'll love me; she's my destination."

GIRL

Yes; sweet.

>   (*More interested*)

Did you *really* tell them at the hospital you were my brother? You told them you were my brother and that's why they let you in? Let you sit by me?

BOY

Yes. I wanted you very much and being your brother made it even more intense—made me hard.

GIRL *(Not too nice)*

So many things do.

BOY *(Smiles)*

Yes. Isn't that nice?

GIRL *(Preoccupied)*

I wonder how that old Gypsy knew so much?

BOY

Who, the one you went to before we met?

GIRL

Yes, the one who told me . . .

BOY *(Sort of reciting)*

What, that you would pass out one day, be put on a stretcher and taken to the hospital, where nothing was found to be wrong—if fainting away is nothing—and that when this happened you would wake up and the nurse would be over you and she would smile and say everything was just fine and that your brother was in the hospital room with you, right by your side . . . that he was hard.

GIRL

She didn't say that—either one, the nurse *or* the Gypsy—the hard part.

BOY

. . . and that when you looked and saw it wasn't your brother . . .

GIRL

. . . not hard to determine, since I don't *have* one . . .

BOY

. . . it wasn't your brother, it would be the boy you would marry?

GIRL

Yes. I wonder how that old Gypsy knew so much?

BOY

Was she really very old? *He* very old? Gypsies look older than they are.

GIRL *(Dogmatic)*

She was *old*. That's what the sign said: "Come in and visit the old Gypsy; have your future told."

BOY

They lie.

GIRL *(Slightly offended)*

No! It was all true! It all came true!

BOY

No: about being old. It might have been a man for all *you* know.

GIRL

I can tell a man from a woman!

BOY

A Gypsy?

GIRL *(Uncertain)*

Well . . .

(More aggressive)

What do you mean "*if* she wakes up"? What do you *mean* by that?

BOY

You could have had a stroke for all *I* knew; you could have been *dead*. But you were so beautiful—so thrilling—I assumed you weren't—wouldn't be. I got off my bike—didn't even look at it, left my clips on—and saw you there and my heart sang, as the song sings. She won't be dead, I said to myself; she'll wake up and I'll be hard and she'll love me and she'll marry me.

GIRL *(Preoccupied again)*

Gypsies are strange people. How *do* they know so much?

BOY

It's easy to foretell the future: you just have to know what's going to happen.

GIRL

Hmmmmm.

BOY

And in the way of a true fairy tale come true no one even stole my bike.

GIRL

I guess those boys weren't around.

BOY

What boys?

GIRL

Oh, never mind.

BOY

Oh; those boys.

GIRL

Never *mind*. What a lovely story.

BOY

I think so. Did the Gypsy say we'd have a baby?

GIRL

No; the Gypsy was . . . well, she wouldn't *talk* about that.

BOY

Did you ask?

GIRL

Of course! "What about a baby?" I said. "What about babies? How many
will we have?"

BOY

And she wouldn't say—*he* wouldn't say?

GIRL

No; she . . . the Gypsy frowned.

BOY

She *frowned*? He *frowned*?

GIRL

"I can't see that," she said; "besides: your time is up."

BOY

Your money, she meant—*he* meant: not your time, your money.

GIRL

Same thing.

BOY

Yes. With Gypsies, yes.

GIRL

Maybe we'd better go back, get some more answers; take the baby *with*
us . . .

BOY

No! Gypsies steal babies!

GIRL *(Laughing)*

They don't!

BOY

You've never heard? It's famous; it's like the money scam.

GIRL

What is *that*?

BOY

You don't know? The money scam? The Gypsy promises to double your money
for you, so you bring it *to* her, or him, to be blessed, so it'll double, or whatever.
You bring it in ten-dollar bills, or something, in a big paper bag, and . . .

GIRL

Why do you do *that*?

BOY

What?

GIRL

Bring it to the Gypsy in a big paper bag!

BOY

To be blessed!

GIRL

No! Why in a big paper bag?

BOY *(Mildly irritated)*

Because that's the way the Gypsy *asks* for it.

GIRL

Oh.

BOY

And the Gypsy puts the paper bag . . .

GIRL

. . . with all the money in it . . .

BOY

. . . yes . . . *on* the table, be*tween* the two of you, and the Gypsy blesses it, and starts chanting, or something, and the music starts, and the lights go all funny . . .

GIRL *(Losing track)*

Wait a minute . . .

BOY

. . . and in the middle of all that the Gypsy pulls the famous switch.

GIRL

What famous switch?!

BOY

Hm? Oh, the famous switch of the bag. In all the chanting and the lights and the music and all, the Gypsy switches bags—takes *your* paper bag with all the money in it and puts another paper bag in its place filled with— what, I don't know—newspapers, or something, cut-up newspapers.

GIRL *(Logical)*

Well, what if you opened it?! You'd see that . . .

BOY

. . . the Gypsy tells you to bury the paper bag in your backyard without opening it and without anyone seeing you, and you're to leave it there for—what?—three weeks, so the magic can work, the money can double, or whatever.

GIRL

Yes, but . . .

BOY

. . . and you do it, because you're an asshole—you wouldn't have put your life savings in a paper bag and handed it to some damn Gypsy if you *weren't* an asshole in the first place. And so, after three weeks you go out and start digging up your backyard, since you've probably forgotten exactly where you've buried the paper bag, you being such an asshole, and your husband asks you what you're doing, and there's nothing for it, and so you say you're digging up the paper bag with all your life savings in it, like the Gypsy told you to do. And your *husband*, who knows a lot more about Gypsies than *you* do, is sitting down by now, his head in his hands, crying. And so you eventually find where you buried it, and you dig it up and you take it over to your husband to show him how the money's doubled, and you open up the bag . . .

GIRL

. . . and it's all cut-up newspaper.

BOY

Right; and the Gypsy's probably in Miami Beach by now driving around in some snazzy convertible.

GIRL *(At a loss for words)*

That's . . . that's . . . *terrible.*

BOY

You bet your life *savings* it is. So: You don't take the baby to the Gypsies.

GIRL

They'd steal it.

BOY

Probably.

GIRL

But, what would they . . . *do* with it?

BOY *(Shrugs)*

Sell it. Eat it.

GIRL *(Disbelieving)*

Noooooooo!

BOY *(Shrugs again)*

OK.

MAN *(Pops in)*

If you're not careful you're going to have the society for the prevention of cruelty to Gypsies after you.

(Exits abruptly)

BOY *(To where he was; nonplussed)*

Why? Why would I?

GIRL

Who *is* that *man*! Why are there so many strange people around here?

BOY (*At* GIRL; *preoccupied*)

What? What?

(*To where* MAN *was*)

Nobody cares about *Gypsies*!

(*To* GIRL)

What strange people?

GIRL

You were talking to a woman earlier, and now this man sticks his head in here and . . .

BOY (*Shrugs*)

I don't know these people. I thought we were talking about the baby.

GIRL

We were; indeed we were. Do we have in-laws we don't know about?

BOY

Not that I know of.

GIRL

Have we rented out rooms?

BOY

I don't believe so.

GIRL

Then why are they here?

(*Suddenly*)

Maybe they're Gypsies! Come to steal the baby!

BOY

Don't *you* be silly. Do they *look* like Gypsies?

GIRL

Well . . .

BOY

Swarthy; big mustaches, cigars, fedoras . . .

GIRL

Like Mexicans?

BOY

No; different. Mexicans wear little derbies.

GIRL

That's Peruvians, and that's women.

BOY (*Mildly annoyed*)

Whatever. Mexicans look . . . Mexican. Gypsies—from photographs I've seen . . . drawings—look like . . . well, like Gypsies.

GIRL

Oh.

(*Relieved*)

Then they're not Gypsies come to steal the baby.

BOY

What I said was, these people don't *look* like Gypsies—from what I know of how Gypsies look—which may not be much. That's what I said.

(*Pause*)

Why would anybody want to steal the baby?

GIRL

For money?

BOY

We don't have any.

GIRL

To sell it, or to eat it?

BOY (*Sighing*)

I said that's what Gypsies are *purported* to do, and I said I didn't think that . . .

GIRL (*Abrupt*)

All *right!*

(*Shy*)

To *hurt* us? To injure us beyond salvation?

BOY (*Pause; very sincere*)

Aren't we too young?

GIRL (*Not wholly convinced*)

I suppose.

(*Baby crying offstage. Alarmed*)

The baby's crying! Do you think someone is . . .

BOY (*Comforting*)

Doesn't that sound like hunger? Isn't that the hungry sound the baby makes?

GIRL (*Somewhat relieved*)

Yes; yes; I suppose so.

(*Moves to exit*)

I'll go feed the baby.

(*Exits*)

BOY

(*Half to himself; very preoccupied*)

Leave some for me.

(Pause. This next speech is to "theoretical people." The audience is not to be addressed directly, nor is anyone else.)

Beyond salvation? Injure us beyond salvation? Hurt us to the point that . . . ?

(To GIRL, *off)*

I'm standing guard.

(She doesn't hear, of course. More to himself now)

I'll guard you; I'll guard the baby.

(Gentle)

If there's anybody out there wants to do this to us—to hurt us so—ask *why*? Ask what we've *done*? I can take pain and loss and all the rest *later*— I *think* I can, when it comes as natural as . . . sleep? But . . . now? We're *happy*; we love each other; I'm hard all the time; we have a baby. We don't even under*stand* each other yet!

(Pause)

So . . . give it some thought. Give us some time.

(Pause)

OK?

GIRL *(Emerges; goes to* BOY)

Wasn't hungry; false alarm.

BOY

(Shrugs) No problem.

(Out again)

OK? Please?

*(*MAN *is propelled on stage, followed by* WOMAN; *clearly they are in the middle of a heated exchange.)*

WOMAN

I was young once, remember? I had a life before you?

MAN

Oh, God!

WOMAN

What you referred to—what you always refer to—as my privileged little life before I met you?

MAN

Oh, God!

(Indicates out)

Not in front of all these people!

(Indicates BOY *and* GIRL *who are peripheral)*

Not in front of the children!

(They stand, sit, move; musical chairs, etc.)

WOMAN

Well, I *did* have. You think no one but you wanted me? Hunh?! (*A pronouncement*) A painter hanged himself for the love of me.

MAN (*Flat contradiction*)

No.

WOMAN

Yes, he *did*. I was eighteen, and moving into ripeness. I was eighteen, as I said, and knowledgeable, and I was at a tea one afternoon—it was summer; it was a resort—and I had on silk and a great hat with ribbons, and I had been to Europe . . .

MAN (*Quietly dogmatic*)

You had *not*.

(*To* BOY *and* GIRL)

She had not!

WOMAN (*Overriding him*)

. . . and I had been to Europe, and I knew the women there went without bras if their breasts were exemplary and if they were young, and I had my lovely breasts.

(*Cups them for him*)

Lovely? Breasts?

(*Tiny pause*)

Nothing?

MAN

Get on with it.

WOMAN (*Smiles*)

And I had my lovely breasts free in the delicious silk, an unlined silk, smooth against my nipples; and I stalked about—I think I had a parasol as well, really doing it up. Very Gainsborough, or perhaps Watteau.

MAN

Jesus!

WOMAN

"Very Gainsborough, or perhaps Watteau," I heard a voice say, just behind me and to the right. I stopped. I mean, who else could the voice be referring to, right?

MAN (*Ironic*)

Right!

WOMAN

"Definitely Watteau," it went on, "definitely Watteau." And I turned my pretty head, and there he was . . . The Painter. Not a man who painted, not a painter, but . . . The Painter: hollow-cheeked, burning eyes, wispy whiskers, long, bony fingers, the voice cavernous, basso, the costume . . . well, do you know Whistler?

(*Afterthought*)

Of course you do.

MAN

Of course I do.

WOMAN

Of course you do.

MAN

What do you take me for?

WOMAN

"You should have a crook and sheep, or an arm basket filled with wild-flowers. I'm going to paint you," he said. "*Are* you!" I said . . .

MAN (*Out*)

I don't believe a word of this.

(*To* BOY *and* GIRL)

Not a word of this is true.

WOMAN

"Yes," he said, "twice." "To get it right?" I joked. "First time a practice swing?" "No," he said, his burning eyes even deeper and sadder, "first as you are, as you are right now, and then, later, naked, your lovely breasts, the dimple of your belly, your milk-pink hips, your burning bush . . . " "Really!" I said. "You go too far!" Phrases like that just . . . came to me then; I could do them with conviction. "Really, sir, you go too far."

MAN (*Back in*)

Milk-pink?

WOMAN (*A trifle embarrassed*)

Well . . . yes.

MAN

You must have read it somewhere.

(*To* BOY *and* GIRL)

She read it somewhere.

WOMAN (*High horse*)

It is what he said!

(*Back to recounting; out*)

I should probably interject here that all my lovers to that moment had been both young and handsome—sturdy, virile boys and young men my own age, well-muscled . . . handsome, as I said. I had not made love with the aged, with cripples, dwarves, or—and I blush at this, I think, in retrospect, at least, for its lack of humor, its lack of generosity—even with the simply plain.

MAN *(Eyes to heaven)*

Christ!

WOMAN *(Back in)*

Needless to say—needles, as I used to say when I was little—*almost* needles to say, nothing was further from my lovely mind than an affair with the gaunt and disheveled painter.

   (Thinks)

Well . . . perhaps death was further from my mind, but not much. I was seeing—as they say—"seeing" a young polo player . . .

MAN *(Out)*

Do you believe *any* of this?

   (To BOY *and* GIRL*)*

Do *you?*

   (Afterthought)

Well, *they* might.

WOMAN

Yes, of course they do . . . a young polo player, whose biceps alone were worth the trip. I was seeing him, and quite involved, almost . . . happy. What did I need with . . . well, with anything else? My days were filled with polo, my nights with rut. Oh, what a wangled teb we weave.

MAN

A what?

WOMAN

A teb; a wangled teb.

MAN

What is *that?*

WOMAN

You figure it out. Anyway, I sat for the painter. He was meticulous, and he worked so slowly. My polo player wondered where I was instead of watching him knock balls through the legs of horses. "I'm being painted as a shepherdess," I said. "You're kidding!" he replied, white teeth flashing, et cetera. "Be careful he doesn't want to paint you in the nude," he warned. "Oh, he does," I smiled, "he does." And Beauty's face darkened—even beneath the tan—and my young heart broke, for I saw that he loved me, and I knew in that moment . . . that I did not love him.

MAN

Oh, you poor dear!

WOMAN

That I *desired* him, yes; I mean, he *was* a splendid lover—slow, patient, thoughtful, but always in command, and driving. Indeed, he was splendid.

MAN *(Out)*

Look at her! You believe this?

WOMAN

Of course they do. *But* . . . I became lovers with the painter. He wasn't much good—in bed, I mean. "I know I'm unworthy of you," he said, "That my touch is unworthy of you, that when I crawl on you like a spider in the night, my bony fingers trembling on your perfect breasts . . . "

MAN *(To* WOMAN*)*

Nobody talks like that!

WOMAN

He did . . . "and when you let me enter in, it is in an act of mercy . . . "

MAN *(Out)*

Nobody! Nobody has *ever* talked like that!

(To BOY *and* GIRL*)*

Nobody. EVER. Don't just stand there with your mouths open! Learn something!

WOMAN

"I know all this and I am strengthened by my weakness." And so on and so forth. And, well, he *was* strengthened; his talent surged; his drawings of me—*and* the paintings—made him, well . . . quite famous. I hang in museums. You didn't know that, *did* you?

MAN *(In)*

You do not.

(Out)

She does not.

(To BOY *and* GIRL*)*

She does not.

WOMAN

I do not? But I began to see something: that *he* was getting far more out of this than *I* was: He had his lovely decoration, plus a model for free, plus a source of income, and *I* was saddled with this . . . skimpy little man with only bones and drive and the oddest breath and . . . and I felt *tricked*. I be*longed* with the polo players and such, the healthy animals.

MAN *(Back in. Sarcastic)*

Of course you did!

WOMAN

I was young and fabulous.

MAN *(Ibid.)*

Yes! Of course you were!

WOMAN

And I suddenly knew that I hadn't gained the days, but I'd merely lost the nights. Do you understand?

(Waits; MAN *merely shakes his head.)*

Where was I?

MAN

Not gained the days but merely lost the nights, or some such rubbish.

WOMAN

. . . not gained the days but merely lost the nights. And so I broke it off. "You're using me," I shrieked at him, pacing his studio, knocking things over. "You don't love *me*; you love the *fact* of me."

(Shakes her head)

Who did I think I was? Who did we *all* think we were? "I can't live without you," he called to me from his window as I flounced from the building. "I'll kill myself!" "Hanh!" I said, and turned on my heel and . . . vanished into the mist, or whatever. And of course he *did*: kill himself, that is. He hanged himself in his atelier, from a rafter.

(Pause)

And how does all *that* strike you? How and where does all *that* grab you?

MAN

(Shakes his head; smiles, applauds)

Very good! Really, very good!

(Out)

Wasn't that good? Didn't she do that well? Come on, give her a hand!

(Encourages, leads audience applause. She curtsies. If there is none, he dismisses audience with a wave of his hand.)

Good. Really very good.

(To BOY *and* GIRL*)*

Didn't you think so?

(Before they can reply: a sudden shift to very businesslike; in)

OK. Let's get on with it.

(To BOY *and* GIRL*; calling)*

Will you two come over here, please?

BOY *(Flat)*

What?

GIRL *(Flat)*

What? What is it?

MAN

Did you like our little performance? Our *intermezzo a due?*

(Before they can answer)
Ah! But where's baby-poo?

GIRL *(Flat)*
Asleep; all fed.

BOY *(Licks lips)*
I got dessert.

WOMAN *(False hearty)*
Oh, you have a baby!

BOY
Yes.

WOMAN
What kind?

BOY *(Eyeing her)*
A small one.

WOMAN
A*ha.*
(Exits left; false stealth)

BOY *(To* MAN*)*
What do you want?

MAN *(Cheerless smile)*
What do we *want.* Well, I would imagine we want what almost everybody wants—eternal life, in great health, no older than we are when we want it; easy money, with enough self-deception to make us feel we've earned it, are worthy people; a government that lets us do whatever we want, serves our private interests and lets us feel we're doing all we can for . . . how do they call it— the less fortunate?; a bigger dick, a more muscular vagina; a baby, perhaps?

BOY
No, no.
(Articulated)
What do you *want?*

MAN
Hm?

BOY
Here; what do you want *here?*

MAN *(Helpless gesture; false)*
I'm not sure that I . . .

BOY
You're *here.*

MAN (*Grudging*)

Yes.

BOY

That . . . woman is here—is with you.

MAN

Everything being *relative* . . .

BOY

Yes.

GIRL (*Suspicious*)

Where *is* she? Where's she *gone!?*
(WOMAN *re-enters, from stage right, very casually, an "OK" finger gesture to* MAN, *a broad wink to him.*)
Oh, *there* she is.

MAN (*To* BOY)

We are both here; yes.

BOY (*Level*)

Why?

MAN

Hm?

BOY (*Still level, if harder*)

Why are you here? What do you want?

MAN (*Cheerless smile*)

What do we *want*. Well, it's really very simple. We've come to take the baby.
(*Silence*)

BOY

What do you mean!?

MAN (*Flat*)

We've come to take the baby.
(*Shorter silence*)

GIRL (*A look of panic*)

What do you mean "you've come to take . . ." Oh, my *God!*
(*Suddenly exits, left*)

BOY (*Eyes on* MAN; *steely*)

I don't understand you.

WOMAN

He doesn't understand you; be clearer.

MAN (*To* WOMAN)

I thought I was being clear.

(*To* BOY)

What is it you don't understand? The noun "baby"? The verb "take"?

WOMAN

You're not being nice.

MAN

You told me to be clear—clearer.

WOMAN

They're not mutually exclusive.

MAN (*Heavy sigh*)

All right.

(*To* BOY)

The baby. The baby?

BOY (*Very innocent*)

Yes?

MAN (*Demonstrates*)

We've come to take it.

BOY

I don't . . .

MAN (*Very explicit*)

A-way; a-way.

GIRL

(*Re-enters from left; hysterical*)

WHERE'S THE BABY?! WHAT HAVE YOU DONE WITH THE BABY?!

(*Silence*)

MAN

What baby?

(*Silence*)

WOMAN

Yes; *what* baby?

(*Tableau*)

CURTAIN

ACT TWO

(No one on stage; otherwise everything as it was at the end of Act One)

MAN

(Enters, waves a little to audience. To someone)
Is this where I was at the end of one—Act One? Right about here?

(Takes exact position as of the end of Act One. Generally; out)
Yes? Good.

(To stragglers)
Hurry back in, now; you don't want to miss the exposition. Well, maybe you do.

(Irritated complaint)
"Honestly! You'd think they'd have it in the *first* act!"

(Thinks about it)
No; you couldn't possibly. Well, let me tell you: intermissions are never long enough, are they. Did you enjoy yourselves while you were out for your cigarettes, or whatever?

(Wrinkles his nose, etc.)
Don't smoke; bad for you. Half a million die of it every year. In this country alone, subsidized murder. Not *you*, of course—someone you know. So; you had your cigarette, or your drink—not *quite* so bad, one or two a day good for the old heart, they say. *Or* your coffee.

(Harpy; shrill)
KEEP AWAKE! KEEP AWAKE! Or merely . . . stretching your legs, having a pee.

(Annoyed woman imitation)
"You'd think they'd build the ladies' restrooms bigger; after all these years you'd think they'd have noticed the lines! *Honestly!*" Or maybe just a phone call? Or a talk with friends—*or* strangers. Whatever.

(Shift of tone)
I must tell you something here: I have a troubling sense of what should be—rather than what *is*. It chokes me up at simpleminded movies—where good things happen to good people? My throat clots, and I think I'm going to

cry. Because I know it can never happen in what they call "real life"? Good things to good people and happy endings? That it's all . . . fantasy? Is that what allows me to believe? To weep in relief? If I saw it *really* happening—all good things to all good people?—would I turn away in horror? Yes, probably: because it could all . . . stop, could go away, be a single instant of glory, desperately cruel. We can't take glory because it shows us the abyss. That is why we cry at movies—because it's *safe* to; it's all so . . . beautifully false. But I have, as I say, this sense of what should be rather than what is. And I file it away; file it away under "unwanted on the voyage, dangerous cargo," for I know it does not apply? Because it is an impediment to . . . what do they say? . . . to "getting through it all"?

(*Smiles grimly; demonstrates shuddering*)

It's troubling, though, I *tell* you. As . . .

(*Gestures*)

. . . as in, well . . . *here*; now; all this. Troubling, but I'll get through it.

(*Snaps fingers*)

OK!! So, where did we leave off? "We've come to take the baby." "I don't understand." "What baby?" et cetera. That was it . . . casual—more or less—straightforward, but casual. "We've come to take the baby." Remember it? Good. We'll see if they let us take the baby from them.

(*In*)

Where were we all?

(*Off*)

Will you come back in now?

(BOY *and* GIRL *re-enter from left,* WOMAN *from right; they take positions identical to their positions on* MAN's *"OK. Let's get on with it"*)

Fine.

(*To* BOY *and* GIRL)

Now you two say "What?" "What is it?" You first, then her, flat, flat, both of you. Say it! "What?" "What is it?"

(*Pause*)

Say it, for God's sake!

BOY (*Flat*)

What?

GIRL (*Flat*)

What? What is it?

MAN (*Approving*)

That's right; that's it.

(*False hearty*)

Good to see you! But where's "the little one"?

GIRL *(Flat)*

Asleep; all fed.

BOY *(Licks lips)*

I got dessert.

WOMAN *(Quiet aside to* MAN*)*

Oh, I get it.
  (To GIRL*; false hearty)*
Oh, you have a baby!

GIRL

Yes.

WOMAN

What kind?

GIRL *(Eyeing her)*

A small one.

WOMAN

Aha.
  (Quick aside to MAN*)*
Is this where I . . .
  (Answering her own question)
. . . yes; yes, it is.
  (To GIRL*)*
A*ha*!
  (Exits left; false stealth)

BOY *(To* MAN*)*

What do you want?

MAN *(Sotto voce aside to audience)*

I love this speech.
  (To BOY*; cheerless smile)*
What do we *want*. Well, I would imagine we want what almost everybody
wants—eternal life, in great health, no older than we are when we want it;
easy money, with enough self-deception to make us feel we've earned it,
are worthy people; a government that lets us do whatever we want, serves
our private interests and lets us feel we're doing all we can for . . . how do
they call it—the less fortunate?; a bigger dick, a more muscular vagina; a
baby, perhaps?

BOY

No, no.
  (Articulated)
What do you *want*?

MAN

Hm?

BOY

Here; what do you want *here*?

MAN (*Helpless gesture; false*)

I'm not sure that I . . .

BOY

You're *here*.

MAN (*Grudging*)

Yes.

BOY

That . . . woman is here—is with you.

MAN

Everything being *rel*ative . . .

BOY

Yes.

GIRL (*Suspicious*)

Where *is* she? Where's she *gone*!?

(WOMAN *re-enters, from stage right, very casually, an OK finger gesture to* MAN, *with a broad wink*)

Oh, *there* she is.

MAN (*To* BOY)

We are both here; yes.

BOY (*Level*)

Why?

MAN

Hm?

BOY (*Still level, if harder*)

Why are you here? What do you want?

MAN (*Cheerless smile*)

What do we *want*. Well, it's really very simple. We've come to take the baby.

(*Silence*)

BOY

What do you mean?

MAN (*Flat*)

We've come to take the baby.

(*Shorter silence*)

GIRL *(A look of panic)*
What do you mean "you've come to take . . ." Oh, my God!!
(Suddenly exits, left)

BOY *(Eyes on* MAN: *steely)*
I don't understand you.
(Brief awareness of GIRL's *action)*

WOMAN
He doesn't understand you; be clearer.

MAN *(To* WOMAN)
I thought I was being clear.
(To BOY)
What is it you don't understand? The noun "baby"? The verb "take"?

WOMAN
You're not being nice.

MAN
You told me to be clear—clearer.

WOMAN
They're not mutually exclusive.

MAN *(Heavy sigh)*
All right.
(To BOY)
The baby. The baby?

BOY *(Very innocent)*
Yes?

MAN *(Demonstrates)*
We've come to take it.

BOY
I don't . . .

MAN *(Very explicit; impatient)*
A-way; a-way.

GIRL
(Re-enters from left; hysterical)
WHERE'S THE BABY??!! WHAT HAVE YOU DONE WITH THE
BABY??!!
(Silence)

MAN
What baby?
(Silence)

WOMAN

Yes; *what* baby?

MAN (*Out, then in*)

There we are! *Here* we go!

GIRL

WHAT HAVE YOU DONE WITH MY BABY??!!

BOY

(*Gathering energy; clearly about to lunge*)

Look, you motherfucker, what have you done to . . .

MAN (*A stopping hand up; very loud*)

STOP!!

(BOY *freezes*)

GIRL (*Sobbing*)

What have you done with my baby?

MAN (*Loud*)

BOTH OF YOU!! NOW JUST STOP!!

(GIRL *whimpers, sobs, but stays still;* BOY *puts his arm around her, never taking his eyes off* MAN)

WOMAN (*Distaste*)

Such a performance! You'd think somebody was hurting somebody—or something!

MAN

(*Keeping his eyes on* BOY; *casual tone*)

Wouldn't you?

WOMAN

You'd think something was amiss, as they say.

MAN (*Ibid*)

Wouldn't you?

GIRL (*Weepy*)

I want my baby.

MAN

Everyone wants his baby.

WOMAN

Her baby.

MAN (*Shrugs*)

Whatever.

(*To* WOMAN; *points at* GIRL: *innocence*)

Her baby? Everyone wants her baby?

WOMAN *(Chuckles)*

No, no; generics again.

BOY

(About to get up, move toward MAN*)*
OK. I've had enough of this now! What the fuck have you done with . . .

MAN *(Hand up)*

Hold!

BOY *(Beginning to move)*
I will not "hold," whatever that means.

WOMAN *(Helpful)*

It's Elizabethan.

BOY *(Confused)*

It's . . . it's *what*?!

MAN

ELIZABETHAN!! Now go sit down. If you care about this baby you behave yourself, yourselves.
(Demonstrates)
If there are two hands—see? two hands?—if there are two hands, we have the upper one. If you have ever had a baby—

BOY

If?

MAN

. . . if that is mother's milk you've been feeding on, and if you wish to see your real or imagined baby again—ever!—

BOY

Real? Or . . .

MAN

. . . if you are wiser than your years, be good.
*(*BOY *does so)*

WOMAN *(To* MAN*)*

You have a way with children.

MAN

As it was with my own.

WOMAN

Oh? You have children?

MAN

Certainly; I have six.

WOMAN

Really!

MAN

Yes: two black, two white, one green, and the other . . . well, I'm not certain, or I've lost track, or whatever.

BOY (*Quietly*)

Bullshit.

WOMAN (*Ignoring* BOY)

Two black?

MAN

Yes.

WOMAN

Half black, half white, what in the bad old days they used to call mulatto?

MAN

No; all black.

WOMAN

But . . .

MAN

This was when I was black.

WOMAN

A*ha*. Was this before you were white? Before . . .

MAN

No; it shifted: two white, one black, one green, et cetera.

WOMAN

I see; I see.

GIRL (*To* MAN)

You have no children.

MAN

Well, that may be, or may have been, or . . . whatever.

WOMAN (*To* GIRL)

Why do you say that?

GIRL (*To* WOMAN)

Nor do you.

WOMAN

Oh?

GIRL

No one who has children . . .

MAN

Had!

GIRL *(Onward)*

. . . would treat us like this—anyone like this.

BOY

She's right, you know.
> *(Pause)*

Had?

MAN *(Playful)*

Well, *having* had doesn't mean one *has*.
> *(Pause)*

Does it?

WOMAN

One green?

MAN

Yes.
> *(Out)*

Does this need explaining?

WOMAN

When you were green?

MAN *(Back in; thinks a moment)*

Well, when *some*one was.

WOMAN

Half green then.

GIRL *(Soft, gentle pleading)*

Please?
> *(BOY quietly shushes her)*

MAN *(Considers it)*

Mmmmm . . . light green.
> *(To BOY and GIRL)*

So, I want you to understand I know about children, about who has them
. . . and who does *not*; how large they may be, how many legs they have—
if they have the number they are supposed to, where they come out of—
the length of the small intestine in a two-week-old . . .

WOMAN

How long?

MAN

Eleven and three-quarter inches. The color of loss, the names most com-
monly not used . . . all the things essential. You don't fool with *me*. Fool

yourselves, fool each *other*, but don't try it with *me*. *I've* touched the golden dick. Have *you*?
(*To* BOY, *specifically*)
Have you? *Have* you? You there?

BOY (*Preoccupied*)

Have I what?

MAN

Touched the golden dick.

BOY

I don't know what you're talking about, mister.
(*Suddenly loud*)
Where's our baby!!??

MAN and WOMAN (*Softly singing*)
Yes, Sir, where's our baby?
No, Sir, we don't mean maybe.
Yes, Sir, where's our baby now?

MAN (*Speaking again*)
Too bad about the dick—the golden dick.
(*As* BOY *prepares to lunge*)
I'd be careful if I were you!
(BOY *lunges;* MAN *flips him on his back on the floor with a judo move; pins* BOY's *neck under his foot*)
I said I'd be careful if I were you!
(*To* GIRL)
Are you going to try something, too?
(GIRL *sobs, shakes her head*)
Good; the lady here is adept at things as well.

WOMAN

I am.

MAN

Everyone's adept at something.
(*To pinned* BOY)
Will you be good?

BOY

Yes.

MAN

Good.
(BOY *gets up, not easily*)

Go to your chair.

    (BOY *does;* GIRL *moves to comfort him*)

Good. Touching.

    (*To* WOMAN)

Goodness, I'm saying "good" a lot, *aren't* I?

WOMAN (Shrugs)

It *sounds* right.

MAN

Good!

    (*To* BOY *and* GIRL)

So! No more shenanigans.

    (*Out*)

Is that Irish? Shenanigans?

    (*If anyone answers, handle it; in any event, go on with this*)

I looked it up once in the dictionary and it didn't say; it said "informal," which I don't believe is a genesis. Though maybe it is . . . the island of informality? The city of shenanigan? I meant to look it up somewhere else, but I . . . lost interest, I guess.

    (*Back in*)

In any event,

    (*To* BOY *and* GIRL)

no more

    (*very pronounced*)

she-nan-i-gans. No?

BOY (Nursing his neck)

No.

MAN

No what?

BOY

No more.

MAN

No more *what*!?

BOY

No more shenanigans.

MAN

Always be precise: saves time, saves paper. Did I hurt you?

BOY

No.

MAN

No wound?

BOY

No.

MAN (*To* BOY *and* GIRL)

If you have no wounds, how can you know if you're alive? If you have no scar, how do you know who you are? Have been?

BOY (*Impatient*)

Come on, mister!

WOMAN (*To* BOY)

Listen to him.

MAN (*To* BOY)

Was your fracture compound? Did it stick out through the skin—like snapped wood?

GIRL (*To* BOY; *shy*)

Did it?

BOY

No!

MAN

If it didn't, who *are* you? Who have you ever *been*?

(*To* GIRL)

Was it a caesarean for the baby? A theoretical caesarean for the theoretical baby?

BOY

Theor . . .

GIRL

No! No wound!

MAN (*To them both*)

Blood? Piercings? Gougings? Wounds, children; wounds. Without wounds what *are* you? You're too young for the batterings time brings us . . .

WOMAN (*Dramatic*)

Oh, God! The batterings!

MAN (*To* WOMAN)

. . . time brings us.

WOMAN

Sorry! . . . time brings us.

(*An aside*)

Oh, God?

MAN

One is enough.

(*To* BOY)

Give me your arm; let me see your wound.

BOY (*Self-protective*)

Hah! You think I'll fall for that!?

MAN

Oh, I wouldn't break your arm; *I* don't want you on your knees—not literally. Ever? No, I don't think so. Break your arm? Nahhhh! Your heart, perhaps. Your heart, yes. Certainly your heart.

WOMAN (*Pleased*)

Oh, the heart!

MAN

Give me your heart, then; I'll break *that*. If you don't have the wound of a
broken heart, how can you know you're alive? If you have no broken heart,
how do you know who you are? Have been? Can ever be?

GIRL

(*To* MAN *and* WOMAN; *crying a little*)

Leave us alone? Please, let me have my baby?

MAN (*Sighs*)

We're going to have to talk about this.

(*Beginning of lecture?*)

What is a baby?

(*Out*)

What is a baby?

(*In and out, now*)

We must, first of all, define a baby. A baby . . . *what*!? A baby mouse? A
baby kangaroo? A baby wolverine? A baby . . . *baby*. A human baby, an
almost, not quite yet human baby—no larger than, well, somewhat larger
than that "great divide."

(*To* BOY)

Hey? Between the something slopes, or something?

BOY (*Curt*)

What?

MAN

Nothing.

(*In and out again*)

You can't go home again? Surely not! They say we want to go back in—
back home—some of us, at any rate. Try it! A minute after out-you-slide—
or whatever—it's all closing up, closing down, 'til the next time. Push you
back in—head first, whatever? Wouldn't work! The water's gone now;
you've been shocked into breathing . . . what?, nothing *you* can see, *could*
see if you had *eyes*—eyes that *opened*.

(*Bravura quote*)

"Oh, blessed eyes that never ope!"
      (*Natural again*)
"Ope"; I've always liked "ope."

                    WOMAN (*Matter-of-fact*)
You're running on.

                              MAN
Yes? I am?

                              WOMAN
"What is a baby?" Then relate *that* to where we are—to this.

                              MAN
Aha!

                         GIRL (*Quiet*)
Please? My baby?

                              MAN
Now, look; if there *is* a baby, and if it is yours, and you can prove it's yours,
we'll handle it.

                      BOY (*Ominously quiet*)
If? Who *are* you? Who are you, really?

                              GIRL
Yes; who *are* you?

                       MAN (*To* BOY)
I am your destination. Remember? Is that familiar?
      (*To* WOMAN)
Now you.

                              WOMAN
      (*Tiny orienting pause; to* GIRL)
Yes. Yes, I go in the back with you, and I am your destination.

                       MAN (*To* BOY)
We do things together, you and I, that no one else has done.

                     WOMAN (*To* GIRL)
You love me; we are each other's . . . whatever.

                   GIRL (*Intense; to* BOY)
None of this is true!

                       MAN (*To* BOY)
The first time you touched me . . .
      (*Indicates*)
there, I almost fainted. It was so . . . unexpected, I suppose.

BOY (*Cold*)

You fuck!

MAN (*Considers*)

Well . . . yes.

WOMAN (*To* GIRL; *dreamy*)

We lay there, you and I, true spoons, the two of us, mouths on each other . . .

GIRL (*Voice shaking*)

No! No!

MAN (*To* BOY)

We are each other's destination. No? Yes?

WOMAN (*To* GIRL)

No? We are not?

MAN (*To both* BOY *and* GIRL)

Or are we Gypsies? Hm?

GIRL (*To* BOY; hysterical)

They're Gypsies!!

BOY

(*Eyes on* MAN; *steely, to comfort*)

No; no, they're not.

MAN (*Pretending bewilderment*)

We're *not!?*

BOY

No!

MAN (*Of* WOMAN)

You don't recognize her fedora and her huge mustache?

WOMAN (*To* GIRL)

You came to me; you brought your life savings in a paper bag.

GIRL

No! I don't *have* any life savings!

BOY (*Pleading; explaining*)

We're very young.

MAN

And therefore you don't have Gypsies?

(*To* GIRL)

She had a Gypsy.

WOMAN

(*To* GIRL)

Yes, you *went* to one.

(Uncertain)
Was it *me*? Was it to me?

BOY

But it wasn't for *that*.

MAN

For *what*?

GIRL

For . . . life savings, and all.

MAN

Well, I should hope not. How dumb can you be?!

WOMAN (*To* MAN, *about* GIRL)
That's for *later*, when you *get* dumb, life-savings-time dumb.

MAN (*Sighs*)

Time; time, the great leveler.
(To BOY; *sweet)*
Tell me *about* you; tell us your history.
(Whispered aside; out)
Exposition.

BOY (*Confused*)

Who? Me?

MAN (*Back in*)

Whatever. You can tell us your history, or she can tell us your history, and
you can tell us hers, and we won't know *what* to disbelieve.

BOY (*A recitation; quiet rage*)

I'm a twenty-three-year-old white, Anglo-Saxon American man . . .

MAN

That's a redundancy. All Anglo-Saxons are white.

BOY

Yes? A twenty-three-year-old Anglo-Saxon American man.

MAN

Boy.

BOY

Boy—yes?—boy, and I'm married to *her*, the light of my life.

WOMAN

Your destination.

BOY (*Confused*)

What?

WOMAN (*Cheerful*)
Your destination! Don't you remember?

MAN (*To* BOY)
I thought it was you and me: that time you touched me . . .
  (*Gestures*)
here, and put your lips to my . . .

BOY (*Loud enough to cover*)
THE LIGHT OF MY LIFE!

MAN and WOMAN (*As if on cue*)
  Roll me over, in the clover,
  Roll me over, lay me down, and do it again.

MAN (*To* BOY *and* GIRL)
Familiar? No?

BOY (*Shaking his head*)
What more do you want? When will you . . .

MAN (*Expansive*)
Ohhhhh, *much* more.

GIRL (*Sudden*)
I want my baby!

WOMAN (*Groucho*)
Everybody wants his baby—her baby—whatever.

MAN (*To* BOY)
Tell us more; tell us what we want to know, and then tell us what we *don't*.
I'd like to know, for example, why you took up with this young woman,
when you obviously despise her.

BOY (*Rage; frustration*)
I *love* her; I love her with all my *heart*!

WOMAN (*To* MAN; *false support of* BOY)
He *loves* her; she loves *him*.

MAN (*To* WOMAN)
Well, *that* may be—that she loves *him*.
  (*To* BOY)
You love *her*?

BOY
YES!!

MAN
Tisk, tisk, tisk! Then, what shall I think of the letter you sent me when we
were apart . . .

BOY

We were never together!

MAN

. . . when we were apart, saying it was all for show, that her family has money, you can't stand the smell of her, the things she makes you do, and . . .

BOY *(Making to lunge)*

You motherfucking . . . !!

MAN *(Warning hand up instantly)*

Hanh!! The baby? Remember the baby?

BOY *(Subsiding)*

You . . .

MAN

Yes: *me*. I am the one, am I not? Am I not the gypsy you love, on your knees before me? Do you not aspire to my huge mustache, to my fedora?

BOY *(Heavy sigh)*

I don't know you, mister.

MAN *(Out)*

They all say that.

WOMAN *(Attorney; to* GIRL*)*

Did you not fake pregnancy to . . . to get him for yourself?

GIRL

No! No! I didn't! We married and *then* I got pregnant!

WOMAN *(Out)*

They all say that.

BOY *(Quietly)*

She was a virgin.

MAN *(Tiny pause; to* BOY*)*

When?

BOY

When I married her; when I met her.

MAN

Which came first?

BOY *(Bewildered)*

What?!

WOMAN *(Helping)*

He means: Did you marry her and *then* meet her, or . . .

BOY

NO!

MAN

No, you did not marry her before you met her, or you did not meet her before you married her?

BOY *(Hands to ears)*

Stop it!

GIRL *(To* BOY*; very shy)*

Did you write him a letter?

BOY *(Exploding)*

I don't *know* the man!!

MAN *(To* GIRL*; soothing)*

A fan letter; fans often write to those they've never met. Hope; hope!

WOMAN *(Echo)*

Hope.

GIRL *(To* BOY*; determined)*

Did you?!

BOY *(To* GIRL*; pleading)*

Of *course* not! I *love* you.

MAN *(To* BOY*; explaining)*

I was one of the Gypsy boys who stopped you on your way back from the gym-gym.

WOMAN *(Nods happily)*

And I was another.

MAN

I was the one who stopped in front of you, the one who spoke to you . . .

WOMAN *(As if quoting)*

You're the one who put the guard dogs on us, *aren't* you.

BOY *(Memory; rote)*

Guards, not guard dogs.

GIRL *(Shakes her head; memory)*

Not a wise answer.

WOMAN

You guys could have paid, you said.

GIRL

Nor that.

BOY *(Dreamy)*

I did?

MAN

Yes, you did, and no hard feelings, you said.

BOY *(Ibid.)*

I did?

WOMAN

Yes; yes, you did.

BOY *(Recalling, still dreamy)*
And I put my arm out . . .

WOMAN

. . . and you put your arm out . . .

MAN

. . . and you put your arm out . . . and CRACK!!!

WOMAN

Crack!

GIRL

Crack!

BOY

It hurt so; it hurt so very much.
　　(GIRL *takes his shoulder to comfort him; he swivels to his knees*
　　beside her chair.)

MAN

And I came up to you . . .

WOMAN

. . . and I came up to you, and I undid my fly and
　　(A trifle uncertain)
what was I going to do?

BOY

I don't know. You're going to piss on me?

MAN

Or maybe it was me, and you know what *I* wanted, what *you* wanted.

WOMAN *(Echo)*

What *you* wanted.

BOY

Or maybe . . . or maybe . . .

GIRL *(Offers her breast to* BOY*)*
Here; here.

BOY

Maybe he *wasn't* going to piss on me. Maybe he was going to . . .

GIRL

Here!!

(BOY *takes her breast in his mouth; brief tableau*)

WOMAN (*Unemphasized fact*)

That is so . . . touching.

MAN

Yes; yes, it is.

MAN and WOMAN

Roll me over, in the clover,
Roll me over, lay me down, and do it again.

WOMAN

That is so . . . touching.

MAN

Yes; yes, it is.

(*Brief pause; slaps hands together*)

OK! Back to work!

(BOY *detaches himself;* GIRL *replaces breast*)

WOMAN (*To* BOY)

Why did you never do that to me? I know you wanted to.

BOY

Pardon?

(*Wiping lips*)

WOMAN

I was eighteen, wasn't I, and moving into ripeness? And I had been to Europe and I knew the women there went without bras if their breasts were exemplary and if they were young, and I had my lovely breasts?

(*Cups them for him*)

Lovely? Breasts?

(*Tiny pause*)

Nothing?

BOY

(*A quick look to see how* GIRL *is reacting*)

Lady, I . . .

WOMAN

Didn't you want to suck them? Everyone else did . . . wanted to.

MAN

Of course he did.

WOMAN *(To* BOY)

Of course you did; of course you wanted to. You said you would paint me;
you said you were a painter.

BOY

Lady . . .

WOMAN

You said you would paint me . . . naked, my lovely breasts, the dimple of
my belly, my milk-pink hips, my burning bush?

(GIRL *begins to weep)*

MAN *(Scoffing)*

Milk-pink?

WOMAN *(A trifle defensive)*

Well . . . yes.

(To BOY)

You were only one of my lovers, of course, one of the sturdy, virile boys,
the young and handsome, well-muscled . . .

GIRL *(To* BOY; *rage and tears)*

You know her!!

BOY

(Trying to comfort her; dogmatic)
No! No, I don't know her!

MAN *(To no one)*

Oh what a wangled teb we weave.

WOMAN

A what?

MAN

A teb; a wangled teb.

WOMAN

What is *that?*

MAN

You remember. He was only one of your lovers, no?

WOMAN

Hm? Oh! Oh; right.

(To BOY)

You were a *splendid* lover, though . . . slow, patient, thoughtful, but always
in command, and driving . . .

GIRL *(To* BOY; *still weeping)*

You *know* her!

BOY

(Pounding his fists on his knees)
I do *not*! I do *not* know her!

MAN

(To WOMAN, *but so* GIRL *will hear)*
When *was* all this? When were you two lovers?

WOMAN *(With a toss of her hand)*
Oh . . . last year, last month, last week, on his way to seeing her at the hospital, on his way from seeing her at the hospital—her and the baby. Earlier today.

MAN

The so-called baby.

WOMAN *(Smiles)*
The so-called baby.

BOY *(Quiet intensity; almost crying)*
I don't know you! I've never been with anyone but her.

MAN *(To* WOMAN*)*
Tell me about his penis; compare notes, so to speak. Show her you know the man through his manhood.

BOY *(Flustered rage)*
She's never seen my penis!

WOMAN *(About to begin)*
Well, all right now, let me see: I've seen penie in my life, and on a scale of one to ten—ten being *very* un*likely*—I would say that he was a . . . oh, a . . .

GIRL *(Exuberant in her invention)*
He doesn't have one! She couldn't have seen it because he doesn't have one! So there!!

BOY *(GIRL nudges him)*
Right! She's right! So there!

GIRL

So there!!
(Giggles)

MAN *(Out)*
They are so inventive, these two.
(Back in; to BOY *and* GIRL*)*
In the sense that the Queen of Spain does not have legs?

BOY *(Cold)*
What?

MAN *(Out; pleasant)*

It is said that once, centuries ago, an envoy from the East came to the Spanish court—with gifts, of course, gifts for the royal family, including fine-spun silk, a novelty back then. "For her Majesty," the envoy said, in his—well, his silkiest tone.

(WOMAN *chuckles appreciatively)*

Thank you. "For her Majesty, silk for her Majesty's legs." The major domo—or whatever he was—Their Majesty's major-domo, sniffed, the story goes, raised his eyebrows at the effrontery, the familiarity, and said, in his haughtiest tone, "The Queen of Spain does not have . . . legs."

(Back in; to BOY *and* GIRL*)*

Is that the sense you mean, that your young man does not have a penis in the sense that the Queen of Spain does not have legs? Or are we dealing here with a bewildering and somber deformity, one which puts into even greater question the matter of a baby?

WOMAN *(Rather puzzled)*

That's something you'd think I would have noticed—or not noticed, rather.

BOY *(Pause)*

Go fuck yourselves.

MAN

Right on!

(He and WOMAN *slap each other's right palms.* GIRL *tries to sneak off, with an "it's OK" gesture to* BOY. MAN *notices; a warning)*

I wouldn't do that!!!

(GIRL *hesitates)*

Leave the so-called baby be! *If* you have a baby—

BOY

I told you, we have a baby.

GIRL

Yes, we have a baby.

MAN

. . . if there *is* a baby, who is to say it has ever been yours? Who is to say you have a right to it? Or that you didn't steal it? Gypsies *do* steal things.

WOMAN

Yes; yes, they do.

MAN *(To* GIRL; *very harsh)*

So . . . SIDDDOWN!!

GIRL *(Sitting; weeping quietly)*

We are not Gypsies.

BOY *("Will this help?")*

No; no, we're not.

WOMAN

Well . . . *some*one is.

MAN *(Seemingly puzzled)*

Yes; yes, that's right . . . *some*one is, *must* be.

(To GIRL; *steely)*

If you can prove it is yours—belongs to you . . . you did not steal it, as Gypsies do . . . belongs to *you* . . .

WOMAN *(Helping)*

. . . and belongs *with* you . . .

MAN *(To* WOMAN*)*

Yes; right; thank you.

WOMAN

Welcome.

GIRL

I *told* you . . .

BOY

She *told* you . . .

MAN *(To* GIRL *again)*

. . . belongs to you, *and* belongs *with* you, then your interest in seeing it *ever* transcends your need to see it now.

(Pause)

No?

GIRL *(Still quietly weeping)*

Yes; yes, it does.

MAN

Good girl; you'll go far—to paraphrase.

BOY

I'll ask you one more time, mister, and only once more, who do you . . .

MAN *(To* BOY *and* GIRL*)*

No; the question is not who I think I am, but who I cannot be—the knowledge we all have of who we all cannot be, singularly, of course. I've lived long enough to understand that *that* is the most important question. Keep it in mind as you go on through it—both of you: what we cannot do; who we cannot be.

*(*WOMAN *begins signing—clearly absurd signing-like gestures)*

MAN

What are you doing?

WOMAN

Signing.

MAN

You know *how*? You know how to *sign*?

WOMAN (*Signing*)

It would seem so.

MAN

When did you learn? And *why*? *Why* did you learn?

WOMAN (*Shrugs; signs*)

It came upon me.

MAN

When?

WOMAN

Just now; I just realized I could do it.

MAN

Sign away.

WOMAN (*Signing; smiling*)

Thank you.

MAN (*Out now*)

Ignore her; I mean pay attention if you want to, but concentrate on *me*. I am talking; she is listening. Well, she is talking, too, in a way, but following *me*. She listens and then talks, almost simultaneously, but not quite. I . . . *talk*. I even listen as I talk—to myself, not to her. I can't sign.

(WOMAN *stops signing*)

You've stopped.

WOMAN

It comes and goes. I've suddenly forgotten. You go on; I'll catch up.

MAN (*Scoffs*)

With *me*? Never!

(*Out again*)

So. Who I cannot be.

(*To* BOY *and* GIRL)

Learn from this, children.

(*Out again*)

I cannot be young again; I cannot be a woman—therefore I cannot have babies, blah, blah, blah, if indeed I *would* have them, or *could*.

(*To* GIRL)

Eh, toots?

GIRL

Leave me alone!

BOY (Gentle pleading)

Leave her alone.

MAN (To GIRL)

But you *asked* . . . or *he* did: who I thought I was, et cetera.

(In and out now)

I would like, above all else, to be . . . historical and free-floating; I regret the people I have not met. I regret Jesus most of all. God! The questions! That's in retrospect, of course . . . mostly. Still: to *really* . . . *hear* him.

(To BOY and GIRL, who just look back)

How many sentences do the scholars think are his in the testaments? Three? A half-dozen?

(Dismissive gesture; back out)

No education. To have *been* there; to have heard him speak.

(To WOMAN)

This is important.

WOMAN

I know, I know; I'll try.

(Begins signing again, badly, then better).

MAN (In and out again; ecstatic)

The Sermon on the Mount! Oh, my God! One could dine out on that . . . *forever*! The truth about the Last Supper? I almost don't dare mention the Crucifixion! Would I have tried to stop it? Would He have made me *not*? Not tried? Was it what he wanted? The proof he needed?

WOMAN (Stops signing)

You go too far!

MAN (Apologetic)

I know, I know; madness lies that way.

GIRL (Quiet begging)

Please?

MAN (To GIRL)

Soon; soon, now.

(To himself, mostly; shakes head)

All the things I know I can never be, can never do, can never . . . *undo*. That's the worst.

(Ponders)

All the things I can never be,

(Harsher now, to BOY and GIRL)

including as sympathetic as you would like to your . . . what?—your "plight"? Your supposed *plight*? You who are probably not what you say you are—*who* you say you are.

BOY (*Weary*)

I've told you . . . a hundred times . . .

MAN

Yes yes yes, I know; you're married—to one another . . . you have this baby.

BOY

Yes!

GIRL

Yes!

MAN (*Dismissive*)

Right; sure; and the Gypsies have taken it—or will, or have thought about it, at the very least, as Gypsies will.

(GIRL *weeps;* BOY *takes her hand*)

BOY (*Very serious; very calm*)

The baby is real; the baby is ours; we went to the hospital for her to have it.

(GIRL *nods, still weeping a little*)

WOMAN

You go to the hospital a *lot.*

MAN (*Remembering*)

Yes! Yes, you do! You came to *see* me; I was on the stretcher; I was unconscious . . .

WOMAN (*To* MAN; *of* BOY)

. . . and he said to himself: "When he wakes up—*if* he wakes up—I'm going to be there . . . "

MAN

. . . and I'll be the first person he sees, and he'll love me; he'll want me and he'll love me; he's my destination.

WOMAN

And he told them he was your brother.

MAN (*To* BOY)

And I woke up, and you were hard.

GIRL

It was me!

BOY

It was her!

GIRL

It was me!

MAN *(Pause)*

Oh?

WOMAN *(Pause)*

Oh?

BOY *(Dogged; almost in tears)*
Yes; yes. It was her; she woke up and I was hard.

MAN *(Surprise)*
It wasn't me?! *I* remember you being hard.

WOMAN *(To* BOY*)*
We all do; we all remember you being hard.

MAN

Dick or no.

WOMAN

Dick or no.

MAN
And out popped the baby, the so-called baby?

BOY

When?

MAN

Then!

WOMAN

When-then.

BOY

No; that was when we *met*!

MAN
I remember; I woke up; the nurse said you were my brother, and you were hard.

BOY *(More dogged)*
No! Not then-then; not that time! When we went to have the baby!

MAN

(Distant)
I don't remember. Was it me? I don't remember.

WOMAN

Maybe it was *me*.

BOY

(To prove his existence; GIRL *cries softly during this)*
I was in the kitchen, and she came in and she said, "My water broke; my water just broke!"

WOMAN

It *was* me! Yes; of course.

BOY

And I bundled her up, and we took a cab to the hospital. I called our baby doctor, and we raced off to the hospital.

MAN *(Shakes his head)*

Everyone's a baby—even the doctor.

WOMAN *(To BOY)*

It isn't *water*, you know.

(*To* GIRL)

It isn't water.

BOY *(Determined)*

. . . and it wasn't long; it didn't take very long.

MAN *(Remembering giving birth)*

But it hurt! Oh, my God, it hurt! How it hurt me!

WOMAN *(Remembering)*

Oh, God, how it hurt me!

BOY *(Ibid.)*

And I held her hand during it, and *I* squeezed and *she* squeezed . . .

(GIRL *begins howling birthing sounds now, punctuating* BOY's *speech; she stays seated; shows no emotion, hands in lap—merely howling*)

. . . and she howled . . . and she howled . . . and she howled . . . and the sound was terrible, but I held on, *we* held on . . . the doctor and the nurses were all there . . . and the blood . . . and the blood came, and I'd never seen so much . . . blood, and then the baby came, the baby's head came . . .

(GIRL *ceases howling*)

and the rest of it . . .

GIRL *(Hands going wide)*

WOOOOOOSSSSSSH!!

MAN *(Ecstasy)*

. . . and I'd never seen so much blood!

WOMAN *(Ecstasy)*

. . . I felt it! The blood, and then the baby . . .

BOY

(*Ignoring them; maybe with a dismissive hand gesture*)

. . . and there it was; there was our baby.

GIRL *(Softer)*

Wooooossssssh.

WOMAN *(Shakes her head)*

Just like in the movies.

MAN

(Agreeing; suddenly understanding)

Yes!

(To BOY*)*

You go to a lot of movies?

BOY *(Bewildered)*

Who? This wasn't a movie!

WOMAN

It looked like one to *me*—all the trappings.

MAN *(To* WOMAN*)*

Yes! *Did*n't it? When I had *my* baby . . .

WOMAN

The black one?

MAN

No; the green one; there was very little blood, no pain . . .

WOMAN

Well, you had a spinal.

MAN

Hmmmm! Yes, that may have had something to do with it. In any event, when I had *my* baby *I* had the Gypsies, too. The Gypsies came to me, too.

WOMAN *(Smiles)*

Too?

MAN *(Smiles)*

Whatever. But I was wise.

(To GIRL*)*

When I took *my* baby to the Gypsy . . .

WOMAN

The old Gypsy *woman.*

MAN *(Aside, to* WOMAN*)*

Whatever.

(To GIRL *again)*

When I took *my* baby to the Gypsy, *I* was smart; when they told me to put the baby in a big paper bag, *I* didn't *do* it.

GIRL *(Weeping)*

No! I *didn't*!

WOMAN *(To* MAN*)*

Of *course* you didn't!

MAN *(Still to* GIRL*)*

I didn't put it on the table, between me and the Gypsy.

WOMAN

Of course you didn't!

MAN

(Still to GIRL*) I* didn't see the lights go all funny, and hear the music.

WOMAN

Of course not!

MAN *(Still to* GIRL*)*

And *I* didn't take the bag and bury it in the backyard for three weeks, so the baby could double, or whatever.

WOMAN

(Out) Twins!

GIRL

No! I didn't!

BOY

She didn't!

WOMAN *(To* MAN*)*

Of course you didn't!

MAN

So that when it came time to dig it up . . .

GIRL *(Weeping)*

I . . . didn't . . . do . . . that!

BOY *(Comforting her)*

No; no; of course you didn't.

WOMAN *(Observing)*

Touching.

MAN

Or whatever.

GIRL

Please. My baby.

MAN *(Pause; brisk now)*

Well, time for the old blanket trick.

WOMAN

Oh; right!

(*Exiting right; to* BOY *and* GIRL)

I'll be right back.

(*Out*)

I'll be right back.

MAN

(*To* BOY *and* GIRL, *as* GIRL *looks apprehensively off right*)

She'll be right back.

(*Out*)

She'll be right back.

BOY

(*After a pause; shy; quietly fearful*)

Are you Gypsies?

MAN (*Laughs; to* BOY)

Do we look like Gypsies? Do we have fedoras and bushy mustaches . . . ?

BOY

Whatever, then. Have you come to hurt us? Beyond salvation? Hurt us to the point that . . . if you want to do this to us, hurt us so, ask *why*! Ask what we've *done*. I can take pain and loss and all the rest *later*; I *think* I can— *we* can—when it comes as natural as . . . sleep? But . . . now? Not now. We're happy; we love each other; I'm hard all the time; we have a baby; we don't even understand each other yet. So . . . give us some time.

(*Pause*)

Please?

MAN

(*After long pause; brisk*) Time's up.

(WOMAN *re-enters with the baby blanket bundle, nuzzling.* GIRL *instinctively reaches toward bundle*)

WOMAN (*Possessive*)

AH!

(GIRL *withdraws*)

BOY (*An echo from before*)

Please?

MAN (*Gentler*)

Time's up.

(WOMAN *hands him the bundle. Out; a barker*)

Ladies and Gentlemen! See what we have here! The baby bundle! The old bundle of baby!

(*Throws it up in the air, catches it;* GIRL *screams*)

BOY (*Desperate*)

Don't do *that*!

WOMAN (*To* BOY; *comforting*)

He knows what he's doing.

MAN (*To* BOY *and* GIRL)

I know what I'm doing.

(*Out again; in when necessary*)

The old baby bundle—treasure of treasures, light of our lives, purpose—
they say—of all the fucking, all the . . . well, all the everything. Now the
really good part, the part we've all been waiting for!

(*He takes the bundle, snaps it open, displays both sides; we see
there is nothing there.*)

Shazaam! You see? Nothing! No baby! Nothing!

(GIRL *goes to blanket;* MAN *gives it to her; she searches it, cuddles
it; weeps. To* GIRL)

You see? Nothing.

BOY (*Pause*)

You *have* decided then: you have decided to hurt us beyond salvation.

MAN (*Objective*)

I said: time's up.

BOY

No matter how young we are? No matter how . . .

WOMAN (*Gentle*)

He said: time's up.

MAN

I said: time's up. Wounds, children, wounds. If you have no wounds, how
can you know you're alive? How can you know who you are?

(BOY *bows his head. To* BOY *and* GIRL)

Let us deal finally, once and for all, with the baby—I put it in quotes,
"baby." I want you to be certain, you have a baby? Have ever *had* a baby.

(*Pause*)

You have a baby?

(GIRL *replies more and more tentatively;* BOY *stays firm. Don't
rush this section*)

BOY

Yes.

GIRL

Yes.

(*Pause*)

MAN

You have a baby?

BOY

Yes.

GIRL

Yes.
(*Pause*)

WOMAN

You have a baby?

BOY

Yes.

GIRL

Yes.
(*Pause*)

MAN

You have a baby?

BOY

Yes.

GIRL

(*Opens mouth; closes it*)

BOY (*Tiny pause*)

Say something!
(*She shakes her head. Increasing intensity, and increased tempo here*)

MAN

I'll ask you once again. You have a baby?

BOY (*To* GIRL)

Tell him.

GIRL (*Finally*)

I don't know.

BOY

Of course you know!

GIRL

No! I don't know!

MAN

Once more: you have a baby?

BOY (*To* GIRL)

Tell him!!

WOMAN (*Gentle*)

Tell me, too.

BOY

Tell her!

MAN

Tell *someone:* you have a baby?

GIRL

(*Long pause; finally; rather shy*)

No; I don't think so.

BOY

But . . . ?

GIRL (*To* BOY; *begging*)

No; no; we don't have one; we don't have a baby.

(*Varying intensities and tempi*)

Please, please, no baby, I can't . . .

BOY (*Rage*)

I was with you when it was born!

GIRL (*Flat*)

No.

BOY

No one before *me*; we *made* it!

MAN (*An aside; quiet; out*)

They all say that.

GIRL (*Flat*)

No.

BOY

I SAW IT! I HELD IT! I WATCHED IT COME OUT OF YOU, ALL
BLOOD . . . !

GIRL

No. Please; no.

WOMAN (*To* GIRL)

You have no baby.

GIRL (*Flat*)

No.

MAN (*To* WOMAN)

What a wise girl.

WOMAN

What a brave girl.

BOY (*Crying now*)

I . . . saw . . . it; I . . . I held it.

   (*Response tempi easy now; all gentle except* BOY)

WOMAN

No.

MAN

No.

GIRL

No.

BOY (*Sobbing*)

Yes.

WOMAN

No.

MAN

No.

GIRL

No.

BOY

Yes.

WOMAN

No.

MAN

No.

GIRL

No.

BOY

No?

WOMAN

No.

MAN

No.

GIRL

No.

BOY (*Pause*)

No.

MAN (*Sighs*)

Well then; we're done.

WOMAN

Yes.

   (MAN *and* WOMAN *begin moving upstage;* MAN *pauses; mild puz-*
   zled look; BOY *and* GIRL *in silent tears—if possible*)

MAN

Tears!

(Out)

Tears!

(To WOMAN)

Tears!

WOMAN (Gentle smile)

Yes: tears.

MAN

(To BOY and GIRL, who are too interior to respond)

Oh what a wangled teb we weave. Wounds, children, wounds. Learn from it. Without wounds, what are you? If you don't have a broken heart . . .

(Shrugs)

We'll leave you, then. Don't get up.

(Taking WOMAN's hand)

Shall we?

WOMAN

Shall we?

(They exit; silence; BOY and GIRL still)

BOY (Still in tears)

No baby?

GIRL (Still in tears)

No.

BOY (More a wish than anything)

I hear it crying!

GIRL (Please)

No; no, you don't.

BOY (Defeat)

No baby.

GIRL (Begging)

No. Maybe later? When we're older . . . when we can take . . . terrible things happening? Not now.

BOY (Pause)

I hear it crying.

GIRL (Pause; same tone as BOY)

I hear it too. I hear it crying too.

(Lights fade)

CURTAIN

The Goat
or,
Who Is Sylvia?
(Notes Toward a
Definition of Tragedy)

For Liz McCann
—because

The Goat Or, Who is Sylvia? had its world premiere in New York City on March 10, 2002, at the John Golden Theatre. It was produced by Elizabeth Ireland McCann, Daryl Roth, Carole Shorenstein Hays, Terry Allen Kramer, Scott Rudin, Bob Boyett, Scott Nederlander, and Sine/ZPI. It was directed by David Esbjornson; the set design was by John Arnone; the lighting design was by Kenneth Posner; the sound design was by Mark Bennett; the costume design was by Elizabeth Hope Clancy; the production stage manager was Erica Schwartz; the general manager was Joey Parnes; the company manager was Elizabeth Blitzer; the casting was done by Bernard Telsey Casting; and the press representative was Sam Rudy of Shirley Herz Associates. The cast was as follows:

MERCEDES RUEHL *as* STEVIE

BILL PULLMAN *as* MARTIN

STEPHEN ROWE *as* ROSS

JEFFREY CARLSON *as* BILLY

On September 13, 2002, the roles of Stevie and Martin were taken over by Sally Field and Bill Irwin, respectively.

PLACE
A living room.

TIME
The present.

SCENE ONE

(The living room. STEVIE *onstage, arranging flowers)*

STEVIE *(Calling offstage)*
What time are they coming?
(No response)
Martin? What time are they coming?

MARTIN *(Offstage)*
What?
(Entering)
What?

STEVIE
(A little smile; a slowish statement)
What . . . time . . . are . . . they . . . coming.

MARTIN
Who?
(Recalling)
Oh! Oh.
(Looks at watch)
Soon; very soon. Why can't I remember anything?

STEVIE *(Finishing flowers)*
What can't you remember?

MARTIN
Anything; nothing; can't remember a thing. This morning—so far!—I couldn't remember where I'd put the new head for the razor; I couldn't recall Ross's son's name—still can't; two cards in my jacket make no sense to me whatever, and I'm not sure I know why I came in here.

STEVIE
Todd.

MARTIN

What?

STEVIE

Ross's son is called Todd.

MARTIN *(Slaps his forehead)*

Right! Why the flowers?

STEVIE

To brighten up the corner . . .

MARTIN

. . . where you *are?* Where *I* am?

STEVIE

. . . where you'll probably be sitting, to make the cameras happy.

MARTIN *(Smelling the flowers)*

What are they?

STEVIE

Cameras?

MARTIN

No; these.

STEVIE

Ranunculus. I.
     (Then)
I: ranunculi.

MARTIN

Pretty. Why don't they smell?

STEVIE

They're secretive; probably too subtle for your forgetful nose.

MARTIN

(Shakes his head, mock concern)
Every sense going! Taste next! Touch; hearing. Hah! Hearing!

STEVIE

What?

MARTIN

What?

STEVIE

And to think you're only fifty. Did you find it?

MARTIN

What?

STEVIE
The new head for the razor.

MARTIN
Right! A new head! I'll need that next—the whole thing.

STEVIE
Why did you want to remember Todd's name?

MARTIN
Well, to begin with, I shouldn't be forgetting it, and when Ross shows up and he asks about Billy I can't say "He's fine; how's . . . you know . . . *your* son . . ."

STEVIE
Todd.

MARTIN
Todd. "How's old Todd?"

STEVIE
Young Todd.

MARTIN
Yes. It's the little slips.

STEVIE
I wouldn't worry about it. Are you going to offer them stuff? Coffee? Beer?

MARTIN *(Preoccupied)*
Probably. Do you think it means anything?

STEVIE
I don't know what "it" is.

MARTIN
That I can't remember anything.

STEVIE
Probably not: you have too much to remember, that's all. You could go in for a checkup . . . if you can remember our doctor's name.

MARTIN *(Nailing it)*
Percy!

STEVIE
Right!

MARTIN *(To himself)*
Who could forget that? Nobody has a doctor named Percy.
  (To STEVIE*)*
What's the matter with me?

STEVIE

You're fifty.

MARTIN

No; more than that.

STEVIE

The old foreboding? The sense that everything going right is a sure sign that everything's going wrong, of all the awful to come? All that?

MARTIN *(Rueful)*

Probably. Why did I come in here?

STEVIE

I heard you in the hall; I called you.

MARTIN

Aha.

STEVIE

What's my *name*?

MARTIN

Pardon?

STEVIE

Who *am* I? Who am *I*?

MARTIN *(Acted)*

You're the love of my life, the mother of my handsome and worrisome son, my playmate, my cook, my bottlewasher. Do you?

STEVIE

What?

MARTIN

Wash my bottles?

STEVIE *(Puzzles it)*

Not as a habit. I may have—washed one of your bottles. Do you have bottles?

MARTIN

Everyone has bottles.

STEVIE

Right. But what's my *name*?

MARTIN *(Pretending confusion)*

Uh . . . Stevie?

STEVIE

Good. Will this be a long one?

MARTIN

A long what?

STEVIE

Interview.

MARTIN

The usual, I guess. Ross said it wasn't going to be a feature—sort of a catch-up.

STEVIE

On your fiftieth.

MARTIN *(Nods)*

On my fiftieth. I wonder if I should tell him that my mind's going? If I can remember.

STEVIE

(Laughs; hugs him from behind)
Your mind's not going.

MARTIN

My what?

STEVIE

Your mind, darling; it's not going . . . anywhere.

MARTIN *(Serious)*

Am I too young for Alzheimer's?

STEVIE

Probably. Isn't it nice to be too young for something?

MARTIN *(Mind elsewhere)*

Um-hum.

STEVIE

The joke is, if you can remember what it's called you don't have it.

MARTIN

Have what?

STEVIE

Alz . . .
(They both laugh; he kisses her forehead)
Oh, you know how to turn a girl on! Forehead kisses!
(Sniffs him)
Where have you been?

MARTIN *(Releases her; preoccupied)*

What time are they coming?

STEVIE

Soon, you said; very soon.

MARTIN

I did? Good.

STEVIE

Did you find it?

MARTIN

What?

STEVIE

The head for your razor.

MARTIN

No; it's around somewhere.
     (Fishes in a pocket, brings out cards)
But these! Now these! What the hell are these!? "Basic Services, Limited."
Basic Services, Limited?? Limited to what!?
     (The other card)
"Clarissa Atherton."
     (Shrugs)
Clarissa Atherton? No number, no . . . email thing? Clarissa Atherton?

STEVIE

Basic services? Clarissa Atherton, basic services?

MARTIN

Hm? Every time someone gives me one of these, I know I'm supposed to
give them one back, and I don't have them. It's embarrassing.

STEVIE

I've told you to have them made . . . cards.

MARTIN

I don't want to.

STEVIE

Then don't. Who is she?

MARTIN

Who?

STEVIE

Clarissa Atherton, basic services. Does she smell funny?

MARTIN

I don't know.
     (Afterthought)
I don't know who she is, as far as I know. Where were we this week?

STEVIE *(Overly casual; stretches)*

Oh, it doesn't matter sweetie. If you're seeing this Atherton woman, this
. . . dominatrix . . . who smells funny . . .

MARTIN

How could I be seeing her—whoever she is? There's nothing on the card.
Dominatrix!?

STEVIE

Why not?

MARTIN

Maybe you know things I don't.

STEVIE

Maybe.

MARTIN

And I probably know one or two things *you* don't.

STEVIE

It evens out.

MARTIN

Yes. Do I look OK?

STEVIE

For the TV? Yes.

MARTIN

Yes.
    (Turning)
Really?

STEVIE

I said: yes; fine.
    (Indicates)
The old prep school tie?

MARTIN *(Genuine, as he looks)*

Is it? Oh, yeah; so it is.

STEVIE *(Not letting him have it)*

No one puts on their prep school tie by accident. *No* one.

MARTIN *(Considers)*

What if you can't remember that's what it is?

STEVIE

No one!! If you do get Alzheimer's, and you get to the stage you don't know
who *I* am, who *Billy* is, who *you* are, for that matter . . .

MARTIN

Billy?

STEVIE *(Laughs)*

Stop it! When you get to the point you can't remember anything, someone will hand you *that*
        (Indicates his tie)
and you'll look at it and you'll say
        (Terrible imitation of aged man)
"Ahhhhh! My prep school tie! My prep school tie!"
        (They chuckle; the doorbell rings/chimes)

MARTIN

Ah! Doom time!

STEVIE *(Quite matter-of-fact)*

If you *are* seeing that woman, I think we'd better talk about it.

MARTIN

(Stops. Long pause; matter-of-fact)
If I *were* . . . we *would.*

STEVIE *(As offhand as possible)*

If not the dominatrix, then some blonde half your age, some . . . chippie, as they used to call them . . .

MARTIN

. . . or, worst of all, someone just like you? As bright; as resourceful; as intrepid; . . . merely . . . new?

STEVIE *(Warm smile; shake of head)*

You win 'em all, don't you.

MARTIN *(Same smile)*

Enough.
        (Door again. The next several speeches are done in a greatly exaggerated Noël Coward play manner: English accents, flamboyant gestures)

STEVIE

Something's going on, isn't it!?

MARTIN

Yes! I've fallen in love!

STEVIE

I knew it!

MARTIN

Hopelessly!

STEVIE

I knew it!

MARTIN

I fought against it!

STEVIE

Oh, you poor darling!

MARTIN

Fought hard!

STEVIE

I suppose you'd better tell me!

MARTIN

I can't! I can't!

STEVIE

Tell me! Tell me!

MARTIN

Her name is Sylvia!

STEVIE

Sylvia? Who is Sylvia?

MARTIN

She's a goat; Sylvia is a goat!
   (*Acting manner dropped; normal tone now; serious, flat*)
She's a goat.

STEVIE

   (*Long pause; she stares, finally smiles. Giggles, chortles, moves
   toward the hall; normal tone*)
You're too much!
   (*Exits*)

MARTIN

I am?
   (*Shrugs; to himself*)
You try to *tell* them; you try to be *honest*. What do they do? They laugh at
you.
   (*Imitation*)
"You're too much!"
   (*Thinks about it*)
I suppose I am.

ROSS

Hey honey.

STEVIE

Hi Ross.

(ROSS *enters with* STEVIE)

ROSS

Hello there, old man!

MARTIN

I'm fifty!

ROSS

It's a term of endearment. Nice flowers.

MARTIN

It is?

ROSS

What? What is?

MARTIN

"Hello there, old man." Ranunculi.

ROSS

Pardon?

STEVIE

The proper plural of ranunculus—the flowers, according to old Martin here.

MARTIN

Some say ranunculuses, but that sounds wrong, even though it's probably perfectly acceptable.

ROSS *(Not interested)*

Aha! Let's move that chair over to the . . . whatever they are . . . the flowers.

(*To* MARTIN)

Are you happy in that chair?

MARTIN

Am I happy in it? I don't even know if I've ever sat in it.

(*To* STEVIE)

Have I? Have I ever sat in it?

STEVIE

You just did, and you sat in it the last time Ross did the program with you.

ROSS

That's *right!*

MARTIN

Yes . . . but was I happy? Did I sit there and did contentment bathe me in its warm light?

ROSS

You got me, fella.

STEVIE

Yes; contentment fell; you sat there and I watched it bathe you in its warm light. I've got to go.

MARTIN

Where are you going?

STEVIE *(No information)*

Out.

MARTIN

Are we in tonight?

STEVIE

Yes. I think Billy's going out.

MARTIN

Naturally!

STEVIE

We're in.
    (Glee)
TV time! I'm getting my hair done, and then I thought I'd stop by the feed store.
    (Exits, giggling)

ROSS

By *what*? She's going to stop by *what*?

MARTIN *(Staring after her)*

Nothing; nowhere.
    (To ROSS*)*
No crew?

ROSS

Just me this time—the old handheld.
    (Setting up camera on a tripod)
You ready for the chair?

MARTIN *(Sing-song)*

Ha, ha.
    (Suddenly remembering)
How's old *Todd!?*

ROSS

"Old Todd?"

MARTIN

You know: old *Todd!*

ROSS

You mean my baby son who just last week it seems I dandled on my knee? *That* old Todd?

MARTIN

Lovely word—dandled. Yes: *that* old Todd.

ROSS

Who I cannot accept having become eighteen?

MARTIN

Whom.

ROSS

Maybe.

MARTIN

Yes; that one. Can any of us? Ever?

ROSS

Pushing me further into middle age?

MARTIN

Yes; that one.

ROSS *(Offhand)*

He's OK.
    (Laughs)
He asked me last week—first time since he was four, or something—why he didn't have a brother, or a sister, or whatever—why April and I never had another kid.

MARTIN

April, May, June—the pastel months. You name girl babies after them.

ROSS *(Doesn't care)*

Right.
    (Does care)
I told him if you do it right the first time, why take a chance on another.

MARTIN

Did he like that one?

ROSS

Seemed to. Of course, I could have told him the whole graduating class got together and vowed that we would all have only one kid each—keep the population down. Speaking of which, how's Billy? How's *yours*—*your* one and only?

MARTIN

(*Attempted throw-away tone*)

Ohhhh, seventeen last week—didn't Todd come to the party? No, I guess he didn't. Real cute kid, Billy, bright as you'd ever want, gay as the nineties.

ROSS

Passing phase. Have you had the old serious talk?

MARTIN

The "You'll get over it once you meet the right girl" lecture? Nah, I'm too smart for that, so's he, so's Billy. I told him to be sure. Says he's sure; loves it, he says.

ROSS

Well, of course he loves it; he's getting laid, for God's sake! Don't worry about him.

MARTIN

Who?

ROSS

Billy! Seventeen; it's a phase.

MARTIN

Like the moon, eh?

ROSS

He'll straighten out—to make a pun.

(*To quash the subject*)

Billy'll come out of it; he'll be OK.

MARTIN

(*Reassuring if a bit patronizing*)

Sure.

ROSS

Voice test? Phone off?

MARTIN

I assume Stevie did it.

ROSS

I hear a kind of . . . rushing sound, like a . . . whooooosh!, or . . . wings, or something.

MARTIN

It's probably the Eumenides.

ROSS

More like the dishwasher. There; it stopped.

MARTIN

Then it probably wasn't the Eumenides: they don't stop.

ROSS *(Agreeing)*

They go right on.

MARTIN

Right.

ROSS

Why is Stevie going to the feed store?

MARTIN

She isn't.

ROSS

Then why did she . . .

MARTIN

It's a joke.

ROSS

A standing joke?

MARTIN

No, a new one; a brand new one.

ROSS

OK? Ready? Ready Martin; here we go; just . . . be yourself.

MARTIN

Really?

ROSS *(A tiny bit testy)*

Well, no; maybe not. Put on your public face.

MARTIN *(Overly cheerful)*

OK!!

ROSS

And don't switch in the middle.

MARTIN *(More)*

OK!!

ROSS *(Under his breath)*

Jesus!

(Announcer voice)

Good evening. This is Ross Tuttle. Welcome to "People Who Matter." Some people have birthdays and no one pays them any mind. Well . . . family, of course, friends. And others . . . well, some people are . . . I was going to say special, but that's a . . . dumb word, for everyone matters, everyone's special. But some people matter in extraordinary ways, in ways which affect the lives of the rest of us—enrich them, inform them. Some people, I guess, are, well . . . more extraordinary than others. Martin Gray—whom you've met on this program before—is such a man, such a person. Good evening, Martin.

MARTIN

Good . . . uh, evening, Ross.

(Sotto voce)

It's mid-afternoon.

ROSS (Quiet snarl)

I know. Shut up!

(Announcer voice)

Three things happened to you this week, Martin. You became the youngest person ever to win the Pritzker Prize, architecture's version of the Nobel. Also this week you were chosen to design The World City, the two hundred billion dollar dream city of the future, financed by U.S. Electronics Technology and set to rise in the wheatfields of our Middle West. Also, this week, you celebrated your fiftieth birthday. Happy birthday, Martin, and congratulations!

MARTIN (Brief pause; casual)

Thanks, Ross.

ROSS

Quite a week, Martin!

MARTIN (A little puzzled)

Yes; yes it was. Quite a week.

ROSS (Big)

How does it feel, Martin?

MARTIN

Becoming fifty?

ROSS (Pushing)

No. All of it. Yes.

MARTIN

Well . . .

ROSS (Sensing no answer is coming)

It must be amazing! No, thrilling!

MARTIN

Turning fifty? No: not really.

ROSS (Not amused)

No! The other! The World City! The Pritzker! All that!

MARTIN (Genuine surprise)

Oh, that! Well, yes . . . amazing, thrilling.

ROSS *(Prompting)*

For one so young.

MARTIN *(Innocent)*

Fifty is young?

ROSS *(Controlling himself)*

For the Pritzker Prize! Where were you when they told you?

MARTIN

I was at the gym; I'd taken all my clothes off, and Stevie called me there.

ROSS

Stevie is your wife.

MARTIN

I know that.

ROSS

How did it make you feel?

MARTIN

Stevie being my wife?

ROSS

No: the Prize.

MARTIN

Well, it was . . . gratifying—not being naked, but . . . hearing about it—the Prize.

ROSS *(Exuberant)*

Weren't you . . . thunderstruck!?

MARTIN

Well, no; they'd hinted at it—the Prize, I mean, and . . .

ROSS *(Heavily prompting)*

But it was pretty wonderful, wasn't it?

MARTIN

(Understanding what to say)

Yes; yes it was pretty wonderful—*is* pretty wonderful.

ROSS

Tell us about The World City.

MARTIN

Well, you just *did:* two hundred billion dollars, and all, the wheatfields of Kansas, or whatever . . .

ROSS

What an honor! What a duo of honors! You're at the . . . pinnacle of your success, Martin . . .

MARTIN *(Considers that)*

You mean it's all downhill from here?

ROSS

CUT! CUT!
  (Camera off. To MARTIN*)*
What's the matter with you!?

MARTIN

Sorry?

ROSS

I can't shoot that! You were a million miles away!!

MARTIN *(Considering)*

That far.

ROSS

You want to try again?

MARTIN

Try what?

ROSS

The taping! The program!

MARTIN

  (As if seeing the camera for the first time)
Oooooh.

ROSS

We're taping!

MARTIN *(Unhappy)*

Yes; I know.

ROSS *(Nicely concerned)*
Something the matter?

MARTIN

I think so. Yes; probably.

ROSS

Do you want to talk about it, as they say?

MARTIN

About what?

ROSS

About what's the matter.

MARTIN *(Concerned)*

Why? What's the matter?

ROSS

You said something was the matter, that you think something's the matter.

MARTIN *(Far away)*

Oh.

ROSS

Forty years, Martin; we've known each other forty years—since we were ten.

MARTIN *(Trying to understand)*

Yes. That gives you something? Rights, or something?

ROSS

I'm your oldest friend.

MARTIN

No; my aesthetics professor at college; I still see him; he's a lot older than you; he's over ninety.

ROSS *(So patient)*

Your longest friend: the person you've known the longest.

MARTIN

No; my Aunt Sarah; she's known me . . .

ROSS *(Trying to stay patient)*

She's not a friend!

MARTIN *(Deep, quiet surprise)*

Oh?

ROSS *(Close to giving up)*

No; she's a relative; relatives are not friends!

MARTIN

Oh, now . . .

ROSS

Are not the same as friends. Jesus!

MARTIN

Aha! Yes; well, you're right. I've known you longer as a friend than anyone.
   (Tiny pause)
Why is that relevant?

ROSS

Because you're troubled, and I thought that as your oldest friend I might be able to . . .

MARTIN

I am? Is that true?

ROSS
You said that something was the matter!

MARTIN *(Not remembering)*
I did, hunh?

ROSS
Why are you so . . . ?
(Can't find the word)

MARTIN
Are you still shooting? Are you still on?

ROSS *(Heavy sigh)*
No. We'll try to do it at the studio later. Sorry.

MARTIN
Can I get up now?

ROSS
If you want to; if you're not happy.

MARTIN
Why are you talking to me like I was a child?

ROSS
Because you're acting like one.

MARTIN *(Innocent)*
I am?

ROSS
Probably the most important week of your life . . .

MARTIN *(Impressed, if uninvolved)*
Really!

ROSS
. . . and you act like you don't know whether you're coming or going, like you don't know where you are.

MARTIN
(Self-absorbed, almost to himself)
Maybe it's . . . love or something.

ROSS
Maybe what is?

MARTIN
Like a child.

ROSS *(Bingo!)*
You're having an affair!

MARTIN

SHHHHHHHH! I mean, Jesus!

ROSS *(Shrugs)*

It's OK; he's not having an affair.

MARTIN

Jesus! Too bad you didn't bring the crew; they'd love this.

ROSS *(Cool)*

They know their business.

MARTIN

And . . . ?

ROSS

And . . . ?

MARTIN

Aren't you guys friendly anymore?

ROSS

They know their business. What do you want me to do—have them over for *dinner*? Have every crew over for dinner?

MARTIN *(Puzzled)*

No, I guess not.
  (Afterthought)
Why *not*?

ROSS

Hm?

MARTIN

Why *not* have them over for dinner?

ROSS

Oh, for God's sake, Martin!

MARTIN *(Hands up, defensively)*

OK! OK! Jesus!

ROSS

It's just that . . . it's just that I don't . . . mix with . . .

MARTIN *(Joyful)*

The *help*?! You don't mix with the *help*!?

ROSS

What *is* wrong with you today!? That's not what I meant, and you *know* it.

MARTIN (*Half-serious, half-joking*)
You're a snob! I guess I've always known that. For all your left-wing, proletarian background, you're a *snob*: worst kind.

ROSS (*A plea; a warning*)
We're best friends, remember?

MARTIN
Meaning . . . ?

ROSS
We like each other.

MARTIN (*"So, that's it!"*)
Ohhhhhhhh!

ROSS
More than anyone.

MARTIN (*Ibid.*)
Ohhhhh!
     (*Considers it*)
Right; yes. Who else can I be cranky with?

ROSS
Stevie?

MARTIN
Ya know, Stevie doesn't take too well to cranky anymore. If she's developed
a flaw, it's that. "Don't be so cranky, Martin."

ROSS
Pity.
     (*They've gentled down now*)

MARTIN (*Shrugs*)
Well . . . *you* know.

ROSS (*Pause*)
So you're in love.

MARTIN
With Stevie? Sure! Twenty-two years now.

ROSS
No, I mean . . . "in love." Ficky-fack! Humpty-doodle!

MARTIN
What on earth are you talking about!? "Humpty-doodle"!?

ROSS
You said you were in love—outside of Stevie, as I read it.

MARTIN *(Genuine)*

Really? I don't remember.

ROSS *(Impatient sigh; abrupt)*

O . . . K! That does it!

MARTIN

(As ROSS *gathers up stuff; true innocence)*

Where are you going?

ROSS *(Staring him down)*

I'm gathering my things and I'm taking my left-wing . . . what was it?

MARTIN

Uh . . . proletarian.

ROSS

. . . proletarian self outta here.

MARTIN

"But, why!" as the . . .

ROSS

Look, I came here to fucking interview you.

MARTIN

Fine.

ROSS

To boost your ego even more than . . .

MARTIN

I have no ego.

ROSS

Bullshit! Even more than where it is already and you fuck that up.

MARTIN

Fine. You say fuck a lot.

ROSS

You say fine a lot.

(He laughs; so does MARTIN*)*

MARTIN

Words beginning with F.

ROSS *(Smiles)*

Yeah.

(Pause)

So; tell me about it.

MARTIN *(Shy)*

About . . . ?

ROSS *(Gently urging)*

Your new love.

MARTIN

Oh; that.

ROSS

Yes.

MARTIN

I don't know that I want to.

ROSS

Yes; you do.

MARTIN

. . . that I can.

ROSS

Try.

MARTIN *(Small smile)*

You're persistent.

ROSS

Best friend.
    (MARTIN *tries to talk; can't*)
Best friend.

MARTIN *(Frustrated explosion)*

OK!! OK!!
    (Heavy, slow sigh; long pause)
I don't know if I ever thought that . . . well, that Stevie and I would be . . .
well, no; we're not.
    (Pause)

ROSS

Are you telling me about it?

MARTIN

I'm starting to . . . or maybe I'm beginning to start.

ROSS

Oh; OK.

MARTIN

As I said, it never occurred to me that anything like this would come
up. 'Cause we've always been good together—good in bed, good out;
always honest, always . . . considerate. I've not been unfaithful our
whole marriage; I want you to know this; never physically untrue, as
they say.

ROSS

That's amazing. It's wonderful, but . . . wow!

MARTIN

Yes: wow. Oh, I've been groped in the kitchen by a cutie or two, late, a party, once or twice, and I've had my hand a couple of places a couple of times, but I've never . . . *done* anything. You follow.

ROSS

Yes; I follow.

MARTIN

It never seemed . . . well, necessary, either to be able to do a comparison, or . . . even for its own sake. I never needed it, I guess. Do you remember that time, that college reunion weekend you and I decided to call that service they'd told us about . . . the gang had told us about?

ROSS *(Rueful laugh)*

The Ladies Aid Society?

MARTIN

Yeah, and you called them, and . . .

ROSS

. . . and we had a couple of bimbos over . . .

MARTIN

Bimbi.

ROSS

Yes?
     (Broad)
Ohhhhh, I remember.

MARTIN

. . . and you were married already, and Stevie and I were dating . . . or going together . . .

ROSS

. . . or whatever.

MARTIN

Yes.

ROSS *(Trying to recall)*

What were their names?

MARTIN

Mine was Alice.

ROSS

Big girl.

MARTIN

Large Alice.

ROSS

Right! Mine was Trudy, or Trixie, or . . .

MARTIN

April.

ROSS

Yes? April?

MARTIN

Yes; April.

ROSS *(Interior)*

Oh, shit; April's called April.

MARTIN *(Registering it)*

Yes; she is.

ROSS

Shit.
   (Pause; recovers)
And we had them up to our room—two beds, two hookers.

MARTIN

Just like when we roomed together.

ROSS

A kind of reunion for the reunion.

MARTIN

Yes, I guess so. And do you remember what happened?

ROSS

I don't know. What happened?

MARTIN

I couldn't do it? Couldn't perform?

ROSS *(Recalls)*

Oh, yeah. You'd never had that problem when we were undergrads! I'd be
pumping away, you pumping away in the next bed.

MARTIN

I hadn't met Stevie.

ROSS *(Soberer)*

Right.

MARTIN

That night at the reunion with large Alice . . .

ROSS

You were going with Stevie . . .

MARTIN

Right.

ROSS

I remember.

MARTIN

I don't know why I ever thought I wanted to . . . *you* know.

ROSS

No. Right.

MARTIN

I was already in love with Stevie and I didn't know how much.

ROSS (*A little deriding*)

Amazing theory: the heart rules the dick. I always thought that the dick was driven by . . .

MARTIN

Don't be cynical.

ROSS

Oh, a new part of my left-wing . . . what?

MARTIN

Proletarian.

ROSS

Yes. My left-wing, proletarian, snobbish, *cynical* self.

MARTIN

Right, and not new.
  (*They both smile*)
You *do* see, don't you? In love with Stevie, she owns every part of me. Look, when I'm traveling, and Stevie's *here*, and I get itchy . . .

ROSS

You give yourself a handjob and you think about Stevie—about you and Stevie.

MARTIN (*Shy*)

Yes.

ROSS (*Shakes his head; noncommittal*)

Wonderful.

MARTIN

I didn't catch your tone.

ROSS

There wasn't any. Go on; how did you fuck it up?

MARTIN *(Truly confused)*

What? Fuck *what* up?

ROSS

Are you playing games?

MARTIN

No. Fuck *what* up?

ROSS *(Serious)*

Your life, apparently—you and Stevie. How'd you fuck it up?

MARTIN *(Pause)*

Oh.
   (Pause)
That.

ROSS *(Impatient)*

Getting an answer out of you . . .

MARTIN

OK! OK! As I told you, I've never been unfaithful, never needed it . . . never . . .

ROSS

Yeah, yeah; right. You told me.

MARTIN

And then . . . one day . . .
   (Stops)

ROSS *(After a silence)*

Yeah!?

MARTIN

And then one day.
   (Says nothing more)

ROSS *(Long pause)*

That's it!?

MARTIN *(Goes ahead)*

And then one day . . . one day . . . well, I was house-hunting—barn hunting, actually. Stevie and I had decided it was time to have a real country place—a farm, maybe—we deserved it. So, I was in the car about sixty miles out from the city. Stevie couldn't come with me.

ROSS

Beyond the suburbs.

MARTIN

Yes; beyond the suburbs. Farms around it, small farms. And I found a wonderful place, a wonderful old farmhouse, and a lot of land.

ROSS

The old back twenty, or whatever it is.

MARTIN

Right! Whatever. And I called Stevie, and told her she had to see it, and I'd put a hold on it 'til she could see it. And Stevie was . . . well, "A farm?" she said, but I said "Wait!" And the real estate guy was OK with that for a while. And I was driving out of the town back to the highway, and I stopped at the top of a hill.

ROSS

Crest.

MARTIN

Right. And I stopped, and the view was . . . well, not spectacular, but . . . wonderful. Fall, you know?, with leaves turning and the town below me and great scudding clouds and those country smells.

ROSS

Cow shit, and all that.

MARTIN *(Broad country parody)*
New-mown hay, fella! The smell a country; the smell a apples!
    (Normal tone again)
The roadside stands, with corn and other stuff piled high, and baskets full of other things—beans and tomatoes and those great white peaches you only get late summer . . .

ROSS *(Broad)*
The whole thing; right.

MARTIN *(Shakes his head)*
Oh, you city boys! And from up there I could trace the roads out toward the farm, and it gave me a kind of shiver.

ROSS

The ludicrous often does.

MARTIN

Anyway . . .

ROSS

Anyway.

MARTIN

Anyway, it was pretty wonderful. And I was getting back in the car, about to get back in the car, all my loot—vegetables and stuff . . .

(*Change of tone to quiet wonder*)

and it was then that I saw her.

(*Sees it*)

Just . . . just looking at me.

ROSS

Daisy Mae! Blonde hair to her shoulders, big tits in the calico blouse, bare midriff, blonde down at the navel, piece a straw in her teeth . . .

MARTIN

(*Gentle, admonishing smile*)

You don't understand.

ROSS

No? No blonde hair? No tits?

MARTIN

No. And there she was, looking at me with those eyes.

ROSS

And it was love.

MARTIN

You don't understand.

ROSS

No? It *wasn't* love?

MARTIN

No. Yes; yes, it was love, but I didn't know it right then.

(*To himself*)

How could I?

ROSS

Right then it was good old lust, eh? Dick starting to get big in your pants . . .

MARTIN (*Sad*)

You *don't* understand.

(*Pause*)

I didn't know *what* it was—what I was feeling. It was . . . it wasn't like anything I'd felt before; it was . . . so . . . amazing, so . . . extraordinary! There she was, just looking at me, with those *eyes* of hers, and . . .

ROSS (*Impatient*)

Well, did you *talk* to her?

MARTIN (*Incredulous laugh*)

Did I *what!?*

ROSS

Did you *talk* to her!?

MARTIN (*Considers it*)

Hunh! Yes; yes, I did. I went up to her, to where she was, and I spoke to her, and she came toward me and . . . and those eyes, and I touched her face, and . . .

(*Abrupt*)

I don't want to talk about it; I can't *talk* about it.

ROSS

All right; let me help you. You're *seeing* her.

MARTIN (*Sad laugh*)

Yes; oh, yes; I'm *seeing* her.

ROSS

You're having an affair with her.

MARTIN (*Confused*)

A what? Having a *what!?*

ROSS (*Hard*)

You're *screwing* her.

MARTIN (*Sudden vision of it*)

Yes; yes; I'm *screwing* her. Oh, Jesus!

ROSS (*Softer*)

And you're in love.

MARTIN

That's it, you see.

ROSS

What is? What do I see?

MARTIN

I *am* seeing her; I *am* having . . . an affair, I guess. No! That's not the right word. I am . . .

(*Winces*)

screwing her, as you put it—all of which is . . . beyond even . . . yes, I'm doing all that.

ROSS (*Prompting*)

. . . and you're in love with her.

MARTIN (*Begins to cry*)

Yes! Yes! I am! I'm in love with her. Oh, Jesus! Oh, Sylvia! Oh, Sylvia!

ROSS *(After a respectful pause)*
I almost dare not ask this, but . . . who is Sylvia?

MARTIN
I can't tell you!

ROSS
Who else *but* me? You can't tell Stevie, it would . . .

MARTIN
NO!!

ROSS
Then, who is she? Who is Sylvia?
(MARTIN *pauses; goes to wallet, brings out photo, looks at it, hesitates, then hands it to* ROSS, *not looking as he does so.* ROSS *takes
photo, looks at it, double-takes, begins a huge guffaw, which becomes
a coughing)*

MARTIN *(Shy)*
Don't laugh. Please; don't laugh.

ROSS
(Staring at photo; straightforward)
This is Sylvia.

MARTIN *(Nods)*
Yes.

ROSS *(Pinning it down)*
This is Sylvia . . . who you're fucking.

MARTIN *(Winces)*
Don't say that.
(It just comes out)
Whom.

ROSS
. . . with whom you're having an affair.

MARTIN *(Soft; nodding)*
Yes.
(Pause)
Yes.

ROSS
How long now?

MARTIN *(Soft)*
Six months.

ROSS

Jesus. You *have* to tell Stevie.

MARTIN

I can't! I couldn't do that!

ROSS

You *have* to . . . and if you don't, I will.

MARTIN *(Begging)*

No! Ross! Please!

ROSS *(Genuine)*

You're in very serious trouble.

MARTIN *(Pause; little boy)*

I am?

ROSS

(Quiet; shaking his head as he looks at the photo)
You sure are, buddy; you sure are.

MARTIN

But, Ross, you don't under . . .

ROSS *(Huge)*

THIS IS A GOAT! YOU'RE HAVING AN AFFAIR WITH A GOAT!
YOU'RE FUCKING A GOAT!

MARTIN *(Long pause; factual)*

Yes.

CURTAIN

SCENE TWO

(The living room; a day later. MARTIN, STEVIE, *and* BILLY; STEVIE *holding a letter)*

BILLY *(To* MARTIN*)*

You're doing *what*?! You're fucking a *goat*?!

MARTIN

(Indicating STEVIE, *who is at window, facing out)*

Billy! Please!

BILLY

Jesus Christ!

MARTIN

Don't swear.

BILLY *(Scoffing laugh)*

Don't *what*?!

MARTIN

Don't swear; you're too young.

BILLY

(Considers a moment, then)

FUCK THAT!!

MARTIN

Billy! Your mother!

BILLY *(Scoffing laugh)*

You're fucking a fucking goat and you tell me not to *swear*?!

MARTIN

You know, your *own* sex life leaves a little to . . .

STEVIE *(Still at window; ice)*

All right, you two!

BILLY *(To* MARTIN*)*

At least what I do is with . . . persons!

STEVIE *(Turning into the room)*

I said, all right, you two!

BILLY

Goat fucker!

MARTIN

Fucking faggot!

STEVIE

I said, all right!
    (A silence)

BILLY *(To* MARTIN*; soft, hurt)*

Fucking faggot? You called me a fucking *faggot*?!

MARTIN *(Gentle; to* BILLY*)*

I'm . . . I'm sorry.

STEVIE *(Even)*

Your father's sorry, Billy.

MARTIN

I'm sorry.
    (To get rid of the whole subject)
You're gay, and that's fine, and I don't give a shit what you put where.
    (Thinks about it)
I don't care one way or the other is what I mean.

BILLY

Yeah! Sure!

STEVIE *(Cool)*

I said your father's sorry for calling you a fucking faggot because he's not
that kind of man. He's a decent, liberal, right-thinking, talented, famous,
gentle man
    (Hard)
who right now would appear to be fucking a goat; and *I* would like to talk
about *that, if* you don't mind. Or . . . even if you *do.*

BILLY *(Nice)*

Sure, Mom; I'm sorry; you go right ahead.

MARTIN *(Sighs)*

Oh, dear.

STEVIE *(Objective)*

Let's review Ross's letter, shall we?
    (Waves it)

MARTIN *(Hurt and enraged)*
How *could* he!! How could he do such a thing?!

STEVIE *(Ice)*
How could he—best friend to both of us, a man you would trust with your wife—no? . . .

MARTIN
. . . sure; sure . . .

STEVIE
How could Ross write me this letter?
(*Waves it again*)

MARTIN
YES!!

STEVIE *(Composed; cool; quoting)*
". . . because I love you, Stevie, as much as I love Martin, because I love you both—respect you, love you—I can't stay silent at a time of crisis for you both, for Martin's public image, and your own deeply devoted . . ."

MARTIN
BULLSHIT!

STEVIE
Yes?

MARTIN
Yes!

STEVIE
So; anyhow; let's not pretend he never wrote the letter; let's not pretend I didn't get it in the mail today—nice that: no electronic nonsense—and let us not pretend that I did not read it.

MARTIN
No; no, of course not.

STEVIE
And let us not pretend that Ross does not tell me that you are having an affair with . . .
(*Looks*)
how does he put it? . . . "an affair with a certain Sylvia who, I am mortified to tell you . . ." He does get flowery, doesn't he!

MARTIN
Yes; yes, he does.

STEVIE
"I am mortified to tell you is a goat."

BILLY

Jesus!

STEVIE and MARTIN

Will you be still!!?

BILLY *(Dramatically cowering)*

Hey! Sure! Jesus!

STEVIE

(Back to business; quoting again)

"You will, of course, be shocked and greatly distressed . . ." No kidding! Uh . . . "shocked and greatly distressed to know of this, but I felt it my obligation to be the one to bear these tidings . . ."

MARTIN *(Some disbelief)*

Tidings?

STEVIE

Yes; "tidings."

MARTIN

Jesus! Of comfort and joy?

STEVIE

" . . . as I'm sure you'd rather hear it all from a dear friend . . ." As opposed to *what*! The ASPCA?!

MARTIN *(Woe)*

Oh, God; oh, God.

STEVIE

"Doubtless, Martin . . . " Doubtless?

MARTIN

Probably.

STEVIE

" . . . doubtless Martin will tell you all I have not, all I cannot."

(To MARTIN*)*

What are friends for, eh?

BILLY *(Really sad)*

Oh, Dad!

MARTIN

Poor Dad?

BILLY

What?

MARTIN

Nothing.

STEVIE *(Level)*

So, now you will tell me all that Ross has not, cannot. After you tell me what friends are for, of course.

MARTIN

Oh . . . Stevie . . .
(Starts to move to her)

STEVIE *(Abrupt; cold)*

Stay away from me; stay there. You smell of goat, you smell of shit, you smell of all I cannot imagine being able to smell. Stay *away* from me!

MARTIN *(Arms wide; hopeless)*

I *love* you!

BILLY *(Softly)*

Jesus.

STEVIE

You *love* me. Let's see if I understand the phrase. You *love* me.

MARTIN

Yes!

STEVIE

But I'm a human being; I have only two breasts; I walk upright; I give milk only on special occasions; I use the toilet.
(Begins to cry)
You love me? I don't understand.

MARTIN *(More hopeless)*

Oh, God!

STEVIE

How can you love me when you love so much less?

MARTIN *(Even more hopeless)*

Oh, God.

BILLY

Fucking a goat?!

MARTIN *(To BILLY; sharp)*

That does it! Out!

BILLY *(To STEVIE; arms wide)*

What did I *say*? I said he was . . .

MARTIN

Enough!

BILLY

For Christ's sake, I . . .

MARTIN

Go to your room!

STEVIE *(Almost laughing)*

Oh, really, Martin!

BILLY *(Incredulous)*

Go to my room?!

MARTIN

Go to your *room*!

BILLY

What am I—eight, or something? Go to my *room*?

STEVIE

You'd better go, Billy. If you stay you might learn something.

MARTIN *(To* STEVIE*)*

Nicely put.

STEVIE *(Coldly)*

Thanks.

BILLY *(To* STEVIE*)*

You want me to leave you here with this . . . this . . . *pervert*?!

STEVIE *(To help)*

Just go to your room, Billy, or go outside, or . . .

MARTIN

. . . or go to one of your public urinals, or one of those death clubs, or . . .

BILLY

KNOCK IT OFF!!

MARTIN

(Impressed) Wow!

BILLY *(Sneering)*

You seem to know a lot about all that.

MARTIN *(Not defensive)*

I *read*.

BILLY

Sure.

(To STEVIE*)*

I'll go if you think it's OK, Ma; I'll go.

(To MARTIN*)*

But not to your . . . "places." I will probably go to my room, and I'll probably close my door, and I'll probably lie down on my bed, and I'll probably
start crying and it'll probably get louder and worse, but you probably won't
hear it—either of you—because you'll be too busy killing each other. But
I'll be there, and my little eight-year-old heart will for certain be breaking—in twain, as they say.

MARTIN *(Some awe; no contempt)*
Very good; very good.

STEVIE *(Preoccupied)*
Yes; very good, Billy.

BILLY *(Fleeing; near tears)*
Jesus Christ!

STEVIE *(As he exits)*
Billy . . .

MARTIN *(Quietly)*
Let him go.
    (Silence; quietly)
Well, now; just you and me.

STEVIE *(Pause)*
Yes.

MARTIN *(Pause)*
I take it you want to talk about it?

STEVIE *(Awful chuckle)*
Oh, God!
    (Afterthought)
You *take* it?

MARTIN
Is that a "yes"?

STEVIE *(Cold; precise)*
I was out shopping today—dress gloves, if you want to know. I still wear
them—for weddings and things . . .

MARTIN *(Puzzled)*
Who's getting married?

STEVIE *(Huge)*
SHUT UP!

MARTIN *(Winces)*
Sorry.

STEVIE *(Normal tone again)*

. . . dress gloves, and then to the fish people for shad roe—it's just come in—and then back home, and you were gone and I heard Billy's music up in his room and there was the mail. You'd gone out before it came—not that it would have mattered: we don't read each other's.

MARTIN

Would that we did.

STEVIE

Oh? I would have found out sooner or later. And there was Ross's letter. "Ross? Writing to me? Whatever for!"

MARTIN *(Softly)*

Oh, God.

STEVIE

. . . and I was standing in the pantry. I'd put the roe away and had left the kitchen and was moving to the dining room on my way to the stairs when I began to read it.

MARTIN

Ross shouldn't have done this. He *knows* he shouldn't have done . . .

STEVIE

(Reading; steady, almost amused)

"Dearest Stevie . . . "

MARTIN

Oh, God.

STEVIE

"This is the hardest letter I've ever had to write."

MARTIN

Sure!

STEVIE

You doubt it? ". . . the hardest letter I've ever had to write, and to my dearest friends. But because I love you, Stevie, as much as I love Martin, because I love you both—respect you, love you—I can't stay silent at a time of crisis for you both, for Martin's public image and your own deeply devoted . . ."

MARTIN

As I said, bullshit.

STEVIE

. . . "self. I must put it baldly, for hinting would only put off the inevitable. Martin—and he told me this himself" . . .

(Aside)

I would have liked to have been listening to *that* conversation!

MARTIN

No you wouldn't.

STEVIE *(Reading again)*

"Martin is having an affair with a certain Sylvia . . . "

(To MARTIN*)*

Oh, God, I thought; at least it's someone I don't know; at least it's not Ross's first wife, the one I thought you might if you were going to . . .

MARTIN *(Surprise)*

Rebecca?

STEVIE

Yes, or maybe your new assistant . . .

MARTIN *(Bewildered)*

Who? Ted Ryan?

STEVIE

No; the *other* one—the one with the hooters.

MARTIN

Oh; Lucy something.

STEVIE

Yes: Lucy "something." You men are the end. Where was I?

(Reads again)

. . . "an affair with a certain Sylvia who, I am mortified to tell you . . . is a goat. You will, of course, be shocked and greatly disturbed to know of this, but I felt it my obligation to be the one to bear these tidings, as I'm sure you'd rather hear it from a dear friend. Doubtless, Martin . . ."
Doubtless?

MARTIN

(Shrugs) Sounds right.

STEVIE

"Doubtless, Martin will tell you all I have not . . . all I cannot. With profound affection for you both, Ross."

(Pause)

Well.

MARTIN

Yes. "Well."

STEVIE *(Not eager; dogged)*

We will now discuss it.

MARTIN (*Heavy sigh*)

Of course, though you won't understand.

STEVIE

Oh? Do you know what I thought—what I thought after I'd read the letter, right to the end?

MARTIN

No, I don't want to know . . . or guess.

STEVIE

Well, I laughed, of course: a grim joke but an awfully funny one. "That Ross, I tell you, that Ross! You go too far, Ross. It's funny . . . in its . . . awful way, but it's way overboard, Ross!" So, I shook my head and laughed—at the awfulness of it, the absurdity, the awfulness; some things are so awful you have to laugh—and then I listened to myself laughing, and I began to wonder why I *was*—*laughing*. "It's not funny when you come right down to it, Ross" Why *was* I laughing? And just like that

(*Snaps her fingers*)

I stopped; I stopped laughing. I realized—probably in the way if you suddenly fell off a building—oh, shit! I've fallen off a building and I'm going to die; I'm going to go splat on the sidewalk; like *that*—that it wasn't a joke at all; it was awful and absurd, but it wasn't a joke. And everything tied in—Ross coming here to interview you yesterday, the funny smell, the Noël Coward bit we did about you having an affair, and with a goat. You said it right out and I laughed. You *told* me! You came right out and fucking *told* me, and I laughed, and I made jokes about going to the feed store, and I *laughed*. I fucking laughed! Until it stopped; until the laughter stopped. Until it all came together—Ross's letter and all the rest: that odd smell . . . the mistress's perfume on you. And so I knew.

MARTIN

Stevie, I'm so . . .

STEVIE

Shut up. And so I knew. And next, of course, came believing it. Knowing it—knowing it's true is one thing, but *believing* what you *know* . . . well, there's the tough part. We all prepare for jolts along the way, disturbances of the peace, the lies, the evasions, the infidelities—*if* they happen.

(*Very off-hand*)

I've never had an affair, by the way, all our years together; not even with a cat, or . . . *any*thing.

MARTIN

Oh, Stevie . . .

STEVIE

We prepare for . . . things, for lessenings, even; inevitable . . . lessenings, and we think we can handle everything, whatever comes along, but we don't know, *do* we!

(*Right at* MARTIN)

Do we!

MARTIN (*Bereaved*)

No; no, we don't.

STEVIE

Fucking *right* we don't!

(*Didactic*)

Something can happen that's outside the rules, that doesn't relate to The Way the Game Is Played. Death before you're ready to even think about it—that's part of the game. A stroke that leaves you sitting looking at an eggplant the week before had been your husband—that's another. Emotional disengagement, gradual, so gradual you don't know it's happening, or sudden—not very often, but occasionally—that's another. You've read about spouses—God! I hate that word!—"spouses" who all of a sudden start wearing dresses—yours, or their own collection—wives gone dyke . . . but if there's one thing you *don't* put on your plate, no matter how exotic your tastes may be is . . . bestiality.

MARTIN

Don't! You don't understand.

STEVIE

The fucking of animals! No, that's one thing you haven't thought about, one thing you've overlooked as a byway on the road of life, as the old soap has it. "Well, I wonder when he'll start cruising livestock. I must ask Mother whether Dad did it and how *she* handled it." No, that's the one thing you haven't thought about—nor could you conceive of.

(*Pause; grimly cheerful*)

So! How was *your* day?

MARTIN

(*Pause; attempting the casual*)

Well . . . I had a good day at the office. Made the design for The World City even larger than . . .

STEVIE (*Fixed smile*)

Oh, good!

MARTIN

. . . and then I stopped by the haberdasher . . .

STEVIE (*Pretending to puzzle*)

Ha-ber-dash-er. That's someone who makes haberdash?

MARTIN

Haber, I think. Dash is part of doing it.

STEVIE

Ah! *Then* what?

MARTIN

Hm? Well, then I drove back home, and . . .

STEVIE

What! You didn't stop by to see your ladyfriend? Get a lick in?

MARTIN

She's in the country. Please, Stevie . . . *don't!*

STEVIE (*Feigned wonder*)

She's in the *country!*

MARTIN

I keep her there.

STEVIE

Where!?

MARTIN

Please! Don't!

STEVIE

Martin, did you ever think you'd come back from your splendid life, walk into your living room and find you had no life left?

MARTIN

Not specifically; no.
    (*Looks down*)

STEVIE

I think we'd better talk about this. If I'm going to kill you I need to know exactly why—all the details.

MARTIN (*Shy*)

You really want to?

STEVIE

What? Kill you?

MARTIN

No; learn about it.

STEVIE (*Big*)

No! I *don't* really want to!
    (*Normal tone again*)

I want the whole day to rewind—start over. I want the reel to reverse: to see the mail on the hall table where Billy's left it, then *not* see it because I haven't opened the door yet—not having gotten the fish yet because I haven't bought the gloves yet because I haven't left the house yet because I haven't gotten out of our bed because I haven't *waked UP YET!!*

(*Quieter*)

But . . . since I can't reverse time . . . yes, I *do* want to know. I'm reeling with it.

(*Pleading*)

Make me not *believe* it! Please, make me *not believe* it.

MARTIN (*Pause*)

Why aren't you crying?

STEVIE

Because this is too serious. Do goats cry, by the way?

MARTIN

I . . . I don't know. I haven't . . .

STEVIE

. . . made her cry yet!? What's the *matter* with you?!

MARTIN (*Begging*)

Stevie . . .

STEVIE (*As if to someone else*)

He can't even make a *goat* cry. What *good* is he? His son's probably weeping as we speak. That was pretty awful what you said to him, Martin, pretty awful. His son's probably lying on his bed, tears flowing; his wife *would* be crying

(*Harder*)

except she can't be that weak right now. And you can't even make a goat cry?! Jeez!

MARTIN (*Dogmatic*)

I didn't say I *couldn't*; I said I *haven't.*

STEVIE

Well, the goats of this world must be very happy. Oh, you kid!

MARTIN (*Starting to leave*)

I can't *have* this conversation. I can't listen to you when you're . . .

STEVIE (*Blocking him*)

You *stay* where you *are!* You will *have* this conversation, and with *me* and right *now!*

MARTIN (*Retreating; sighing*)

Where shall I start?

STEVIE (*A threat*)

Right at the beginning!

(*Afterthought*)

Why do you call her Sylvia, by the way? Did she have a tag, or something? Or, was it more: Who is Sylvia,

What is she

That all our goats commend her . . .

MARTIN (*Trying to be rational*)

No, it just seemed right. Very good, by the way.

STEVIE

Thank you. You saw this . . . *thing* . . . this goat, and you said to yourself "This is Sylvia." Or did you talk to it: "Hello, Sylvia." How the hell did you know it was a she—was a female? Bag of nipples dragging in the dung? Or, isn't this your first?!

MARTIN (*Very quiet*)

She is my first; she is my only. But you don't understand. You . . .

STEVIE (*Contemptuous*)

Awww; I'm trying not to throw up.

MARTIN

Well, if that's the way you . . .

STEVIE

No!! Tell me.

MARTIN (*Sighs*)

All right. As I said to Ross . . .

STEVIE (*Broad parody*)

"As I said to Ross . . . " *NO!* Not "As I said to Ross." To *me!* As you say to *me!*

MARTIN (*Annoyed*)

In any event . . .

STEVIE

Not "in any event!" No! *This* event!

MARTIN (*Won't let it go*)

As I said to Ross . . .

STEVIE (*Impatient acquiescence*)

Very well; as you said to Ross.

MARTIN

Thank you. As I said to Ross, I'd gone to the country . . . to find the place we wanted, our . . . country *place.*

STEVIE (*Fact*)

You went out a lot.

MARTIN

Well, if you're after Utopia . . .
  (*Shrugs*)

STEVIE

Sure.

MARTIN

. . . unless you're one of those people finds it right off: "That's it; that's the place." Unless you're one of those, you've got to nose around.

STEVIE

Is that an ugly phrase?—"nose around"?

MARTIN (*Not too certain*)

I don't think so. Search. Is that better?
  (STEVIE *Shrugs*)
Search; look around. Close enough in to make it practical for our country needs. No more than an hour or so from . . .

MARTIN

You're the one who said it. Verdancy: flowers and green leaves against steel and stone. OK?

STEVIE (*Shrugs*)

OK.
  (*Angry*)
And it's lovely. Now get to the *goat!*

MARTIN

I'm *getting* there. I'm *getting* to her.

STEVIE

Stop calling it *her!*

MARTIN (*Defending*)

That is what she *is!* It is a *she! She* is a *she!*

STEVIE (*Pathetic sneer*)

I suppose I should be grateful it wasn't a *male, isn't* a male goat.

MARTIN

Funny you should ask—as they say. There was a place I went to . . .

STEVIE

Oh?

MARTIN

Well, when I realized something was wrong. I mean, when I realized people would *think* something was wrong, that what I was doing wasn't . . .

STEVIE (*Dispassionate*)

I *am* going to kill you.

MARTIN (*Preoccupied*)

Yes; probably. It was a therapy place, a place people went to . . . to talk about it, about what they were doing . . . and with whom.

STEVIE

What! Not *whom! What!* With *what!*

MARTIN (*Sharp*)

Whatever! A place! Please! Let me finish this!

(STEVIE *is silent*)

A place to talk about it; like A.A., like Alcoholics Anonymous.

STEVIE (*Sneers*)

Goat-fuckers Anonymous?

MARTIN (*Oddly shocked*)

Please!

(STEVIE *hoots. Quieter*)

Please?

STEVIE

Sorry. Destroy me.

MARTIN

It had no cute name; no A.A.; no . . . no nothing. Just . . . a place.

STEVIE

How did you find it?

MARTIN

Online.

STEVIE (*Toneless*)

Of course.

MARTIN

I went there . . . and there were—what?—ten of us . . . a group leader, of course.

STEVIE

What was *he* fucking? *Who;* sorry.

MARTIN

He was cured, he said—odd phrase. Was off it.

STEVIE (*Very calm*)

Very well. What *had* he been fucking?

MARTIN (*Matter-of-fact*)

A pig. A young pig.

(STEVIE *rises, finds a big ceramic table plate, smashes it, resits, or whatever*)

STEVIE *(Without emotion)*

Go on.

MARTIN *(Indicates)*

Is there going to be a lot of that?

STEVIE

Probably.

MARTIN

You don't want Billy down here; some things . . .

STEVIE *(Steaming)*

Some things are . . . *what?!* Private? Sacred? Husband telling wifey about a very peculiar therapy session? A *pig?!*

MARTIN *(A little embarrassed)*

A small one, he said.

STEVIE

Jesus!

    (BILLY *rushes in from the hall)*

BILLY

You two OK?

MARTIN

Yes-we're-fine-go-away-Billy.

BILLY

Who's throwing things?

STEVIE

I am; your mother is throwing things.

BILLY

Is there going to be more?

STEVIE

I imagine so.

BILLY *(Retrieving a small vase)*

I gave you this one; I think I'll take it upstairs.

STEVIE *(As BILLY turns to go)*

I would have noticed, Billy.

BILLY *(Shaking his head)*

Sure. You guys hold it down.

    (Exits)

STEVIE *(After him)*

I *would* have.
     (Uncertain)
I *think* I would have.

MARTIN *(Pause)*

So, anyway; it was this place.

STEVIE *(Reconcentrating)*

A pig? Really?

MARTIN

Well, everyone had . . . *you* know . . .

STEVIE

. . . some*one*, or some*thing*.

MARTIN

Yes.

STEVIE *(Lightbulb)*

And was Clarissa Atherton there?

MARTIN

Who? Yes! That's where I got the card, and . . .

STEVIE

And what is *she* fucking? *Who*?

MARTIN *(Matter-of-fact)*

A dog, I think.
     (STEVIE finds a vase, crashes it to the floor)

STEVIE

A dog you *think*.

MARTIN

Why would she lie? Why would anyone there lie?

STEVIE

Damned if *I* know.

MARTIN *(Sighs)*

And so I went there, and . . .

STEVIE

(There is chaos behind the civility, of course)
Did you all take your . . . friends with you—your pigs, your dogs, your
goats, your . . .

MARTIN

No. We weren't there to talk about *them*; we were there about ourselves,
our . . . our problems, as they called them.

STEVIE
The livestock was all happy, you mean.

MARTIN
Well, no; there was this one . . . goose, I think it was . . .
    (STEVIE *finds a vase, crashes it to the floor*)
Shall we go outside?

STEVIE *(Hands on hips)*
Get *on* with it.

MARTIN *(So calm)*
All right; there was this one goose . . .

STEVIE
Not geese! *Not* pigs! *Not* dogs! *Goats!* The subject is *goats!*

MARTIN
The subject is *a* goat; the subject is Sylvia.
    (*He sees* STEVIE *looking for something to throw*)
No! Don't; please! Just listen! Sit and listen!

STEVIE
    (*Has a small bowl in her hands; sits*)
All right. I'm listening.

MARTIN
I said, most of the people there were having problems, were . . . ashamed,
or—what is the word?—conflicted . . . were . . . needed to talk about it
while . . . while I went there, I guess, to find out why they were all there.

STEVIE
    (*As if the language were unfamiliar*)
Pardon?

MARTIN
I didn't understand why they were there—why they were all so . . . unhappy;
what was wrong with . . . with . . . being in love . . . like that.
    (STEVIE *gently separates hands, letting bowl fall between her legs,
    break*)
There's so much I have to explain.

STEVIE *(Deep, quiet irony)*
Oh?

MARTIN *(Rises, moves a little away)*
You must promise to be still. Sit there and please listen, and then maybe
when I've finished you . . . just listen; please.

STEVIE *(Sad smile)*
How could I not?

MARTIN

I went there . . . because I couldn't come to *you* with it.

STEVIE

Oh?

MARTIN

Well . . . *think* about it.

STEVIE *(Does)*

I suppose you're right.

MARTIN

And most of them had a problem, had a long history. The man with the pig was a farmboy, and he and his brothers, when they were kids, just . . . *did* it . . . *naturally*; it was what they did . . . with the pigs.

(Knits brow)

Or piglets, perhaps; that wasn't clear.

STEVIE

Naturally; of course.

MARTIN

Are you agreeing?

STEVIE

No. Just get on with it.

MARTIN

It was what they did. Maybe it was better than . . .

STEVIE

. . . than with each other, or their sisters, or their grandmothers? You've got to be kidding!

MARTIN

No one got hurt.

STEVIE

HUNH!!

MARTIN

We'll talk about that.

STEVIE

You *bet* we will!

MARTIN *(Sighs)*

Most of them had a reason, the man with the pig more a matter of . . . habit than anything else, I guess . . . comfort, familiarity.

STEVIE *(Eyes heavenward)*

Jesus!

MARTIN

Though he was off it . . . "cured," as he put it, which I found odd.

STEVIE

Of course.

MARTIN

I mean . . . if he was happy . . .

> (STEVIE *knocks over the small side table where she is sitting, never taking her eyes off* MARTIN)

STEVIE *(Ironic)*

Ooops!

MARTIN

When he was doing it, I mean. Must you? Though I suppose he wasn't . . . no longer was happy.

STEVIE *(Feigned surprise)*

You mean you didn't *ask* him?

MARTIN

No; no, I didn't. The lady with the German Shepherd . . .

STEVIE

Clarissa?

MARTIN

No; another one. The lady with the Shepherd, it turned out she had been raped by her father *and* her brother when she was twelve, or so . . . continually raped, one watching the other, she told us . . .

STEVIE

. . . and so she took up with a *dog?!*

MARTIN *(No opinion)*

Yes; it would seem. The man with the goose was . . . hideously ugly—I could barely look at him—and I suppose he thought he could never . . . *you* know.

STEVIE *(Cool)*

Do I?

MARTIN

Try and imagine.

STEVIE *(Calm; sad)*

I doubt I can.

MARTIN

Try: so ugly, no woman—no *man*—would even *think* of . . . "doing it" with you—*ever*.

STEVIE

One in the hand, et cetera. But . . . a goose!?

MARTIN (*Sad smile*)

Not everyone is satisfied that way . . . one in the hand. No matter. And *I* was unhappy there, for *they* were all unhappy.

STEVIE

My goodness.

MARTIN

And I didn't know why.

STEVIE (*Considers it*)

Really? I think we've hit upon why I'm going to kill you.

MARTIN (*Onward*)

There's something else I want you to understand.

STEVIE (*Sarcasm*)

Oh? Something else?

MARTIN

It's something I told Ross.

STEVIE

Not him again.

MARTIN

He *is* my best friend.

STEVIE (*Actress-y*)

Oh? And I thought *I* was!

MARTIN (*Undeterred; calm*)

I told him that in all our time together—yours and mine—all our marriage—I've never been unfaithful.

STEVIE (*A beat; fake astonishment*)

Hunh!!

MARTIN (*Onward*)

Never in all our years. Oh, early on, one of your friends would grope me in the kitchen at a party, or . . .

STEVIE

I love my friends; they have taste.

MARTIN

Never unfaithful; never once. I've never even wanted to. We're so good together, you and I.

STEVIE

A perfect fit, eh?

MARTIN *(Sincere)*

Yes!

STEVIE

You'd never imagine that a marriage could be so perfect.

MARTIN

Yes! I mean *no*; I *hadn't*.

STEVIE *(Advertisement)*

Great sex, good cook, even does windows.

MARTIN

Be serious!

STEVIE

No! It's too serious for that.
  (Afterthought)
Fuck you, by the way.

MARTIN

Never once! People looked at me, said "What's the matter with you?!"
"Don't you have any . . . you know, lust?" And "Sure," I said, "I've got
plenty. All for Stevie."

STEVIE

  (Shakes her head; sing-song)
La-di-da; la-di-fuckin'-da!

MARTIN *(Rage)*

Listen to me!

STEVIE *(Army drill)*

Yes, sir!
  (Softer)
Yes, sir.

MARTIN

All the men I knew were "having affairs" . . . *seeing* other women, and
laughing about it—at the club, on the train. I felt . . . well, I almost felt like
a misfit. "What's the matter with you, Martin!? You mean you're only doing
it with your wife!? What kind of man *are* you?!"

STEVIE

You men *must* be fun together.

MARTIN

Odd man out. I only wanted *you*.

STEVIE *(Pause; quietly)*

And *I* have something to tell *you*.

MARTIN (*Anticipating, with dread*)

Oh, no! Don't tell me that you've been with . . .

STEVIE (*Hands up; shakes her head*)

Hush. In all our marriage I've never even wanted anyone but you.

MARTIN (*Deeply sad*)

Oh, Stevie.

STEVIE

My mother told me—we really *were* good friends; I'm sorry you never knew her.

MARTIN

I am, too.

STEVIE

We talked together like sisters, by God; we talked the night away, two "girls" talking; we were that good friends, but she sure knew how to be a "parent" when she needed to, when she wanted to keep me very . . . level. And she said to me—I never told you this—"Be sure you marry someone you're in love with—deeply and wholly in love with—but be careful who you fall in love with, because you might marry him."

(MARTIN *chuckles, quietly, ruefully*)

"Your father and I have the best marriage anyone could possibly have," she said to me, over and over. "Be sure you do, too."

MARTIN

Stevie, I . . .

STEVIE

"Be careful who you marry," she said to me. And I *was*. I *fell* in love with you? No . . . I rose into love with you and have—what—*cherished?* you, all these years, been proud of all you've done, been happy with our . . . funny son, been . . . well, happy. I guess that's the word. No, I don't guess; I *know*.

(*Begins to cry*)

I've been happy.

(*More*)

Look at me, Mother; I've married the man I loved

(*More*)

and I've been . . . so . . . happy.

MARTIN (*Moves to her; touches her*)

Oh, Stevie . . .

STEVIE

(*Huge; swipes objects off the coffee table*)

GET YOUR GOAT-FUCKING HANDS OFF ME!!!

(*Retreats to wall, arms wide, sobbing greatly*)

MARTIN
(Reacts as if he's touched a hot stove)
All right! No more!

STEVIE
Yes! *More!* Finish it! Vomit it all up! Puke it out all over me. I'll never be less ready. So . . . *do* it! *DO* IT!! I've laid it all out for you; I'm naked on the table; take all your knives! Cut me! Scar me forever!

MARTIN *(Thinks a moment)*
Before or *after* I vomit on you?
(Gently; hands up to appease)
Sorry; sorry.

STEVIE *(A shaking voice)*
Women in deep woe often mix their metaphors.

MARTIN *(Pacifying)*
Yes; yes.

STEVIE
Get *on* with it!
(Afterthought)
Very good, by the way.

MARTIN *(Rue)*
Thanks.

STEVIE
. . . and hopelessly inappropriate.

MARTIN
Yes; sorry.

STEVIE *(Casually overturns a chair)*
Get on with it, I said.

MARTIN
Are you going to do that with *all* the furniture?

STEVIE *(Looks around)*
I think so. You may have to help me with some of it.

MARTIN
Truce! Truce!

STEVIE
(Takes a painting, breaks it over something)
NO! NO TRUCE! *All* of it! Now!

MARTIN
That was my mother's painting.

STEVIE

It still is!

(Prompting)

You found us our lovely country place.

MARTIN (Girds)

And the day I found it—I called you. You remember: I told you I'd put a hold on it.

STEVIE

I'll never forget.

MARTIN

And I was driving out of the town, back to the highway, and I stopped at the top of a hill . . .

STEVIE

Crest.

MARTIN

What!? Who are you!?

STEVIE

You stopped at the crest of a hill—on it, actually.

MARTIN

Yes. And I stopped, and the view was . . . wonderful. Not spectacular, but wonderful—fall, the leaves turning . . .

STEVIE (Staring at him)

A regular bucolic.

MARTIN

Yes; a regular bucolic. I stopped and got us things—vegetables and things. You remember.

STEVIE (Denial)

No; I don't.

MARTIN (Realizing, going on)

No matter. And it was then that I saw her.

STEVIE (Grotesque incomprehension)

Who!?

MARTIN (Deeply sad)

Oh, Stevie . . .

STEVIE (Heavy irony)

Who!? Who could you have seen!?

MARTIN (Dogged)

I'm going on with this. You asked. I'm going to get it all out.

STEVIE *(Eyes hard on him)*
Serves *me* right, I guess.

MARTIN
And I closed the trunk of the car, with all that I'd gotten—
   (Pause)
. . . and it was then that I saw her. And she was looking at me with . . . with
those eyes.

STEVIE *(Staring at him)*
Oh, those eyes!
   (Afterthought)
THEM eyes!

MARTIN *(Slow; deliberate)*
And what I felt was . . . it was unlike anything I'd ever felt before. It was
so . . . amazing. There she was.

STEVIE *(Grotesque enthusiasm)*
Who!? Who!?

MARTIN
Don't. She was looking at me with those eyes of hers and . . . I melted, I
think. I think that's what I did: I melted.

STEVIE *(Hideous enthusiasm)*
You melted!!

MARTIN *(Waves her off)*
I'd never seen such an expression. It was pure . . . and trusting and . . . and
innocent; so . . . so guileless.

STEVIE *(Sardonic echo)*
Guileless; innocent; pure. You've never seen children, or anything? You
never saw Billy when he was a kid?

MARTIN *(Pleading)*
Of course I did. Don't *mock* me.

STEVIE *(Shooting harsh chuckle)*
Don't mock *me.*

MARTIN
I . . . I went over to where she was—to the fence where she was, and I
knelt there, eye level . . .

STEVIE *(Quiet loathing)*
Goat level.

MARTIN *(Angry; didactic)*
I will *finish* this! You *asked* for it, and you're going to *get* it! So . . . shut
your tragic mouth!

(STEVIE *does a sharp intake of breath, puts her fingers over her mouth*)

All right. Listen to me. It was as if an alien came out of whatever it was, and it . . . took me with it, and it was . . . an ecstasy and a purity, and a . . . love of a . . .

(*Dogmatic*)

un-i-mag-in-able kind, and it relates to nothing *whatever*, to nothing that can be *related* to! Don't you see!? Don't you see the . . . don't you see the "thing" that happened to me? What nobody understands? Why I can't feel what I'm supposed to!? Because it relates to nothing? It can't have happened! It did, but it *can't* have!

(STEVIE *shakes her head*)

What are you doing?

STEVIE (*Removes fingers*)

Being tragic. I bet a psychiatrist would love all this.

MARTIN

I knelt there, eye level, and there was a . . . a what!? . . . an understanding so intense, so natural . . .

STEVIE

There are some things you *can* remember, eh?

MARTIN

(*Closes his eyes, reopens them*)

. . . an understanding so . . .

STEVIE

(*Awful, high-pitched little voice*)

I can't remember why I come into rooms, where I put the thing for the razor . . .

MARTIN (*Refusing to be drawn in*)

. . . an understanding so natural, so intense that I will *never* forget it, as intense as the night you and I finally came at the same time. What was it . . . a month after we began?

(*Where is she, emotionally?*)

Stevie? It wasn't happening . . . but it *was!*

STEVIE

(*Shaking her head; oddly objective*)

How *much* do you hate me?

MARTIN (*Hopeless*)

I *love* you.

(*Pause*)

And I love *her*.

    (Pause)

And there it is.

    (STEVIE *howls three times, slowly, deliberately; a combination of rage and hurt)*

STEVIE (Then; calmly)

Go on.

MARTIN (Apologetic)

I have to do it.

STEVIE

Yes?

    (MARTIN *nods)*

Right.

MARTIN (Starting again)

And there was a connection there—a communication—that, well . . . an epiphany, I guess comes closest, and I knew what was going to happen.

STEVIE

    (Mildly interested in the fact)

I think I'm going to be sick.

MARTIN

Please don't.

    (Back to it)

Epiphany! And when it happens there's no retreating, no holding back. I put my hands through the wires of the fence and she came toward me, slipped her face between my hands, brought her nose to mine at the wires and . . . and nuzzled.

STEVIE

I am a grown woman; a grown married woman.

    (As if she's never heard the word before)

Nuzzled; nuzzled.

MARTIN

Her breath . . . her breath was . . . so sweet, warm and . . .

    (Hears something; stops)

STEVIE

Go on. Tell the grown-up married woman . . .

MARTIN (Warning hand up)

I hear Billy.

    (BILLY *enters)*

BILLY

Are you hitting her!?
   (*Sees the carnage*)
What the fuck!?

STEVIE

We're redecorating, honey. No, he's not, by the way—hitting me. I'm hitting myself.

BILLY (*Near tears*)

I hear you two! I'm up there and I *hear* you! STOP IT! JESUS GOD, STOP IT!!

MARTIN (*Gentle*)

We will, Billy; we're not quite done.

STEVIE

Go away, Billy. Go out and play.

BILLY

Go out and . . . ?

STEVIE (*Harder*)

Leave the house! Leave us alone!

BILLY

But . . .

MARTIN (*Calm*)

Do what your Mother says. "Go out and play." Make mudpies; climb a tree . . .

BILLY (*A finger in* MARTIN's *face*)

If I come back and find you've hurt her, I'll . . . I'll . . .
   (BILLY *lunges at* MARTIN, *shoves him, recoils.* MARTIN *steps forward, stops.* BILLY *sobs, runs from the room. We hear the front door slam*)

STEVIE (*After*)

Mudpies?

MARTIN

Well . . . whatever.

STEVIE (*Calm*)

What *will* you do if he comes back and finds you've hurt me? . . . *when* he comes back and finds you've hurt me?

MARTIN (*Absorbed in something*)

What?

STEVIE *(Smiles)*

Down from the trees, hands all muddy?
   (Sad)
Nothing.
   (Cold)
You were in the middle of your epiphany.

MARTIN *(Sighs)*

Yes.

STEVIE *(Sad)*

God, I wish you were stupid.

MARTIN *(He, too)*

Yes; I wish *you* were stupid, too.

STEVIE *(Pause; businesslike)*

Epiphany!

MARTIN

Yes. It was at that moment that I realized . . .

STEVIE

. . . that you and the fucking goat were destined for one another!

MARTIN

. . . that she and I were . . .
   (Softly; embarrassed)
that she and I were going to go to bed together.

STEVIE

To stall together! To hay! *Not* to bed!

MARTIN *(Sits)*

Whatever. That what could not happen was *going* to. That we wanted each
other very much, that I had to have her, that I . . .
   (STEVIE *screams—a deep-throated rage—and lunges at* MARTIN.
   He rises, grabs her wrists and shoves her into a chair. She attempts
   to get up, but he shoves her back again)
Now stop it! Let me finish!

STEVIE

You'll be fucking Billy next.

MARTIN *(Ice)*

He's not my type.

STEVIE *(Rising again. Rage)*

He's not your type!? He's not your fucking type!?

MARTIN

No; he's not.

(She is about to strike him)

You're my type.

(The shock of this stays her gesture; we see her confusion)

You're my type.

STEVIE (Stands where she is; hard)

Thank you!

MARTIN

You're welcome.

(A gesture)

Oh, Stevie, I . . .

STEVIE

I'm your type and so is she; so is the goat.

(Harder)

So long as it's female, eh? So long as it's got a cunt it's all right with you!

MARTIN (Huge)

A SOUL!! Don't you know the difference!? Not a cunt, a soul!

STEVIE (After a little; tears again)

You can't fuck a soul.

MARTIN

No; and it isn't about fucking.

STEVIE

YES!!

MARTIN (As gentle as possible)

No; no, Stevie, it isn't.

STEVIE (Pause; then, even more sure)

Yes! It is about fucking! It is about you being an animal!

MARTIN (Thinks a moment; quietly)

I thought I was.

STEVIE (Contempt)

Hunh!

MARTIN

I thought I was; I thought we all were . . . animals.

STEVIE (Cold rage)

We stay with our own kind!

MARTIN *(Gentle; rational)*
Oh, we fall in love with *many* other creatures . . . dogs and cats, and . . .

STEVIE
We don't *fuck* them! You're a monster!

MARTIN *(Pinning it down)*
I am a deeply troubled, greatly divided . . .

STEVIE *(No quarter)*
Animal fucker!

MARTIN
Sylvia and I . . .

STEVIE *(Hideous)*
You're going to tell me she *wants* you.

MARTIN *(Simply put)*
Yes.

STEVIE
What does she do—back into you making awful little bleating sounds?

MARTIN
That's sheep.

STEVIE
Whatever!! Presented herself? Down on her forelegs, her head turned, her eyes on you, her . . .

MARTIN
Stop it! I won't go into the specifics of our sex with you!

STEVIE *(Contempt)*
Thank you! You take advantage of this . . . creature!? You . . . *rape* this . . . animal and convince yourself that it has to do with love!?

MARTIN *(Helpless)*
I love her . . . and she loves me, and . . .

STEVIE
(A huge animal sound: rage; sweeps the bookcase of whatever is on it, or overturns a piece of furniture. Silence; then starting quietly, building)
Now, you listen to me. I have listened to you. I have heard you tell me how much you love me, how you've never even wanted another woman, how we have been a more perfect marriage than chance would even *allow*. We're both too bright for *most* of the shit. We see the deep and awful humor of things go over the heads of most people; we see what's hideously wrong in what most people accept as normal; we have both the joys and the sorrows

of all that. We have a straight line through life, right all the way to dying, but that's OK because it's a good line . . . so long as we don't screw up.

MARTIN

I know; I know.

STEVIE (*Don't interrupt me!*)

Shut up; so long as we don't screw up.

(*Points at him*)

And *you've* screwed *up!*

MARTIN

Stevie, I . . .

STEVIE

I said, shut up. Do you know *how* you've done it? How you've screwed up?

MARTIN (*Mumbled*)

Because I was at the vegetable stand one day, and I looked over to my right and I saw . . .

STEVIE (*Hard and slow*)

Because you've broken something and it can't be fixed!

MARTIN

Stevie . . .

STEVIE

Fall out of love with me? Fine! No, not fine, but that can be fixed . . . time . . . whatever! But tell me you love me and an animal—both of us!—equally? The same way? That you go from my bed—*our* bed . . .

(*Aside-ish*)

it's amazing, you know, how good we are, still, how we please each other *and* ourselves so . . . fully, so . . . fresh each time . . .

(*Aside over*)

. . . you go from our bed, wash your dick, get in your car and go to her, and do with her what I cannot imagine myself imagining? Or—worse! . . . that you've come *from* her, to *my* bed!? To *our* bed!? . . . and you do with me what I *can* imagine . . . love . . . *want* you for!?

MARTIN (*Deep sadness*)

Oh, Stevie . . .

STEVIE (*Not listening*)

That you can do these two things . . . and not understand how it . . . SHAT-TERS THE GLASS!!?? How it cannot be dealt with—how stop and forgiveness have nothing to do with it? and how *I* am destroyed? How *you* are? How I cannot admit it though I *know* it!? How I cannot deny it because I cannot *admit* it!? Cannot admit it, because it is outside of denying!?

MARTIN

Stevie, I . . . I promise you, I'll stop; I'll . . .

STEVIE

How stopping has nothing to do with having started?! How nothing has anything to do with anything!?

(Tears—if there—stop)

You have brought me down, you goat-fucker; you love of my life! You have brought me down to *nothing!*

(Accusatory finger right at him)

You have brought me down, and, Christ!, I'll bring you down with me!

(Brief pause; she turns on her heel, exits. We hear the front door slam.)

MARTIN

(After she leaves; after he hears the door; little boy)

Stevie?

(Pause)

Stevie?

CURTAIN

SCENE THREE

(*An hour or so later.* MARTIN *is sitting in the ruins. Maybe he is examining a broken piece of something. The room is as it was at the end of Scene Two. The front door slams;* BILLY *enters;* MARTIN *rises and stands in the middle of the room.*)

BILLY (*Looking around*)

Wow!

MARTIN (*Realizing* BILLY *is there*)

Yes; wow.

BILLY (*Seemingly casual*)

You guys really had it out, hunh.

MARTIN (*Subdued; almost laughing*)

Oh, yes.

BILLY

Where is she?

MARTIN

Hm? Who?

BILLY

(*Not friendly; overly articulated*)

My mother. Where is my mother?

MARTIN (*Mocking*)

Where is "my mother"? Not "Mother—where's mother?" Not that, but . . . "Where is my mother?"

BILLY (*Anger rising*)

Whatever! Where *is* she? Where is *my mother?*

MARTIN (*Arms out; helplessly*)

I . . . I . . .

BILLY *(Angrier)*

Where *is* she?! What did you do . . . kill her?

MARTIN *(Softly)*

Yes; I think so.

BILLY

(Dropping something he has picked up)
What!!?

MARTIN

(Quietly, with a restraining hand)
Stop. No. No, I did not kill her—of *course* not—but I think I might as well
have. I think we've killed each other.

BILLY *(Driving)*

Where *is* she!?

MARTIN *(Simply)*

I don't know.

BILLY

What do you mean you don't . . .

MARTIN *(Loud)*

She left!

BILLY

What do you mean she left? Where . . .

MARTIN *(Snappish)*

Stop asking me what I mean!
    (Quieter)
She said what she wanted to say; she finished . . . and she left. She slammed
the front door and left. I assume she drove somewhere.

BILLY

Yeah, the wagon's gone.
    (Harder)
Where *is* she!?

MARTIN *(Loud)*

She *left!* I don't know where she *is!* It's English! "She left." It's English. No,
I did not kill her, yes, I think I did, I think we killed each other. That's
English, too: one of your courses!

BILLY

(Is his rage close to tears? Probably)
I know who you *are.* I know you're my father. I know who you are, and I
know who you're supposed to be, but . . .

MARTIN

You, too?

BILLY

Hunh?

MARTIN

You don't know who I *am* anymore.

BILLY *(Flat)*

No.

MARTIN

Well . . . neither does your mother.

BILLY

(Trying to explain, but, still, rage underneath)
Parents fight; I know that; all kids know that. There are good times and rotten ones, and sometimes the blanket is pulled out from under you, and . . .

MARTIN *(Can't help saying it)*

You're mixing your metaphors.

BILLY *(Furious)*

What!?

MARTIN

Never mind; probably not the best time to bring it up. You were saying . . . "There are good times and rotten ones"?

BILLY

Yes.
    (Quick sarcasm)
Thanks.

MARTIN *(Noncommittal)*

Welcome.

BILLY

But sometimes the whatever is pulled out from under you.

MARTIN

Rug, I think.

BILLY

Right! Now shut the fuck up!
    (MARTIN opens his mouth, closes it. Spits out)
Semanticist!

MARTIN

Very good! Where did you learn that?

BILLY

I go to a good school. Remember?

MARTIN

Yes, but still . . .

BILLY

I said, shut the fuck up!

MARTIN *(Subsiding)*

Right.

BILLY

There are good times, and there are rotten ones. There are times we are so . . . deep in content, in happiness, that we think we'll probably drown in it but we won't mind. There are *some* of those—not too many. There are times we don't know what the fuck's going on—*to* us, *with* us, *about* us—and that's most of the time. I'm talking about us so-called adolescents.

MARTIN

I know.

BILLY

And then there are the times we wish we were old enough to . . . just walk out the door and start all over again, somewhere else—blank it all out.

MARTIN*(Quietly)*

And this?

BILLY *(Hard)*

One guess, you *fuck*!!
    (Huge)
What have you done with my *mother!!??*

MARTIN *(Calm)*

We finished our conversation
    (Gestures at ruined room)
—you see how we talk?—we finished our conversation, and she said a final . . . *thing,* and she left. She walked out, out the front door, slam.

BILLY

How long ago?

MARTIN *(Shrugs)*

An hour; maybe more; maybe two. I'm not very good at time and stuff right now.

BILLY

Two hours? And you haven't . . .

MARTIN *(A little angry himself)*
What!? Called the police?
(Awful imitation of distress)
"Oh, Officer, help me! My wife just found out I've been doing it with live-stock, and she's run off, and can you help me find her?" What!? Take off after her!? She's a grown woman; she could be having her hair done, for all I know.

BILLY *(Dogged)*
What did she *say* to you?

MARTIN *(Rueful chuckle)*
Oh . . . quite a few things.

BILLY *(Bigger)*
When she left! What did she say when she left!?

MARTIN
Something about . . . bringing me down—or whatever.

BILLY
Be specific.

MARTIN
Well, it's hard to be specific. We *were* busy after all, and . . .

BILLY *(Big)*
Exactly what she said, and *now!*

MARTIN *(Clears his throat)*
"You have brought me down, and . . . I will bring you down with me."

BILLY *(Puzzled; trying to get it)*
What does that *mean?*

MARTIN *(Almost sweet)*
No one's ever brought you down? No, I suppose not—not yet. It means . . .
(Fails)
it means what it says: that you have done to me what cannot be undone and . . . and you won't get away with it.
(BILLY stands for a moment and then spontaneously cries for a little, stops)

BILLY *(Wiping his eyes)*
I see.

MARTIN *(Further explanation)*
You destroy me—I destroy you.

BILLY
Yes; I see.

(Indicates wreckage)

Then there's no point in setting all this right.

MARTIN *(Sad chuckle)*

It does look pretty awful, *doesn't* it.

BILLY

Let's do it anyway.

MARTIN

Set the stage for the next round?

(Some self-pity and irony)

Hunh! *What* next round!? It's all behind me, isn't it?—everything? All hope . . . all . . . "salvation?"

(Fast litany)

Dead-end-rock-bottom-out-with-the-garbage-flushed-down-the-toilet-ground-up-spit-out-over-the-edge-with-heavy weights, down-down-sunk . . . whatever? All hope, everything? Gone? Right?

BILLY *(Shrugs)*

Whatever.

(BILLY begins to right a few things, not much; then quits)

What is it going to be then? Divorce?

MARTIN *(Simply)*

I don't know, Billy; I don't know that there are any rules for where we are.

BILLY

Beyond all the rules, eh?

MARTIN *(Some rue)*

I think so.

BILLY

I wouldn't know. I guess I've never been in love. *Yet*, I mean. Oh, lots of crushes, and all.

MARTIN

Only twice for me—your mother and . . . Sylvia.

BILLY

You're really holding onto this, *aren't* you.

MARTIN

To . . . ?

BILLY *(Sneering)*

This goat! This big love affair!

MARTIN *(Shrugs)*

It's true.

BILLY

Grow up!

MARTIN

Ah! Is *that* it!

(BILLY *laughs, in spite of himself.* MARTIN *tries to right a chair*)

Help me with this.

(BILLY *helps him*)

Thanks.

BILLY (*Shrugs*)

Any time.

(*Pause*)

They asked us at school—when? Last week, last month?—they asked each of us in this class to talk about how normal our lives were, how . . . how conventional it all was and how did we feel about it.

MARTIN

What kind of school *is* this!?

BILLY (*Shrugs*)

You chose it; you two chose it. And a lot of the guys got up and talked about—you know—our home lives, how our parents get on, and all; and it wasn't very special except the guys whose parents are divorced or one has died or gone crazy, or whatever.

MARTIN

Really? Crazy?

BILLY

Sure. Good private school. All guys, too; thanks. I mean, it was all about what you'd expect. Maybe everybody left all the juicy stuff out, or they didn't know it.

(*Picks up a shard*)

Where does this go?

MARTIN

Trash, I suspect.

BILLY (*Looks at it*)

Too bad.

(*Drops it*)

So, it was all pretty dull, pretty much what you'd expect.

MARTIN

I take it you haven't gotten up and spoken yet.

BILLY (*Noncommittal*)

Nope. Haven't.

(Waits a little)
You know what I'm going to tell them—when I get up there on my hind
legs?

MARTIN

(Winces) Do I *want* to know?

BILLY

Sure; you're a big guy.

MARTIN

I am diminished.

BILLY

Yeah? Well . . . whatever. I think what I'll tell them is this: that I've been
living with two people about as splendid as you can get; that if I'd been
born to other people, it couldn't have been any better.
      (MARTIN sighs heavily, puts a protesting hand up)
No; really; I mean it. You two guys are about as good as they come. You're
smart, and fair, and you have a sense of humor—both of you—and . . . and
you're Democrats. You *are* Democrats, aren't you?

MARTIN

More than *they* are, sometimes.

BILLY

That's what I thought, and you've figured out that raising a kid does *not*
include making him into a carbon copy of *you*, that you're letting me
think you're putting up with me being gay far better than you probably
really are.

MARTIN

Oh, now . . .

BILLY

Thank you, by the way.

MARTIN

It's the least.

BILLY *(Nodding)*

Right.

MARTIN *(Feigned surprise)*

You're *gay!?*

BILLY *(Smiles)*

Shut up. Anyway, you've let me have it better than a lot of kids, better than
a lot of "Moms and Dads" have, a lot closer to what being grown up will
look like—as far as I can tell. Good guidance; it's great to see how two people can love each other . . .

MARTIN

Don't!

BILLY

At least that's what I thought—until yesterday, until the shit hit the fan!

MARTIN

Billy, please don't.

BILLY (*Big crying underneath*)

. . . until the shit hit the fan, and the talk I was going to do at school became history.

(*Exaggerated*)

What will I say *now!?* Goodness me! The Good Ship Lollipop has gone and sunk.

(*More normal tone*)

What will I say!? Well, let's see: I came home yesterday and everything had been great—absolutely normal, therefore great. Great parents, great house, great trees, great cars—you know: the old "great."

(*Bigger now, more exaggerated*)

But then today I come home, and what do I *find?* I find my great Mom and my great Dad talking about a letter from great good friend Ross . . .

MARTIN (*Deep anger*)

Fuck Ross!!

BILLY

Yes? A letter from great good friend Ross written to great good Mom about how great good Dad has been out in the barnyard fucking animals!!

MARTIN

Don't . . . *do* this.

BILLY

Animals! Well, one in particular. A goat! A fucking goat! You see, guys, your stories are swell or whatever, but I've got one'll knock your socks off, as they used to say, wipe the tattoos right off your butts. Ya see, while great old Mom and great old Dad have been doing the great old parent thing, one of them has been underneath the house, down in the cellar, digging a pit so deep!, so wide!, so . . . HUGE! . . . we'll all fall in and

(*Crying now*)

and never . . . be . . . able . . . to . . . climb . . . out . . . again—no matter how much we want to, how hard we try. And you see, kids, fellow students, you see, I love these people. I love the man who's been down there digging—when he's not giving it to a goat! I love this man! I love him!

(*Drops whatever he's holding, moves to* MARTIN, *arms out*)

I love him!

(Wraps his arms around MARTIN, *who doesn't know what to do. Starts kissing* MARTIN *on the hands, then on the neck, crying all the while. Then it turns—or does it?—and he kisses* MARTIN *full on the mouth—a deep, sobbing, sexual kiss.* ROSS *has entered, stands watching.* MARTIN *tries to disengage from* BILLY, *but* BILLY *moans, holds on. Finally* MARTIN *shoves him away.* BILLY *stands there, still sobbing, arms around nothing. They have not seen* ROSS.*)*

MARTIN

Don't *do* that!!

BILLY

I *love* you!

MARTIN

Sure you do, you . . . you . . .

BILLY

Faggot? You faggot?

MARTIN *(Enraged)*

That's not what I was going to say!!

BILLY *(So sad; so sincere)*

Dad! I *love* you! Hold me! Please!

MARTIN *(Holds him; strokes him)*

Shhhhhh; shhhh; shhhhh now.

BILLY *(Disengaging finally)*

I'm sorry; I didn't mean to . . .

MARTIN

No; it's all right.
    (Arms out)
Here; let me hold you.
    *(*BILLY *moves to him again; a momentary silent embrace)*

ROSS

Excuse me.
    (They are startled, split. Maybe BILLY *stumbles over something.)*
I'm sorry; I didn't mean to interrupt your little . . .

MARTIN *(Cold fury)*

What!? See a man and his son kissing? That would go nicely in one of your fucking letters. Judas! Get out of here!

BILLY *(To* ROSS)*

It wasn't what you think!

MARTIN *(At* BILLY*)*

Yes! Yes, it was! Don't apologize.

(To ROSS*)*

Too bad you couldn't have brought your fucking TV crew over! Don't you and *your* son ever kiss? Don't you and—what's his name?—*Todd* love one another?

ROSS *(Hard; contemptuous)*

Not *that* way!

MARTIN *(Angry and reckless)*

That way!? *What* way!?

(Points vigorously at BILLY*)*

This boy is hurt! I've hurt him, and he still loves me! You fucker! He loves his father, and if it . . . clicks over and becomes—what?—sexual for . . . just a moment . . . so what!? So fucking what!? He's hurt and he's lonely and mind your own fucking business!

ROSS *(A sneer)*

You're sicker than I thought.

MARTIN

No! I'm hysterical!

BILLY *(Rueful wonder)*

It *did.* It clicked over, and you were just another . . .

MARTIN

It's all right.

BILLY

. . . another man. I get confused . . . sex and love; loving and . . .

(To ROSS*)*

I probably do want to sleep with him.

(Rueful laugh)

I want to sleep with everyone.

MARTIN *(To quiet him)*

It's all right.

BILLY *(Still to* ROSS*)*

Except you, probably.

ROSS

Jesus! Sick! What is it . . . contagious?

BILLY *(Confused)*

What? Is what?

MARTIN *(Moves over to comfort* BILLY*)*

There was a man told me once—a friend; we went to the same gym—he told me he had his kid on his lap one day—not even old enough to be a boy or a girl: a baby—and he had . . . *it* on his lap, and it was gurgling at him and making giggling sounds, and he had it with his arms around it,

(Demonstrates)

in his lap, shifting it a little from side to side to make it happier, to make it giggle more . . . and all at once he realized he was getting hard.

ROSS

Jesus!

BILLY

Oh my God . . .

MARTIN

. . . that the baby in his lap was making him hard—not arousing him; it wasn't sexual, but it was happening.

ROSS

Jesus!

MARTIN

. . . his dick was rising to the baby in his lap—his baby; his lap. And when he realized what was happening, he thought he would die; his pulse was going a mile a minute; his ears were ringing—loud! Very *loud!* And he was going to faint; he *knew* it, and then the moment passed, and he knew it had all been an accident, that it meant . . . nothing—that nothing was connected to anything else. His wife came in; she smiled; he smiled and handed her the baby. And that was it; it was over.

(Shrugs)

Things happen. Besides—I'm hysterical. Remember?

ROSS

What are you doing? *Defending* yourself?! Jesus. You're sick.

MARTIN *(Contempt)*

Do you have any other words? Sick and Jesus? Is that all you have?

BILLY *(Shy)*

Was it me? Was it me, Dad? Was the baby me?

MARTIN

(To BILLY; *after a pause; gently)*

Hush.

BILLY *(Almost frightened)*

Was it?

MARTIN *(Turning to* ROSS*)*
So, what do you want here now, motherfucker!? Judas!?

ROSS
Stevie called—what? An hour ago? More? She said you needed me; she said to come over.

MARTIN
I don't! Get out!
(Surprise)
She *called* you?

ROSS
Yes.
(Shakes his head)
Getting hard with a baby! Is there anything you people don't get off on!?

BILLY *(Once more)*
Was it, Dad?

MARTIN *(So clearly a lie; gently)*
Of course not, Billy.
(To ROSS; *hard, eyes narrowing)*
Is there anything "we people" don't get off on? Is there anything anyone doesn't get off on, whether we admit it or not—whether we *know* it or not? Remember Saint Sebastian with all the arrows shot into him? He probably came! God knows the faithful did! Shall I go on!? You want to hear about the cross!?

BILLY *(Quietly; smiling)*
No, of course it wasn't . . . wasn't me.

ROSS
(Shaking his head; sad, but with a lip curled)
Sick; sick; sick.

MARTIN *(At* ROSS; *growing rage)*
I'll tell you what's sick! Writing that fucking letter to Stevie—why doesn't matter!!—that's what's sick! I *tell* you about it; I share it with you, the . . . the . . . whole . . . awful . . . thing, because I think I've lost it, maybe; I *tell* you; I *share* it with you because you're . . . what!? . . . you're my best friend in the whole world? Because I needed to tell *somebody*, somebody with his head on straight enough to hear it? I *tell* you, and you fucking turn around and . . .

ROSS
I *had* to!!

MARTIN
No! You *didn't!* You didn't *have* to!

ROSS *(Dogmatic)*

I couldn't let you *continue*!

MARTIN *(Near tears)*

I could have worked it out. I could have stopped, and no one would have known. Except you, motherfucker. Mister one strike and you're out. I could have . . .

ROSS

No! You couldn't!

MARTIN

I could have worked it out! And now nothing can *ever* be put back together! *Ever*!

BILLY *(Trying to help)*

Dad . . .

MARTIN *(Savage)*

You shut up!

(BILLY *winces*. MARTIN *reacts*)

Oh, God! I'm sorry.

(To ROSS*)*

Yes; all right, it *was* sick, and yes, it *was* compulsive, and . . .

ROSS

IS! Not *was*! IS!

MARTIN *(Stopped in his tracks)*

I . . . I . . .

ROSS

IS!

MARTIN *(Gathering himself)*

Is. All right. *Is. Is* sick; *is* compulsive.

ROSS *(Pushing)*

And it was *wrong*!

MARTIN

It was . . . it was . . . what?

ROSS

Wrong! Deeply, destructively *wrong*!

MARTIN

Whatever you want.

(Rage growing)

But I could have handled it! You didn't have to bring it all down! You didn't have to destroy both of us; you didn't have to destroy Stevie, too!

ROSS

Me!? *Me* bring you down!? This isn't . . . embezzlement, honey; this isn't stealing from helpless widows; this isn't going to whores and coming down with the clap, or whatever, you know. This isn't the stuff that stops a career in its tracks for a little while—humiliation, public remorse, and then back up again. This is *beyond* that—*way* beyond it! You go on and you'll slip up one day. Somebody'll see you. Somebody'll surprise you one day, in whatever barn you put her in, no matter where you put her. Somebody'll see you, on your knees behind the damn animal; your pants around your ankles. Somebody will *catch* you at it.

BILLY

Let him alone. For God's sake, Ross . . .

ROSS *(Waving* BILLY *off; to* MARTIN*)*

Do you know there are prison terms for this? Some states they kill you for it? Do you know what they'd *do* to you. The press? Everybody? Down it all comes—your career; your life . . . everything.

(So cold; so rational)

For fucking a goat.

(Shakes his head sadly; BILLY *is weeping quietly)*

MARTIN *(Long pause)*

Is *that* what it is, then? That people will *know!?* That people will find *out!?* That I can do whatever I want, and that's what matters!? That people will find *out!?* Fuck the . . . thing it*self!?* Fuck what it *means!?* That people will find *out!?*

ROSS

Your soul is your own business. The rest I can *help* you with.

MARTIN

Of course it's my business, and clearly you don't have one.

ROSS *(Mild interest)*

Oh?

MARTIN

So that's what it comes down to, eh? . . . what we can get away with?

ROSS

Sure.

MARTIN *(Heavy irony)*

Oh, thank God! It's so simple! I thought it was . . . I thought it had to do with love and loss, and it's only about . . . getting *by*. Well, Stevie and I have been wrestling with the wrong angel! When she comes back—*if* she comes back—I'll have to set her straight about what matters.

(Intense; not looking at ROSS *or* BILLY; *pounding his hands on his knees perhaps)*

Does nobody understand what happened!?

ROSS

Oh, for Christ's sake, Martin!

BILLY

Dad . . .

MARTIN *(Crying a little)*

Why can't anyone understand this . . . that I am *alone* . . . all . . . *alone!*

(A silence. Then we hear a sound at the door.)

BILLY

Mom?

*(*BILLY *going into the hall. Gone)*

MARTIN *(Pause; to* ROSS, *begging)*

You *do* understand; *don't* you.

ROSS *(Long pause; shakes his head)*

No.

*(*STEVIE *is dragging a dead goat. The goat's throat is cut; the blood is down* STEVIE'*s dress, on her arms. She stops)*

Oh, my God.

MARTIN

What have you done!?

STEVIE

Here.

BILLY

(Generally; to no one; helpless; a quiet plea)

Help. Help.

ROSS

Oh, my God.

*(*MARTIN *moves toward* STEVIE*)*

MARTIN

What have you done!? Oh, my God, what have you *done*!?

*(*BILLY *is crying.* STEVIE *regards* MARTIN *for a moment;* ROSS *is immobile.)*

STEVIE

(Turns to face him; evenly, without emotion)

I went where Ross told me I would find . . . your friend. I found her. I killed her. I brought her here to you.

(Odd little question)

No?

MARTIN *(A profound cry)*

ANNNNNNH!

STEVIE

Why are you surprised? What did you expect me to do?

MARTIN *(Crying)*

What did she *do!?* What did she ever *do!?*

(To STEVIE*)*

I ask you: what did she ever *do*!?

STEVIE *(Pause; quietly)*

She loved you . . . you say. As much as *I* do.

MARTIN *(To* STEVIE; *empty)*

I'm sorry.

(To BILLY; *empty)*

I'm sorry.

(Then . . .)

I'm sorry.

BILLY

(To one, then the other; no reaction from them)

Dad? Mom?

(Tableau)

CURTAIN

Occupant

Occupant began preview performances on February 5, 2002, at the Signature Theatre (James Houghton, artistic director; Bruce E. Whitacre, managing director) in New York City. It was directed by Anthony Page; the set was by Christine Jones; the costumes were by Jane Greenwood; the lighting was by Pat Collins; the production state manager was Renee Lutz; the assistant stage manager was Tammy Scozzafava; casting was by Jerry Beaver and Associates, LTD; the press representative was The Publicity Office. The cast was as follows:

ANNE BANCROFT *as* LOUISE NEVELSON

NEAL HUFF *as* THE MAN

Due to illness, Anne Bancroft was not able to continue in her role as Lousie Nevelson, so the production never officially opened.

Occupant officially opened on June 5, 2008, at the Signature Theatre (James Houghton, artistic director; Beth Whitaker, associate artistic director; Erika Mallin, executive director; Adam Bernstein, general manager) in New York City. It was directed by Pam MacKinnon; the set was by Christine Jones; the costumes were by Jane Greenwood; the lighting was by David Lander; the production stage manager was Lloyd David, Jr.; the assistant stage manager was Chandra LaViolette; casting was by Will Cantler (Telsey & Co.); the press representative was Matt Ross (Boneau/Bryan-Brown). The cast was as follows:

MERCEDES RUEHL *as* LOUISE NEVELSON

LARRY BRYGGMAN *as* THE MAN

CHARACTERS

NEVELSON
much like the later photographs

THE MAN
40's; pleasant

THE SET

Two or three platforms stretching across the stage. Ultimately Nevelson's sculpture will fill edges, how and when to be determined. Very little else; maybe a bench. Tan carpet overall?

ACT ONE

(MAN *comes on stage*)

MAN

Good evening [or good day] Ladies and gentlemen . . .
   (*Indicating*)
the great American sculptor. . . . Louise Nevelson.
   (NEVELSON *enters, to applause*)

NEVELSON *(Improvising)*

Thank you; thank you; thank you; etc.
   (*Sees* MAN *is behaving oddly*)
You're nervous, dear?

MAN

A little bit. I've never interviewed someone who is dead before.

NEVELSON

Yeah? Well, I haven't *been* interviewed since I'm dead. So . . . we're both
nervous. We'll get through it.
   (*Indicates*)
Go on.

MAN

Louise Nevelson was born in . . .

NEVELSON

Wait; wait. People don't know who I am?

MAN

Hm?

NEVELSON

You have to introduce me? People don't know who I am? They look at me
up here like this and they don't say "Look, that's Louise Nevelson"?

MAN

Some; probably.

NEVELSON

Some! Look, dear, everybody knows who I am; everybody . . .

MAN

Did, maybe. Time passes. You're not as . . . recognizable now as you were.

NEVELSON

You're kidding!

MAN

No; time *passes*.

NEVELSON *(Arguing)*

People who know about art, who know about sculpture . . .

MAN

Yes! People who *knew* you *know* you.

NEVELSON

Everybody . . .

MAN

. . . who knows who you *were* knows who you *are*. I mean . . . who do you think you are? No offense.

NEVELSON

No, of course not. None taken. Is that what they say . . . none taken?

MAN

Yes, sometimes. I mean, people go to a museum, they look at your work, maybe, and maybe they know it's by you, but how many people go to museums? God, half the people in this country don't know who their *senators* are much less who does the sculpture they . . .

NEVELSON

All right! Nobody knows who I am! Fine! Let it alone!

MAN *(Placating)*

Everybody knows who you are if they know anything, but I bet I could go right outside and ask the first twenty people walking by, "Pardon me, who is Louise Nevelson?"

NEVELSON

All right!

MAN

. . . and maybe one will have heard of you. And try the wheatfields of Kansas, or wherever.

NEVELSON

I said . . . all right!

MAN

So: anybody who *knew* you *knows* you—and they know everybody else, too. They know Henry Moore, and Calder, and Stella and Bourgeois . . .

NEVELSON *(Feigned)*

Who?

MAN

Bourgeois; Louise Bourgeois.

NEVELSON *(Beat)*

Never heard of her.
    (Out)
Who is *she*?

MAN *(Laughs)*

Now, now!
    (Previous tone)
The people who know you know you. And I bet even then a lot more know what you look like than what you do—did.
    (Points to photo—which we see)
They know *that* a lot more than they know your work.

NEVELSON *(In)*

All right! So I'm invisible! Or I don't exist! Which do you want?

MAN *(Sighs)*

I just want to tell a few things.

NEVELSON *(Shrugs)*

So . . . go ahead.
    (Indicates audience)
Tell them.

MAN *(Mildly put out)*

Thank you.

NEVELSON *(Disbelief)*

More people know my picture than what I do . . . what I did?

MAN

You're a very famous image, Louise . . . you were. Time passes, you know.

NEVELSON

Tell me! What is it now?
    (She refers to present year)

MAN

Two thousand and eight
    (or whatever it is at performance)

NEVELSON

Shit! I'm dead seventeen

   (or whatever is correct)

years now and nobody knows who I am?

MAN

That's not what I said. What I said was . . .

NEVELSON *(Impatient)*

I know, I know, I know. I heard you. Nobody knows anything about anything except maybe one or two people. You might as well not exist—have
existed . . .

MAN *(Gently needling)*

Well, sure, if fame is the only thing that matters.

NEVELSON

Fuck you.

MAN *(Amused)*

Now, now.

NEVELSON

Not fame—recognition of what you've done that matters.

MAN

OK.

   (Out)

Louise Nevelson . . . great American sculptor.

   (In)

All right?

NEVELSON *(Shrugs)*

Sure.

MAN

I mean . . .

NEVELSON *(Speculating)*

Louise Nevelson. Yes, of course. What was the rest?

MAN

Great American Sculptor.

NEVELSON

Great? Well, you said it; I didn't.

MAN

What *is* this . . . false modesty?

NEVELSON *(Pique)*

I said you said it! *I* know who I am; *I* know how good my stuff is . . . but you never heard me call myself great. What I *think*—what I *know*—and what I *say* about what I *think*—what I *know* . . .

MAN

All right! All right!

NEVELSON

There was a long time people said what I did was crap.

MAN

I know.

NEVELSON

So, I kept on doing it and finally they came around—some of them did, most of them; maybe not the Berg boys . . .

MAN *(Out)*

The Berg boys—Greenberg and Rosenberg. Clement Greenberg and Harold Rosenberg, the two most important art critics in town. Tastemakers; dictators.

NEVELSON

Right; not those two, but most of them came around—eventually. They came around, but *I* never said it in public: "I am the great Louise Nevelson." No matter *what* I thought.

MAN *(Laughs. In)*

OK! OK! Any arguments? Is "great" OK?

NEVELSON *(Shrugs)*

Naaaaaah; it's OK. What was the rest . . . American? American sculptor? American? Sure, when I was what—twenty, twenty-one? I was Russian.

MAN

No, no; you came over when you were six, and so . . .

NEVELSON

Four and a half.

MAN

Six. Six, to be exact.

NEVELSON

Four and a half!

MAN

No.

NEVELSON

You'd think I'd know.

MAN

Yes; one would. You were six.

NEVELSON *(Grudging)*

Sooooooo . . . maybe I was six, but I didn't become a citizen until . . .

MAN *(Heavy sigh)*

. . . until you got married. OK!

NEVELSON

I was born in Russia!

MAN

. . . and you came over here when you were six! You're American!

NEVELSON

I was born in Kiev.

MAN

No, you weren't.

NEVELSON

No?

MAN

No: Jews weren't allowed in Kiev. You were born *near* Kiev.

NEVELSON

So?

MAN

So.

NEVELSON

So, I was Russian—for all the good it did.

MAN

Let's drop it.

NEVELSON

OK.

MAN

Do facts *mean* anything to you?

NEVELSON *(Shrugs)*

They can be useful.
    (Out)
No?

MAN

Anyway . . . sculptor: great American sculptor? Is that OK? Sculptor?

NEVELSON *(In)*

What else! Of course: sculptor. What else is there?

MAN (*Settling it*)

Louise Nevelson—great American sculptor.

NEVELSON

Fine; good. Great American sculptor. Good.
  (*Pause*)
You know, dear, if you're born someplace and you don't feel *right* there . . .

MAN (*Helping*)

. . . . Near Kiev? Jewish? Pogroms?

NEVELSON

Whatever. And you come over here . . .

MAN

Rockland, Maine . . .

NEVELSON

 . . . whatever, and you don't feel right there either, and you move to New York City when you get married, and you don't feel right there *either*—with *anything*—what do you do?
  (*Out*)
What do you *do*? You don't fit in—so you make everything fit to you. That's what you do.
  (*In*)
That's what you do.

MAN

Yes.

NEVELSON

That's what you do.

MAN

I know.
  (*Out*)
Leah Berliawsky—shtetl, near Kiev, 1899. Father Isaac, Mother Minna Zeisel Smolerank.

NEVELSON (*To herself, primarily*)

What a marvelous name: Minna, Zeisel, Smolerank.
  (*To* MAN)
She didn't want to marry him, you know—my mother. He scared her; he was older; she was fifteen.

MAN

Sixteen.

NEVELSON

Whatever! Whatever makes the most sense.

MAN

The best story?

NEVELSON *(Out)*

Ignore him. He scared her; he pursued her, she couldn't get away from him. So . . . she married him.

MAN *(In)*

What a nice story.

NEVELSON

Thank you.

MAN

You want us to believe it?

NEVELSON *(Shrugs)*

Suit yourself.

MAN

I bet she liked him . . . good-looking guy. I bet she wanted to marry him all along.

NEVELSON *(In)*

Don't be too sure. We don't always do what we do because we know what we're doing. Or we do know what we're doing, but it's for other reasons.

MAN *(Broad)*

Could you possibly be talking about your *own* marriage?

NEVELSON

If the shoe fits . . . .
     (Afterthought)
Wait, if the shoe fits, you should probably get a larger size—or a smaller one. I don't remember.

MAN

Whichever.

NEVELSON

Whichever.
     (Out)
Which is it?—smaller? larger?

MAN

The saying is . . . if the shoe fits, wear it.

NEVELSON *(Pause; suspicious)*

What are you *after*?

MAN

Hm?

NEVELSON

What are you . . . doing?

MAN

I don't . . .

NEVELSON

You're after something.

MAN (*Genuine*)

You. I'm after you.

NEVELSON (*Smiles*)

Yeah? Who's *that*? Who am *I*? I'm a lot of people, honey, and I shift all the time. You got a tough row to hoe, mister. Is that the expression?

MAN

Yes.

NEVELSON

And what does it mean? What tough row?

MAN

You're vamping.

NEVELSON

I'm what?

MAN

You're avoiding me.

NEVELSON

Maybe I don't like what you're doing—what you're after.

MAN

You're so . . . .
    (*Dismissive gesture*)
never mind.
    (*New attack*)
Russian! You say you're Russian!? You never even *spoke* Russian!

NEVELSON

We spoke Yiddish.

MAN

Yes!

NEVELSON (*Not too pleasant*)

We were Jews; we lived in a shtetl! It was Russia; we were Jews!

MAN

Yes, and so everybody kept leaving—everybody who could! Your father, his brothers . . .

NEVELSON

Of course! America, the land of . . . whatever . . . We spoke Yiddish; we were Jews. We couldn't even own land in Russia. Why would we speak Russian? .

MAN (*A little dubious*)

And it was better in *Maine*, in Rockland, *Maine*? Down into Maine from Canada? Your father—him and his brothers? Why not New York?

NEVELSON

Anywhere, probably; anywhere you could get. He sent money for us, finally —for my mother and the rest of us; he saved up; he sent us passage.

MAN

Is it true that when he left you all to go to America you were so upset you wouldn't speak at all for over a year?

NEVELSON

Where did you hear that!? Maybe; maybe not. Couldn't, not wouldn't; I was abandoned.

MAN

With your whole family around you? . . . your mother, your sister, your brother? You say you were . . .

NEVELSON

He left! He left us! He was the one I talked to!

MAN

Yes? Really? You missed him that much, eh? You, three years old, or four, or whatever?

NEVELSON

Well . . . something. I am a very shy woman, you know.

(*Out*)

I am; I'm very shy.

MAN (*Scoffing*)

Yeah; sure.

NEVELSON (*Quiet*)

You don't know anything.

(*Out*)

He doesn't know anything.

MAN (*Hand up, in surrender*)

All right; you're very shy. So you got to Maine . . .

NEVELSON

So we got to Maine, and there were maybe three families—all Jews, and the rest were—what did they call them?—Yankees?

MAN

Yes: Yankees. More persecution.

NEVELSON

Hm? Well, yeah; some; a little
    (*Out*)
I mean, you live all huddled together; you don't speak English; you feel strange; maybe that makes you a stranger—you feel like one. But you go on, and you —what is the word?— you assimilate. You try to assimilate. You learn English; you go to school; you huddle together, but you reach out.

MAN

To the Yankees? You reach out to the Yankees?

NEVELSON (*In*)

To whatever's out there. You know you'll never fit in; you know you'll always be a . . . an exotic, is that the word?— but you go ahead as if you didn't know that. You get ahead. You help your parents and you get ahead.

MAN

Your father makes out pretty well—furniture and stuff. What's the joke . . . we buy junk; we sell antiques?

NEVELSON (*Sour*)

Yes? Is that the joke? I don't know.

MAN

And he buys land . . .

NEVELSON (*More enthusiastic*)

Yes! He bought land. Just think of that! A Jew could buy land in Rockland, Maine. He worked himself up.

MAN

And on top of that . . .

NEVELSON (*Angry*)

Why do we have to go through all this!? We were poor; we were cold; we didn't have glass in the windows! We pulled ourselves up. My father made the most of it—the most of everything. He worked his ass off. He threw me in the ocean to make me swim! He was like that—whatever he *did* he *did*. We assimilated. Nachman became Nathan, Chaya became Anita, and I became Louise.

MAN

Leah to Louise.

NEVELSON

But we never changed our last name! Berliawsky; that stayed! What were we supposed to become—Berkley, or something? No! We were proud! My mother dressed us up when we went out walking, or to school, whenever we went out. She put me in wonderful clothes; she found them; she made them. I loved them. People would stare at me as I walked to school: who's that princess? I was regal, and I was extravagant. So, my mother was a little crazy the way she got us up but, by God, people knew we were there!

MAN

Which has something to do with the way you dress now?

NEVELSON

What! You think I dress funny? I dress like *me*. I always *did*; I always *have*.

MAN *(Apologetic)*

I know; I know.

NEVELSON

People look at us; they see what we show them. I dress like *me*, so that's what they see—*me*.

MAN

You're how you dress?

NEVELSON

I'm the total of everything I do.

MAN *(To pin it down)*

You dress to be noticed.

NEVELSON *(Sarcasm)*

No; I dress to be invisible! Of course I dress to be noticed. I expect people to *look* at me—at *me* and what I *do*!

MAN

They're the same thing?

NEVELSON *(Out)*

Who is this guy!? You understand, no?

(In)

They understand.

MAN

Yes, I do, too. I want to be sure you do.

NEVELSON *(Instead of replying)*

I gotta go pee.

(Exits)

MAN *(Stands)*

It's just that . . . .

(Watching her go)

It's just that she's a very complicated woman. What's the old joke . . . true if interesting? And what did Blanche Dubois in *Streetcar* say . . . I tell what ought to be true? Or is it she forgets? Or maybe she doesn't care? I think it's a little bit of each, and maybe true isn't what we're after, or maybe true is what applies. As I say, she's a very complicated woman. But . . . life is pretty complicated, too. You know, there's a lot written about her. There were a lot of stories and interviews stretching over a long time, and things shifted: a lot of contradictions, a lot of evasions, a lot of . . . careful misrememberings, a lot of scores being settled, and a lot of . . . well . . . outright lies.

NEVELSON *(Re-entering)*

I heard that.

MAN *(Mouth open in astonishment)*

You weren't peeing at all.

NEVELSON

No?

MAN

No, you were listening!

NEVELSON

So?

MAN

How much did you hear?

NEVELSON

Enough; some.

MAN

Sorry.

NEVELSON

A lot of outright *lies*?

MAN

Well . . .

NEVELSON

Listen, dear; tell me something . . . who *am* I?

MAN

Hm?

NEVELSON

What was my name . . . when I was born?

MAN

Leah Berliawsky.

NEVELSON

And . . . ?

MAN

. . . and you became Louise Nevelson.

NEVELSON *(Nods)*

OK. With any luck you turn into whoever you want to *be*, and with even *better* luck you turn into whoever you *should* be. No, you got somebody in you right from the start, and if you're lucky you figure out who it is and you *become* it. People who don't *become* are . . . well, look around you. So, don't talk to me about facts.

MAN

But there *are* facts, and . . .

NEVELSON

. . . and *most* of them are *OK*.

MAN

Oh. So . . . you always knew you were going to become Louise Nevelson.

NEVELSON

Don't be stupid! I knew I was going to become somebody very special. No . . . that I *was* somebody very special.

MAN

But you didn't know then that . . .

NEVELSON

. . . but I had no idea what it *was*—what the special *was*—just that it *was*. I had to grow into it, I guess. If I'd known when I was a little girl that one day . . .

MAN

But you started drawing! You were just a kid!

NEVELSON *(Derisive wave)*

Nyyaah! All kids draw; all kids are creative—naturally—even the dumb ones.

MAN

But you've bragged about how you started drawing when you . . .

NEVELSON

Bragged!?

MAN

Mentioned; talked about it.

NEVELSON

I did hunh?

(Shrugs)

So? Maybe I did.

MAN

And . . . so . . . ?

NEVELSON

And so nothing. What did *I* know? That was a long time ago. I took piano lessons, too. I took singing lessons.

(A sudden remembrance)

Oh! Did I ever tell you that when I was a little baby—maybe a month old—the great Sholom Aleichem—his sister lived next to my parents—he came to see us. And . . .

(Indicates audience)

Does anybody here know who he is, who he was?

MAN (Out)

Great Yiddish writer; Russian.

(In)

Yes, I think so.

NEVELSON

He came to visit, this was in Russia, and he took me up in his hands and he said to my family that I was destined for greatness—a baby; a little baby.

MAN

Built for greatness was the way I heard it. Built.

NEVELSON

Built? Destined? So?

MAN

There's a difference, maybe.

NEVELSON (Cool)

Translation, probably.

(Effusive; gesturing)

The great Sholom Aleichem, holding me aloft! "Destined for greatness."

MAN (Shakes his head; grudgingly)

That's pretty impressive.

NEVELSON

You're damn right!

MAN (Slight smile)

True if interesting?

NEVELSON *(Sharp)*

What!?

MAN

Nothing. When did you decide?

NEVELSON

What?

MAN

That you were an artist.

NEVELSON

I don't think that way.

MAN

Oh, come on!

NEVELSON

I don't!

MAN

One of your biographies says when you were nine you knew . . .

NEVELSON *(Dismissive)*

Oh, that! That we kids were in the library and some librarian or teacher or something asked us what we wanted to be when we grew up and I suddenly said, "I'm going to be a sculptor"? And it frightened me and I started crying and ran home? That one?

MAN *(Smiles)*

Yeah; that one.

NEVELSON

I wonder if that happened, or I dreamed it? I mean I always knew I was different, that I was . . . special, but special doesn't always mean happy, or talented or . . . or whatever. Special can be one eye in the center of your forehead.

MAN

Cyclops.

NEVELSON

Hm? What? Special is . . . special, and I always knew that.

MAN *(Holds up invisible baby)*

"Destined for greatness."

NEVELSON

Yeah, but with two eyes and two ears and one mouth and all the rest; normal, except . . . different. And let me tell you, there wasn't much time to figure it all out. We were poor, and we had to raise ourselves!

MAN

Yeah, and your family did pretty well.

NEVELSON

My father worked his ass off, and we all helped, and . . .

MAN

. . . and by the time you were fifteen he owned half of Rockland.

NEVELSON *(Laughs)*

Not quite. Fifty-one parcels of property. Fifty-one! Isn't that something? The immigrant Jew from the Ukraine?

MAN

Pretty impressive. Is there any truth to the story your father wanted to buy a fine house for you all to live in, and you went with him to look at it, and you were sixteen, maybe, and you told him it was too fine? That it embarrassed you?

NEVELSON *(Thinks)*

Maybe; vaguely. That it was wrong—for us, probably; for me. It was . . . oppressive? Overwhelming? I've never wanted anything to *own* me—or *any*one. I've never wanted to *belong* to anything—or any*one*, I guess.

MAN

. . . which brings us to the subject of your marriage, I would imagine.

NEVELSON

So soon?

MAN

Yes.

NEVELSON *(Sad)*

So soon.

MAN

Do you want to tell it, or shall I?

NEVELSON

You can start . . .

MAN

And if what I know doesn't jibe with . . .

NEVELSON

Just get on with it.

MAN

OK.

NEVELSON

If I don't like the way it's going I'll fix it.

MAN

I bet you will.

(Small pause)

OK. So. You turned into a real beautiful young lady, didn't you.

NEVELSON *(Factual)*

Unh-hunh.

MAN

. . . tall, great figure, great face . . .

NEVELSON

Unh-hunh. Yep, for all the good it did. I was still a Jew from Russia. You think the other girls at school had me to their parties? Not on your life!

MAN

It was probably their parents.

NEVELSON

Maybe, but I didn't have many friends.
   (Chuckles)
Here's a funny story! I was tall, as you say, and not bad looking, and my skin wasn't that pasty white so many of the girls had—what you could see through the acne—it was darker, and clear, and . . . healthy-looking. And, one day, one of the mothers was walking her daughter to school came up to me and ran her thumb over my cheek—to see if I had makeup on! But I didn't; it was just me . . . healthy-looking and . . . different . . . They didn't want me around. I was invited to one party once—they had to—it was at some home, for the basketball team, and I was captain because I was so tall, and I got so nervous—being invited—that I pee'd in my pants right there.

MAN

Jesus! Did you date . . . at all?

NEVELSON *(Scoffing)*

Hanh! Are you kidding? One of the boys at school—he was a basketball player; so was I, remember? I was tall, and athletic?—the teacher at school, the coach, maybe, told him to take me to something—a prom? I don't remember—and he said, "I don't want to take that Jew," and he wouldn't.
   (MAN shakes his head)
So; no, it wasn't too happy a time. I mean, I had my family, my sisters, and my brother and . . .

MAN

The nest.

NEVELSON

Yeah; the nest.

MAN *(Casual)*
But sooner or later birds leave the nest? Or get pushed out?

NEVELSON
Sure. Plus—didn't I tell you this?—feeling special and all I was . . .
impatient, I guess. There was a big world out there; so why was I doing
all the stuff I was doing—the art lessons, the singing lessons, the piano
lessons—and I was good at all of them . . . very good . . . all the—what
is it called?—the extra-curricular stuff ever since I was little, if it wasn't
supposed to . . . turn into something. *Mean* something.

MAN
Lots of kids do art and stuff, but it doesn't do anything to their lives.

NEVELSON
Sure, but it doesn't make everyone feel . . . that *special*, as special as *I* did.

MAN
"Destined for greatness."

NEVELSON
Something! I guess I knew I had to . . . move on.

MAN
And away.

NEVELSON *(Defensive)*
I loved my family!

MAN
Sure.

NEVELSON
I mean, my mother was sick a lot—disturbed, you know?—but we all loved
each other. My father scared me a little, but we all loved each other. We'd
been through so much.

MAN
But there was moving on to do.

NEVELSON *(Definition)*
There was getting to where you were supposed to be—wherever that was.

MAN
There was moving *on* . . . and there was moving *up*.

NEVELSON
What?

MAN
Up. Moving *up.*

NEVELSON
Well, yeah; sure. You better yourself.

MAN

I've read that not all marriages in the old world, as they call it, that not all marriages were based entirely on love.

NEVELSON *(Noncommittal)*

Oh?

MAN

Yeah, that sometimes sons and daughters married as a kind of moving up in the world.

NEVELSON *(Ibid.)*

Yeah?

MAN

Yeah, that a lot of marriages were—how shall I put it?—business arrangements.

NEVELSON *(Ibid.)*

Yeah; I've heard that.

MAN

So; so, Miss Berliawsky, tell me about the Nevelson family.

NEVELSON

Don't be funny.

MAN *(Smiles)*

Sorry. So, *tell* me about them; tell me about all of *that*.

NEVELSON

"All of that"?

MAN

Engagement; leaving home; marriage; a son; disenchantment.

NEVELSON

I don't want to talk about it.

MAN

Yes, but . . .

NEVELSON

I said, I don't want to talk about it! It's too important.

MAN

You have to!

NEVELSON

"I have to"!?
(Out)
Did you hear this? I have to talk about it?

MAN (*Consults notes*)

Let me see; you were nineteen, I think.

NEVELSON (*Out*)

Pay no attention to him.

MAN (*Out; notes*)

In nineteen-seventeen Louise Berliawsky met Bernard Nevelson, a Lithuanian Jew, born in Latvia, in eighteen . . .

NEVELSON (*In; angry*)

All right! I'll *tell* it! *I'll* tell it. *I'll* do it. What are we going to do—talk about everything? Every fucking thing!?

MAN (*Shrugs*)

Only what matters.

NEVELSON

Everything matters!

MAN

And so . . .

NEVELSON (*Softer*)

Let me do it.

MAN

Do it.

NEVELSON (*Quiet*)

All right.
    (*Out*)

I'll tell it my way . . . so you'll understand. I'd finished school, and I was doing some—what do they call it?—*temp* work at an office—a lawyer's office.

MAN (*Out; an aside*)

Legal stenographer.
    (*Sotto voce*)

She actually managed to graduate from school.

NEVELSON (*To* MAN)

Shut up!

MAN (*False*)

Sorry.

NEVELSON

Jesus!
    (*Out*)

Legal stenographer; all right, but temp work, just to keep busy, to bring in

a little money—for myself. And one day, a man walked into the office—a
client, probably.

(*In*)

A client?

MAN

Oh, I'm allowed to talk?

NEVELSON

Forget it.

(*Out*)

This man walked in—fifty maybe; tall; thin; a little balding, and for some
reason I knew he was a Jew; I knew he wasn't from "around"; and he
walked in, and I spoke to him in Yiddish, right away, just like that! In
Yiddish! And I was right; he was a Jew, a Lithuanian Jew, and was in the
shipping business—he had ships. I don't know why I knew he was Jewish,
but I *know* things. I have insights and I trust them. I liked this man; I was
shy, but I felt OK with him. He was—what?—fifty? There was a kind of . . .
electricity? . . . between us? I liked him. He invited me to have dinner with
him that night, at the hotel he was staying at . . . .

(*In*)

The Thorndyke, was it?

MAN

Yes.

NEVELSON

Thanks.

(*Out*)

. . . along with a sea captain he had with him—for one of his ships, I think.
I told you I was shy, and here was this older man—and I'd never been in
a hotel in my life, and what if he pirated me away on one of his ships!

MAN

How naive *were* you!?

NEVELSON (*In; hard*)

Very!

MAN

How did your family feel about this—you going to dinner. You *told* them.

NEVELSON (*In*)

I'm telling it!

(*Out*)

They seemed to think it was OK. He was older; he was a businessman.

(*In*)

I think they checked with the lawyer—where I was . . . whatever.

MAN *(Out)*

Pretty quick work.

NEVELSON *(In; sharp)*

What!?

MAN

Go on. So what was this . . . your first date?

NEVELSON

It wasn't a date; it was a . . . social engagement.

MAN *(Smiles; out)*

Oh!

NEVELSON *(Out; waving him off)*

It was a social engagement, and it was nice, and the food was great—a little greasy, maybe, but good—and it was a hotel—china and mirrors—and I was all dressed up and it was wonderful . . .

(In)

I guess it was my first time being a grownup. He walked back home with me, and he said hello to my family.

(Out)

And the next day I was told he'd left—went back to New York. And then he started writing me, writing me letters, about his family, about his brothers, about his business—his ships—about being married, and he and his wife were planning to have their first baby—that they hadn't wanted kids at first, but now they were thinking about it! He wrote me these letters, but I didn't answer them, because I was suspicious, in spite of all he said, because I'd read about those things, about robber barons having young mistresses, and so forth, and I wasn't about to get into that kind of life. So, I didn't answer his letters.

MAN *(To NEVELSON)*

And maybe in part because you could barely spell. Some education!

NEVELSON *(Out)*

And maybe because I was ashamed of my spelling.

(In)

YES!

(Out)

So, I didn't answer his letters, but about a year after I'd had dinner and all with Bernard, I got a letter from him saying his youngest brother was coming to Rockland on business—for the family—and would I like to meet him.

MAN

And your whole life changed.

NEVELSON *(In)*

Yes, and my whole life changed.

(Out)

My whole life changed.

MAN *(Nicely)*

Tell about it.

NEVELSON *(To herself, really)*

It's very weird.

MAN

I know.

NEVELSON *(Out)*

You don't know how weird. Here's what's weird, what's so weird. When he got to Rockland—the brother, Charles, did—he called us—on the phone! we had one!—and said could I have dinner with him. My mother answered; I wasn't home. I got home and my mother told me the brother had called, and I knew . . . and I knew that I would—that I would marry him.

MAN *(Out)*

Charles Nevelson, thirty-seven years old, five foot *four?*

(To NEVELSON*)*

He really looked up to you, eh?

NEVELSON

I said, don't be funny.

MAN *(Out)*

Five foot four, stocky, thirty seven years old, under his brother's thumb.

(In)

Why *ever* did you marry him?

NEVELSON *(In)*

I don't know; I just knew I would. Sometimes you know things. It was all wanted—my family, Bernard; I could tell that. They all wanted it,

(Shrugs)

so I guess I wanted it, too.

MAN

Oh, come on! You? Miss Free Spirit?

NEVELSON *(In and out; uncomfortable)*

I guess it was a kind of a . . . a way up, a way out. I've *told* you; I'm very intuitive. Something comes up like that—I realize I've already decided without knowing I'd done it. It all came together—all the reasons—and I *knew.* I *knew* he would ask me to marry him, and I knew I would.

MAN

Marriage at first sight. Amazing. Right there at dinner.

NEVELSON

It was that simple.
  (*Out*)
It was . . . that simple.

MAN (*Not pleasant*)

That . . . simple.

NEVELSON (*In*)

Well . . . whatever.

MAN (*Ibid.*)

A way out? A way up?

NEVELSON

Sure.

MAN (*Pinning it down*)

So you had dinner with him—this stranger. At the same hotel?

NEVELSON

I think so; maybe; I don't know.

MAN (*Puzzled*)

And so . . . you had dinner with this . . . short, plumpish, balding man almost twice as old as you, and he asked you to marry him and you said yes.

NEVELSON

Yes.

MAN

Before dessert?

NEVELSON (*A little dreamlike*)

What? No; during.

MAN

And you said yes.

NEVELSON

Yes.

MAN

. . . even though it was Bernard you were attracted to.

NEVELSON (*Annoyed*)

We *did* that. He was *married*.

MAN

Still, you said yes.

NEVELSON *(Fact)*

Yes.

MAN *(Wanting to disbelieve)*

What did you see in him—in this Charles?

NEVELSON *(Pause)*

A passport, I guess.

(*Out; intense*)

You, understand, no? A way out . . . up? We were immigrants; I wasn't even a citizen, and here was this rich Nevelson family deciding I belonged with *them*—that they wanted me to be part of *their* life . . . in New York!

MAN *(Pause)*

Well, maybe it was simple.

NEVELSON *(In; intense)*

Were you around in nineteen-twenty?

MAN

No.

NEVELSON

Were you ever an immigrant?

MAN

No.

NEVELSON

Were you ever a Jew?

MAN

No.

NEVELSON

Were you ever a girl?

MAN

No; of course not.

NEVELSON

Then don't talk to me about simple. There were lots of reasons, and they all

(*Gestures*)

. . . intertwined.

(*Out*)

He doesn't *understand* anything.

MAN *(A little sarcastic)*

Right! You were suffering up there in Rockland, and . . .

NEVELSON (*In*)

Not suffering, for Christ's sake! It was all right, I guess, for most people, but I was . . .

(*Gently*)

I was very special.

MAN

And your family probably wanted it.

NEVELSON (*A little sad*)

Sure; they wanted it.

MAN

Too?

NEVELSON (*A beat*)

Too.

MAN

And so your whole life changed.

NEVELSON

Yes; and so my whole life changed.

(*Long pause*)

Into a pile of shit.

MAN (*Awe*)

Wow!

NEVELSON

Hm?

MAN

Wow.

NEVELSON (*Apologetic*)

Slowly; not at first. Why, do you find that too dramatic?

MAN

No; pretty good, but, still . . . wow!

NEVELSON

Thanks.

MAN (*Ironic*)

Out and up, and into a pile of shit?

NEVELSON

Yeah, well. Things are seldom what they seem.

MAN

And skim milk masquerades as cream?

NEVELSON

Right; but later. We didn't get married right away. You didn't in those days.
I was engaged for over a year.

MAN

I take it you two . . . "kept your distance"?

NEVELSON

What does that mean?
    (*Out*)
What does that mean?

MAN

I'm talking about . . . sex.

NEVELSON (*In*)

Well, don't!

MAN

I mean . . .

NEVELSON

Back in those days every girl who got married was a virgin—went to the
altar intact.

MAN

Yes, but . . .

NEVELSON

. . . whether they were or not.

MAN

Oh, I see!

NEVELSON

NO, you *don't*! You *don't* see.
    (*Pause*)
All right; yes; I was.
    (*Out*)
I *was*. It was how I was raised; it was how I was brought up.

MAN

Thank you.

NEVELSON

You're welcome.

MAN

It's nice to get something cleared up.

NEVELSON (*Chuckles*)

Oh, now. He brought me and my mother to New York—Charles did—and he showed us around the city. He brought us there for several weeks, and he took us everywhere, the whole family did—you know, we'd never been there, my mother or me—and it was so . . . opening.

(*Out*)

I mean, the great buildings, the stores, the places people lived, the concerts, the museums, the opera—and the Statue of Liberty! The water, and the sky, and this wonderful, oversized thing! It looked like she reached to heaven!

(*In*)

All the way to heaven.

MAN (*Smiles*)

You liked it, eh? New York?

NEVELSON

It was . . . well, it was everything I'd *thought* it would be. It was where I belonged, and I *knew* it.

(*Out*)

No matter what! It was where I had to be. I moved there and I lived there . . . forever. I saw Europe later and it was wonderful, but New York . . .

(*Shakes her head*)

that was *it*!

(*In*)

That really was *it*!

MAN

Great.

(*Urging on*)

And so eventually you got married.

NEVELSON (*Laughs*)

In Boston, at the Copley Plaza.

(*Out*)

Halfway between New York and Rockland. I figured everyone could go halfway. And I wore a wonderful lace dress—down to my ankles—and a huge pink hat!

MAN

You must have looked great!

NEVELSON (*In*)

Yes; I looked great. I think it was the pink hat.

MAN

Wasn't there some problem with the engagement ring?

NEVELSON

Well . . . in a way, yeah.

MAN

You didn't like it?

NEVELSON *(Shrugs)*

It was a perfectly nice one carat diamond ring, bought at good store.

MAN

So?

NEVELSON

So . . . the Nevelsons had a lot of money and I wasn't a tiny little thing. You could barely see it! I mean . . . big girl, big ring.

MAN *(Agreeing)*

Everything in proportion.

NEVELSON

Exactly! Everything in proportion. But the big rich Nevelson family had the feeling that ostentation was vulgar, or something. Still!

MAN

Still!

NEVELSON *(Out)*

And it wasn't I wanted a big ring—to show off, or whatever. I don't wear rings and stuff. It was the . . . principle.

MAN

Yes.

NEVELSON *(Under her breath)*

Cheap little . . .

MAN

What!?

NEVELSON *(In)*

Ring! Cheap little *ring*. That *still* burns me up.

MAN

Tsk, tsk, tsk.

NEVELSON

Tsk, tsk, tsk. Right!

MAN

So, you *did* get married.

NEVELSON

Yeah; we got married.
      (Out)
We went to Havana on our honeymoon.

MAN

Tell me about it.

NEVELSON *(In)*

Havana? You want to know about Havana? Nice city, great people.

MAN *(Laughs)*

No . . . your marriage.

NEVELSON *(Shakes her head)*

You *do* want to talk about sex, don't you.
   (Out)
Isn't he something?

MAN

Well, not if you don't . . .

NEVELSON *(In; imitating)*

"Well, not if you don't . . . " Yes! You *do*! All right let's get it out of the way.
   (Sincere)
Sex and I were fine together; I want you to understand that. I liked sex—
once I knew what it was all about.
   (Out)
I mean, sometimes I did think it was a little strange, a man bouncing up
and down on top of you like that, but it was OK, and I had my share.

MAN

I have a list of your supposed lovers.

NEVELSON *(In)*

I bet you do.
   (Out)
I bet he has.

MAN *(Out)*

Quite a group.

NEVELSON *(Out)*

Listen to him!
   (In)
That list: you probably got people on there I never met, and some should
be on it you don't even know about . . . Sex is fine; it's splendid, but there's
stuff goes with it that no one should put up with.

MAN

Yes?

NEVELSON

Possession! Ownership! For sex you get possession of someone? You get to
tell them what to do, how to live? No thank you, sir.

MAN

And Charles tried to . . . tried to do *what*?

NEVELSON

When I married him he promised me a kind of life . . . We'd be married, yes. But I was supposed to go on with my life, with my studies, my painting lessons, my singing, my . . .

MAN

He *promised* you?

NEVELSON

Hm? Well, maybe I thought he did; maybe that's what I expected, so maybe I thought I'd been promised.

MAN

Marriage is a contract.

NEVELSON

Yeah? Maybe, but it doesn't give you . . . ownership. You don't own somebody just because you marry them. I tried to fit *in*; I tried to become all the . . . *stuff* he wanted me to be—all the social life, the parties, the . . . the . . . the domestic arrangements? Wife of the rich man, dress up, go out; be with him all the time . . . the wife.
　　(Out)
I had my own life I wanted. I wanted to grow into *being* somebody. I didn't want to be told what I *could* do and what I couldn't—what looked proper and what didn't.

MAN

You married into a society that was . . .

NEVELSON

. . . that wanted to approve everything I did! I tried! I played the game, but . . . it wasn't me.

MAN

You were expected to fit in.

NEVELSON

Yeah, to a lot of things I didn't *need*, didn't *want*.

MAN

That's life?

NEVELSON

I'd look into the mirror—the big gilt mirror in the entrance hall were we lived—on Central Park West—and I'd look at myself—all dressed to go out, fine dress, long fur coat, hair all done up, and I'd look, and I'd say, "Who's that!? Who's that *woman*?" I didn't recognize me.

MAN

You looked great, of course.

NEVELSON *(In)*

Well, the woman in the mirror looked great, but . . . who *was* she?

MAN *(Urging on)*

And then . . .

NEVELSON

Yeah, and then I got pregnant.
   (To herself; angry)
How did I *do* that!? How did I let myself *do* that!?

MAN *(Sort of a question)*

Charles was the father, of course.

NEVELSON *(In rage)*

Of course Charles was the father! What do you think I *am*!?

MAN

Well, there are rumors that there were affairs.

NEVELSON

Yeah, I've heard them too—read them, but later! That was later! It was
Charles and me; *me*—good, faithful wife.

MAN

It never occurred to you you'd get pregnant?

NEVELSON

I guess not.

MAN

But . . .

NEVELSON

It wasn't something I wanted, so I guess I thought it would never happen,
or maybe I didn't think about it, or . . .

MAN

. . . or maybe you forgot to . . .

NEVELSON

Drop it!

MAN

OK.

NEVELSON

Anyway, there I was—pregnant; and I didn't want to be, and . . .

MAN

You didn't . . .

NEVELSON

What!? Try to get rid of it?

MAN

Yes.

NEVELSON *(Out)*

It never occurred to me! Never!

MAN *(Calming her)*

OK.

NEVELSON *(In)*

In spite of what it did to my mother. Pregnant! Pregnant! Four of us kids. It became her whole life, and look what it did to *her*!

MAN

What did it do?

NEVELSON

I don't want to get into it!
    (Out)
She was a good woman.

MAN *(Priming)*

And so, you were going to have a baby.

NEVELSON *(In)*

Well, that was what was expected, wasn't it? Good strong girl? Strengthen the line?

MAN

I read that you insisted on a Caesarean—big healthy girl like you.

NEVELSON

Yeah.
    (Out)
The shrinks could have a field day with that one.

MAN

Did have.

NEVELSON

Right! No, I didn't want a baby, and I was a rotten mother.
    (Out)
But I loved him—Mike; we called him Mike: Myron, Mike.

MAN

Yeah, you were a rotten mother, weren't you.

NEVELSON *(In)*

OK! OK! All those stories!

MAN

. . . how you almost let him drown at the beach—a tiny baby: you walked off and let him . . .

NEVELSON

I said: OK!

MAN

. . . and how a couple of years later you almost backed over him in the *car*? He was playing, and you almost backed *over* him?

NEVELSON

Yes!

MAN

And he was slow learning to speak, because you wouldn't *talk* to him?

NEVELSON

Yes! All of it!
     (*Pause; softer*)
Don't you get it? I was—what?—I was . . . going down, going under.

MAN (*Out*)

Right, and so were the Nevelsons—the empire collapsing?—less and less money all the time?
     (*In*)
You have to move to smaller and smaller places—to Brooklyn, finally?

NEVELSON

I was going under!

MAN

Right.

NEVELSON (*Out*)

I got sick; I had to go to bed for a year!

MAN (*Like reading a list*)

Depression; sciatica, abscesses, boils . . .

NEVELSON (*In; rage*)

My blood was boiling!
     (*Quieter*)
I was going down.
     (*Out*)
I tried—for *years*. I kept on going as best I could. I was the wife; I *tried*; I was a mother; I *tried*! But it was all . . . going down.

MAN (*Gentle*)

Down; not . . . up.

NEVELSON *(In)*

Hm? Oh; right.

(*Out*)

I guess I was having a . . . what do they call it? . . . . a breakdown? A nervous breakdown? A slow . . . a very, very slow nervous breakdown—the walls around me? The darkness? The darkness always crowding me?

MAN

Did you think about killing yourself?

NEVELSON *(Pause; nodding; in)*

Sure. Of course I did. For the first time.

MAN

Oh?

NEVELSON

There were others . . . later.

MAN *(Real curiosity)*

What kept you from doing it?

NEVELSON

Damned if I know.

(*Pause; sudden awareness; to herself, mainly*)

Maybe it was the horse.

MAN

The what?

NEVELSON

The horse; the big black horse.

MAN *(Confused)*

I'm sorry, I don't . . .

NEVELSON

The horse.

(*Out*)

I was—what?—eleven, maybe, and I was coming home from school.

MAN

In Rockland.

NEVELSON

Of course in Rockland! Where do you think?

(*Out*)

I was coming home from school, and I was eleven maybe, and all of a sudden there was this huge black horse . . . running, alone, with no harness, or carriage. Maybe it'd broken away from the stable. And there it was— huge, bigger than any horse I'd ever seen. All black, and against the green everywhere—everything was in foliage, everything was in bloom—I was running home from school, and I ran to keep up with the horse, the . . . huge black horse. But I couldn't, of course; so I stopped and watched as long as I could . . . until it vanished. I've never forgotten that. Nothing has ever affected me like that. Ever.

MAN

My goodness.

NEVELSON

It was free.

MAN

Yes.

NEVELSON

Nothing.

MAN *(Impressed)*

Well.

NEVELSON

Except maybe when I was fifteen, I think. There was a neighbor who had a relative visiting—a boy. And he was known to be a good-for-nothing—the boy—He was slender, and he already looked decadent, though he must have been my age. Blue eyes; he had blue eyes. And I remember looking in his eyes and seeing depths which I've never seen again.

(Pause)

MAN

My goodness
(Sudden thought)
Is all this true?

NEVELSON

Hm? What?

MAN

The horse; the huge black horse. Is all this true? Forget the boy. The black horse: is all this true?

NEVELSON *(Noncommittal)*

Well, what do *you* think?

MAN *(Genuine; slow)*

I don't know.

NEVELSON

It's interesting, isn't it.

MAN *(Sudden awareness)*

True if interesting!?

NEVELSON *(Preoccupied)*

Hm? What did you say?

MAN

True if interesting!? The black horse? The boy?

NEVELSON *(Genuine smile)*

Oh, no; it's all true. The black horse: all true. And the boy: I never saw him again. That may be the only time I've ever been in love.

MAN *(Quite disturbed)*

I think I need to . . . I think we should have an intermission.

(Out)

We'll have an intermission.

NEVELSON *(Starting to exit)*

Oh, good.

CURTAIN

ACT TWO

(Stage empty; MAN *enters)*

MAN *(Out)*

Welcome back. If you're wondering why I called an intermission back there when I did, it was . . . well, very simply, I was getting confused and I wanted to think about some things, get a little . . . *un*confused—a little *less* confused than I was. I mean . . . look, I've heard the story about the black horse before; I've read about it; it's in at least two books, but in each time it's not a quote; it's a retelling of what she *said* happened—what she *said* the event was. It wasn't a report of what happened; I mean, no one was *there*. Each time it was a slightly different report of what she *said* happened. It's troubling, you know? You say things enough and people believe them. They may be *true*, but if you've got someone you know makes things up, and admits to it, is probably *proud* of it! . . . well, then, the weirdest thing happens: what's true, what's *really* true gets a kind of an edge about it, a kind of . . . where's what's really *really* true and what is embroidery, or what's just slightly misremembered—no intention. The downright lies are different; they're calculated, usually, made up for a reason—to disprove a fact, or . . . make everything just a little . . . ambiguous. And does this get us anywhere? Well, maybe it does . . . if you like quicksand.

(NEVELSON *enters, having heard the last bit)*

NEVELSON

You are *really something.*

MAN

Every time I start talking about you, in you sneak. Do you wait? Do you wait until I get close to the point I'm trying to make, and then . . . ?

NEVELSON

No, I come back in when I'm finished doing whatever I'm doing. I was fixing my makeup.

MAN

You don't wear makeup.

NEVELSON

My eyes! My eyes! My fucking eyelashes!

(Out)

I wear sable eyelashes: I wear two sets on each eye. No powder; no paint; no lipstick—in spite of what some people say—just the sable eyelashes.

MAN

Why sable?

NEVELSON *(Amazed)*

Why sable!? Are you crazy!? I had a great sable coat; I had a big sable spread for my bed.

(Out)

The eyes are . . . what? the entry to the soul? Well, I don't know about that, but they sure do call attention to themselves—the eyes—if you've got two sets of sable eyelashes on 'em.

MAN

Did you ever try three sets?

NEVELSON *(In)*

Yes; of course. I couldn't keep my eyes open.

(They both chuckle)

Everybody thought I was asleep—standing up, walking around and talking, dead asleep.

MAN *(To confirm)*

You wore them when you worked; not just socially.

NEVELSON *(Out)*

Socially? What's socially?

(In)

No . . . all the time. In the morning when I got up

(Out)

. . . *if* I got up, if I wasn't spending the day in bed, the *week* maybe.

MAN

Drinking? Is this about drinking, about the binges?

NEVELSON *(To* MAN; *straightforward)*

What drinking? *What* binges?

(Out)

Isn't he something?

(In)

Who the hell are you anyway?

(Out)

You gotta be real careful with these types, these "interviewers." Especially if you're dead. They take all sorts of liberties.

(In)

Drank? Who drank?

MAN
(Almost says something, doesn't; then)
I . . . we'll talk about it . . . another time . . . later.

NEVELSON
Talk about what? I don't know what you're talking about.

MAN *(Hands up; defeated; smiling)*
OK. OK.

NEVELSON *(Out)*
Where was I?

MAN
In the morning, when you got up, *if* you got up, if you weren't for some reason spending the *week* . . .

NEVELSON *(Gets it)*
Oh; OK.
(Out)
What I always did was . . . look pretty. I never went anywhere I didn't look pretty—when I was a little girl; when I was married; all during the bad times; later. I never went anywhere I didn't look pretty. What if somebody sees you! You're going to a party . . . you look pretty. You're going into your studio to work; you put on your levis and . . . what? . . . a wonderful lace shawl, and a jockey's cap, maybe? Nothing special, but . . . pretty. You know?

MAN
And always the eyelashes.

NEVELSON *(In)*
And always the eyelashes. The focus.

MAN
And that started when?

NEVELSON
Hm?
(Shrugs)
I don't know.

MAN
All that was later. I want to get back to where we were.

NEVELSON
And where was that?

MAN
The collapse of the marriage, the nervous breakdown . . .

NEVELSON

We *did* all that.
   (*Out*)
Didn't we?

MAN

I want to pick up from there.

NEVELSON (*In*)

You mean go over it all again!?
   (*Out*)
Jesus!

MAN

No; make some sense of it.

NEVELSON (*In*)

Hah! Good luck!

MAN

I want to try.

NEVELSON (*Shrugs*)

Suit yourself. And what was all that stuff you were going on about the
horse, and what's true, what isn't? All that stuff again?

MAN

The horse, yes.

NEVELSON

Black.

MAN

Yes; black; the black horse . . .

NEVELSON

I'll never forget it.
   (*Out*)
I knew I'd never catch it, I guess.

MAN (*Snorts*)

Metaphor!

NEVELSON (*In*)

Hm?

MAN

You were—what?—you were eleven!? And you were thinking in metaphors!?
"I knew I'd never catch it," et cetera? Is that the way you were thinking
when you were eleven?

NEVELSON *(Slow smile)*

I don't remember.
(Out)
Do I.
(Chuckles)

MAN *(Hands up)*
All right; all right! But what about the boy?

NEVELSON *(In)*
Who? What boy?

MAN
The boy; the boy when you were fifteen—the decadent boy and those eyes
you looked into. Blue eyes and
(Checks notes)
what did you say? . . . And I remember looking into his eyes and seeing
scary depths which I never saw again . . . ever . . . anywhere.

NEVELSON *(Cool)*
You're adding.

MAN
Still. Depths you never saw again?
(Beat)
Ever?

NEVELSON *(Uncovered)*
No; never.
(Defensive)
I thought you didn't care about him!

MAN
No; but you did.
(Beat)
Didn't you.

NEVELSON *(Slow smile)*
I don't remember.
(Out)
Do I.
(Chuckles)

MAN *(Gentle)*
Did you love him?
(No response)
Louise?

NEVELSON (*Preoccupied*)

Hm?

MAN

The boy. Did you love him?

NEVELSON (*Open*)

I saw him only once. What does love have to do with it?

MAN

I don't know. What does love have to do with anything? Talk to me about love, Louise. Who did you love? Really love?

NEVELSON (*Gorge rising*)

You don't know anything about anything, you and your books! Love? I loved my *family*; I love my *friends*, I . . .

MAN

And Mike? Did you love Mike?

NEVELSON (*Angry*)

Of course I loved him! He was my son! Of course I loved him! I was a rotten mother—I told you that—and I didn't want him—not *him*—didn't not want *him*—I loved him, but I didn't want to be a mother. I didn't want to be . . .

MAN

Held down.

NEVELSON (*Softer*)

Whatever.
    (*Out*)
He was a good boy. I don't know how he ever forgave me. I sent him off to live with the family.

MAN

In Maine.

NEVELSON

Yeah; in Maine; in Rockland. He went to good schools there. They took him back twice—his father did—came up to Rockland and persuaded my family to let them; put him in Jewish schools in New York, but he *hated* it! Both times he *hated* it!
    (*Clearly wants to abandon the subject. Out*)
He was a good boy; he grew up OK. He was strong—like his mother.

MAN

He took up art, didn't he. He became a sculptor.

NEVELSON (*In; smiles*)

Isn't that something!?

(Out; pleased)

He did sculpture, weekends. He made structures; they were art and they were furniture. I kept one in my bedroom on Spring Street. It was wood and it looked like a . . . person, a . . . a cubist person. He was good!

MAN *(Casual)*

As good as his mother?

NEVELSON *(In)*

. . . what?

MAN

As good as his mother.

NEVELSON *(Pause; odd chuckle)*

Don't be silly!

(Pause; realizes)

Why did you make me say that!?

MAN *(Offhand)*

Oh, because you have no mind of your own, because you'll say anything anyone wants you to, because you don't think before you speak, because . . .

NEVELSON *(Furious)*

Because you tricked me!

(Out)

Mike's art was good; it had integrity. Mike was a good son, a lot better than I deserved. He made a good life for himself, a good family. He was a good, steady man. And he put up with me. With *me!*

(In)

OK? Can we get on to something else?

MAN *(Shrugs)*

Sure.

NEVELSON *(Out)*

I mean . . . come on!

MAN

So! You had your nervous breakdown, your . . . long . . . long nervous breakdown.

NEVELSON *(In. Eyes narrowing)*

Are you mocking me?

MAN

No, but I'm interested that you didn't make a final break with it all for ten years, and even after *that* you came back a couple of times.

NEVELSON

So?

MAN *(Smiles)*

That's a really long nervous breakdown.

NEVELSON

Look; don't you know *any*thing? You have—what*ever* it is—you have—call it whatever you want—there are only two ways to handle it, this . . . this awful knowledge that everything's fucked up. You go bonkers, or you go numb. And if you go numb you can sleepwalk your way through it for a very long time. People know something's wrong, but they don't know what, and they don't know how awful the stuff inside is . . .

(Pokes her chest)

inside *you*! You can go on a very long time and nobody can hear you screaming. You know? It goes in and out, bad to very bad, very bad back to . . . to what? . . . tolerable? Yeah; OK; tolerable. Psychiatry was coming in and a friend, a good friend, said I should do it. But I said no; *no*! That's for *weak* people. I'm good, tough stock. I'll get through it. And I *did*.

(In)

And I *did*.

MAN

Eventually.

NEVELSON

What do you *want*!? Jesus!

MAN

Ten years!

NEVELSON

You're a good girl; you try. Sometimes you scream so they can hear you; sometimes you do so they can't. Ten years; yeah.

MAN

Piano lessons; singing lessons; drawing lessons; shopping lessons! The whole time!

NEVELSON *(Laughs)*

Ah! You heard all about that.

MAN *(Pleased disbelief)*

The worse the Nevelsons' business troubles got, the more stuff you bought?

NEVELSON *(Pleased)*

Yeah!

MAN

Crystal? Silverware? Rugs? Antiques?

NEVELSON

Yeah, and I was good at it. I had a good eye. I only got the really good stuff.

MAN

And when it got really hairy—when you were down to a couple of rooms in Brooklyn—you *still* went to the fancy markets in Manhattan and had all the food *delivered*!?

NEVELSON *(Reasonable)*

Yeah, well . . . they promised me a rose garden.
    (They both laugh)

MAN

You should have gone into analysis.

NEVELSON

Naah; I knew what I wanted; I just didn't know what it was.

MAN

It might have helped.

NEVELSON

No! I learned a couple of things along the way—eventually, some later than others—and what I learned most was . . . you've got to do it yourself. Try to stand up, and if it turns out you can't stand up straight without crutches, go out and learn how to make crutches. Make your own.

MAN *(Applauds a little)*

Very good!

NEVELSON

Thank you.

MAN

How did Charles take to all this—the lessons, the shopping, the . . .

NEVELSON *(Matter of fact)*

We fought. All the time. "Stop shopping; you're driving me into the poor-house! Stop ignoring Mike . . ."

MAN

Myron.

NEVELSON *(In)*

Yes.
    (Out)
"Who are you fucking!?" Believe me, it wasn't a good time.

MAN

You almost make me feel sorry for him.

NEVELSON *(In)*

Who?

MAN

Charles; the whole damn bunch of 'em.

NEVELSON *(Considers)*

I guess I wasn't easy.

MAN *(Very casual)*

Were you?

NEVELSON

Hm?

MAN

Were you? Did Charles have a point?

NEVELSON

Did the little fat bald man have a point?

MAN

You're not nice.

NEVELSON

I never claimed it. Did Charles have a point? Was I sleeping around?

MAN

Yes.

NEVELSON *(Smile)*

Wouldn't *you* like to know.

MAN

Yes; as a matter of fact I would. None of the books about you . . .

NEVELSON

Well, you . . . you decide whatever you want. Who goes around talking about their sex lives in public!?

MAN

A lot of people.

NEVELSON

Yeah? Well, I'm not one of them. Whatever there was—if there was anything—didn't help and didn't hurt.

MAN

No boy with the blue eyes—deepest you'd ever seen, or whatever?

NEVELSON

Lay off him! No; no deep blue eyes. No nothing, probably.

MAN

And so ten years into it you finally broke off and went to Europe.

NEVELSON

Yeah, but before that I'd met somebody—the Princess Norina Matchabelli; she was Italian and she was an actress and she was married to this Russian Noble got thrown out with the revolution, and they were stuck in New York. They were broke, and so she started teaching, and I took lessons.

MAN

Was she any good?

NEVELSON (*Considers it*)

Well, maybe if you wanted to act in Russian. But she did something. She taught me about some of the Eastern stuff—the philosophers, the mystics.

MAN

Oh, no!

NEVELSON

Krishnamurti and the others.
        (*Man shakes his head*)
Don't make fun! What they said to me was this—the Eastern ones—"live for yourself; live *fully*; be . . . your*self.*" The transcendental end didn't interest me too much. "Be your*self*; be *only* yourself." The Princess introduced me to a lot of people. Frederick Kiesler was one. What a mind he had!

MAN (*Out*)

Frederick Kiesler—Freiderich, actually; Austrian; architect, artist, visionary . . .

NEVELSON (*Out*)

He took me around. He showed me art I'd never seen, never even imagined—Picasso, Klee . . .

MAN

His widow said you two maybe had an affair.

NEVELSON (*In*)

He was tiny! He barely came up to my *waist*!

MAN

So?

NEVELSON (*Dismissive*)

Forget it!
        (*Afterthought*)
Bright man. I liked him. He knew what was going on. God knows *I* didn't.

MAN

And so you went to Europe.

NEVELSON

Yeah, I went to study with Hans Hofmann; he was the big guy then. Everybody said he was the best art teacher around. He was a pretty good artist himself.

MAN

I know.

NEVELSON

You know his work? He sort of went out of fashion after a while.

MAN

I know; but I know.

NEVELSON

I was at the Arts Student League in New York. They let me in; I was good.
      (*Out*)
I mean, good for what anybody knew back then. God, nobody knew about Europe, about Picasso, about . . . anybody. But I heard about Hofmann, and he was teaching in Berlin . . . Germany, and I decided I had to go to him.

MAN

In Berlin!

NEVELSON (*In*)

Yeah.

MAN

I'm sure Charles liked that.

NEVELSON

He said no. "You're a wife; you're a mother; you stay where you belong."

MAN

In spite of everything.

NEVELSON

In spite of everything; yeah. So, I went to my family; they were doing O.K. There was money—well, not a lot, but there was money.

MAN

And they paid for your trip to Europe!?

NEVELSON

Yeah; they knew that everything was wrong. It was my mother, mostly. She understood.

MAN

Right; sure.

NEVELSON

She never had the freedom to . . . to do what she wanted. Not that I think she ever knew what it *was* . . . what she wanted. They paid for it—the trip.

MAN

So, you up and left?

NEVELSON *(Out)*

Why doesn't he understand anything? What do you have to do? (In) I parked Mike in Maine; I told Charles I was going whether he liked it or not, and . . .I went.

MAN

Didn't he threaten to—what, divorce you?

NEVELSON *(Dogma)*

You didn't divorce. Respectable, upper-middle-class New York Jews? Don't be dumb.

MAN

You did get divorced eventually—a lot later.

NEVELSON *(Dismisses it)*

He found a woman he wanted to marry—a nice woman, probably. I never met her.

MAN

They say you did.

NEVELSON *(Shrugs)*

Then maybe I did.

MAN

And so you went to Berlin.

NEVELSON *(In)*

And so I went to Berlin.

MAN

And how was Hofmann?

NEVELSON

He was a shit! The Nazis were coming, and all Hofmann wanted to do was get out of Germany. He was a Jew. So the only students he paid any attention to were those he thought could help him. The rest of us he just ignored.

MAN

He also told you you had no talent, that you'd never make it as an artist.

NEVELSON

I said: he was a shit . . . So I left his class and I discovered Europe—the cities, the museums, the people!

MAN

You were happy.

NEVELSON

No, I wasn't happy. I was alone; I didn't know anybody; I'd been thrown out of Hofmann's art class; little Mike was writing me letters saying come home, mommy, I miss you; my money was running out! Of course I wasn't happy!
(*Out*)
Happy? Is he crazy? But every once in a while something would happen that would . . . what? . . . take me out of myself—take me beyond . . . *me*.
(*Out*)
Like when I was back in New York and I was at the Metropolitan Museum and I walked into a show of costumes for the Japanese Noh theatre!

MAN (*Out; ironic*)

Ah, the famous Japanese robe.

NEVELSON (*In*)

Be quiet!

MAN (*Smiles*)

Sorry.

NEVELSON (*Out*)

Now, let me tell you there are things in us we find parallel outside us, and it was that way with these robes. Each robe was a universe. I can tell you exactly where they were. The exhibition was on the south side of the balcony, and the manikins didn't have any heads, and I went upstairs and I looked at them—the forms—and then I looked at the material. Some of them had gold cloth with medallions, and the cloth was so finely woven that the likes of it I never saw before; and the medallion was gold, so it was gold on gold. I looked at it all, and I sat down without thinking and I had a barrel of tears in the left eye and a barrel of tears in the right eye . . . and then my nose was running, so there was another barrel of that, and I wanted to go to the bathroom, so there was another barrel. Everything opened up . . . and I knew, and I said, Oh, my God, life is worth living if a civilization can give us this. And so I sat there and wept, and wept and sat. And I went home, and it gave me a whole new life.

MAN

A whole new life?

NEVELSON

Well, a little bit of *light*. Sometimes things *happen* and they change everything and you don't know *why* . . . but you *do*; you *do* know why . . . only somewhere inside.

MAN

Moments of . . . revelation.

NEVELSON

Don't be pretentious.
  (*Afterthought*)
Yes; you have them; you have these. I had some.
  (*Out*)
Doesn't it happen to you, too? These . . . moments. Yes? No?
  (*They reply, or do not; improvise*)

MAN

They *are* revelation, then.

NEVELSON (*In*)

Sure; the mystics; Picasso; the Japanese robes. There are . . . things.

MAN

Things . . . people.

NEVELSON

I knew a lot of people—later—famous people, great people, and I had the chance to meet Picasso—more than once—but I couldn't *do* it.

MAN

No?

NEVELSON

No; he was too great; he meant too much to me. There are people like that.

MAN

Were there others?

NEVELSON

I don't remember. Maybe, but not like that.

MAN

From what they tell me maybe you wouldn't have liked him.

NEVELSON

It isn't the people; it's what they *do*. I knew Celine. Did you know that?

MAN (*Astonished*)

The French writer!? The Jew-hater!? The Nazi!?

NEVELSON

Yes; well . . . you see? He had a great mind; he taught me a lot, and he wanted to marry me, but I said to him why is it you Jew haters always want to marry Jewish women? Go away!

MAN

And so he went.

NEVELSON

I told him I think I'd admire you better dead than alive.

MAN

O . . . K . . . So; you came back to America, after Hoffman .

NEVELSON *(High horse)*

Yes, I came back for a while—to see Mike, in Maine, to make sure he was O.K.

MAN

Right.

NEVELSON

But before I came back I had another—what do you call it?—revelation.

MAN

One on top of the other!

NEVELSON

I jump around. Before I came back I was in Paris, and there was this thing called the Musee de L'homme . . .

    (Out)

this museum of so-called primitive art. It changed my life as much as Picasso did, and it changed *his* life, too.

MAN *(Out)*

It was a museum of African sculpture. Picasso and Braque saw it when it opened, in nineteen-oh-nine.

NEVELSON *(In)*

Yes; way back. The meeting: think of it! Cubism and the so-called primitive.

    (Out)

It knocked Picasso out, and it knocked me out, too. This was before I went to Mexico—way before—before I saw the Mayan and the Aztec temples. Primitive!? That museum had some of the most sophisticated and power-ful art I'd ever see. Picasso's cubism and this so-called primitive art. These two things; *they* changed me, too.

MAN

It's interesting that none of that African work was made as art.

NEVELSON *(In)*

Yes!

MAN

That it was all utilitarian.

NEVELSON *(Indicating)*

Tell them what that means.

MAN

Uh . . .

    (Out)

Do you need this? That it was all useful?, made to be used? The masks were made to be worn in dance ceremonies?

NEVELSON *(Out)*

Not just stuck on a wall to be looked at.

MAN *(In)*

Yes.

(Out)

Nobody said, "Hey, we're making *art*." They were making things to be used as part of everyday life.

NEVELSON *(Still out)*

It knocked me out. Things knock you out. Nobody in Africa'd studied with Hans Hofmann; nobody'd been to a museum; nobody'd ever heard the word "art," and there it was: pure power; pure art! I tell you!

MAN *(In)*

So, what did it *do* to you . . . to *your* stuff?

NEVELSON *(In)*

Not much; not right away; not for a long time. I'm slow; things get in there and work their way back up.

(Out)

Do you know how long it took me from the time I came back from Europe that first time to the time I really felt—what!?—fulfilled? No! To when I said to myself, "You've done it! You've done it! You've become Louise Nevelson!"

MAN

How long?

NEVELSON *(In; slowly)*

Twenty-seven years!

MAN

That's a long time in the wilderness.

NEVELSON

Ahhh, wilderness came and went. Some times were bad, some times were OK, but twenty-seven years till I knew I'd done it. Twenty-seven years.

MAN

Well, then, that's a lot of self-confidence.

NEVELSON

Self-confidence!? Four times I tried to kill myself, or I thought about it—wished I *could*. I lived off my family; Mike sent me money. Self-confidence!?

MAN

How'd you keep on going?

NEVELSON

I didn't know any better.

(Out)

No, that's not right. This is what I know: you're an immigrant Jew; you're raised in a family scrapes its way up from poverty to . . . respectability and eventually even some . . . affluence; you're raised with these values; you marry . . . *up*; you marry into a wealthy, upper-crust Jewish world. Forget it collapses when the market goes bust; forget that you've married into a world and that's one more thing, one more thing you take on and it falls apart—your whole world—the whole thing you were supposed to—what—*agree* to, become a part of? And it's all about the damn specialness you've felt about yourself ever since you were a little girl. You're special; you're talented; you're going to be somebody.

MAN

Be somebody?

NEVELSON *(In)*

Your*self*! Be your special *self*! OK?

MAN

OK.

NEVELSON *(Out)*

You've known this from the beginning; you're very special; you're going to *be* somebody. No! You're going to be your*self*. You're going to find out who that "you" is—what that "you" is—and you're going to . . . *occupy* that *space* . . . if it kills you.

MAN

And it almost does?

NEVELSON *(In; softly)*

Damn close.

(Out)

I was humiliated. They raised me to be . . . to be—what?—self-reliant, and here I was practically begging them for food. And the whole marriage—arranged, or whatever?— what did I do to that!?

MAN *(Gentle)*

What you had to.

NEVELSON *(In)*

Yeah, what turned out to be what I *had* to—not that I knew it while I was doing it. That was just . . . thrashing; thrashing around!

(Out)

And so there it all was, special Louise, not so special Leah, really screwed up, ruined her marriage, living in New York City—hand to mouth—pretending to be an artist.

MAN

Weren't you working? I mean . . . making stuff?

NEVELSON *(In)*

Yeah; sure; and I even had stuff in shows, now and again: drawings, pottery, small . . . sculptural pieces, in places nobody ever heard of or went to, and nobody ever bought anything. And even when I had a show somebody came to see, you know what the critics said?

MAN

Yes.

NEVELSON

Yes?

(Indicating audience)

Tell 'em!

MAN *(Out)*

I quote: "We learned the artist is a woman in time to check our enthusiasm . . ."

NEVELSON *(Almost under her breath)*

Son of a bitch.

MAN

"Had it been otherwise we might have hailed these sculptural expressions as by surely a great figure among moderns."

NEVELSON

Can you imagine?

(Out)

I'd only put my last name on the pieces . . . Nevelson, but he found out.

MAN *(In)*

Well, there were a couple of good reviews, too . . . a couple of not bad ones.

NEVELSON *(In)*

It's only the rotten ones stick with you.

MAN

How true.

NEVELSON *(Out)*

This show was at Nierendorf—a good gallery, and he took a chance on me. I'd gone into his gallery one day—cold!—and I said, "Mister Nierendorf, I want an exhibition in your gallery." And he said, "But I don't know your work; I don't know who you are." And I said, "Well, you can come and see my work." And he did; he came to where I was living and he looked at the work very thoughtfully, and then he said, very quietly, "You can have a show in three weeks."

MAN

You think somebody had cancelled?

NEVELSON *(In)*

Never look a gift horse in the mouth.

MAN

Even a big black one?

NEVELSON

Very funny.
 (Out)
"You can have a show in three weeks." He took a chance on me; it was the first time he'd ever shown an American artist.

MAN

Well, that was something.

NEVELSON *(In)*

Sure. Big deal. He sold . . . nothing.
 (Out)
He gave me another show a year later and then he died. Nobody bought anything.

MAN

But your family knew you were having shows.

NEVELSON

You know what somebody in the Nevelson family said? They said she probably pays for the shows—how was I supposed to do *that!?* I could barely get *food!*—or maybe she—you know—maybe she gives, what do they call them? "special favors"?

MAN

That's not nice.

NEVELSON

Tell me!

MAN

You *did* have it rough.

NEVELSON

I was a woman! I had another show—I don't remember where—paintings and little sculptural pieces, and nobody even mentioned I wasn't a man, and still nothing sold. Nobody bought a fucking thing. And they sent it all back to me—all of it—and what was I going to do? . . . so I took all they'd sent back and a hundred more paintings I had, and I took them off the stretchers and I *burned* them, and I destroyed the sculptures, too, and I gave all my tools to Mike, all my sculptural tools.

Maybe he could use them, I thought. It wasn't a good time; it was a long, bad time.

MAN

Did you ever think maybe you were no good?

NEVELSON *(Pause; in)*

I don't remember. No, I don't think I ever thought that, but I did think I'd maybe never get where I knew I could—to that space I knew I was supposed to stand in.

MAN

Occupy.

NEVELSON

Hm? Yeah; occupy. I met a nice guy, though—during that show, a really nice guy.

MAN

Was it love?

NEVELSON

Well, a love affair; went on a while.

MAN

But was it love? They tell me you frightened a lot of men. They thought they wouldn't be up to you.

NEVELSON

Yeah?

MAN

Sure; you were big and gorgeous and crazy, and . . .

NEVELSON

Well, maybe most of them weren't up to me, but I've met a few in my time I've . . . well, let me put it this way: I'm not Emily Dickinson.

MAN

But I was talking about love.

NEVELSON *(Pause)*

You learn after a while that there isn't room for everything.

MAN

Pity.

NEVELSON

And if you're any good you learn the difference between alone and lonely.

MAN

You've never been lonely?

NEVELSON

Sure; I was a *lot*, before I figured out who I was.

MAN *(Pinning it down)*

Not since.

NEVELSON

As I said: there isn't room for everything. I've had lots of men, lots of love affairs . . . well, some. All interesting people.

MAN

Including some art dealers?

NEVELSON

I'd had enough of fat, bald men. I liked real men, maybe a little younger than me, *real . . . men*. You learn a lot about sex being a dancer. Did you know I studied dance for over ten years?

MAN

Yes; I knew. Martha Graham?

NEVELSON

I knew her; I watched her. I didn't study there. Of course you knew I did all that. You know a lot about me.

MAN

And some of it's even true.

NEVELSON *(Out; after gesturing him off)*

You learn a lot about your body, what it's capable of, what it needs . . . from dance. Sex is good! It's healthy, and it's nourishing.

(In)

I really did; I thought sex was great—in its place, when it was needed, when it was . . . useful.

MAN *(Smiles)*

Like so much else.

NEVELSON *(Tough agreement)*

Yes; like so much else.

MAN

You never wanted another child?

NEVELSON

No! I screwed up once, and then there wasn't room for it.

MAN

Meaning . . . ?

NEVELSON *(Out)*

How many times do I have to tell him!?

(In)

Meaning, I didn't know who I was yet, so there's no hand for anybody to take hold of. And when I *knew* . . . it was too late . . . or I was too set.

MAN

You're tough.

NEVELSON *(Pause)*

You're damn right.

MAN

A survivor.

NEVELSON

Nobody's going to do it for you. There were really bad times—aside from the work, the . . . the stuff that hurt. There was broke, as I told you, and humiliation and . . . do you know how tough it was to be an artist and a woman?

MAN

You've told me.

NEVELSON

I know I've told you!

MAN

Even today.
      (Out)
Even today women have a harder time than men—sales prices half men's, nowhere near as many museum shows? Grudging acceptance?

NEVELSON *(Out)*

The weaker sex; bullshit! You're not weak if you can survive all that. But it was tough. We made a group of women artists, and we showed together, and that just made it worse. Solidarity? Hunh!

MAN

Yes. I mean no.

NEVELSON

Make up your mind.
      (Out; sudden choking up)
And then my mother died!

MAN *(Sober)*

Yes.

NEVELSON

I almost didn't get through *that* one. I think I went to bed for six months. The poor woman!

MAN *(Genuine)*

It's nice she was able to leave you a little money.

NEVELSON *(In)*

Yes; yes, it was.

(Out)

Enough to buy a little place of my own, so I didn't have to live in those holes anymore. She knew; she understood. I rented half of it out . . .

MAN

To Peggy Guggenheim.

NEVELSON *(In)*

Yes

(Out)

and I kept the rest as a studio and a place for Mike to come if he wanted.

MAN

Did he? Much?

NEVELSON

No; not too much; some.

(Eager for a new subject)

And so, as I told you, it was a long time!

MAN *(Almost not believing)*

Twenty-seven years?

NEVELSON

Well, until the real breakthrough. Before that there was some progress, through all the bad stuff. But the first twenty years were really tough.

MAN

Twenty years—according to all the reports—of drinking and sleeping around and lying and conniving and . . .

NEVELSON *(Out; to cover him)*

. . . and painting and drawing and making pieces and keeping my eyes open—especially the ones in the back of my head . . .

MAN

. . . and meeting all the wonderful people—the ones who were doing all the same things you were.

NEVELSON

Yeah, and some of them came through, got through it; some of them made it.

MAN

It was tough for *most* of you.

NEVELSON *(In)*

More for some. Now listen: about the drinking . . .

MAN *(False surprise)*

Drinking? What drinking?

NEVELSON

Cut it out. We Jews don't drink like other people; *you* know that.

   (Out)

But then I'm not *like* other people—other Jews, other *any*body. I used to sit around with the alkies sometimes, and I'd watch and I'd listen, and they had a kind of camaraderie, a whole world that made sense to them. They didn't seem lonely, and I was so lonely sometimes I'd make friends with a rat. But I wasn't a drunk; you have to understand that.

   (In)

Sometimes . . . sometimes, if you're pushing yourself real hard, if your mind's spinning, you just have to . . . relax. Sometimes you just have to . . . go lie down.

MAN

For a week, maybe.

NEVELSON *(Thinks about it)*

Maybe. Yeah, maybe a week and then you're all rested and you can go on.

MAN

Makes sense.

NEVELSON *(Some surprise)*

Really?

MAN

Well; for you, sure.

NEVELSON

And then I got sick.

MAN

Oh?

NEVELSON

I had to have an operation.

   (Modest; points)

. . . down there.

MAN

The cervix?

NEVELSON

It was a tumor; women get them; it was fine.

MAN

A hysterectomy.

NEVELSON

Yeah; funny word for it. I wasn't hysterical; I was concerned, maybe. They cut it all out. They cut my past out.

　(Laughs glumly)

MAN *(Genuine)*

Gee.

NEVELSON *(Sighs)*

Well, it let me concentrate more—on what was important.

MAN

The breakthrough; get to the breakthrough.

NEVELSON *(Sighs again)*

OK.

　(Out)

This is a lecture.

　(In)

Do you want to . . .

MAN

No; I want to hear everything—especially this.

NEVELSON *(Shrugs)*

OK.

　(Afterthought)

You're sure!

MAN

Yes!

NEVELSON

OK.

　(Out)

OK. I want to talk to you about wood. I was wandering around one day and I saw some wood lying in the street—discarded stuff—and I said that looks nice and so I carted it home and put it in my studio. And then I did it the next day; oh, that looks nice, and so I took it home. And I had people *help* me. We'd go out for a walk and find wood—broken chairs, banisters, flat pieces, anything—and I'd collect it. I'd worked with wood before. I mean, I'd made sculpture out of wood and ceramic and all, but this was something else. I filled my house with it! My studio! My living area! Mike's room! My kitchen! The hallways! Everywhere! Finally it was floor to ceiling . . . piled up, everywhere! I moved the furniture out so I could have wood. I knew I was going to do *something* with it, but I didn't know *what*. And finally I did. What is all this good wood doing lying around my house in piles? Why is it *lying* there? Why don't I . . . and suddenly I knew! Stand it up! Make it all vertical! And it began to happen.

(Wood sculpture starts to appear)

Small at first, and then bigger.

(More sculpture is revealed)

And then I got the idea of stacking up wooden boxes and putting wood inside *them*.

(We see more)

And suddenly there it all was!

(We see it)

and it was wonderful! It was a whole world! And I looked at it and I started to dance.

(She does)

And I danced, and I danced. I never felt more free in my life!

(Stops; points)

There it was! My world! And I went on.

(We see more)

Black; black; and then I did white, and then I did gold. And there it was.

(Pointing)

There it all was.

(The stage is now filled with her work)

All of a sudden I had become *me*, and I was *that*!

(Points)

End of lecture.

(If audience applauds, handle it. MAN *applauds, slowly, nodding. In)*

Thank you; thank you.

MAN

Just like that.

NEVELSON

Well, no; not just like that. It took a few years, but it was better and better,

(Out)

and people looked and I had show after show and everything sold, and museums gave me whole *rooms* to fill, and . . .

(Quieter)

and I became very famous . . . and I stayed that way.

(Looks at walls)

Look at this, look at this . . . world. Isn't . . . that *something*?

(If audience applauds)

Thank you; thank you.

MAN

And all the bad years were over, and all the stuff you went through was . . .

NEVELSON *(In)*

Never forgotten! You never forget all that—and a lot you never forgive.

(Out)

But if you finally come *into* yourself like I did, if you finally know the space you . . . occupy . . . well, then . . . you go on. You don't relax; you don't . . . bask in it. Now they want you; you're famous and they're throwing around words like great and magnificent, and so you go right *on*. You work harder than ever. You turn the world into one huge Nevelson. It was . . . fucking . . . wonderful.

(In)

And what was wonderful was what I'd always known would happen—deep inside of me—if I could only ever find it, if I could only hang on.

MAN *(Sincere)*

I'm glad you did.

NEVELSON *(Chuckles)*

Yeah; me too. And I outlived just about everybody—except Mike.

MAN

And how did he feel about it all?

NEVELSON

I don't want to go into it.

MAN

But . . .

NEVELSON *(Determined)*

I said, I don't want to go into it! It was . . . complicated! He and I had problems; I . . . I don't want to go *into* it! He was *happy* for me! *Leave* it!

MAN

Well, he surely must have been happy you left him your entire estate.

NEVELSON *(Cold)*

Yeah; well, it probably made up for a lot. You do what you can. Let's get off this!

MAN *(Grudging)*

O . . . K.

NEVELSON

And so.

MAN

And so?

NEVELSON *(Cheerful again)*

And so I became . . . well, I became a celebrity, on top of it all.

MAN

That surprised you?

NEVELSON

Hm?

MAN

You didn't work at it?

NEVELSON

Listen, dear: I learned: you use everything you can. If I was at the opening of one of my shows, I'd dress up really fine, so people would know I was there.

MAN

So people couldn't *not* notice you were there.

NEVELSON

Look! There's *Nevelson*! There's the *artist*! There she *is*!

MAN

Never hurts, I suppose.

NEVELSON

I told you before: I wasn't Emily Dickinson.

MAN

That was about sex.

NEVELSON

That was about everything.

MAN

A lot of people thought you were overdoing it.

NEVELSON

Sour grapes. MAN
What did you *need*? You had fame; you had money. What did you need —friends?

NEVELSON (*Pause*)

No; not really.

MAN

Love?

NEVELSON (*Pause*)

No; not really.

MAN

What did you need then?

NEVELSON (*Pause*)

Wood.

MAN *(Pause)*

Yes.

(New tone)

You were famous for a long time.

NEVELSON

Yes.

MAN

And it was a great ride?

NEVELSON

A lot of it.

MAN

Not all?

NEVELSON

Once you get known, the vipers come out from under the rocks—if that's where vipers come out from under.

MAN

I don't know; probably; sounds good.

NEVELSON

No matter. Dealers you've had shows with deep in the past claim contracts they've never had, or hold on to work after you've left them? There are lawsuits; there are claims made. And the envy starts:

(Out)

"Oh, her assistants make all her work. She can't do it herself—a woman, and drunk all the time. And you know she never pays for her fancy clothes. She . . . forgets." Shit like that.

(In)

And no matter how it's going, there are always a few knocks. The Met leaves you out of a show of the big U.S. artists. A couple of powerful critics never let you in the club, and the more you do—especially if you try to do something a little new—the more the carping starts: the shit!

MAN

You made a lot of enemies along the way.

NEVELSON

And a lot of new ones once I got there. But I finally got a good dealer—a young guy just starting out.

MAN

He made you rich.

NEVELSON *(In)*

No; *I* made me rich.

MAN

Touché!
   (Beat)
OK. What else?

NEVELSON

You tell me. What else?

MAN

Were the depressions all gone? And did the week-long "lie-downs" ever
stop? The drinking?

NEVELSON

Not on your life! Something would always come up, throw a monkey-
wrench in there. I guess I didn't change all that much when things got better; it just became more . . . tolerable. And there was death to think
about—dying.

MAN

I didn't know that ever worried you.

NEVELSON

No, but you get into your eighties you think about it more.

MAN

Still . . . what a ride!

NEVELSON (*Out; laughs*)

One lady informed me once—what, a few years before I died?—she was a
journalist—we'd been talking about stuff I collected—this big collection of
American Indian bowls and robes I had, and she'd read somewhere that
I'd said that if I was reincarnated—not that I believed in that stuff—that
if I was reincarnated I wanted to come back as an American Indian—
because I loved everything American Indian. So she asked me if I still felt
the same way. She asked me what I wanted to come back as.
   (*In*)
And you know what I said?

MAN

No.

NEVELSON

I said I wanted to come back as Louise Nevelson.

MAN

A much better idea.

NEVELSON (*Sober; in*)

Is that comfort?

MAN

Isn't it?

NEVELSON

I suppose.
  (*Pause*)

MAN

Eventually you got very sick . . .

NEVELSON

Yeah, I sure did.
  (*Out*)
I smoked! I smoked a lot! I smoked all the time!

MAN

Thanks for not smoking now.

NEVELSON (*In*)

Do the dead smoke? Do the dead have cigarettes? Is the cigarette lobby that big!?
  (*Out*)
All the time—whenever I was conscious I had a cigarette in my mouth. They showed me an album once, pictures of me, and there wasn't one I didn't have a cigarette in my mouth. Don't smoke!
  (*In*)
Yeah; lung cancer.

MAN

Which they removed, gave you radiation, said it was all better.

NEVELSON

Yeah, and it was—for a while, and then the headaches started.
  (*Out*)
It had . . .
  (*In*)
What is the word?

MAN

Metastasized.

NEVELSON

Yes; that.
  (*Out*)
It had come back, and this time in my head. I went downhill pretty quick.

MAN

You were eighty-eight!

NEVELSON

Still!

MAN (*Laughs*)

I heard a funny story!

NEVELSON

Well; cheer me *up*.

MAN

It's that when you were in the hospital for the last time, someone came to visit you and said she didn't even have to ask where your room was—that everybody in the hospital knew?

NEVELSON

I remember.

MAN

And that she came to your room and there was your name on the door as big as life . . . Louise Nevelson, in capital letters?

NEVELSON

As big as *death* maybe. Yes; I remember.

MAN

And that you had them take your name off the door . . . ?

NEVELSON

Yes; there's no privacy anywhere.

MAN

And what did you have put up there instead?

NEVELSON (*Smiles*)

Occupant.

MAN (*Smiles*)

Yes; Occupant . . .
  (*Pause*)
So; you died. They say you fought it, you fought it real hard.

NEVELSON

The pain was terrible.
  (*Out*)
But it always is in losing battles.

MAN

You were cremated.

NEVELSON

Sure. If they'd buried me, someone would have probably put up some sculpture or something I would have hated.

MAN

And there's a rumor that when you died your nurse tied your big toes together—some primitive ritual?

NEVELSON *(Disbelief)*

Noooooo!
   (Out)
So *what*! So my soul wouldn't sneak out from between my legs!?
   (In)
People will say anything. Do you believe that?

MAN

Search me.

NEVELSON *(To herself; snorting)*

Tied my big *toes* together!

MAN

They gave you a big memorial service at the Metropolitan Museum.

NEVELSON *(Pleased)*

Did they!

MAN

There were two hundred and fifty people there, and a lot of your friends spoke.

NEVELSON

I wish I'd been there!

MAN *(Pause)*

So. It was a good life?

NEVELSON *(Considers)*

Some; parts of it; enough; yes: enough.

MAN *(Points at the wall of sculpture)*

You'd better go back up there—occupy your space.

NEVELSON

Are we finished?

MAN

Just about.
   (She crosses. Out)
Ladies and Gentlemen . . . the great American sculptor . . . Louise Nevelson.

CURTAIN

Knock! Knock! Who's There!?

AUTHOR'S NOTE

People should come upon this play by accident. They should be walking somewhere in the theatre—in a hallway, from the restrooms, a remote part of the lobby, etc. They will probably begin to *hear* it before they "see" it. What we need for the set is (and this can be real or fake, depending upon circumstance) a boarded-up doorway. I mean the doorway should look real (should have a knob, etc.) and should be framed as a normal doorway is. The boarding-up I speak of should clearly be a hasty and imperfect one— a couple of 2x4's nailed across it, whatever. It is important that the sound come from behind the door. It should be a little muffled but quite intelligible. The words, as opposed to the knock-knocks, are recorded, of course, and come from a speaker behind the door, I would imagine. The knock-knocks are sounds, and they should come from behind the door, too. Nobody says "knock-knock"; they are sounds. How this is coordinated with the dialogue is not my problem but we, the audience, standing in front of the door, should sense the thumping from within. Ideally, if we were to touch the door, we would feel the thumping, as well. The comment "repeat endlessly" means exactly that. The entire play should be performed over and over again whenever the theatre is accessible to the patrons.

Knock! Knock! Who's There!? was first performed at the McCarter Theatre Center (Emily Mann, artistic director; Liz Engelman, literary director) in Princeton, N.J. on October 25, 2003, with Bruce Weber, *New York Times* theatre critic, as the voice.

(Knock! Knock! Pause. Knock! Knock!)

Help! Help!

(Knock! Knock! Knock!)

Help! *(Pause)* Hello?

(Knock. Knock.)

Is anyone there? *(Pause)* Help. *(Pause)* Hello? Hello?

(Knock. Knock. Knock. Knock)

Help! Someone's locked me in here! Let me out!

(Knock. Knock)

I have to be at the performance! I'm a critic! Help! Help!

(Knock. Knock)

Is there anyone there? *(Pause)* Help?

(Knock. Knock. Knock)

I'm a critic! Let me out!

(Knock. Knock)

Help! *(Pause)* Help!

(Repeat endlessly)

 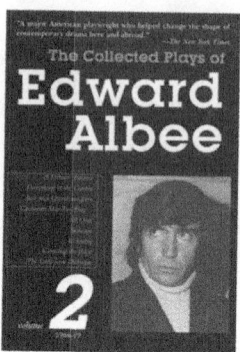